# ADVENTISM CHALLENGED

## The Gathering Storm

Book One

Russell R. Standish
Founder, Remnant Ministry

Colin D. Standish
President, Hartland Institute

Published and Distributed by
Hartland Publications
Box 1
Rapidan, Virginia, U.S.A.

© Copyright 1986, 2000 by Russell and Colin Standish.
All rights reserved.

ISBN 0-923309-65-9

Printed and bound in the United States of America

Originally published in two volumes entitled:
THE GATHERING STORM
BOOK 6A

THE STORM BURSTS
BOOK 6B

Published and distributed by
Hartland Publications
Box 1, Rapidan, VA 22733
1-800-774-3566

Table of Contents

Book One

# THE GATHERING STORM

Chapter

| | Dedication | vii |
|---|---|---|
| 1 | Response to a Challenge | 1 |
| 2 | Background | 5 |
| 3 | Nineteen Fifty-Six | 16 |
| 4 | Initial Reaction to Barnhouse-Martin Dialogue | 19 |
| 5 | Fundamental Doctrinal Changes | 23 |
| 6 | Further Doctrinal Dilution | 28 |
| 7 | Bible Doctrine Despised | 31 |
| 8 | Champion When Champions Were Few | 35 |
| 9 | Robert Brinsmead | 39 |
| 10 | Robert Brinsmead's Early Doctrines | 44 |
| 11 | The Seminary | 48 |
| 12 | Educational Changes in Australia | 52 |
| 13 | Desmond Ford Defends the Church | 55 |
| 14 | Opposition to the New Theology | 57 |
| 15 | The Rise of the Theologians | 61 |
| 16 | Brinsmead Changes Direction | 65 |
| 17 | The Nineteen Seventy-three Annual Council | 68 |
| 18 | Opposition Surfaces | 72 |
| 19 | Old Errors Emphasized | 74 |
| 20 | An Octogenarian Throws Down the Challenge | 77 |
| 21 | Division in Quandary | 80 |
| 22 | Learning from History | 87 |
| 23 | The Review and Herald Special—an Adventist Landmark | 89 |
| 24 | The Committee of Concerned Laymen | 96 |
| 25 | Before the Biblical Research Institute | 103 |
| 26 | The Biblical Research Institute—Second Day | 109 |
| 27 | The Findings of the Biblical Research Institute | 113 |
| 28 | The Palmdale Meeting Mooted | 116 |
| 29 | Conflicting Concepts | 118 |
| 30 | The Palmdale Conference | 122 |
| 31 | The Controversy Continues | 126 |
| 32 | An Emotive Reaction to Old Truths | 131 |

| 33 | Curious Questions | 137 |
| 34 | A Secret Letter | 141 |
| 35 | A Four-Pronged Attack | 145 |
| 36 | The Victorian Conference Targeted | 150 |
| 37 | Victorian Pastors Disunited | 154 |
| 38 | The Clippard-Slandish Brochure | 160 |
| 39 | Anglicans and Adventists—The Twofold Union | 163 |
| 40 | Truth Mixed with Error | 168 |
| 41 | Jesus, The Model Man | 170 |
| 42 | Australasian Division Responds | 174 |
| 43 | The Lesson Quarterly Outside Australia | 180 |
| 44 | Adventism Attacked | 183 |
| 45 | General Conference Youth Leader Condemned | 187 |
| 46 | Secret Papers Published | 189 |
| 47 | The Gathering Storm | 192 |

Book Two
# THE STORM BURSTS

Chapter
48  Nineteen Fifty-Six Revisited ................................................................. 197
49  The Shaking of Adventism ..................................................................... 200
50  Personnel Changes ................................................................................. 210
51  Australian Pastors Attack the Truth ....................................................... 216
52  Further Attacks on Truth ........................................................................ 223
53  Armidale Church .................................................................................... 229
54  Persecution ............................................................................................. 232
55  Pastors Deprived of the Pulpit ............................................................... 239
56  New Theology Spread by Old Apostate Protestant .............................. 245
57  The Retirement of Pastor Robert Pierson .............................................. 249
58  Adventist Laymen's Fellowship ............................................................ 252
59  Righteousness by Faith Consultation .................................................... 255
60  The Forum Revelation ........................................................................... 258
61  Glacier View ........................................................................................... 264
62  Editor Denounces the Sanctuary Doctrine ............................................ 270
63  Dispelling Darkness ............................................................................... 275
64  Moral Degeneracy .................................................................................. 278
65  American Leader in Australia ................................................................ 283
66  Little Change in Avondale College ....................................................... 286
67  Ways with Words ................................................................................... 291
68  The Printed Page .................................................................................... 294
69  Adventist Observer ................................................................................ 298
70  God's Work Falters ................................................................................ 304
71  Prophetic Fulfillment ............................................................................. 307
72  China Enlightens the World .................................................................. 310
73  The Atlanta Affirmation ........................................................................ 315
74  The Spirit of Prophecy ........................................................................... 319
75  The Davenport Affair ............................................................................. 322
76  Column Inches ....................................................................................... 325
77  Cartoons Return ..................................................................................... 330
78  Pacific Union College ............................................................................ 332
79  Songs of Blasphemy .............................................................................. 336
80  Efforts to Shake Student Confidence .................................................... 338
81  Moral Laxity at Pacific Union College ................................................. 341
82  Students Respond at Pacific Union College ......................................... 346
83  Southern Missionary College ................................................................ 349

| | | |
|---|---|---|
| 84 | Consensus | 354 |
| 85 | Publications | 357 |
| 86 | Another Sabbath School Quarterly Controversy | 361 |
| 87 | Smokescreens | 364 |
| 88 | Lack of Fundamental Faith: A Phenomenon of the Eighties | 374 |
| 89 | God's Word | 378 |
| 90 | Conclusion | 382 |

## Appendixes

| | | |
|---|---|---|
| A | Worldwide Concern | 391 |
| B | Conflicting Concepts | 402 |
| C | Correspondence with Church Editor | 404 |
| D | Reply to Australasian Division Spokesman | 408 |
| E | Misinformation | 410 |
| F | Counterfeit Baptismal Vows | 412 |
| G | Changed Convictions | 414 |
| H | Pastor W. W. Fletcher | 416 |
| I | A Statement of Protest Concerning a Letter to Elder Duncan Eva from the Australasian Signs Editor | 418 |

# DEDICATION

To the memory of Hilda Marie Joyce Standish (1912–1974)

Our mother was born into a home that was not significant for its harmony or happiness. The last of 11 children, her parents were aged 47 and 42, respectively, at the time of her birth. Twelve years earlier our grandmother, then a faithful Methodist, had accepted the great truths of the Adventist faith. She had had the privilege of listening to Sister White speak just prior to her departure from Australia. Our grandfather, on the other hand, had violently opposed our grandmother's change of faith. It was into this home, where disharmony reigned, that our mother was born.

The influences of the home were thus mixed, and for a short period as a late teenager our mother was sorely tempted to follow the path of the worldling. But at this time she truly accepted the Lord. She was only a young woman of 21 years of age when we were born. We remember her so well as a young woman full of energy and vivaciousness. At church picnics there was never the least doubt as to which young woman was the most capable at the games played and who joined in the most enthusiastically. It was this same energy and enthusiasm which she devoted to the work of her God. Whether playing the church organ, singing, visiting, reading poetry, or leading out in the Sabbath School, she performed all not only with unusual skill but also with an explosive enthusiasm which carried all with her.

For her the Seventh-day Adventist message meant all. No effort was spared to promote it. Whether it was soliciting Ingathering funds in the century heat of summer, distributing leaflets announcing an oncoming evangelistic effort, meeting folk on her *Signs* round, she did all to promote the dissemination of the greatest message ever given to mankind. We were never left with the slightest doubt that our mother believed present truth to the very marrow of her bones. It was her human influence, along with our father's, which did so much to turn two wayward lads to look to Jesus as their Saviour.

When she was 61 years old, God saw fit to ask her to lay down life's burdens. Her death was sudden and thus unexpected. For us it was a terrible shock, softened by the certainty of God's redeeming grace. Prior to her death, our mother had begun to perceive the inroads of the *new theology* into our faith. Lifelong fidelity caused her to express her stand on the side of truth at an early stage. It would not have been our mother if she had not. A few hours prior to her death she read the affirmation of the 1973 Annual Council. That stand for truth filled her heart with peace. It is thus fitting that we dedicate this volume with tender love and immense appreciation to the memory of the mother whom God in an act of the most wonderful favor gave to us.

# 1 Response to a Challenge

THIS volume deals with the history of the present doctrinal controversy in God's Church. In the opinion of some, this conflict is a matter which should remain in the domain of the theologians in our Church. It is thus necessary to explain why two church members, unschooled in the niceties of theological debate, should venture to enter this arena. Admittedly we have not done so because we believe that we possessed unusual skills or insights into the truths of God. We did not do so from a belief that no one else could have defended the truth in a superior fashion; and some, we freely admit, have. But strangely we have noted but few who have written in defense of the truth, now under the most telling attacks since its exposition by that noble band of Adventist pioneers. There has been a pervading sentiment, apparently accepted by many, which suggests that to proclaim the specifics of our faith at this time of crisis will cause further damage to the Church we love and will bring greater divisions into our midst.

An examination of previous crises in God's work indicates that on no occasion has God commanded His people to be silent at a time of doctrinal crisis. Virtually every prophet of God was commissioned to cry aloud at such times. In this history of our own Church, never have we retreated from attacks on the pure faith. The errors of Canright, the holy flesh movement, Kellogg, Ballenger and others, were not met by silence. Had this policy been followed, there is little doubt that the schisms they produced would not have been minimized, but rather magnified manyfold. Yet today the shelves of our Adventist Book Centers, in many countries, are curiously empty of material specifically designed to meet errors now demonstrated by time to be leading thousands of God's people out of the faith toward eternal loss.

In relation to the Kellogg apostasy, Sister White quite properly pinpointed the apostasy as the cause of the division within the Church. She did not condemn the proclamation of truth at that time. Rather she urged upon workers the need to act in defense of the truth. Notice how different was the divine plan for combating the alpha of apostasy from many of the plans of men to settle the present controversy.

> Will the men in our institutions keep silent, allowing insidious fallacies to be promulgated to the ruin of souls? The sentiments of the enemy are being scattered everywhere. Seeds of discord, of unbelief, of infidelity, are being sown broadcast. Shall our medical missionaries raise no barrier against this

evil? Is it not time that we asked ourselves, Shall we allow the adversary to lead us to give up the work of proclaiming the truth? Shall we allow him to keep us from being channels through which the blessings of the gospel, as a current of life, shall flow to the world? Let every man now arouse, and work as he has opportunity. Let him speak words in season and out of season, and look to Christ for encouragement and strength in welldoing.
(*1SM 195*).

In such a situation we believe that God calls on all men who claim to be His children to arise and defend His great message of love for mankind. When we went forward in baptism in October 1950, a few days prior to our seventeenth birthday, inherent in that decision was a covenant to stand for the principles of doctrine to which we had assented. When Colin was ordained to the gospel ministry in 1971, and Russell nine years later, each accepted the charge to defend the faith. Such commitments beg no excuses to waver from the line of duty. We could not face our Maker should we do so.

We do acknowledge, however, that to write a history of a contemporary event has many drawbacks. The perspective which time alone permits is of necessity absent. Only our heavenly Father knows the nature of the conclusions of this matter. This we cannot know. Charges of bias can hardly be refuted, particularly when the historians have made no attempt to conceal their stand and involvement on the issues under dispute.[1] Yet contemporary histories do lend themselves to the production of a record of events seen through the eyes of participants. Of even greater import in the present crisis is the knowledge that in the past some, doubtful about the issues at stake, have through an understanding of the history of the controversy, been confirmed in the truth.

Our initial entry into the field of history of what for want of a better term has been designated by many the *new theology*, began on a hot, humid day in Bangkok, Thailand, in March 1979. Colin, returning to the United States with his wife, Cheryl, from furlough in Australia, was visiting Russell and his wife, Enid, at their mission post in Bangkok. Russell had just returned from the Thailand Mission Triennial Session at Pattaya on the fabled Gulf of Thailand. There Mrs. Schuler, wife of Dr. Schuler who was practicing in our hospital in Hat Yai, 700 miles to the south, urged him to place on tape his knowledge of the development of the *new theology*. Colin had had similar requests made to him during his visit to Australia. After some initial discussion and planning, we produced three cassette tapes of a total duration of three and a half hours. In all truth we did not anticipate a large listening audience, but we did feel that some people would be interested in the information the tapes contained.

It should be recorded that March 1979 was seven full months before Dr. Desmond Ford's now famous lecture to the Forum Group at Pacific Union College on October 27, 1979.[2] Glacier View and the various conferences and publications which ensued could not have been anticipated at that time. Indeed, Dr. Ford was still one of the most sought-after speakers within our Church in March of that year. Thus the tapes were addressing an audience, in most cases, still unaware of the course the *new theology* was taking.

The tapes left our hands untitled, and within a few months had been spread around by the thousands. A number of tape ministries chose to actively distribute them. In both the United States and Australia abridged transcripts were made and published. It was the late Brother Paul Miller of Oregon who first coined the title *The Bangkok Tapes*, a name which has been adopted by popular usage. When we attended the General Conference Session at Dallas in April 1980, we were astounded to be met by numerous delegates expressing their appreciation for the information contained in the tapes. Presidents of some conferences in North America informed us that they had sent copies to all their pastors. The greatest joy, however, came to us in letters from sincere men and women who informed us that they had found a firmer hold on the truths of God from the material they had gleaned from *The Bangkok Tapes*.

Of course the letters were not unanimous in expressing appreciation. It would be a matter of puzzlement to us if no discordant note had been sounded. Although we had made every effort to be as kind and as Christian in our statements concerning personalities (as opposed to doctrinal errors) as we could, a number felt incensed on behalf of some mentioned. Disturbed that our words concerning men may not have truly reflected our faith, we listened and relistened to those tapes ourselves, and enlisted the advice of a number of brethren more experienced in God's truth than we. We felt that we had not harmed anyone's reputation, and in this our brethren concurred. But nevertheless we must grant that it is only natural to feel hurt when one's beliefs are placed under attack. Thus it was understandable that some of those who had espoused the *new theology* would be affronted by that which was spoken.

In this volume we have attempted to treat men and women as kindly as we ourselves would wish. We have used names as sparingly as possible, even risking attacks upon the veracity of the material presented to do so. But names have to be mentioned on occasions, or the history would be hollow. Could one write a history of the Napoleonic Wars and entirely ignore the role of Napoleon Bonaparte? In our own church history no one has succeeded in writing a history of the holy flesh movement while ignoring Pastor S. S. Davis, who introduced the doctrine, and Pastor R. S. Donnell, the president of the Indiana Conference in 1900, who espoused and promoted it.[3] Pastor J. O. Corliss, who wrote a stout defense of our faith to counter the accusations of D. M. Canright, naturally named names in his presentation. Similarly Pastor A. G. Daniells' contemporary history of the pantheistic error in our church was not written in a vacuum, ignoring the contributions of Dr. John Harvey Kellogg and Pastor Alonzo T. Jones.[4] Pastor E. E. Andross did not ignore Pastor Albion F. Ballenger in his defense of truth against Ballenger's attack upon the sanctuary doctrine.[5] Similarly, when *Ministry* reported the affairs of the Glacier

View Conference which examined the teaching of the *new theology*, Dr. Desmond Ford's name was not omitted.[6] Also in the contemporary history of our Church, *The White Truth* and Robert Olsen's writings did not ignore the name of Walter Rea in the defense of the doctrine of the Spirit of Prophecy. Thus both past and contemporary church history have verified the value of some level of personal identification in pointing out those who are principally involved in the destruction of the faith.

Although this history is not presented as a dry collection of documents, it is nevertheless based upon documented evidence. This procedure is only proper. In many instances reference is made to these materials. In most cases direct quotations are incorporated. The authors hold thousands of papers of documentary evidence related to this problem in the Church. For example, for the period 1976–78 alone, we possess over 3,000 pages of documents bound in ten large volumes. Veracity demands a history, not of hearsay or opinion, but of fact. Under God's blessing we have striven to enlighten rather than to cloud the facts. Where opinions are cited this fact has been made obvious.

## Chapter 1 Endnotes

1. See Chapter 2.
2. It is not a matter of great recall for the authors to remember this date, for it fell on their forty-sixth birthday.
3. A. L. White, *Ellen G. White*, Vol. 5, 100–108
4. A. G. Daniells, *How the Denomination was Saved from Pantheism*
5. E. E. Andross, *Studies in the Sanctuary*, 1911
6. *Ministry*, October 1980. Many persons have placed their views on open record. There is no merit in preserving confidentiality in such cases.

# 2 Background

IN January 1950 we left home to enroll in the primary teacher training course at Avondale College.[1] In those days the course was known by the rather august title of the Theological Normal Course. We were just beyond our sixteenth birthday and were not a little awed by the place. The principal, Dr. William G. Murdoch, later to become renowned as the Dean of the Theological Seminary at Andrews University, appeared to us to be a man of such immense learning and academic achievement that deep respect was automatic. We had never previously met anyone in possession of a Doctor of Philosophy degree, and Dr. Murdoch's possession of this qualification impressed us immensely.[2] Dr. Murdoch was the first president of Avondale College to hold a doctorate degree. All his successors, of course, have been similarly qualified.

Dr. Gordon McDowell and Dr. Lionel Turner, who had in 1949 been awarded doctorate degrees in the United States, returned to Avondale College upon the completion of these degrees. Only recently our Bible teachers, Pastors Alfred Kranz and Nelson Burns, had returned with master's degrees obtained at the Theological Seminary in Washington. These changes in the academic qualifications of the teaching staff of the College were to have far-reaching effects upon its course. Previously the majority of the lecturers had no degrees at all and were selected on the basis of their experience and proven worth.

The sudden upgrading of the qualifications of the staff of lecturers reflected changes occurring in our colleges in the United States. Until the mid-1930s our colleges employed professors more qualified by experience than by academic attainments. With the acceptance of accreditation, however, it had become mandatory, in satisfying the accreditation board's criteria, to upgrade the academic qualification of the staff. As in the case of those receiving their upgrading from Australia, initially much care was taken in selecting men of proven dedication to receive such training. As time went on it became more and more difficult to select men who had first shown themselves successful in their calling. As the pressures to upgrade all areas of college programs were increasingly exerted, it became necessary to select some faculty members who had high academic qualifications but who had not had sufficient time to prove their dedication to the Advent message. In many cases such men and women subsequently proved their worth to the cause, although markedly handicapped by a lack of practical experience in their field. Others, on the other hand, failed to meet the stringent standards necessary for one preparing young people for the highest of all callings—service in the cause of their Master. It was among some of this latter group that the seeds of the *new theology* were to germinate.

Although Avondale College granted no degrees in 1950, for such was the preserve of state universities only, this fact did not preclude the enrollment of a number of students of outstanding ability. Many of these students subsequently achieved high academic distinctions, and even more important, rendered dedicated and humble service to their Lord. Without dispute, the most able student at the college in 1950 was Desmond Ford, who was that year completing the ministerial course. Not only did Des have an outstanding academic record, but he was also highly spiritual and a speaker of the first order. Yet he was still in his very early twenties. There was no question in our minds that here was a prince of the Church in blossom. Furthermore, Des was possessed of a very kindly and helpful personality. It was impossible to dislike him.

We watched Des' course with great interest, first as a ministerial intern in 1951 under Pastor George Burnside in his Newcastle Crusade, and then as a church pastor in the North New South Wales Conference. As news filtered through of his successes, it caused us no surprise. We heard of his open discussion with Pastor Bergen, a Church of Christ pastor who specialized in attacking the Adventist faith. All reports of those in attendance were that Des handled the pastor's objections to God's truth with consummate ease.

We were not surprised when, following Avondale College's affiliation with Pacific Union College, we found that Des had returned to complete his bachelor's degree and had been sponsored to undertake post-graduate studies in the United States. Upon his return from the United States at the beginning of the sixties, Des was inundated with speaking appointments. No denominational speaker was more sought after in Australia. Invariably his audiences were thrilled by his messages. We were aware of no words of dissent.

At this time we were students at the University of Sydney. Colin was undertaking postgraduate studies in psychology while Russell was completing his medical course. In 1960 Russell had been elected president of the Sydney University Seventh-day Adventist Students' Society. Colin was voted into the same office the following year. We believed that the number one function of the Society was to establish the verities of the faith among the more than eighty Seventh-day Adventists then attending Sydney University. As part of that aim ministers were selected to make presentations which upheld the truth in its purity.

It was only to be anticipated that at the top of the list of those whom we valued for this purpose was Des, now at the prime of his powers as a man in his early thirties and chairman of the theology department at Avondale College. Thus it was that in 1961 Colin invited Des to speak at a Friday evening service on the subject of the value of the Spirit of Prophecy to the Church. We approached that meeting with great anticipation, fully expecting a faith-strengthening discourse. To our dismay Des introduced a thought which to us seemed contrary to the plainest teachings of Sister White.

Perhaps it would be best if we let a contemporary account of the meeting set forth that which disturbed us greatly:

> Doctor Ford said that while Sister White was thought-inspired, she used her own phraseology in expressing her thoughts. In doing this, he suggested, she sometimes included erroneous expressions in her work. Dr. Ford cited several instances of this. For instance, she mentioned the faculties in a manner which accepted the now discredited Faculty-approach to psychology. Also she referred to Paul as the author of "Hebrews" when the best evidence now indicates that this book was a Pauline sermon recorded by a fellow Christian. Dr. Ford's third instance certainly led to much discussion when he suggested that her reference to a 6,000-year-old world was in error. In defence of his position, Dr. Ford referred to Luke 3 where a list of the patriarchs includes a second Cainan, not listed in Genesis. It was thus suggested that Genesis records only the important patriarchs and thus the antediluvian period was in excess of that suggested by classical chronological determinations. Indeed, Dr. Ford suggested the date of 8,000 B.C. as being closer to the truth, accepting the last Ice Age to be 10,000 years ago. This latter fact was ascertained following the meetings as was his suggestion that the Flood occurred about 3,500 B.C. rather than the generally accepted 2,000–2,500 B.C.[3]

Since we were aware that on at least 16 occasions [4] Sister White asserts that the earth was created approximately 6,000 years ago, and on a further 14 occasions [5] she refers to Christ's birth and ministry as occurring at about 4,000 years after Creation Week, we could not but see this sermon as a direct challenge to the inspiration of the words of the Spirit of Prophecy. To say the least we were stunned. A short conversation with Des at the conclusion of the meeting did nothing to ameliorate our concerns.

Yet our respect for Des remained. We did not doubt his integrity and his sincerity. Our belief was understandable since at this time Dr. Ford was still preaching that which could only be described as historic Adventism. Even five years later he preached that, "Our message is sanctification. God wants a people such as described in Revelation 14:1–5, without fault before the throne of God, without guile. They are people in whom sanctification had its perfect work." (Sermon delivered by Dr. D. Ford at the Greater Sydney Conference Camp Meeting, 1966)

When Sydney University in 1962 hosted the initial convention of Australian and New Zealand Universities Seventh-day Adventist Students' Societies, Des was among the first speakers we invited to address the group of delegates. But a nagging doubt persisted.

In 1965 Colin was appointed chairman of the Educational Department at Avondale College, a position he retained for the next five years. During this period Des and he were contemporary faculty members and thus had the opportunity to dialogue on doctrinal questions. It was in 1965 that the first ripples of concern for Des' Sanctuary teachings were heard. Someone, still unknown to us, wrote an anonymous warning asserting that error on the Sanctuary doctrine was being taught at Avondale College. It was also in this year that Pastor Burnside, then the Division ministerial secretary, first discerned that a number of recent graduates from the theology course did not believe our doctrine of the Sanctuary, expressing the alternative view that Jesus entered the most holy place of the heavenly Sanctuary at His ascension, then to commence the second-apartment ministry.

Rumors of these matters reached Colin's ears, but at the time it seemed as if the theology department was more concerned by discussions of such matters as whether God could save the heathen who, while never having heard the name of Christ, still lived up to the minimal light available; and the timing of the universal death decree. From time to time, however, other members of the theology department expressed anxiety to Colin over Des' class presentations. It was felt that because of his undoubted excellence of presentation, Des' material and views were more readily accepted by the students than was that of other theology lecturers. Yet they believed that they were holding the line of doctrinal purity, only to see it being eroded in the adjacent lecture room.

But in direct conversations with Des, Colin found it sometimes difficult to pinpoint specific doctrinal aberrations. Nevertheless, he was not left with the full assurance that the future pastors of the flock were being instructed as they ought. Colin was more than a little perturbed by this situation, for the education students also took religion courses from Des. It was Colin's conviction that he must do all in his power to prepare Christian educators whose convictions were securely founded upon the pillars of our faith. Many of the rumors which reached his ears provided him with less than full confidence that in all classes this same goal was being achieved.

With Colin's appointment as president of West Indies College in Jamaica in 1970 and Russell's service in Malaysia from 1967, we lost a good deal of contact with the developing storm of doctrinal controversy, although from time to time snippets of news came through.

Thus when Russell and his wife, Enid, and their family returned to Australia in December 1973, he was largely ignorant of the rapid escalation of what had become termed *new theology*. A series of conversations with respected senior pastors soon changed that situation.

Shortly after their return, Russell was strolling along the Comenarra Parkway just behind the Sydney Adventist Hospital. There he met Pastor George Burnside and exchanged the normal pleasantries. After a short discussion of general news Pastor Burnside unburdened himself concerning the errors which he perceived were being taught at Avondale College. It was obvious that he felt this problem very keenly. Since much of Pastor Burnside's revelation was unknown to Russell, he naturally found it difficult to accept that such a situation had arisen without a halt having been called. Pastor Burnside's major concern centered upon the Sanctuary doctrine, although he did mention the matter of the age of the earth, a topic which sent Russell's mind back twelve years, and of which he was well aware.

Still, despite the very high respect Russell had for Pastor Burnside, he did not treat the revelations with the seriousness they merited. Reestablishing his family in the homeland occupied so much of his attention that the matter was permitted to recede into the recesses of his mind.

Several weeks later Russell walked into the foyer of the Sydney Adventist Hospital and there met Pastor Frank Basham. Since he was an uncle of Colin's wife, Cheryl, the meeting was an enthusiastic one. But after a high-spirited conversation Pastor Basham suddenly turned grave as he recounted his deep sorrow over what he too had noticed were the results of the ministry of the current teachings of the theology department at Avondale. This revelation naturally resurrected the matter in Russell's mind and added to his growing curiosity as to the real state of the doctrinal controversy now well developed within the Church. Pastor Basham, while mentioning the Sanctuary, added yet another matter to the growing list of doctrinal woes, for he felt that the basic problem was a departure from truth on the doctrine of righteousness by faith.

One day, less than a month after Russell's discussion with Pastor Basham, he was attending his inpatients in the hospital when a nurse passed him a note. The signature was that of Pastor J. W. Kent. He was then already well over a decade beyond his three score and ten but still keen of mind and still in possession of his remarkable gift of expression in the English language. He had met with an accident to his foot caused by a motor mower. Believing that the request to see him simply indicated a desire for a sick visit, Russell gladly complied. Russell indeed had ample time from his "busy schedule to visit an old man" as requested. Pastor Kent's request was Russell's command, for he had been the first conference president that we as very young lads could recall. Russell soon learned, however, that this was to be more than a sick-bed visit. Pastor Kent poured out his grief over the deteriorating doctrinal situation within our Church. His words paralleled those of the other dedicated pastors who had chosen to speak to Russell upon the matter.

It was a wedding invitation which brought Russell a step closer to recognizing the extreme gravity of the doctrinal crisis in Australia. Following the conclusion of the wedding ceremony, which was held in the Avondale Memorial Church, Russell and his wife, Enid, met Pastor O. K. Anderson, an old-time family friend who had been our church pastor when we were teenagers. He had also baptized our grandfather. Pastor Anderson possessed that rare type of personality which is most malleable on all issues of little significance, but unshakable on matters of faith. Thus Enid and Russell spent a considerable time laughing and chatting, fully enjoying Pastor Anderson's company. But then turning toward Avondale College which stood picturesquely about a mile distant, Pastor Anderson pointed to the institution, expressing his depth of anguish generated by the failure, as he perceived it, of the

Avondale College theology department to teach the truths of God. These Pastor Anderson had the profound joy to preach for half a century.

On returning to Sydney Russell received a phone call from Pastor Llewellyn Jones of Melbourne. They had worked together in Malaysia and when Pastor Jones expressed concern about his wife's health, Russell gladly agreed to admit her to the Sydney Adventist Hospital for diagnostic tests. Pastor Jones accompanied his wife on the 600-mile trip. When Russell and he met, of course, the matter of paramount concern to Pastor Jones was the health of Mrs. Jones. After her condition stabilized, Pastor Jones inquired concerning Russell's opinion of a series of articles which Dr. Ford had published in the Australasian *Signs of the Times*. These articles were expositions of the prophecies of Daniel. Russell had to admit that he had given the articles no real study at all, although he had briefly scanned one or two of them. Pastor Jones offered a written appraisal of the material which he had prepared. Until this time Russell had been unaware that there was any question on Dr. Ford's prophetic interpretation. It did not take long to notice that Dr. Ford's view of the crucial prophecies of Daniel chapters 8 and 9 differed widely from that accepted by God's people for over a century. The expositions of Dr. Ford provided no basis for the investigative judgment, and thus no Sanctuary message.

In the meantime Colin had moved to Columbia Union College, one mile from the General Conference Headquarters in 1973. Information was gathering at the General Conference that all was not well in Australia. Naturally Colin met with frequent questioning as to what the real situation was. General Conference representatives who visited Australia appeared to find little to confirm the growing volume of letters emanating from Australia urging the General Conference to intervene in some way in the doctrinal crisis. To many in Australia it seemed that the only purpose their letters served was to improve the stamp collections of those who received them. The people did not understand the delicate position of the General Conference in such matters. Discreetly and patiently the General Conference moved to unravel fact from fiction. It was a tedious and sensitive procedure. At first it seemed that perhaps the problems rested in the agitation of a small group of radical pastors and lay people. But as the ground swell of concern grew and letters arrived from such men as Pastor Herbert White, who had retired as one of the General Conference publishing department leaders at the 1975 session of the General Conference, and Pastor Erwin Roenfelt, previously president of the Northern European Division, and Pastor Roy Anderson, formerly ministerial director of the General Conference, men well known for their moderation and fidelity, leaders in the world headquarters became perplexed.

On February 3 and 4, 1976, Russell was one of sixteen brethren (eleven pastors and five laymen) who were given a hearing by the Biblical Research Institute of the Australasian Division. This session was most enlightening. Until this time Russell had not heard Des' views on the sanctuary or righteousness by faith at first hand.[6] He had only consented to attend to present the case that Creation Week occurred about 6,000 years ago. For Russell the highlight of this meeting was the stout defense of the fundamentals of our faith offered by men who had won thousands to the truth of God. It was an experience never to be forgotten. But it did also reveal the tragic fact that the fears of these senior pastors had not been overdrawn. Word by word their allegations of doctrinal aberration were confirmed.

It seemed urgent, to those gathered, that Pastors Burnside and John Keith attend the proposed meeting at Palmdale, California, at which, after much negotiation, representatives of the General Conference and the Australasian Division would attend. The Australasian Division, however, felt this plan was inadvisable. This reaction led to intense disappointment for those who feared that the true nature of this problem in the Church might not surface at that meeting.

In response to this situation Dr. John Clifford, a Melbourne physician who had attended the Biblical Research Institute meeting, proposed to Russell that they co-author a manuscript which was given the rather cumbersome title of *Conflicting Concepts of Righteousness by Faith in the Seventh-day Adventist Church—Australasian Division.* Inevitably it became known by the first two words of the title, or simply just *CC.* The primary purpose of this publication was to inform the General Conference brethren of the serious position of our doctrinal status in Australia, as perceived by those who believed that such a state existed. For this purpose only eleven copies were printed, but later a concerned believer in Australia printed a full edition with the authors' consent, and a group of lay people attending the Paradise Church in California published an American edition. The authors had but six weeks to prepare the material, and both were involved in very heavy work schedules. But the deadline was kept, and the material arrived in Palmdale at the commencement of that now historic but little documented meeting.

Although the authors received encouraging letters from two of the three General Conference brethren (Pastors Robert Pierson and Kenneth Wood) to whom the manuscripts were addressed (the third, Pastor Duncan Eva, made no reply), each author was totally unprepared for the deluge of protest the book engendered in their homeland. It was as if an attempt had been made to destroy a sacred institution. Three full-scale rebuttals were prepared and circulated. Secret letters were sent to church leaders throughout the land warning of the dire perils inherent in paying the least attention to the materials presented. One fact became evident: fifteen years of the teaching of error in the Avondale College theology department had borne a baleful fruit, for now there remained few within the ministry to rise up and defend the precious truths of God so wonderfully revealed to our spiritual forefathers. Almost alone were the senior pastors to herald the old message. It was true that numbers of ministers in the latter years of their ministries confided an appreciation of the stand that had been taken for the old landmarks, but even many of these did not dare to express this view openly for fear of retribution.

Any impartial evaluation of *Conflicting Concepts* would reveal that it contained no personal attacks. In fact, it could be evaluated as quite innocuous in this respect.

Yet it cannot be denied that, to many, *Conflicting Concepts* was a most inflammatory document. Dr. Clifford and Russell were astounded that almost every innocent typist's error seemed to be seized upon as if it were a scheming design to misrepresent the position of those introducing the *new theology*. So much of an issue did this book become that in one of the large conferences[7] the ministry was called together to show their unanimity by voting to condemn *Conflicting Concepts* and to support Dr. Ford's doctrinal positions. But God had His true ones in that group, men who would not yield to such pressure to betray their faith. One by one they took their stand and the meeting disbanded without a vote being called for, since it became plain to see that the ministry of that Conference was in total discord on the matter of the principles of the faith.

This reaction did nothing to stifle the fears which we harbored concerning the peril to the fundamentals of the faith at that time. Initially it appeared as if but few still valued the old pathways. In many ways *Conflicting Concepts* was a message before its time. Many folk could not, in 1976, find any flaws in that which was being taught at Avondale. Among these were men and women who loved God and His last-day message, but for whom the errors were woven with such subtlety that discernment was well-nigh impossible. Such folk would have been astounded if anyone had prophesied that within four years Dr. Ford's ministerial credentials would be withdrawn. They heard nothing which indicated to them that the sanctuary doctrine they so ardently believed, the writings of God's messenger they so cherished and the obedience they well knew God demanded, were under scorching attack. And God in His mercy permitted yet a thousand and more days for the error to develop lest any of these good people should fail to understand.

Nevertheless the book did serve a most useful purpose. By various means it spread to many nations of the world, nations for which at that time the name Desmond Ford meant nothing. One Australian pastor even found the book in the possession of a Finnish pastor living near the Arctic Circle. How the book reached there remains a mystery to us. But in the United States it early alerted many to the dangers inherent in Desmond Ford's appointment to the theology department of Pacific Union College, a post he took up a year after the appearance of *Conflicting Concepts*.

In 1978 Colin and Cheryl returned to Australia for the first time in five years. Although they were aware of the fact that grave doctrinal issues had arisen, the reality outstripped their expectations. As Colin preached in church after church and found the upheavals that the *new theology* had wrought, his heart was torn, for when he had left Australia for overseas service nine years earlier the doctrinal stance of the overwhelming majority of church members still centered on the pillars of our faith. These were unquestioned. As a group, our pastors and evangelists were still boldly proclaiming the three angels' messages. He returned to find doubt and even open unbelief on the part of many church members. Others were in a state of mental torment over their faith. Large numbers of ministers no longer saw the Adventist faith as qualitatively unique. To them it was simply another Christian denomination distinguished only by holding doctrines closer to Bible truths than others. For some it did not even hold that advantage. The thought that the Seventh-day Adventist Church contained God's remnant, commissioned to proclaim God's concluding message to sinners, had well nigh vanished from their hearts.

Appalled by what he discovered, Colin called a meeting of concerned pastors and lay people early in 1979. This group of over one hundred believers met in a hall in the Sydney suburb of Turramurra, two or three miles from the headquarters of the Australasian Division. Earnest prayers ascended for guidance. Study groups were formed and possible solutions discussed. For these brethren and sisters it was no longer acceptable to have the specifics of God's last message muted, and even denied. They could not stand by idly as church congregations listened week after week to sermons that could comfortably have been preached by a speaker in virtually any other church of Christendom. They looked with nostalgia to the days when Adventist preachers fed their flocks with messages that promoted holy living and filled the hearers with a deep desire for Christ's return. Some of these preachers attended the meeting, their voices modified by the many years of crying aloud, but their faith undimmed by the passage of time. The purity of faith so notable a feature of God's Australian Church following the blessing of the location of Sister White in our homeland for nine years was not to be lost in cowardly silence, for these men were still in love with God and His message.

Just prior to the Turramurra meeting Colin and an old school friend, Carl Branster, had shared their observations on the state of the Australian Church as they strolled along a beach on the central coast of New South Wales. There massive waves of the Pacific Ocean echoed the might of their Creator as they broke with thunderous roar on the peaceful white sand fringing the land. It was from this simple discussion that the concept of a laymen's group promoting the preaching of the old truths in a manner which would return men and women to—

> . . . the path of the just (Isaiah 26:7)—

germinated.

Carl, now a successful Sydney businessman, dedicated to his Church, seemed ideal for assisting such a project. Further discussions with our brother-in-law, David Pennington, a Sydney-based plastic surgeon, and others confirmed the feasibility of such a move. From this emerged the Adventist Laymen's Fellowship (ALF), an organization which has brought to Australia, at least twice annually, speakers who have thrilled God's people with the old-time faith. [8] These Vision Valley Meetings [9] have grown in stature as hundreds of God's people have gathered to savor the precious message of present truth. [10]

A few months following the formation of ALF came Ford's Forum presentation with its ensuing consequences. Moves to proclaim anew our faith were already afoot in the United States. In 1979 the General Conference had gathered a group together in order to reestablish our position on righteousness by faith. Colin was a member of that group. He felt, with others, the moving of the Holy Spirit in that gathering as study group after study group asserted that alone which Scripture verifies.

As the inevitable procession was taken through Glacier View, disavowal of Dr. Ford's teachings, loss of credentials and finally annulment of his ordination, we watched with a gnawing anguish of heart. While we could not fault the decision of our brethren in these matters, none of this altered our vision of a man seen over thirty years previously through the eyes of admiring sixteen-year-olds. To us Des was still the old college mate, the youth bursting with potential; still the man of unmeasurable God-bestowed talents; the supreme orator, the quicksilver debater, but most of all, as ourselves, a man much in need of the very truths which he saw fit to reject. No doctrinal disagreement could remove from our hearts the bond of Christian charity we held for Des.

And it is the human tragedy of the *new theology* which impels us to write, lest others be snared by its errors. While Des is the most notable, the most visible casualty of the *new theology*, others just as precious to their Redeemer and to their loved ones have imbibed its philosophies. Many of these have stepped further down the ladder of error until the Sabbath, baptism and virtually all Scriptural truths are ignored, and it would seem that the very elements of the Christian faith have ceased to be held of value. Some of these men and women will once more respond to the pleadings of the Holy Spirit and eventually join the host of the redeemed. Praise God for His saving power. Let no believer by word or action contribute to the erection of any barrier to such a return. It seems easy for us to feel great resentment against those who, once having joined hands with us in the blessed hope, apostatize. But does this attitude represent a pure faith? In the day of judgment former believers face greater accountability than those who have never professed faith in the truth.[11] Should not this fact direct our every action that it be redemptive rather than destructive?

These men are not to be viewed as traitors to God's cause; He alone can judge. They are rather souls, like ourselves, for whom our blessed Saviour died, men and women for whom heaven is still a prospect, for whom the truth can render a transformation of mind and heart by the infilling of God's Holy Spirit.

> But I keep under my body, and bring it into subjection; lest that by any means, when I have preached to others, I myself should be a castaway. (1 Corinthians 9:27)

> Brethren, if a man be overtaken in a fault, ye which are spiritual, restore such an one in the spirit of meekness, considering thyself, lest thou also be tempted. (Galatians 6:1)

## Chapter 2 Endnotes

1. Then called The Australasian Missionary College.
2. Ph.D.'s were not introduced into the Australian Universities until the 1950s. Prior to that time the only doctorates available were higher doctorates such as Doctor of Letters, Doctor of Science, Doctor of Laws, and like degrees. These doctorates were of such a standard that they were rarely awarded. For example by the 1970s Sydney University had awarded, in its 120 years of existence, only two Doctor of Letters degrees by examination.
3. SUSDASS Bulletin, Vol. 2. No. 8, pp. 1, 2
4. 3*SG* 92; 2*T* 172; 3*T* 492; 2*SP* 93; 4*SP* 371; *GC* (Author's Introduction); *GC* 581; *GC* 522–553; *GC* 656; *GC* 659; *GC* 659 (*a second reference*); *GC* 673; *PP* 51; *PP* 352; *CH* 19; *DA* 413; *DA* 413 (*a second reference*)
5. *GC* (Author's Introduction); *1SM* 267; *1SM* 267 (*a second reference*); *1SM* 269; *RH* Aug 18, 1974; *1SM* 280; *2SP* 88; *GC* 328; *GC* 546; *Ms* 43, 1897; *DA* 49; *DA* 117; *DA* 652; *DA* 759
6. In fact in 1975 Dr. Ford and Russell had been the guest speakers at a day-long youth rally in Melbourne, and Russell had heard a summary of Des' views then. But this was his first occasion to hear a detailed presentation.
7. The Victorian Conference
8. Speakers have included men such as George Burnside, Austin Cooke, Erwin Gane, Richard Lange, Ralph Larson, Morris Lewis, Mervyn Maxwell, Bill May, LeRoy Moore, Lewis Walton, Charles Wheeling and Colin himself.
9. Named after the location where the meetings have been held.
10. At the first Vision Valley Meeting of 1984 a total of 1,200 believers attended causing one officer of the Greater Sydney Conference to demand of the pastors of that Conference that they commence preaching doctrine in order to recapture the attention of the laity.
11. See 2 Peter 2:20–22.

# 3

# Nineteen Fifty-Six

THE year 1956 was a significant one in the history of the Seventh-day Adventist Church. Although the full significance of the events of that year were not immediately apparent, nevertheless the period of the following quarter of a century clearly demonstrated that events of that year were to have an enormous influence upon the doctrinal affairs of the Church in the years to come.

We were young men 23 years of age in 1956 when these events occurred. Russell was a member of the headquarters church of the Australasian Division at Wahroonga in Sydney. One Sabbath he was alerted by a statement from the Division secretary, Pastor L. C. Naden, which indicated that an evangelical Protestant magazine entitled *Eternity* had declared that Seventh-day Adventists had been found to be part of the body of Christ. The speaker was very enthusiastic about this matter and saw it as a breakthrough in fraternal relations between a large body of Protestantism in the United States and the Seventh-day Adventist Church. [1]

Russell was totally unacquainted with the background which had produced this declaration, but he did feel uneasy that such a publication would speak in such friendly terms concerning God's remnant Church. It must be remembered that in 1956 the ecumenical spirit which today seems to pervade Christianity, at least on a superficial level, was far less in evidence then and that members of smaller Christian churches often suffered much scorn from the lips of those in the larger denominations. Seventh-day Adventists had quite naturally been the recipients of more than their share of contempt from these organizations. Thus it was most surprising indeed to find this sudden change in attitude. The question naturally arose in the minds of some as to why an evangelical Protestant group would adopt such a benign attitude toward a Church which firmly believed that the Protestant churches became part of Babylon when they rejected the message of 1844, and that failure to keep the Sabbath day holy will eventually constitute the mark of the beast. Another question which raised itself was the right of any organization to decide who or what was part of the body of Christ. Many Seventh-day Adventists felt no enthusiasm for such a declaration coming from the churches which in many instances failed to heed the specific truths of Scripture. True members of the Seventh-day Adventist Church, of course, are part of the body of Christ, but they do not obtain that distinction on the basis of the opinions of leaders in other churches. God has inspired His servant to write concerning His church,

> [The church] . . . enfeebled and defective, needing to be reproved, warned, and counseled, is the only object upon earth upon which Christ bestows His supreme regard. (*TM* 49)

What then was the background to *Eternity* magazine's unique pronouncement? The history unfolded gradually over the next year or two. A young graduate student, Walter Martin, was in the process of writing a thesis on the major Christian sects which he regarded as non-Christian. [2] These included Jehovah's Witnesses, Christian Scientists, Mormons and Seventh-day Adventists. In order to gather his material and to be accurate and fair in his presentation of the beliefs of Seventh-day Adventists Mr. (now Dr.) Martin felt it necessary to discuss our beliefs with a number of Adventist theologians and administrators. He sought the advice of Dr. Donald Barnhouse, editor of *Eternity* magazine, in order to make contacts with representative Seventh-day Adventists.

Dr. Barnhouse was the pastor of the Tenth Presbyterian Church in Philadelphia, Pennsylvania, and had in 1949 presented a talk on the radio. This talk had been heard by the president of the East Pennsylvania Conference of Seventh-day Adventists, Pastor T. E. Unruh. He had felt helped by the presentation and had written to Dr. Barnhouse expressing his appreciation for the material presented. Barnhouse was rather surprised, for he had felt that no Seventh-day Adventist could have accepted that which he had stated. This matter was still in his mind when Martin came to seek his assistance. It was therefore recommended that the president of the East Pennsylvania Conference be contacted in order to see whether he could arrange for a meeting between Martin and representative Adventist leaders that he might hear firsthand what was our position on a number of distinctive doctrines.

Pastor Unruh was very enthusiastic about meeting this request and had soon contacted the General Conference and made the arrangements as requested. To these men Martin presented a series of specific questions concerning our beliefs, and a representative group of Seventh-day Adventist leaders provided answers to these questions. The questions asked and the answers provided may be readily reviewed, for they were published in 1957 in the form of a book entitled *Adventists Answer Questions on Doctrine*. In common terminology this book became known by the last three words of its title. It was presented as an authoritative statement of Seventh-day Adventist beliefs and remained so for almost a decade and a half. By the mid-1970s, however, a number of church leaders expressed concern over some of the answers presented in that book, and it has not been reprinted since that time. These doubts were typified in an article by Dr. Herbert Douglass, then associate editor of the *Adventist Review* who in 1975 wrote: "The historic view regarding the human nature of Christ as best set forth in *The Desire of Ages* is now being given its proper emphasis here in Washington, and the aberrant position since the publication of *Questions on Doctrine* is now being seen in its proper light—an unacceptable position for Seventh-day Adventists in view of the E. G. White counsel." [3]

It must not be thought that *Questions on Doctrine* was wholly or even substantially in error. Many sections clearly, indeed expertly, set forth God's truth. But it did contain serious aberrations of Adventist truth. Perhaps the most noticeable changes concerned the presentation of the Adventist understanding of the nature of Christ and the consequent view on Righteousness by Faith. Further, many believed that the Adventist views of the mark of the beast, Babylon, the Sanctuary and the Spirit of Prophecy were serious muted.

Barnhouse and Martin were pleasantly surprised with the doctrinal alterations which they noted in the answers to their questions and felt that these were of sufficient significance to merit the announcement which they made indicating Adventism should be removed from the category of *sects* and placed among the group of true believers in Christ. While no Seventh-day Adventist would go out of his way in order to induce scorn from those of other faiths, nevertheless many began to ask whether the acclaim which had been received had cost the Church too much in doctrinal integrity. Certainly that question began to grow as in the subsequent years the long-term results of these changes became fully appreciated.

## Chapter 3 Endnotes

1. It is strange indeed how enthusiastically Seventh-day Adventist have responded to the least interest shown in them by official church organizations. This fact has also been demonstrated by the Church's growing relationship with the World Council of Churches (WCC). Our first conversations with the WCC began in 1965. Since that time we have contributed to more and more committees of this organization. Since the WCC is clearly not of God we would do well to totally eschew contacts with it. Such are unequal yokes. That we went so far as to present an official church gold medal to Pope Paul VI indicates a most disturbing trend.
2. *Kingdom of the Cults* by Walter Martin
3. See also *Fraud of the Unfallen Nature* by Dr. Ralph Larson.

# 4 Initial Reaction to Barnhouse-Martin Dialogue

THERE was little doubt that many church leaders were very joyous over the results of the Barnhouse-Martin dialogue. It was felt that at long last Seventh-day Adventists were receiving the recognition merited by their clear expositions of Scripture and their fidelity to its principles. At this early stage little did our leaders perceive just how thorny would be the road which was to lead from those discussions. Many believed that this recognition would make our faith more acceptable to the people and thus increase conversions. Perhaps the General Conference president of the day, Pastor R. R. Figuhr, expressed as well as any the initial euphoria which was felt at headquarters over the *Eternity* magazine's statement which seemed to lift Seventh-day Adventists to a denomination of credibility and prominence. Pastor Figuhr presented his thoughts in the *Review and Herald* in an article which appeared on December 13, 1956. It was entitled "A Non-Adventist Examines Our Beliefs—The Background of Articles Appearing in Eternity Magazine." Speaking of *Eternity* magazine and its writers, Pastor Figuhr stated, "But they are doing us a very great favor, for which we can never feel sufficiently grateful." While Pastor Figuhr's statement received worldwide acclaim in 1956, there would be today tens of thousands of Seventh-day Adventists who would totally disagree with that preliminary judgment.

Pastor Figuhr felt very grateful for the publication's statement that Seventh-day Adventists were true Christians. "But to have sincere Christians publish that we too must be looked upon as true Christians, while at the same time recognizing certain fundamental differences, is for us something out of the ordinary." (*Ibid.*) Of course it must be remembered that 1956 provided an entirely different religious climate from that which we experience today. Pope Pius XII still had three years of his pontificate remaining. There was no ecumenical spirit among the leaders of the Catholic Church, and Protestants felt little different about this matter. It should be remembered that it was not until the reign of Pope Pius XII's successor, Pope John XXIII, who occupied the papal seat from 1959 to 1963, that the winds of change began with the formulation of the Vatican II Council. The subsequent new-look Catholicism completely duped the Protestant churches into the belief that the Catholic Church was now much more trustworthy and that the ideal of union with it was one that should be fostered. This spirit had its side effects, still evident today, in that the members of smaller denominations were treated with more kindness and respect. Previously there had been much derision and much attack upon those who belonged to these smaller Christian faiths.

Many readers may be too young to remember the sectarian bitterness that still prevailed in the 1950s. Some of this bitterness was directed toward the Seventh-day Adventists. In order to illustrate this situation we cite a matter from our own experience. In Sydney a member of a strict off-shoot from the Presbyterian Church, Mr. Campbell, published a newspaper entitled *The Rock*. This weekly paper attacked Catholics and their faith with terrible bitterness. On many Sundays we heard Mr. Campbell speaking in the Sydney domain (Sydney's equivalent of Hyde Park Corner in London). At these meetings he would give forth a tirade against the Catholic Church and the activities of the priests and nuns. He even stood for parliament on a number of occasions as the Protestant candidate. *The Rock* was avidly read by many persons who shared Mr. Campbell's views. In the 1950s it had a circulation of over 40,000 weekly.

In 1974, during Russell's term as a physician at the Sydney Adventist Hospital, a man in his late sixties who was obviously quite ill, came to consult with him in his clinic. Just as Russell was about to examine him the man said, "Do you know who I am?" Russell's only knowledge of the patient was that which was written upon his medical chart. Russell was therefore quite surprised when he made the preposterous claim, "I'm public enemy number one!" For a moment Russell wondered what was the nature of the man with whom he was dealing. Soon the boast was clarified as Mr. Campbell thrust into his overcoat pocket and produced two copies of *The Rock*. Russell was astounded to see these papers, as he imagined that its publication had long since ceased, since he had neither seen nor heard of it for well over a decade. With his action Mr. Campbell stated, "I'm the editor of *The Rock*." As Russell discussed this publication with his patient he discovered that the paper which had 20 years earlier been distributed at the rate of 40,000 per week now had a distribution of only 2,000 per month, an enormous drop in circulation. When Russell inquired as to the reason for this loss of popularity, Mr. Campbell summed it up in a single word which he himself had coined—the *ecumaniacs*. This small episode certainly illustrates just what had taken place in inter-church relationships in the years between 1956 and 1974.

Thus when Pastor Figuhr expressed such surprise that we were treated so kindly and fairly by the representatives of other Protestant churches, he was doing so in a climate in which it was usual for Adventists to receive little but poor publicity from such people. It was only to be expected that there would be a sense of relief and satisfaction in this turn of events. As time has shown, the changing attitude did not come without a price having been paid, and that price was the modification of a number of our crucial doctrines. Pastor Figuhr did not perceive this fact, and he expressed great confidence that no alteration in our beliefs had been made and that truth had been upheld. "In framing the answers we exercised great care to do so within the denominationally accepted 'Statement of Beliefs.' The answers are not in any sense a modification or alteration of what Seventh-day Adventists proclaim to the world as their belief. Rather they are a carefully worded series of answers to questions frankly put to us." (*Ibid.*)

There is little doubt that Pastor Figuhr and many others at that time sincerely believed the veracity of this statement. But careful study has revealed that this concept was far from a correct analysis. Certainly in the areas of the Sanctuary and the nature of Christ marked modifications had occurred. It was these changes which were the precursors of the terrible theological upheavals which were to occur in the 70s and 80s. Yet apparently at this very early stage there were few objections to the answers which were given. How different this reaction was from subsequent ones! This situation was probably due to the fact that many of those who were consulted were men who were in academic positions and who had, as early as 1956, been influenced by the theology of the evangelicals. Also there is evidence that few men in senior administrative positions had the time to thoroughly examine the contents of *Questions on Doctrine*, despite the fact that its contents had been circulated to them before the book was published. Thus Pastor Figuhr was able to state, "It has been very reassuring to note that no objections or questions of any importance have been raised by those of our number who have read the answers. On the contrary, a general voice of approval and deep appreciation has been the result." (*Ibid.*)

Although Pastor Figuhr could not have foreseen the seeds of dissent and misunderstanding in what was presented to these evangelicals, nevertheless in this very article the crux of the problem which was to haunt the Church for more than a quarter of a century and beyond, was summed up in a few words. "The great point of misunderstanding has been in the matter of the Seventh-day Adventists' belief concerning Christ—His nature, the completeness of His atoning sacrifice, and His mission as our sole hope of salvation. We have been charged with being legalists, who believe in salvation by our works, either entirely or in part. This has been a point of very serious misunderstanding." (*Ibid.*) In this brief statement Pastor Figuhr highlighted three vital and interrelated doctrines—the nature of Christ, the atonement, and righteousness by faith. These doctrines were to become the focus of intense scrutiny in the decades ahead.

The reason that we had been misunderstood on these doctrines was not that they had been poorly expressed by us as some have contended, but that the evangelicals simply did not believe the truth of God on these issues. What was needed was not a clearer or changed statement of our beliefs on these doctrines, but rather a change in the hearts of the evangelicals. That it was the Seventh-day Adventists who took the initiative in change was a matter of enormous consequence. Soon the Church was to find that there were voices of dissent, men and women who would not concur with the changes which had been wrought albeit in all sincerity, but nevertheless without sanction of Scripture.

Soon the Church was to see the rise of groups defending the old principles of the faith on one hand, and on the other hand the emergence of those who were not content to remain where the authors of *Questions on Doctrine* had ceased.[1] These dissensients were prepared to take those doctrinal changes to their logical conclusion, and by so doing completely destroy the Sanctuary message, and the great truth of righteousness by faith.

While Seventh-day Adventists were slow to perceive the implications of the views set forth in *Questions on Doctrine*, these implications were clearly discerned by the evangelicals. Unlike the vast majority of Seventh-day Adventists, the evangelicals had no hesitation in asserting that in *Questions on Doctrine* the Church had overthrown some of its long-established doctrines. In speaking of the doctrines of Herbert W. Armstrong (leader of the Worldwide Church of God), Dr. Walter Martin had this to day: "Nowhere does the Bible teach that the atonement of Christ is yet to be completed! This particular doctrine is drawn from the early writings of Seventh-day Adventists, with whom, as we have mentioned, Mr. Armstrong was associated at one time. It is to the credit of the Adventists that their organization has officially repudiated this position, maintaining that the atonement has already been completed." (*Martin Speaks Out on the Cults*, 152)

With undeniable changes in such a crucial pillar of the Seventh-day Adventist Church, it was inevitable that God would raise up a voice of protest to arouse His sleeping saints. The Church did not have to wait long to hear that voice.[2]

### Chapter 4 Endnotes

1. For example, a senior member of the theology department at Avondale College stated, in a meeting of the Adventist Forum in Sydney in 1979 addressed by Geoffrey Paxton, that he "breathed a sigh of relief when *Questions on Doctrine* was published." For many persuaded by apostate Protestant thinking, this opened a Pandora's box.
2. See chapter 8 entitled "Champion when Champions Were Few."

# 5 Fundamental Doctrinal Changes

WHEN *Questions on Doctrine* was published in 1957, earnest endeavors were made to assure God's people that no changes in doctrine had been incorporated into that book. In an advertisement for *Questions on Doctrine* it was stated, "Not a new pronouncement of faith and doctrine. Every answer given comes within the framework of fundamental beliefs of Seventh-day Adventists as outlined in the *Church Manual*." (*The Ministry*, December 1957)

But the evidence was otherwise. Non-Adventist writers, not restricted in their analysis by a desire to assure God's people that no change of doctrine had taken place, repeatedly revealed that such modifications had in reality occurred. One such writer stated that he "as a research polemicist had no hesitation whatsoever in stating that those previous positions so widely seized upon by the enemies of Adventism have been totally repudiated by the Seventh-day Adventist denomination for some years." (Walter Martin, "Seventh-day Adventism Today," *Our Hope*, November 1956) Mr. Martin set out four doctrines opposed by the Evangelicals which were the ones repudiated and altered. These were:

1. "That the atonement of Christ was not completed upon the cross" (*ibid.*).
2. "That salvation is the result of grace plus works of the law" (*ibid.*).
3. "That the Lord Jesus Christ was a created being, not from all eternity" (*ibid.*).
4. "That He partook of man's sinful fallen nature at incarnation" (*ibid.*).

These four statements form a curious set. Numbers two and three were never held by the Church as a whole, never advocated in the Spirit of Prophecy and never incorporated into a statement of faith. Why Martin confused the issue by this mixed selection is unknown. That he had a most perceptive and detailed knowledge of our doctrines cannot be doubted from his other writings. He cannot have been unaware that points two and three were held by only a few members in the early years of our Church, who were unrepresentative of the general body of believers.

Item two is an apparently complex subject. Adventists, however, consistently adhere to the simple Bible truth that salvation is based upon grace alone.

> For by grace are ye saved through faith; and that not of yourselves: it is the gift of God. (Ephesians 2:8)

Nevertheless, Seventh-day Adventists cannot overlook the clear testimony of Scripture which plainly states that, although salvation is entirely an act of the grace of God to which no amount of good works can ever make the least contribution, God does place a condition upon the receipt of that grace. That condition is obedience to His law. The very Decalogue itself includes this truth.

> And showing mercy unto thousands of them that love me, and keep my commandments (Exodus 20:6)

Jesus, Himself, enshrined this fact in His own teachings.

> If ye keep my commandments, ye shall abide in my love; even as I have kept my Father's commandments, and abide in his love. (John 15:10)

Paul also referred to this fact in his letters to Titus and to the Corinthian church.

> Not by works of righteousness which we have done, but according to his mercy he saved us, by the washing of regeneration, and renewing of the Holy Ghost. (Titus 3:5)

> Circumcision is nothing, and uncircumcision is nothing, but the keeping of the commandments of God. (1 Corinthians 7:19)

However, the items of faith listed as one and four most certainly are precious truths held by Seventh-day Adventists from their early beginnings. In the type the atonement was not completed by the sacrifice.

> Then shall he kill the goat of the sin offering, that is for the people, and bring his blood within the veil, and do with that blood as he did with the blood of the bullock, and sprinkle it upon the mercy seat, and before the mercy seat: and he shall make an atonement for the holy place, because of the uncleanness of the children of Israel. (Leviticus 16:15, 16)

> And the bullock for the sin offering, and the goat for the sin offering, whose blood was brought in to make atonement in the holy place, shall one carry forth without the camp. (Leviticus 16:27)

Paul, writing to the Jewish Christians, reminded them of the continuing nature of Christ's atoning acts for them.

> Wherefore he is able also to save them to the uttermost that come unto God by him, seeing he ever liveth to make intercession for them. (Hebrews 7:25)

Manifestly Seventh-day Adventists are on solid Scriptural grounds in accepting the truth that the sacrifice did not complete the atonement.

This fact too is true of the doctrine of Christ's assumption of our fallen human nature.

> Forasmuch then as the children are partakers of flesh and blood, he also himself likewise took part of the same; that through death he might destroy him that had the power of death, that is, the devil; and deliver them who through fear of death were all their lifetime subject to bondage. For verily he took not on him

the nature of angels; but he took on him the seed of Abraham. Wherefore in all things it behoved him to be make like unto his brethren, that he might be a merciful and faithful high priest in things pertaining to God, to make reconciliation for the sins of the people. For in that he himself hath suffered being tempted, he is able to succour them that are tempted. (Hebrews 2:14–18)

It will be noted that Martin, by combining two doctrines we do not hold with two that we most certainly do, had possibly unwittingly strengthened his complaint. Non-Adventists would have been appalled at the thought that we hold points two and three, and this reaction would encourage them to overlook the veracity of the other two doctrines.

Walter Martin emphasized his conviction that Seventh-day Adventists had moved their doctrinal positions toward those of the evangelicals. "The Adventists had a definite theological platform, which for many years remained almost constant. In recent years, however, there has been a definite movement towards a more explicit declaration of belief in the principles of the Christian faith and the tenets of Christian theology." (Martin, *The Truth About Seventh-day Adventism*, 235)

Another voice perceived the doctrinal changes in Adventism. "Investigation that has lasted throughout nearly a year has convinced us that we were mistaken, that Seventh-day Adventism has been undergoing a change throughout the past decade." (E. Schuyler English, "Seventh-day Adventism," *Our Hope*, November 1956, p. 271)

Behind the scenes some of our own men were aware of the changes. At least one appeared afraid that our lay people would oppose them if aroused before the groundwork for the change was laid. The General Conference ministerial association secretary wrote to the president of the North New Zealand Conference concerning the new view of the nature of Christ, "If you would suffer me this little word of counsel as a friend, I would suggest that you hold those thoughts in your heart and not make an issue of them until we, as a people, come to the place where we understand this doctrine as clearly as we should, and, as clearly as we do other points of faith. . . . I am confident that the time is near when this great mystery of godliness will be understood better by us as a people. But until then it would seem wise if we could confine ourselves to a prayerful discussion of it between us as workers." (Letter to R. A. Greive, president of the North New Zealand Conference, dated January 19, 1956)

It was just this lack of openness with the laity which prevented the necessary response which would have halted the printing of *Questions on Doctrine*. There is little doubt that the earnest members of the laity, unfettered by considerations related to their denominational careers, would have sent forth speedily such a volume of protest that the printing would have been stayed. But God's people were never consulted. [2]

The comparatively few denominational leaders whose views were sought were often too busy to give adequate study to the material or were, in some cases, reticent to cause upset to those brethren in positions higher than their own. Some, however, did not share this reticence. One of the associate editors of the *Review and Herald* (Dr. R. Cottrell) did properly point out one serious doctrinal error in *Questions on Doctrine* to one of its editors. This editor of the book *Questions on Doctrine* had upheld before the workers of the Southwestern Union Conference the notion that the atonement was completed at the cross. "Your presentation, however, carries the thought that the cross is central in the work of atonement. The same thought is emphasized again and again in the new book *Questions on Doctrine*, but I am confident . . . that the emphasis in is the wrong place. Paul stated that the central features of the work of atonement and the plan of salvation is seen in our High Priest ministering in the Sanctuary above. . . . It appears most unfortunate that in the portions of the book *Questions on Doctrine* dealing with Christ's ministry in the sanctuary, the word 'atonement' appears to be scrupulously avoided." (Letter written by R. F. Cottrell, February 23, 1958)

Cottrell left no doubt that he too believed that changes had been incorporated into *Questions on Doctrine*. In the same letter he protested that "it would appear that in your numerous conversations with Dr. Walter Martin, you have been insidiously led to compromise the truth, so as to state it in terms acceptable to the popular evangelical churches. You have evidently endeavored to give the doctrine of the atonement 'a new look'; but it appears as a doubtful, dubious look, and one which our heavenly Father cannot approve." (*Ibid.*)

Thus the two monumental changes of doctrine set forth in *Questions on Doctrine* were:
1. The assertion that the atonement was completed at the cross and that Christ's work in the heavenly Sanctuary was merely the application of the benefits of the atonement.
2. The claim that Christ possessed the sinless nature possessed by Adam prior to the fall.

These two changes provided fertile ground for those who wished to destroy the Sanctuary message and God's claim upon the loyal obedience of His children. Both are inextricably related. It will be recalled that on the day of atonement the high priest made an atonement for the people with a specific purpose in view.

> For on that day shall the priest make an atonement for you, to cleanse you, that ye may be clean from all your sins before the Lord. (Leviticus 16:30)

If the atonement was completed at the cross, then indeed this high priestly function must of necessity apply to justification alone. This conclusion must logically be so, for the vast majority of mankind were not living in A.D. 31. But if the atonement extended to all Christ's acts of salvation, then indeed this work of cleansing was performed in the believer in the sanctification process, as well as by imputation in Christ's great acts of justification.

On the other hand, if the believer's obedience was neither required from, nor even possible in, a truly converted Christian, then Christ's work in the sanctuary was lessened immeasurably, and Sister White's statement must consist of empty words:

> While the investigative judgment is going forward in heaven, while the sins of penitent believers are being removed from the sanctuary, there is to be a special work of purification, of putting away of sin, among God's people upon earth. (*GC* 425)

Further, Christ would cease to be a valid Example, for He did measure up to this high standard of obedience. If He was not our Example in this respect, then there would have been no point in His assuming our fallen nature. Thus these two matters are logically related.[3]

## Chapter 5 Endnotes

1. For excellent documentation on the title of this chapter, "Fundamental Doctrinal Changes," we recommend Vance Ferrell's *The Beginning of the End*. Many quotations in this chapter come from this work.
2. This failure to recognize the enormous value of our laity in matters pertaining to doctrine has caused considerable hurt. Even more alarming is the fact that this measure has deprived God's Church of the input of that element most likely to uphold the pillars of the faith.
3. Trends toward popular evangelical theology may be detected prior to 1956. This, significantly, paralleled the push of our educated men to study for theological degrees outside the Seventh-day Adventist educational system. In the 1949 edition of *Bible Readings for the Home Circle*, the editor, D. E. Rebok, edited out all references to the fallen nature of Christ.

# 6

# Further Doctrinal Dilution

IN addition to the two major changes mentioned in the previous chapter a number of other less evident, but nevertheless highly significant, doctrinal modifications were introduced at the time of the 1956 discussions with the evangelicals. With the advantage of hindsight it can now be discerned that these changes were also preparing the platform of error upon which the *new theology* was to thrive a quarter of a century later.

Among these matters was the value of the Spirit of Prophecy. Great emphasis was laid upon the fact that Sister White's writings were not regarded on a level with Scripture and that she was not a prophet of equal standing with Isaiah, Jeremiah and other Biblical prophets.[1] Further it was said that her writings were only relevant to Seventh-day Adventists and not to other Christians.[2]

In these statements lay the seeds of rejection of the Spirit of Prophecy by many present-day members of the Seventh-day Adventist Church. It is inconceivable that God would send the world a "minor" prophet at the end of time. This present time is the most perilous era in the world's history, a time for the mightiest of prophets. In 1978 Dr. Dunbar Smith, then director of health for the Far Eastern Division, and Russell were travelling to visit our clinic in Maetang in the north of Thailand. As they discussed the things of God, Dr. Smith offered the opinion that we may discover in the kingdom of heaven that Sister White was the greatest of all the prophets. This thought had so escaped Russell up to that point that Dr. Smith's opinion initially shocked him greatly. But deeper contemplation of it impressed him that this indeed was a decided possibility.

In another area our belief was muted. Adventists firmly believe that the Bible clearly specifies two characteristics of the remnant Church.

> And the dragon was wroth with the woman, and went to make war with the remnant of her seed, which keep the commandments of God and have the testimony of Jesus Christ. (Revelation 12:17)

Thus no desecrator of the fourth commandment can possibly be part of the remnant church. Of course these, upon repentance and obedience to God's law and truly believing in the testimonies of Jesus, can join the remnant in Jesus' strength. This latter fact was quite properly emphasized in the reply to the question, "Do Adventists maintain that they alone are the only true witnesses of the living God in our age and that their observance of the seventh-day Sabbath is one of the major marks that identify them as God's remnant church?" (*Questions on Doctrine*, p. 186)

In part, the reply to this question stated:

> We believe that all who serve God in full sincerity, in terms of all the revealed will of God that they now understand, are presently potential members of that final "remnant" company as defined in Revelation 12:17. We believe it to be the solemn task and joyous privilege of the advent movement to make God's last testing truths so clear and so pervasive as to draw all of God's children into that prophetically foretold company making ready for the day of God. (*Ibid.*, 196)

The authors believe this statement to be an excellent reply as far as it goes. Our concern, however, is that it did fail to precisely pinpoint the specific characteristics of the remnant. This failure was probably due to the apprehension that such identifying factors would have been regarded as offensive to the evangelicals.

In yet another answer our understanding of the churches designated as constituting Babylon was not set forth with clarity. The emphasis upon the fact that many devout people, as yet unacquainted with the fuller truths God has for them, are not part of Babylon, could not be questioned. But no effort was made to point out that the churches which the questioners represented had already become Babylon by their rejection of present truth.

> Many of the Protestant churches are following Rome's example of iniquitous connection with "the kings of the earth"—the state churches, by their relation to secular governments; and other denominations by seeking the favor of the world. And the term "Babylon"—confusion—may be appropriately applied to these bodies, all professing to draw their doctrines from the Bible, yet divided into almost innumerable sects, with widely conflicting creeds and theories. (*GC* 383)

The scapegoat service was also misrepresented. The clear symbolism of Leviticus 16 indicates that—

> Since Satan is the instigator of sin, the direct instigator of all the sins that caused the death of the Son of God, justice demands that Satan shall suffer the final punishment. Christ's work for the redemption of men and the purification of the universe from sin, will be closed by the removal of sin from the heavenly sanctuary, and the placing of these sins upon Satan, who will bear the final penalty. (*PP* 358)

However, in answer to the evangelicals it was stated that "Satan makes no atonement for our sins [of course this portion of the statement is perfectly correct]. But Satan will ultimately have to bear the retributive punishment for his responsibility in the sins of all men, both righteous and wicked." (*Questions on Doctrine*, 400)

This statement was incorrect. Satan actually bears the punishment of the repented sins of the redeemed, not simply the part he has played in tempting all to sin.[3]

It is thus only that sin and sinners can be no more. This fact in no way sets Satan apart as our saviour. Such a contention would be as absurd as it is blasphemous. Rather, the sins which have been transferred to the sanctuary must be removed in order for that structure to be cleansed.

Perhaps it was one aim they set themselves which proved to be the major stumbling block for the authors of *Questions on Doctrine*. These authors stated concerning this presentation that "The goal was to set forth our basic beliefs in terminology currently used in theological circles." (*Ibid*. 8) It seems that all who have made this attempt have inevitably reduced the richness of our body of doctrine. Today we hear this same aim expressed more and more often. The authors have yet to see one such attempt which did not cause our message to be diluted.

## Chapter 6 Endnotes

1. Replying to a question concerning whether those who discussed our doctrines with him believed that Sister White's inspiration was on a par with Isaiah or Jeremiah, Donald Barnhouse stated, "Of course not. Certainly not. They're intelligent men, and they are Christians." (Telephone conversation with Al Hudson, May 16, 1958)
2. "That we do not think of them [Sister White's writings] as of universal application as in the Bible, but particularly for Seventh-day Adventists." (*Questions on Doctrine* 89)
3. The crushing weight of his responsibility in the sins of the whole world —of the wicked as well as of the righteous—must be rolled back upon him [Satan]. Simple justice demands that while Christ suffers for my guilt, Satan must also be punished as the instigator of sin. (*Questions on Doctrine* 399)

# 7 Bible Doctrine Despised

ALTHOUGH Drs. Barnhouse and Martin represented themselves as friends of the Seventh-day Adventist Church, and were so regarded by many church leaders, they most certainly were not friendly to the specific truths enunciated by our Church. Dr. Barnhouse particularly was at times most scathing in his remarks. Indeed he appeared to actively hate those doctrines which are the pillars of our faith. [1] Martin offered the opinion that the evangelistic success of our Church "has not been due to the proclamation of their 'special truths.'" (Martin, *The Truth about Seventh-day Adventists*, 218) This certainly was a major blind spot in Martin's thinking.

Martin, in pressing for fellowship with Seventh-day Adventists, stated that "This writer, a Baptist minister, in no sense endorses the 'special truths' of the Adventist message." (*Ibid.*, 236) Specifically singling out the Sabbath, he went on to declare that "we must not allow these aberrations to blind us to the facts that clearly reveal Seventh-day Adventists to be sincere Christians." (*Ibid.*)

A number of our doctrines were particularly repugnant to Martin and Barnhouse. These include

1. Obedience to the Decalogue [2]

   They take a position (to us very illogical) that the Ten Commandments are to be obeyed." (Barnhouse, "Are Seventh-day Adventists Christians?" *Eternity*, September 1956)

2. The investigative judgment

   "The latter doctrine [the investigative judgment], to me, is the most colossal, psychological, face-saving phenomenon in religious history." (*Ibid.*)

3. The nature of Christ

   The belief that Jesus took a fallen nature is "completely repugnant to the Church at large." (*Ibid.*)

4. The Remnant Church

   "We cannot accept the 'remnant church' concept with its exclusivism." (Martin, *The Truth about Seventh-day Adventism*, 212)

5. Creation

"The Adventists tenaciously hold the six-day creation concept. That is, six 24-hour days during which God created the earth. . . . Without contradicting Genesis, scientific evidence indicates that this was not the case." (*Ibid.* 157)

6. The Spirit of Prophecy

"God Almighty never spake through a woman. You can't justify a woman preaching and usurping authority over a man. It can't be done." (Donald Barnhouse in telephone conversation with Al Hudson, May 16, 1958).³

"She [Sister White] was just a good woman who was greatly blessed and greatly mistaken, frequently." (*Ibid.*)

7. Free Choice

"They [the Seventh-day Adventists who dialogued with Barnhouse and Martin] believe that I am a born-again person. That I am saved and have eternal life. They know that I hold the Calvinistic position that I am saved forever and can never be lost." (*Ibid.*)

8. The Sabbath

"Do you think that I cursing Saturday as the Sabbath, cursing everything that is of the law, and wanting grace alone, and wanting to live in holiness, believing that all sin is removed by the blood of Jesus Christ alone, do you believe that therefore I am a lost soul? (*Ibid.*)

"In the name of Jesus Christ, I curse the Seventh-day Sabbath." (Dr. Barnhouse in an address in late 1959 in Peru. Reported by a Seventh-day Adventist medical missionary. Recorded in Vance Ferrell's *The Beginning of the End*, No. 16)

9. The State of the Dead

Barnhouse described the failure to accept the doctrine of the immortality of the soul as "folly." (Barnhouse's telephone conversation with Al Hudson, May 16, 1958)

It is little wonder that Barnhouse offered the opinion that "their [Seventh-day Adventists'] doctrines are about the screwiest of any group of Christians in the world." (Barnhouse's telephone conversation with Al Hudson, May 16, 1958)

Seventh-day Adventists have a perfect right to question whether they should place any value whatsoever upon the theological opinions of those so out of harmony with Bible truth. Is it possible to have real spiritual fellowship with one who places a curse upon the fourth commandment of God's holy Law? When such a man declares that the direction of our change in doctrine is valid, should not this assertion cause us immediately to reassess the direction we have taken? When we come closer to a man who has declared "I hate Saturday as a Sabbath religious day. I hate it because Christ hates it!" (*Ibid.*) we are surely treading upon dangerous ground.

As we look over the first eight points listed above, we find that all have been attacked by a great number of those who espouse the *new theology*. What is certain is that that which now has become known as the *new theology* is neither new, nor indeed, is it good theology. It is also evident that doctrinal changes accepted to please these evangelicals have logical implications. It is no coincidence that we now find that Seventh-day Adventists who are espousing the *new theology* have accepted erroneous doctrines which are precisely the same as those held by Barnhouse and Martin. They all follow from the same false premise.

Further, Donald Barnhouse in particular, did little for the reputation of some of our leaders. Speaking of Sister White, Al Hudson queried, "And you don't think Elder Froom and Richards [H. M. S. Senior] and the others take my position? That she is a true prophet?" (*Ibid.*) To this question Barnhouse replied, "Of course they don't. None of them do." (*Ibid.*) To the best knowledge of the authors, Barnhouse's answer was an absolute falsehood. This assessment is also almost certainly true of Barnhouse's assertion that all the men he dealt with believed that Sister White wrote considerable error. When Hudson said that he had not encountered such errors in her writings, Barnhouse exclaimed, "Oh brother, you are a dupe. You are not as honest as the people at Takoma Park." (*Ibid.*) Hudson followed with a question, "They feel she has written error?" (*Ibid.*) In reply, Barnhouse asserted, "Of course they do. Every one of these men have said this to me. Every man. Every man. They believe that she was raised up to God to be a great blessing, and that the Spirit of prophecy was upon her, but they all agree that she wrote error in some places." (*Ibid.*)

Barnhouse also attributed to our leaders a libel upon God's people which the authors feel defies credibility. "They [the men involved in these evangelical conferences] explained to Mr. Martin that they had among their number certain members of their 'lunatic fringe,' even as there are similar wide-eyed irresponsibles in every field of fundamental Christianity." (Barnhouse, "Are Seventh-day Adventists Christians?" *Eternity*, September 1956) Since this statement followed mention of topics such as the significance of the Sabbath and the identification of the mark of the beast as being Sunday worship and Christ's possession of a fallen human nature, such a designation as "lunatic fringe" would ascribe to the Seventh-day Adventist Church a very large fringe indeed!

Undoubtedly the men who held these conferences with the evangelicals believed they were advancing the prestige of our Church, and thus its appeal to Christians of other faiths. But the sorry result of this approach are now on record for all to study. The most wide-ranging and persistent schism this church has ever experienced has been the result. Further, in those countries where the doctrinal changes have been most accepted, the success of our evangelistic efforts has been greatly reduced. Few would be encouraged to join a church which was the same as the mainline churches in all essentials. In reality, we differ in every major respect from these churches, for God has provided us with a unique message. Apart from our clear differences on such doctrines as the Sabbath, the Sanctuary and the state of the dead, we differ on virtually every aspect of our understanding of the salvation process. We reject predestination. These evangelicals espouse it. We reject the "once saved always saved" principle; they accept it. We believe that God empowers obedience; these evangelicals deny it. We believe Christ gave us a perfect example of Christian living; they oppose this view. In short, Seventh-day Adventists believe the plain words of Scripture; these men, on the other hand, believe human inventions.

### Chapter 7 Endnotes

1. Sister White specified these pillars as the Sabbath, the Sanctuary, the state of the dead and obedience to God's law. (*CW* 30, 31)
2. Martin described this doctrine as "their effort to bring us under bondage." (Martin, *The Truth about Seventh-day Adventism*, 201)
3. Perhaps in the 1980s, his own church not having escaped the inroads of feminism, Barnhouse would have withheld this sexist view. Not only was it manifestly incorrect, but it does show the thinking of a previous era.

# 8 Champion When Champions Were Few

THE perceived changes in *Questions on Doctrine* did not escape the notice of a number of devoted Seventh-day Adventist believers. With many, however, the concern was muted and they played little part in remedying the problem which had arisen. One who made his voice heard in defense of the old doctrinal truths was Pastor Milian Lauritz Andreasen. Andreasen was already eighty years of age in 1956. He was Danish by birth, at an early age migrating to the United States, and had made a significant contribution to the Seventh-day Adventist Church. He retired from denominational service in 1950, having spent nine years as field secretary of the General Conference. Previously he had been the president of the Minnesota Conference 1924–1931, president of Union College 1931–1938, and a professor of the Theological Seminary 1938–1949.

Andreasen, although only six years from the end of his life, was still mentally alert and energetic in his defense of the Seventh-day Adventist faith. As he read *Questions on Doctrine* he felt that there had been a significant compromise in the doctrines of the Church and he set out to defend that which he believed to be the truth of God. It was not a popular mission which he undertook, for it soon became evident that there were many in positions of authority who were prepared to defend that which had been written in *Questions on Doctrine*. Thus while many believers quietly sympathized with Andreasen's position, few were prepared to stand up and support him openly. A recent biography of Andreasen published by the *Review and Herald* is appropriately titled *Without Fear or Favor*. Indeed, it can truly be said of Pastor Andreasen that he stood boldly when champions were few. Perhaps it would be a fitting reminder to us who remain if this epitaph were to be added to his tombstone.

For his fidelity Pastor Andreasen was stripped of his ministerial credentials, a matter which grieved him deeply, for he had given many years of faithful service to the Church he loved. Ten days after his death on February 19, 1962, the General Conference Committee voted to restore Pastor Andreasen's ministerial credentials. This posthumous action was entirely merited, but regrettably too late.

Andreasen set forth his views in a document entitled *Letters to the Churches*. It is true that some of his allegations were of a most startling nature. He asserted, for example, that there was "an attempt to tamper with the *Testimonies* by having inserted in some of the volumes notes and explanations that would make it appear that Sister White was in harmony with, or at least not opposed to, the new theology advocated in the *Ministry* and the book, *Questions on Doctrine.*" (M. L. Andreasen, *Letters to the Churches*, 45) To our knowledge this accusation has never been verified, and certainly nothing in the subsequent years had appeared in the *Testimonies* to indicate that such a plan was implemented.[1] It is interesting that Pastor Andreasen used the term *new theology* back at that time and there is certainly an undeniable link between *Questions on Doctrine* and the *new theology* today. He was most perceptive in seeing how the changing emphasis of our denomination would produce serious doctrinal errors. At the conclusion of his *Letters to the Churches* he had this to say:

> But more than even this is involved in the new theology; it places an indictment against God as the author of a scheme to deceive both men and Satan. Here is the situation.
>
> Satan has consistently maintained that God is unjust in requiring men to obey His law, which he claims is impossible. God has maintained that it CAN be done, and to substantiate His claim offered to send His Son to this world to prove His contention. The Son did come and kept the law and challenged men to convict Him of sin. He was found to be sinless, holy and without blame. He proved that the law could be kept and God stood vindicated; and His requirement that men keep His commandments was found to be just. God had won, and Satan was defeated.
>
> But there was a hitch in this; for Satan claimed that God had not played fair; he had favored His Son, had "exempted" Him from the results of the working of the great law of heredity to which all other men were subject; He had exempted Christ "from the inherited passions and pollutions that corrupt the natural descendants of Adam." (*Questions on Doctrine*, 383) He had not exempted mankind in general, but Christ only. That, of course, invalidated Christ's work on earth. He was no longer one of us who had demonstrated the power of God to keep men from sinning. He was a deceiver whom God had given preferred treatment and was not afflicted with inherited passions as men are.
>
> Satan had little difficulty in having men accept this view; the Catholic Church accepted it; in due time, the evangelicals gave their consent, and in 1956 the leaders of the Adventist Church also adopted this view. It was the matter of "exemption" that caused Peter to take Christ aside and say, "Be it far from thee, Lord, this shall not be unto thee," which so raised the wrath of Christ that he told Peter, "Get thee behind me, Satan." (Matt. 16:22, 23) Christ did not want to be exempt. He told Peter "thou savourest not the things that be of God." So some today savor not the things of God. They think it is merely a matter of semantics.[2] God pity such and open their eyes to the things that be of God. With the surrender of the Adventist leaders to the monstrous doctrine of

an "exempt" Christ, Satan's last opposition has surrendered. We pray again, may God save His people. (M. L. Andreasen, Letters to the Churches 66, 67)

It can be seen from this statement that Andreasen fully understood the significance of the alteration in the doctrine of the nature of Christ. Many of the church leaders whom he accused of having surrendered the last opposition to Satan's despicable lie were in fact oblivious of what had been suggested in the book, *Questions on Doctrine*. Others, perceiving to some extent its meaning, did not see as clearly as Andreasen the significance of accepting the view that Jesus had the nature of Adam before the fall. It was only natural that Andreasen's forthright condemnation of the leadership of the Church should cause concern and lead to the actions which were taken against him.

But sometimes those of us who are placed in positions of leadership need the rebukes of our brethren, and we should not feel threatened by such rebukes from men of dedication and experience. After all, the rebukes of many of the prophets of old were couched in terms often far less restrained than those of Pastor Andreasen. The authors themselves have benefited from the counsel and rebukes of men of experience, even though at the time these have seemed to be unjust and exaggerated. The passage of time has revealed the necessity for such strong advice. Perhaps the test of the true mettle of leaders when rebuked is their actions toward those whose reputations and positions they are in a position to harm. How often we are all tempted to rebuke those unable to retaliate, because of their positions of weakness! On the other hand, we may be strongly tempted to severely treat such when they rebuke us, for we stand in a position of strength. It is quite certain that Christ would not assert such an advantage.

One statement which Andreasen made in passing was to influence a whole generation of Seventh-day Adventists. He had stated that "this denomination needs to go back to the instruction given in 1888, which was scorned." (M. L. Andreasen, *ibid.* 67)

Pastor Andreasen died without seeing any significant results from his protestations in defense of truth. But in the mid-1970s his concerns stood vindicated as some church leaders took up the defense of those doctrines which were so precious in his sight. Numerous church members began their search of the critical messages of 1888. Thousands of earnest believers, in many cases unaware of Andreasen's contribution to the preservation of the truth, gladly echo and re-echo these precious messages around the world.

## Chapter 8 Endnotes

1. A careful analysis, however, of the usage of Sister White's writings on the subject of the nature of Christ in the book *Movement of Destiny* leads one to the conclusion that her writings were misused to establish a position Sister White very clearly never held.
2. It is instructional to see how early in the doctrinal crisis all the arguments arose. The charge that the problem was merely one of semantics became the catchword of all who were unwilling to study the issues or who did not wish to be convicted of precious truth.

# 9
## Robert Brinsmead

ROBERT Brinsmead enrolled in the theology course at the Australasian Missionary College (Avondale College) in the mid-1950s. He had come from the north coast of New South Wales, an area renowned for the amount of doctrinal interest displayed by its church members. Although Robert came from a rural background he seemed to attract much attention at the college because of his clear insights into Scriptural matters, his obvious high intelligence and his ability to express his views succinctly, clearly and convincingly. He caught the attention of a number of the members of the faculty and many of his fellow students eagerly listened to his discourses. In another era Robert Brinsmead might have become the leading evangelist in the Seventh-day Adventist Church. If we were looking at the events in the Seventh-day Adventist Church from a secular viewpoint, we could be forgiven for offering the opinion that Robert Brinsmead was born either two decades too late or two decades too early. The tenor of that which he preached in the mid-1950s as a young man would have found ready acceptance in 1935 and perhaps even in 1975,[1] but it did not meet the mind of a people who had come to accept the book *Questions on Doctrine* as representing basic Adventist teachings.

Brinsmead was well aware of Pastor Andreasen's stand against the so-called *new theology* of the Church. Like Andreasen he was convinced that the Spirit of Prophecy taught that Christ came to this earth with a fallen nature and in this nature He lived a life free from sin. Brinsmead believed, at that time, that Jesus had demonstrated that sinful man, when filled with the Holy Spirit, could keep every one of God's commandments. He also took up the challenge which Andreasen had laid down to study afresh the messages of Dr. Waggoner and Pastor Jones presented at the historic Minneapolis Conference of 1888. In studying these messages Brinsmead found that these men had a clear perception of righteousness by faith.

By presenting this view Robert Brinsmead was doing nothing more than uplifting the old Adventist positions on the nature of Christ and righteousness by faith. Every *Sabbath School Quarterly* which referred to the nature of Christ during the lifetime of Sister White had stated quite unequivocally that Christ came to the earth with a fallen nature. Studies in 1896, 1902, 1909, 1913 and 1914 had all emphasized this truth. It had also been the basis of the statement of Christ's human nature in the early editions of such representative denominational publications as *Bible Readings for the Home Circle*.[2]

The 1915 edition of *Bible Readings for the Home Circle* stated in the clearest terms the Seventh-day Adventist position on this vital doctrine. This book should be read with care, for it demonstrates how far many of God's people have strayed from our original truths. The rejection of these truths provides the reason behind the tragic doctrinal problems within our Church today.

> In His humanity Christ partook of our sinful, fallen nature. If not, then He was not "made like unto His brethren," was not "in all points tempted like as we are," did not overcome as we have to overcome, and is not, therefore, the complete and perfect Saviour man needs and must have to be saved. The idea that Christ was born of an immaculate or sinless mother, inherited no tendencies to sin, and for this reason did not sin, removes Him from the realm of a fallen world, and from the very place where help is needed. On His human side, Christ inherited just what every child of Adam inherits, — a sinful nature. On the divine side, from His very conception He was begotten and born of the Spirit. And all this was done to place mankind on vantage-ground, and to demonstrate that *in the same way* everyone who is "born of the Spirit" may gain like victories over sin in his own sinful flesh. Thus each one is to overcome *as Christ overcame*. Rev. 3:21. Without this birth there can be no victory over temptation, and no salvation from sin. John 3:3–7. (*Bible Readings for the Home Circle*, 1915 edition printed by the Signs Publishing Company, Australia, 174)

All these older positions acceptably set out the fact that those who wish to give Jesus an advantage over us in the battle with sin did so in order to distort the law of God by accepting the change in the day of worship, and that they followed the Augustinian error that it was impossible for Christians to keep His law. Thus the true understanding of the nature of Christ stood as a bastion against the view that God could not empower obedience to His law.

Brinsmead pointed out that the Sunday keepers could readily accept such appalling error, for they fail to uplift the sanctity of the entire Ten Commandments of God. The fact, however, that some Seventh-day Adventists in the middle twentieth century should also accept this error was very difficult to explain. Certainly the view that Jesus took a nature similar to that of Adam before he fell is found nowhere in Scripture, and it is specifically opposed in the book *The Desire of Ages*.[3] It seems that this view found its way into the Adventist Church through the teaching of some who had trained in theological lines in universities which upheld this erroneous view of the nature of Christ. Here we see the danger of men and women seeking to understand truth through the academic artifices of those who have little understanding of the Scripture and who are more inclined to follow the traditions of men. Such a view of course appealed to some who felt that their battle with sin was such that they would never be victors. However, to God's people, who, although recognizing their own total failure, placed their faith in God's firm assurances, the promise of victory remained a blessed treasure.

The doctrinal controversy which arose in the latter half of the 1950s produced both Brinsmead's moment of opportunity and, so far as his relationship with the Seventh-day Adventist Church was concerned, his undoing.

Robert Brinsmead, who was then a young man in his twenties, possessed a penchant for emphasizing those doctrines of the Seventh-day Adventist Church which are distinctive. At the time when many Seventh-day Adventists were anxious to further cement the amiable relationships with evangelical Protestantism initiated by Barnhouse and Martin, Brinsmead was no little embarrassment. In the book *Questions on Doctrine* a large group of doctrines we held in common with the evangelicals were listed together with the few we held with a minority of other conservative Christians, and five which were stated to be unique to the Seventh-day Adventist Church. These five seemed so few when compared with the many which we held in common with the evangelicals that for some time they were almost lost in the flush of joy over the Protestant recognition of our faith and its offer of respectability. Nevertheless these doctrines were extremely important, for they included the investigative judgment, one of the most significant pillars of our faith.

In his speaking, Brinsmead placed his emphasis upon the Sanctuary, the nature of Christ, the investigative judgment, the three angels' messages, the loud cry, the latter rain, the close of probation, the prophecies of the Apocalypse, and other uniquely Adventist doctrines. Nothing was more likely to upset our precarious approval by the evangelical Protestants than the sort of topics which attracted Brinsmead's attention. By many he was seen as a brash young humbug, while others admired him as a courageous spokesman for the old, unadulterated Seventh-day Adventist faith. For one so young, Brinsmead's influence proved to be not insignificant. Many were surprised at some of the changes they had noted in *Questions on Doctrine* and saw Brinsmead as an able spokesman for their point of view. Andreasen had attracted no sizeable support for his protests, but this young Australian, grasping Andreasen's mantle, found ready hearers.

Because of this support Brinsmead was able to gather around himself an enthusiastic group of young pastors and laymen. This development naturally caused concern to the church leadership and steps were taken to remove these men from their positions of responsibility within the Church and from church membership itself. Many church leaders were not very lucid in their defense of their doctrinal position, and so only a few of Brinsmead's followers were disfellowshiped on the grounds of professing false doctrine. The majority were disfellowshiped because it was said that they failed to loyally support properly constituted church authority.[4] It was far easier for church pastors to demonstrate "disloyalty" than doctrinal deviation in the one they were determined to disfellowship.

In the 1980s it is difficult to believe the emotive reaction which the name *Brinsmead* conjured up in the minds of the majority of Seventh-day Adventists in

Australia two decades earlier. To have the name Brinsmead associated with a church member was akin to being termed "pink" in the McCarthy era in the United States. One incident illustrates the reactions which were engendered by the fear of the encroachment of Brinsmead's views within the Church. This incident occurred in a church in the city of Melbourne. One follower of Brinsmead, Mr. Ray Martin, had three beautiful young daughters who were quite gifted musically. When the church's thirteenth Sabbath children's program was to be presented, the church pastor banned these three girls from participating in the presentation. In defense of the decision, this pastor stated that God had destroyed the Amalekites' children for their parents' sin.

Any church member who was seen to be friendly with any person sympathetic to the views of Robert Brinsmead was eyed with very great suspicion. Elaborate efforts were made in some churches to exclude such people—the vast majority of whom were perfectly loyal Seventh-day Adventists—from church office. The selection committees were manipulated in order to select a nominating committee which could be guaranteed to exclude from office all those who were perceived to be insufficiently antagonistic to Robert Brinsmead's activities. These measures did little more than arouse enmity toward Brinsmead's followers on the part of some church members and sympathy for them on the part of others.

Brinsmead's followers became known as "Awakeners" following their selection of the title *Sanctuary Awakening Fellowship* for their semi-organization. The Awakeners themselves, although content to remain Seventh-day Adventists, did undertake activities which were schismatic, at least in part. Some preferred to send their tithes for the support of the defrocked ministry. This tithe money was accepted by these men and used. This action led to much justified criticism of the Sanctuary Awakening Fellowship. Some of these ex-pastors also baptized believers. Another source of disturbance was the many cottage meetings held by Awakeners and the annual camps held just on the Queensland side of its border with New South Wales. Brinsmead's views spread with unexpected rapidity throughout the Adventist Church worldwide. There was a receptive audience for his views among Seventh-day Adventists distraught by the changes evidenced in *Questions on Doctrine*. Soon many wealthy Adventists, particularly in the United States, were supplying the necessary means for the production and distribution of his *Present Truth* [5] magazine. Thus by the mid-to-late 1960s, the name Brinsmead was well known throughout most of the Adventist world, and he engendered not a little concern among those whose duty it was to lead the Church of God.

## Chapter 9 Endnotes

1. While this statement was not true of the Australasian Division of that time, it is a matter of record that the Statement of the 1973 Annual Council and the 1974 *Review and Herald Special on Righteousness by Faith* both proclaimed the old Adventist positions.
2. In 1949 a new edition of *Bible Readings for the Home Circle* was prepared which completely altered the statement concerning Christ's fallen human nature, and represented the nature of Christ more like the current Protestant view that Christ came with an unfallen nature.
3. The *Desire of Ages* 49 and 117 where the view that Christ possessed Adam's nature before the fall is considered and promptly rejected as error, and the truth that Christ possessed fallen, degenerate human nature is asserted.
4. As an elder of the Avondale College Church in the late 1960s, Colin was the only Board member to vote against the disfellowshiping of a young Brinsmead supporter when the only grounds that could be found was his refusal to follow all the dictates of the church leaders, although he did give assurances that he would do so when there was no conflict with Scripture. Later other Board members privately concurred with Colin's vote. However they had not dared to express this opinion in the presence of the college president.

# 10    Robert Brinsmead's Early Doctrines

ROBERT Brinsmead early set out those matters which he determined to be the doctrinal issues which he would raise. These were as follows:
"1. Christ entered the most holy place in 1844 to make a special atonement to blot out the sins of His people.
2. The Church has not entered by faith into this special atoning work of Jesus.
3. The Church can now enter into this great experience of the cleansing of the Sanctuary.
4. When the records of sin in heaven are blotted out by the atoning blood of Christ, they will no more be remembered or come into the minds of God's people. The parable of Joshua and the Angel in Zechariah outlines this wonderful experience.
5. This experience of the blotting out of sins (cleansing of the Sanctuary) must precede the reception of the latter rain.
6. God's people are called to gather at the Sanctuary to seek this special experience before the decree (Rev. 13) goes forth."[1]

It was within the details of these doctrinal matters that some found fault. Others, particularly those influenced by the evangelical accord, found fault with every one of the six points cited above. These objectors soon found fault with the entire sanctuary message.

In addition to his emphasis on a number of distinctive Adventist truths, Robert Brinsmead introduced some doctrinal concepts which appeared to be uniquely his own. Prominent among these was his view that the true believers would have perfection (some said *absolute perfection*) bestowed upon them by a miraculous act during the outpouring of the latter rain. These purified individuals, Brinsmead taught, would then go forth to give the loud-cry message. So much emphasis was placed upon this matter that it is somewhat difficult to be certain whether Brinsmead failed to teach as some now believe [2]—that obedience was required and empowered by God *now*.[3]

This view of Christian perfection was to have two long-term effects—effects which could not have been predicted at that time. The first of these consequences was of relatively minor significance. One of Brinsmead's Australian associates,

Fred Wright, could see Brinsmead's error in looking beyond the present for Christian perfection and gathered a following out of the Sanctuary Awakening Fellowship in the early 1960s. Wright went so far as to declare the Adventist Church Babylon. Nevertheless his following also spread across the Pacific but never reached the level of support which Brinsmead gained. Even in Australia, Wright's following outside the state of Queensland and the Northern Rivers district of New South Wales was small.

The personal experience of one of the authors (Russell) indicates the tragic situation of some of those who followed Wright. A dear old man came as a patient to see Russell while he was serving as a physician at the Warburton Sanitarium and Hospital in Victoria. It was a bitterly cold winter's day in 1967 and the patient was dressed appropriately in a heavy overcoat. With obvious discomfort and embarrassment as he was leaving, he quickly put his hand in his coat and took out some literature, thrusting it into Russell's hands, saying as he did so, "Would you please read this for me, Doctor?" It was material prepared by Fred Wright. His offer was accepted with a deep sense that this man was truly trying to be of help in the spiritual life of the recipient. While the authors have never found any place for offshoot groups, it has never been our policy to be rude or unChristlike to brethren and sisters who believe otherwise than ourselves. Later, while serving as a physician in the Penang Adventist Hospital in Malaysia, Russell was deeply saddened to read the death notice of this man in the *Australasian Record*. Almost without exception such obituaries are written by the officiating pastor. In this case, however, the obituary had been written by his sister. Russell has often pondered the circumstances whereby no pastor presided at the burial of this dear man, but has not been able to ascertain the reason.

The second and much more significant consequence of Brinsmead's false view of the timing of Christian perfection was that it was later to lead him to accept his current erroneous position that man can reach such a state only when glorified at the Second Coming of Christ. It seems that once the attainment of perfection was placed in the future, it was a simple matter to change the time of its attainment from the time of the latter rain to that of the Second Coming. This view of course was well pleasing to the Evangelical Protestants, and led Brinsmead to repudiate all the matters which he had so ably defended in the early days of his movement.

A second concept introduced by Brinsmead was the view of the cleansing of the soul temple. It cannot be successfully argued that such is not necessary. However, Brinsmead seemed to become more speculative when he separated this cleansing from the cleansing promised upon true confession and repentance.

> If we confess our sins, he is faithful and just to forgive us our sins, and to cleanse us from all unrighteousness. (1 John 1:9)

It was the supposedly more thorough cleansing of the soul temple which Brinsmead claimed occurred at the time of the infilling of the latter rain. Some students of

Brinsmead's views have put forward the view that this continuance of our unclean soul temple after forgiveness provided the kernel for his later acceptance of the Augustinian notion of original sin.[4] While this doctrine stated that men lose eternal life because of Adam's sin, it also emphasizes a fallen nature which is not cleansed by Christ's work within the repentant sinner. While Brinsmead originally believed that only the latter rain experience could achieve this cleansing, Catholics teach that the act of baptism achieves this end. This reasoning of course explains their practice of infant baptism. There are, nevertheless, some obvious parallels between the two views.

Robert Brinsmead certainly did one great service to the Church of God in Australia and also overseas. He made available to many a most significant manuscript written in 1950 by two American missionaries to Africa, Pastors Robert Wieland and Donald Short. This manuscript was entitled *1888 Re-Examined*. This book stood for over three decades against a growing tendency on the part of some to provide a false interpretation of the message and the outcome of the momentous Minneapolis Conference of 1888. There is no doubt that it was the rejection of the 1888 message of Righteousness by Faith which prepared the way for the 1956 presentation of error on this vital subject in an official publication of the Church. In 1950 the Lord, perhaps anticipating this rejection of truth, led Wieland and Short to examine this important topic. Unfortunately this valuable work was significantly revised for the centennial of the 1888 General Conference Session. In the revision, the seeds of the error now to be found in the teachings of the 1888 Message Study Committee and in the teachings of Elder Jack Siqueira were sown.

## Chapter 10 Endnotes

1. Letter written by Robert Brinsmead to W. R. Beach, Secretary of the General Conference, dated Jan. 17, 1961
2. See Pastor Frank Basham's paper presented to the Australasian Division Biblical Research Institute, Feb. 3, 1976.
3. It must be stated that men who were thoroughly acquainted with Robert Brinsmead's teaching seem to differ quite markedly over the relatively small, but nevertheless important, segment of Brinsmead's early teachings which was erroneous. Vance Ferrell identified six areas of error propounded in this early period, *viz* (i) That the conscious mind is equivalent to the first apartment of the Sanctuary. (ii) That the unconscious mind is equivalent to the second apartment of the Sanctuary. (iii) That the European Common Market fulfilled the prophecy of Revelation 17. (iv) That man cannot really put away sin until the investigative judgment. (v) That before the investigative judgment men can only pray for repentance. (vi) Belief in original sin. On the other hand Bob White, who "was at practically every Brinsmead lecture from 1961 to 1971" (*Layworker*, Feb. 1984, p. 39), claimed that Ferrell had misunderstood Brinsmead's early position. White only conceded point (vi), although his objections to points (i), (ii) and (iii) were rather minor. However White most decidedly objected to Ferrell's points (iv) and (v). (*Ibid.*)
4. In fact, in the 1960s one of Brinsmead's ablest allies, Peter Jarnes of the theology department of Union College, Nebraska, did introduce the notion of original sin, while still, at that time, defending Brinsmead's initial position.

# 11 The Seminary

WHEN the Seventh-day Adventist Church first trained ministers and other laborers in the cause of God, little attention was given to the possession of degrees. Rather, workers were selected for service on the basis of suitability and perceived calling. As time progressed, however, it was seen necessary to grant degrees at the baccalaureate level. This situation persisted for a number of years. It was noticed that some graduates at this level later attended non-Adventist institutions in order to study for postgraduate degrees. It was only logical, it seemed, that the Church should provide this type of education for such workers in an atmosphere where truth rather than a mixture of truth and error was given. Thus the Theological Seminary was established in 1942. [1]

Initially the Theological Seminary was located in what is now the south building of the General Conference. In the 1950s, however, it had accumulated a group of liberal teachers who were significantly affected by higher criticism. This situation was due to the fact that they had trained in institutions where their professors held such views. Some of these seminary professors greatly concerned the leadership of the General Conference, for it soon became evident that they were teaching their Seminary students those views which they themselves espoused. Confidence in the inspiration of the Word of God was effectively eroded in many cases. Dr. Ford himself in speaking to Colin referred to one of these professors, Dr. Earl Hilgert, suggesting that he "wasn't really a Seventh-day Adventist." Dr. Ford was in a position to know the situation, for he had studied under the man. That his assessment was almost certainly correct was verified by the fact that this professor later left God's Church and joined the Presbyterian Church. Indeed, one by one each of these liberal professors left the Seminary over the period of a decade and the General Conference seized these opportunities to appoint men of a different caliber.

The new class of Seminary lecturers, who began to be appointed in the late 1950s and the 1960s, consisted of men who in general pleased the leadership of the General Conference. Their acceptance was understandable, for they were like a breath of fresh air after the purveyors of higher criticism. They were Bible- and Christ-centered in their teaching and preaching. There was no open questioning of the Word of God. They placed great emphasis upon the sacrifice of Jesus on Calvary. It was difficult, at least initially, to fault their teachings. But whereas many early professors of the Seminary had been blatant in their deviation from truth, many (although not all) of the new Seminary teachers were also out of harmony with some of the basic Adventist teachings. These men had not sat at the feet of higher critics but had studied under so-called reformational theologians. These theologians claimed to be teaching the very truths brought by men such as Luther, Calvin and Zwingli under the power of God. Naturally, much of what was taught was sound material, but it was evident to those with insight that these professors, influenced by this school of theology, muted their teaching of such topics as the work of Jesus in the heavenly Sanctuary and the ministry of His blood before the mercy seat. These topics of course were not ignored, but their full import and emphasis were not presented.

Thus, little by little, subtle changes came into the beliefs of the men and women who studied under these teachers. There was a gradual weakening of the authority of the Spirit of Prophecy in doctrinal matters and a lessening of interest and confidence in the Sanctuary message. When Dr. Ford attended the Seminary, he did so not in the period when higher criticism was at its peak but in the period in which the reformational theologians had gained the ascendancy. He was such an outstanding student that he immediately gained the attention of his professors who could see that he was a man of exceptional talent. One of his contemporaries, Pastor Hilton Fisher, recalled that when he was a fellow student with Desmond Ford one professor was so impressed with Dr. Ford's gift that he appeared to direct his lectures largely to him, while the other students, who were of lesser capacity, felt that they were left to pick up the crumbs. There is little doubt that it was here that Dr. Ford began to formulate his concepts upon the topics of the nature of Christ and of the inability of man to overcome sin, for these views have been consistent principles of the reformational school of theology.

The history of churches presenting postgraduate education in the field of theology has been such that there is a great need for concern. Churches which have been renowned for their fidelity to the principles of God's faith have little by little seen these principles vanish as more and more of their ministerial force has been subjected to postgraduate theological training. Some would suggest that the study of Scripture cannot stand such minute investigation. Such a contention could never come from anyone who holds the Scriptures as precious and holy. The most minute study under the power of the Holy Spirit will reveal only greater verities and further confirm the student. But it does seem that the theological techniques of investigating Scripture as used by theologians tend to be so constructed, that in the normal course of events, they direct away from truth and toward error.

The Seventh-day Adventist Church is not immune to such forces, as has been clearly seen over the last three decades. Harold Lindsell, a former editor of *Christianity Today* and himself a devout Baptist, has shown very perceptively in his book *The Battle for the Bible* the process which occurred in Fuller College in the United States. This College had been erected with the specific aim to promote the fundamentalist belief in the Scripture. Yet, despite the most diligent effort, little by little, and later very speedily indeed, the College was populated by professors who absolutely denied the fundamentalist approach to the interpretation of Scripture. It seems that only a miracle of God can prevent such progressions. What is required is the greatest vigilance on the part of the leadership of such institutions.

Andrews University, in which the Theological Seminary in North America is located, and other institutions in other parts of the world which also have seminaries, need year by year to examine the teaching of their professors in order to see that the purity of the truth is maintained. Very often we put the possession of a doctorate in theology before other considerations in our selection of leaders and professors in the seminaries. This policy is a grave mistake. We have participated in discussions concerning the appointments in one or two of our seminaries, and we have noticed that even fine leaders, who truly believe the faith that we have and who do not want to see any attack upon that faith, will nevertheless accept the names of persons who, as a few inquiries would show, are totally unsuited for the aims which they wish to uphold. There are times when it is far easier for us to appoint men to our institutions who are uncommitted to our truth than it is to appoint men of outstanding ability who forthrightly defend the truth. Why this should be so is a matter of great concern. One thing is certain: the history of our Theological Seminaries has been a very rocky one indeed. There is hardly a sincere and knowledgeable Seventh-day Adventist who has not expressed concern over some of the appointments that have been made and some of the clearly erroneous material which has emanated from these institutions. The Seventh-day Adventist Church will never be strong until such deviations from truth are eradicated.

Much of the error was introduced on the wave of appeals for academic freedom. Many accepted this claim as a right of the academics and did not critically examine it. But—

> The cry for academic freedom is generated by those who would deny parents the freedom to have their children receive an education based upon the stated principles of the institution to which they have entrusted their children and for which they have made many financial sacrifices. Many professors deny their students the freedom to learn Seventh-day Adventist principles untrammeled by doubt and innuendo. They further deny the employing institution the right to pursue the aims inherent in its establishment. This is tyranny of the worst form, for it usurps a freedom for the professor at the expense of those who have a God-given right to exert it. Much of that which masquerades as academic freedom is, when unmasked, in very fact, *academic coercion*. (Dr. C. Standish, "Academic Freedom in the Adventist School System," *Landmarks*, January 1984).

## Chapter 11 Endnote

1. The first action to establish a Seminary was taken in 1932; however, it was not until 1937 that preliminary courses were given. The date 1942 marks the year in which the Master of Arts degree was first authorized. The Bachelor of Divinity soon followed (1959). The Seminary moved from Washington to Andrews University in 1960.

# 12 Educational Changes in Australia

UNTIL the mid-1950s Avondale College granted no degrees. All graduates were issued diplomas which had minimal acceptance outside the Seventh-day Adventist Church. This procedure was consistent with the original aim of Adventist colleges to train young men and women for denominational service rather than for secular employment. The educational system in Australia was vastly different from that existing in the United States, being much more closely allied to the British educational plan. In this system the education of children was closely supervised by the State, which on a secular level provided an excellent standard of education. In order to complete high school successfully, one had to sit for government examinations and be successful in those examinations. Virtually no credit was given for the work which had been carried out during the academic year, and the student's future was almost entirely determined upon the set of examinations for which he sat at the conclusion of his twelfth year of education. There were colleges of higher education, but these differed in intent from the type of college system in the United States. Those wishing higher education proceeded directly from school to university, where each commenced his course immediately. Thus the medical course was commenced upon leaving school and was completed after a period of six years' training. Similarly engineers, lawyers, dentists, veterinary surgeons, agricultural scientists, scientists, economists and other such professionals commenced their studies at the university directly from school. Those wishing to study in fields such as history, English, philosophy, psychology, likewise commenced a bachelor of arts degree, which was academically just as taxing as any of the other courses which have been cited. It was not the prerogative of non-state colleges at that time to issue any degrees whatsoever.

Even in high school the matter of education was very different from that of some overseas countries. The Australian system of education was not based upon the premise that the average student had the right to complete twelve grades of education. Indeed, such a student was encouraged to leave school after ten grades. Thus the matriculation examinations were set at such a level that only the top twenty-five percent of students possessed the ability, if sufficient effort was expended, to pass the examination. Because of these factors, in 1950 approximately only seven percent of students entering high school completed the matriculation.

Avondale College at that time accepted applicants with varying academic backgrounds, the vast majority of whom quite naturally had not attained their matriculation. Many of these studied diligently and obtained this qualification while at college and went forth to follow outstanding academic careers. Those completing the courses in Avondale were given diplomas which were appropriate to their course of study. Particularly in the field of theology some young graduates felt extremely limited by the fact they could not easily take advantage of the increasing postgraduate courses presented by the Theological Seminary then situated in Washington D.C. These matters were given consideration and moves were made to forge an affiliation with Pacific Union College. The affiliation was completed in 1954. In this way it was possible for students of Avondale College to receive the bachelor of arts degree in either theology or education granted by Pacific Union College. Graduates from these courses were then eligible to study for their master's degrees in the United States.

We attended Avondale College in 1950 and 1951, studying primarily school teaching and graduated from the two-year diploma course which was then called the Theological Normal Course. In 1950 an attempt had been made with good success to prepare science students with a degree acceptable within Australia. This was done by enrolling these students in the London University bachelor of science correspondence course and instructing them in the matters of the curriculum of that course at Avondale College. This procedure was of some help to our schools in preparing science teachers and indeed the first three students in this course distinguished themselves and eventually obtained Ph.D. degrees.[1] In theology, however, the University of London for obvious reasons could not suffice.

Desmond Ford was a final-year theology student in 1950, and thus we had the privilege of being fellow students with him. Since he was older than we and considerably more gifted, we naturally respected him very highly indeed. He was an able speaker even at that time and possessed a prodigious knowledge of the Scriptures. His godly character was in evidence at that time, and we only wish that we could look back at our own time in college as having set a similar example of rectitude. We never doubted that Desmond would make an enormous impact upon the church of God. Naturally in 1950 at the time of his graduation he was issued a ministerial diploma. Had he stayed another year or two he probably would have earned the licentiate of theology. This degree was an interim effort to upgrade the academic standards of the theology course.

Desmond went into the evangelistic field, having the good fortune to work with Pastor George Burnside in his Newcastle evangelistic effort. Pastor Burnside was the most successful evangelist in Australia at that time. After a few years as pastor-evangelist, Des' academic gifts were recognized, and he was granted permission to return to Avondale College in the mid-1950s in order to complete one year's further education, after which he was granted his bachelor's degree from Pacific Union College.

It was at this time that he met Robert Brinsmead, who was studying as an undergraduate in the college. It is not often that men of such outstanding talents are found in a single college as contemporaries. There is no doubt that Brinsmead and Ford spent considerable time in discussions, for each was interested in the other's acute perceptions. Upon completion of his bachelor's degree, Ford was sponsored to the Theological Seminary where he studied for his master's degree. Here he fell very strongly under the influence of Dr. Edward Heppenstall, whose theological classes he attended. Graduating with his master's degree he went to the University of Michigan, and in a very short time was awarded a Ph.D. degree in rhetoric. In 1960 he returned to Australia to head the theology department at Avondale College.

Chapter 12 Endnote

1. Dr. Laurence Draper, Dr. Eric Magnusson and Dr. Kenneth Thompson

# 13 Desmond Ford Defends the Church

AS has been indicated in chapter 2 of this book, early after his return from the United States, Dr. Ford demonstrated a less than full acceptance of the words of the Spirit of Prophecy. He denied the oft-repeated words in the Spirit of Prophecy which indicated that creation week occurred approximately six thousand years ago.[1] Although it was not immediately evident, it now seems that he had also accepted while overseas the view that Christ possessed the nature of Adam before the fall and the corollary of that belief, namely, that man cannot fully obey the law of God until glorification occurs at the Second Coming. These views might have led Dr. Ford to trace a course which would have demanded his resignation from church employment in the nineteen-sixties, had it not been for two circumstances at that time. These dual factors have been referred to previously. The first was the publication of *Questions on Doctrine*, and the second was the rise to prominence of Robert Brinsmead and the Sanctuary Awakening Fellowship. *Questions on Doctrine* permitted a much wider spectrum of doctrinal views to be accepted, and Robert Brinsmead provided an "enemy" to fight.

So articulate were Brinsmead's attacks on *Questions on Doctrine* that the Australasian Church desperately searched for a man of caliber to counter his views in order to minimize the defection of church members to the Sanctuary Awakening Fellowship. Naturally the eyes of many turned toward Desmond Ford, for here was someone of similar intellectual caliber who could cross swords with Brinsmead more effectively than had been demonstrated by many of the other pastors. Thus Dr. Ford was cast in the role of defending the Church against the attacks upon it by Robert Brinsmead and a number of his able assistants. Dr. Ford's acceptance of this assigned duty was not entirely wholehearted. It was true that Ford's belief in the evangelical view that man could not obey the law of God prior to the Second Coming, and his acceptance even of the notion that Jesus had to have a nature superior to our own in order to obey the Decalogue, provided a firm basis for his denunciation of Robert Brinsmead's concept of the nature of Christ and his pronouncement that perfection will be bestowed at the time of the latter rain. Nevertheless, another matter made this role of public antagonist to Robert Brinsmead distasteful.

Dr. Ford had married a wonderful Christian girl, Gwen Booth, who tragically developed a terminal illness. This illness led to considerable pain and discomfort which were not fully ameliorated by the physicians in attendance. Because of this,

Gwen sought the aid of Robert Brinsmead's sister, Mrs. Hope Taylor, who, using hydrotherapy and other simple methods, certainly did bring a degree of comfort to Gwen. The care given to her was not only effective but was also bestowed with much tenderness and love. It was only natural that this situation brought Dr. Ford and Robert Brinsmead into close contact and developed a mutual respect between them, though their doctrinal positions remained, at least superficially, far apart.

Dr. Ford made a number of visits to the north coast of New South Wales in order to visit his wife, and there were many discussions in the quietude of the rural environment during these visits. It cannot be overlooked, however, that the embarrassment which Robert Brinsmead caused the Australian Church also provided Ford's opportunity. Some were so desperate to denounce Brinsmead's views that it almost seemed that any plausible doctrinal view gained credence so long as it was contrary to the views of Robert Brinsmead. It was in this climate that a number of views new to Seventh-day Adventists, but long held by some of the Protestant churches, received an airing within our ranks. One of these, of course, was Ford's newly acquired view that man will continue in sin until the Second Coming. This doctrine, anathema to a previous generation of Seventh-day Adventists, was seen as a neat counter to Brinsmead's claim that the perfection of Christian character would be obtained during the outpouring of the latter rain. Since Ford's view was also more acceptable to the evangelical Protestant churches whose favor had recently been gained, it accorded well with the current atmosphere within the Church.

It is most instructive for God's people to examine these facts, for they demonstrate very plainly how circumstances can be molded by the enemy of truth in such a way that that which could never be accepted under ordinary circumstances becomes a cherished view of the unwary, for it suits the prevailing conditions. It should not be thought that all efforts to confound the Brinsmead error on the timing of Christian perfection were based on false doctrines. At the same time that Ford was countering error with error, others were asserting truth in order to expose the Brinsmead position. One notable instance of this occurred in the 1960s when a public discussion by two church pastors was held. Both of these men vigorously attacked Brinsmead's position, but from entirely different standpoints. Thus Pastor Frank Basham asserted the biblical view that God requires and empowers victory over sin in the life *now*. On the other hand the other pastor, following Ford's view, stated that Christians would continue in sin until the Second Coming. While these two views are in fact the center of the current doctrinal controversy within God's Church, both were happily accepted at that meeting since they equally provided an alternative to Brinsmead's doctrine.

## Chapter 13 Endnote

1. Ford has not been alone in this denial. Unfortunately his disregard for the words of God's servant on the age of the earth continues. See "How Accurate is Bible Chronology?" *Ministry*, March 1984.

# 14

## Opposition to the New Theology

BY 1965 men of perception saw the direction that Dr. Ford's teaching was taking. The stirrings of opposition were slow to surface, many fearing lest they be misunderstood as supporting Robert Brinsmead's views, as they attempted to warn of the even more insidious error which was coming into the Church. These fears were not unfounded. Numbers of devoted Seventh-day Adventists were falsely categorized as followers of Brinsmead on the basis of their objections to errors presented within the Church. This accusation so discouraged many good souls that the voice of truth was almost wholly muted at a time when it was desperately needed. Bible truths such as Christian perfection, the Sanctuary message and other beliefs came to be considered erroneous simply because Brinsmead taught them.

Other true believers remained silent because Ford presented his errors with such ease and wove them into the framework of precious truth in such a way that for many the discernment of error was well-nigh impossible.

It was not on the area of righteousness by faith that these early complaints concerning Ford's doctrines centered. Ford's views of non-victorious living led him to question the Sanctuary doctrine, for righteousness by faith and the Sanctuary are so linked that one cannot hold error in one area without transferring error to the other.

One, who to this day remains anonymous and is unknown to us, circulated a three-page paper, dated September 9, 1965 at Cooranbong, the village in which Avondale College is situated. This person certainly had insight at a time when many were fixing their gaze elsewhere. The author of this paper commenced, "I have hesitated to write on this subject for quite a time, but the conviction grows that I must make known the situation, so that something can be done to arrest the apostasy. So here is the picture as I see it from my home near Avondale."

The paper then set forth some general objections to the worldly trends noted by its author at the college, and then pointed out two serious errors of doctrine taught by the Theology Department. On these matters he stated, "Many are becoming concerned at the easy way the old teaching of the age of the earth is being laughed at by the Doctor of Theology, who says in effect, 'The Spirit of Prophecy may say it is 6,000 years from creation, but I say it could be 7,000 or 8,000 or 9,000 or even 10,000 years ago.' It is apparent that this idea originated with the head of the Bible Department by the one who loves to speak of 'Adventist Scholarship.'" That this writer was clearly referring to Dr. Ford is made plain by another statement from the paper. "Yet a man gets a degree in speech and then sets himself up as the last word in theology and wants to ride over the writings of inspiration."

Following this complaint concerning Ford's view of the age of the earth, this anonymous writer proceeded to utilize one page to set forth his fears concerning Ford's view of the Sanctuary. His concern is well summed up in the single paragraph which follows: "Dr. Ford would have us believe that the heavenly Sanctuary is only an object lesson with no real articles of furniture. In fact, it does not even have walls; in other words, there is no Sanctuary in heaven. Do we have an enemy within our ranks who would overthrow the very foundations of this movement?"

Anonymous letters in general receive scant attention, but this one was an exception, so widely distributed was the paper and so patently correct the charges. It presented a great difficulty for those who were presenting Dr. Ford as the answer to the Brinsmead apostasy within the Church. Thus it was seen as inappropriate to permit Dr. Ford's credibility to be diminished at a time when he was so much needed as a bastion against a problem bedeviling the Church. However, in spite of all the efforts to uphold Dr. Ford's hands and to repudiate the accusations which were made in the anonymous letter, Dr. Ford's standing as an Adventist purist never again reached the level of support which had previously characterized his messages.

Among the first to express open apprehension of Ford's teachings at Avondale College was Pastor George Burnside, the Division ministerial secretary. Naturally he was well acquainted with Dr. Ford since Ford had been an intern on his evangelical team in 1951. Pastor Burnside was one who had long stood in defense of the scriptural doctrine of the Sanctuary. He had witnessed much damage which had been caused to the Church of God by those who questioned the Sanctuary truth together with obedience to God's law, and inevitably the validity of the writings of the Spirit of Prophecy. In Pastor Burnside's own homeland he had seen in the late 1950s the president of the North New Zealand Conference, Pastor Robert Greive, apostatize on these very points of Adventist understanding. The Church had quickly recognized the error and had dismissed him from the ministry. Tragically a number of other promising young workers were lost to God's truth at the same time. Of course Robert Greive's position was not new within the Adventist Church. He had accepted Albion Ballenger's view which had been shown to be false by Sister White in the year 1905. Australian church leader, Pastor W. W. Fletcher, in the late 1920s, while teaching at Avondale College, also had espoused these views and had been lost to the work of God. He had been a most capable leader and had, between 1921 and 1923, been president of the Southern Asia Division.[1] Thus it seemed that the Church in Australia was never long free of this particular line of apostasy. In the case of Desmond Ford, however, the situation, for reasons which we have previously mentioned, was greatly different, and he was to have success in propagating his views far beyond that achieved by any of his predecessors. On more than one occasion, ex-pastor Robert Greive, in writing, expressed amazement that Ford was upheld while he had been dismissed for propagating precisely the same doctrines.

There was a further reason why Dr. Ford's presentation of these very same doctrines met with prolonged tolerance and success within the Australasian Church. He demonstrated much greater care than did either Fletcher or Greive in Australia or Ballenger in the United States in making his views public. Indeed, much of the early concern for Dr. Ford's presentations was initiated by the statements of his students who asserted that they had been taught that which Adventists could not approve. Yet when Dr. Ford spoke in public, little if any of this error was detectable in his sermons.

In 1965 Pastor Burnside was a guest speaker at the Victorian Conference camp meeting. After preaching on the Sanctuary he was confronted by five ministerial interns (four of them subsequently left the ministry) who told him that they could not agree with his presentation. Since Pastor Burnside had presented the Adventist position on the Sanctuary, he was perplexed by their disagreement with his presentation. Questioning them further, he found that each believed that Christ had entered into the second apartment at the time of His ascension. It was discovered that these men asserted that they had been taught this matter by Dr. Ford during his theology classes at Avondale College.

Concerned about this revelation, Pastor Burnside discussed the matter with Pastor John Keith, president of the Trans-Commonwealth Union (now Trans-Australian Union) Conference and Pastor Leo Rose, president of the Victorian Conference. They too interviewed the young men and confirmed Pastor Burnside's findings.

Upon his return to the Division headquarters, Pastor Burnside conveyed his discovery to the Division leadership. Pastor L. C. Naden, the Division president, promptly arranged for a meeting with Dr. Ford. At this meeting Dr. Ford protested that he could not be judged on the basis of what some of his students said concerning his teaching, and his answers were such that Pastor Naden felt reassured that Ford was standing on the side of truth. Pastor Burnside, who attended the meeting, felt less assured but nevertheless was not in a position to place his finger upon anything specific since Dr. Ford had denied the teaching of falsehood in this area. However, as Pastor Burnside continued to itinerate around the Division he found that these five interns in the Victorian Conference were not isolated cases. Thus he began to form the opinion that the material Dr. Ford was teaching within his classrooms was very different from that which he presented to the public. Because of this discovery he commenced to press his concerns with the Division leadership.

There was a natural reluctance on the part of the Division administration to heed Pastor Burnside's warnings since Dr. Ford had possessed all the credentials of an honorable man, and when he gave undertakings of fidelity to the Adventist faith, the men in leadership felt reassured. Further, there was no desire on their part to cause a misunderstanding with the laity who had come to rely on Dr. Ford's position as being that which stood as a biblical defense against the Brinsmead views. Pastor Burnside continued to wrestle with new problems which he saw in the field emanating from the teaching of the *new theology*. Nevertheless he found scant support for his desire to see the truth of God taught in the theology department of Avondale College. It is true that a number of the men who were also teaching in that department privately expressed their grievances, for they too were aware that error was being taught.[2] However, none dared to openly confront the situation, for it had become impolitic to do so by the 1960s.

It would be most improper to speculate as to the reasons for subsequent events. What is certain, however, is that following his public expression of concern, Pastor Burnside was relieved of his post as ministerial secretary of the Australasian Division at the General Conference Session in Atlantic City in 1970. This action was a great blessing to him and to God's cause, for he was now able to devote much more of his time to his one great love, spreading the message of God's love for mankind, in the post of assistant ministerial secretary of the Greater Sydney Conference.

Chapter 14 Endnotes

1. See Appendix H.
2. Among these were Pastors Alfred Jorgensen, Raymond Stanley, and in the early 1970s, Leonard Tolhurst.

# 15

# The Rise of the Theologians

IN the early history of the Seventh-day Adventist Church, doctrinal truth was arrived at by much prayer and study among earnest Bible students who had had little or no formal training in the niceties of theology. When unanimity could not be found, frequently Sister White was given a vision which settled the doctrinal matter for the sincere believer. Thus truth was arrived at, and a body of doctrine adopted which received almost universal acceptance by church members.

Early Seventh-day Adventists entered into a system of college education to prepare men and women for denominational service. Although the first few years of Adventist education were indeed very shaky, by the end of the nineteenth century the professors chosen were normally men of great experience who were confirmed in the faith by their diligent study of the Word of God and their devoted spiritual life. In the 1930s, however, a change came into the educational system of the Seventh-day Adventist Church. The factor which led to this change stemmed from the accreditation of the medical school at Loma Linda. It was believed that unless the pre-medical courses of the denomination were accredited the medical course itself could not be accredited. This belief led to much anguish on the part of church leaders who very perceptively saw the dangers of seeking accreditation. Nevertheless, they also recognized the need to train Christian physicians.[1] With this goal in mind it was decided to select two institutions to seek accreditation, thus permitting the training of young people in the pre-medical course. Pacific Union College was selected in the West and Emmanuel Missionary College (Andrews University) in the East. Thus the door was left wide open so that courses at Loma Linda University could receive accreditation.

In a short period of time, however, all Adventist colleges in the United States had been accredited. In order for the colleges to comply with accreditation board criteria, the need arose for teachers to study in outside universities, including study in the area of theology. Thus a group of Seventh-day Adventists arose in the Church who were to have an influence upon the doctrinal direction of the church body.

Unlike their predecessors, these men were not necessarily those who had studied deeply the Seventh-day Adventist doctrines. In many cases they were men who had studied far more deeply matters which were the concerns of Christian denominations whose beliefs often differed markedly from those of the Seventh-day Adventist Church. As more and more of these teachers with postgraduate theological degrees were found in the Church, there was a decided tendency to look to these men to decide doctrinal issues. Naturally many of them gave judgments colored by the errors they had been taught in outside universities.

Thus while the doctrines of the Church had been relatively stable for several decades, by the 1960s doubts and changes were brought into the Church. These changes were largely introduced by the theologians. Later the theologians were asked to settle the disputes which their doctrinal changes engendered. It was only natural they would tend to come out on the side of the errors which they had initiated. One example of this process can be seen in a letter written from the Australasian Division to the General Conference in 1965. The writer stated, "And now in the area of the Sanctuary. For years the theologians in this country (who imbibed their doctrinal views from the pioneers who came from the USA) have had a very literal concept of the Sanctuary, its furnishings, apartments, et cetera. Two of our former missionaries and leaders in the work here left us because they could not hold to these views. I refer to W. W. Fletcher and R. A. Greive. It is felt by some in Australasia today, both the above were not far removed doctrinally in their views of the Sanctuary from some of our present theologians in the USA.

"We have sent some of our men to the Seminary, to Andrews University, and, in addition, we have had a Seminary Extension School conducted in this field. In all places, I am informed, emphasis is placed today on symbolism and phases of ministry rather than a literal application of the Sanctuary truth as taught by the pioneers. (Now this may be perfectly correct. I am not contending for either view in this statement.) In addition, there is an exchange of views as between the theologians in our colleges with a consequent presentation of the same to our students of theology. These students, when they become interns in the various conferences, soon discover to their dismay that they are at variance doctrinally with their older brethren in the ministry. Recently, in our own Division, in one of the state conferences, this very thing happened with the result that the local conference committee has placed these students under restraint from airing their views until such time as a statement arrives from the G. C. outlining what we do believe in respect to the Sanctuary truth, as to whether or not there is a literal Sanctuary in heaven." [2]

One of the interesting features of this letter was the openness with which the change in theology was mentioned, for it differed significantly from public statements when these matters were raised. It was usual in public for leadership to state that there was absolutely no change in the Church's position. It will be noticed that this letter was penned just four months prior to the appearance of the anonymous letter pointing out Dr. Ford's changed stand on the Sanctuary. The general response to the anonymous letter was to reassure the flock that no change had in fact taken place. But here clearly was evidence that the presence of such changes and their relationship to the Fletcher and Greive apostasies were well known and understood by top leadership within the Australasian Division at the time the anonymous letter was circulated.

Dr. Ford's contribution to bringing this new concept to Australia had been set out in a letter from the same author to Pastor H. W. Lowe at the General Conference a few days earlier. He was referring to the incident cited earlier in this book in which certain interns in the Victorian Conference challenged Pastor Burnside: "We have recently received word from the Victorian Conference where a number of ministerial interns have recently been employed, a statement of concern over the views of these interns in respect to this important doctrine of the Church. The Victorian Conference has taken an action which calls for a statement from the General Conference in respect to the denominational teaching on this important subject. I wonder whether it might be easier for you good folk to state whether or not Dr. Ford's outline is the present view of the denomination in respect to this important doctrine or whether the General Conference is not in harmony with this statement, and if so where it differs from Brother Ford in its view.

"We are very anxious, Brother Lowe, to steady the field down. You know that the Australasian Division is rather sensitive about teachings on the Sanctuary, for in this area some of our leading men in days gone by have lost their way, and in this regard I am referring to men like W. W. Fletcher and R. A. Greive. Could you regard this as an urgent request and let me know without too much delay the opinion of the General Conference men, particularly our theologians, in respect to same?" [3]

For those who recall that period it is somewhat surprising that men in leadership were so cognizant of the changes which were taking place in a doctrine which is such a central pillar of our faith. Most lay people were of the opinion that the church leadership believed that no changes were occurring. A plea was made as follows: "Brother Figuhr, could not most of this embarrassment be prevented if Bible Conferences were called at regular intervals at which some of the theologians from each Division of the world field could be present to participate in such studies and discussions?" [4] It will be seen here that the plea is for theologians to be accorded the right to make the decision on doctrine. Yet, as was quoted earlier from the same letter, it was obvious that these changes had been brought into the Church by these very same theologians in the United States. It hardly seems proper that those who were initiating changes should be accorded the privilege of being arbiters of whether those changes are scriptural or not. Clearly such judges could hardly be free of bias.

It was this growing emphasis on the words of theologians which produced another problem within the Seventh-day Adventist Church in Australia. The anonymous letter of 1965 which attacked Dr. Ford's teaching at Avondale College, it will be recalled, contained a barb. The author stated, "Yet a man gets a degree in speech . . ." This instance was not the only time that Dr. Ford apparently heard these words. He stated that a number of theologians in the United States would not take his contributions to denominational publications seriously because his doctorate degree was in the area of rhetoric rather than in theology. This circumstance influenced Dr. Ford to seek approval to study for a second doctorate, this time in the area of theology. The Australasian Division acceded to this request, and Dr. Ford enrolled in the University of Manchester in England to study for the degree he had requested.

The University of Manchester theological department was strongly influenced by Professor F. F. Bruce, a member of the Plymouth Brethren faith. These Christians strongly believe in the doctrine of the perseverance of the saints (once saved always saved) and in the Futurist interpretation of prophecy. It was Professor Bruce who later wrote the foreword to Dr. Ford's book on the prophecies of Daniel.

Chapter 15 Endnotes

1. That accreditation is unnecessary is shown by the fact that no courses (including the medical course) at Harvard University are accredited despite the high reputation of its graduates.
2. Letter from the president of the Australasian Division to the president of the General Conference dated May 13, 1965
3. Letter from the president of the Australasian Division to Pastor H. W. Lowe, May 7, 1965
4. Letter from Australasian Division president to the president of the General Conference, May 30, 1965

# 16    Brinsmead Changes Direction

IN the very early 1970s Robert Brinsmead slowly began to amend his views. He had studied deeply into Reformed Theology and became impressed from this study that the gospel consisted of nothing more than the objective fact of Christ's death on Calvary for our sins, and that acceptance of this doctrine represented both righteousness by faith and justification by faith. Following this dramatic change of emphasis, Brinsmead, a most logical thinker, was compelled to renounce his former view of Christian perfection, replacing it with the view of the evangelical Protestants that perfection of character will not occur until the Second Coming. This conclusion led him to accept the Augustinian idea that because of the sinfulness of our natures, continuance in sin is inevitable until glorification. Logically this view demanded a reevaluation of Christ's human nature, for if we could not cease to sin because of our possession of a fallen nature, then this too would have been true of Christ if He had possessed a fallen nature. Since Scripture undeniably teaches Christ's sinlessness, Brinsmead deduced that He would not have possessed the nature of fallen man. Thus the point of doctrine set forth in *Questions on Doctrine* which Brinsmead had so strongly taken issue with in the sixties, now became part and parcel of his own theological thinking.

Just what factors or people influenced Brinsmead's change in doctrine is not altogether clear to us. What is certain is that Dr. Ford widely claimed that Brinsmead's reappraisal of his doctrines was largely due to his own influence upon Brinsmead. Brinsmead made no studied effort to deny this claim. Further, Brinsmead had an extraordinary ability, even when defending the distinctive doctrines of the Seventh-day Adventist Church, to have his works read widely outside the Church. We have vivid memories of seeing Brinsmead's commentary on the book of Revelation being sold from many of the bookstands in Sydney. We could only marvel at this success, for religious books find very little favor in Australia in such settings. Brinsmead was able to direct much material to clergymen and lay people of other faiths. These associations presented both opportunities and dangers. There are wonderful opportunities if we work *for* these people, but serious dangers when we work *with* them. Imperceptibly Brinsmead moved from the door of opportunity to the site of danger. The line of demarcation can be so thin as to be almost imperceptible, and yet the distinction is all-important. Thus it soon became evident that instead of influencing

Protestants Brinsmead became greatly influenced by them. One such case was his association with the Anglican pastor, Geoffrey Paxton, to whom reference is made later.

Understandably Brinsmead's changes in doctrine came as a great surprise to a great number of his supporters. The majority of these people had thoroughly studied the doctrines he formerly espoused and were convinced that they were scriptural. Yet in Australia most of these apparently sincere people changed their doctrinal beliefs to conform with Brinsmead's new understanding. It would be quite unfair to suggest that the majority lacked conviction. What was certain was that Brinsmead was a lucid and convincing writer. He is also an unpolished but penetrating and logical speaker relying on a vast knowledge of his subject and an encyclopedic memory to convince his audience. No doubt these undeniable talents were utilized to their fullest in bringing a new doctrinal perception to the majority of his followers. Second, and very significantly, there was an esprit de corps among those who classified themselves as belonging to the Sanctuary Awakening Fellowship. They had accepted much ridicule and even persecution. This circumstance had fused bonds which for many were difficult to break. The thought of severing friendships fused in adversity was almost unthinkable to many.

Nevertheless, with some, acceptance of Brinsmead's new views came only after much heart searching. Indeed, when Brinsmead first presented his views at one of his camp meetings in Australia, a number of his most loyal followers initially refused to accept them. Emotions became greatly strained and it was only after Brinsmead, overcome by the great pressure of the situation, broke down and wept that some ceased their opposition. This episode does emphasize the fearful consequences of persecuting individuals for their conscientiously held convictions. It is very possible that had love and care been shown to those who followed Brinsmead at that time, many would have retained a warmth of sentiment toward the Church and would have returned to it once they saw the direction Brinsmead was taking. But many felt that, should they sever their connection with the Sanctuary Awakening Fellowship, they would have no place of comfort or rest.

Now that the two most audible voices in Australian Adventism were speaking as a single voice, this unity seemed to present almost insuperable obstacles to the presentation of truth in the country. This situation was compounded by the fact that some brethren, noting Brinsmead's transformed position and Ford's support of it, rapidly directed their attacks away from him and permitted a degree of respectability to surround the name *Brinsmead*. Indeed, moves were made to reestablish Brinsmead's membership within the Seventh-day Adventist Church.

All these changes occurred so rapidly that many people could not keep pace with the ins and outs of individuals within the pale of the Seventh-day Adventist Church. Indeed, Brinsmead might well have become a member of the Church once more had it not been for the inexplicable demand that he first be re-baptized. This demand, which is not always required of converts of other faiths who have been previously baptized and was not required of Seventh-day Adventists who returned from the Reform Seventh-day Adventist Church, was said to have been imposed in order to test Brinsmead's repentance for the harm he had done the Seventh-day Adventist Church. Brinsmead, perhaps quite properly, refused this demand. The real problem was that his new beliefs took him even further away from the Seventh-day Adventist Church, and it was most improper to make any moves whatsoever to support his readmission to membership while he was holding doctrines so contrary to God's truth.

To many observers it seemed that Brinsmead was not overly concerned by his failure to regain his former membership. No doubt his status outside the Church gave him much greater freedom of action and lost him very little of the great support he gathered within the Church. Indeed, this support was now greater than ever. Certainly Brinsmead and Ford, uniting in presenting a similar message, one within the Church and one without, produced a formidable combination. It would not be unfair to state that in many respects they were unequaled within the Seventh-day Adventist Church. Brinsmead's talents have been mentioned. While Ford's ability to write convincingly fell far short of Brinsmead's, he did have an exceptional gift in speaking. His recall of numerous statements, his agility in bringing these together in tantalizing sequences, and his ability to think far more rapidly than virtually all members of his audience, combined to give an air of veracity to his contentions. To this ability was added that indefinable quality which is termed *charisma*. This gift led many to wait on his every pronouncement, expressing deep admiration for the "sound" of his talk without taking full cognizance of the danger contained within it.

# 17 The Nineteen Seventy-three Annual Council

IN the early 1970s the leadership of God's Church began a call for reformation and revival. Pastor Robert Pierson, then General Conference president, initiated the call. This challenge to our church membership was taken up in the editorials and articles in the *Adventist Review*. At the Annual Council of the General Conference held in 1973 a most earnest plea to God's people was adopted by the delegates in session. In our lifetime a more stirring appeal has never been made to God's people. The tone of this appeal was set in the first paragraph: "We believe that the return of Jesus has been long delayed, that the reasons for the delay are not wrapped in mysteries, and that the primary consideration before the Seventh-day Adventist Church is to re-order its priorities individually and corporately so that our Lord's return may be hastened." The Annual Council then turned its attention to the great message of 1888 and questioned, "What has happened to the message and experience that by 1892 had brought the beginning of the earth's final message of warning and appeal?"

The leaders of God's Church answered their own question very frankly. There was no arrogant effort to put all the blame on the laity. The Church leadership fully and humbly acknowledged its own deficiencies; nevertheless the failures so evident in God's people were not overlooked. The statement from the Annual Council made the following points: "As a body the Church still is in the Laodicean condition as set forth by the True Witness in Rev. 3:14–19. Therefore in attempting to find the specific present causes for failure and delay, the Council has noted three main factors:

"1. Leaders and people have not fully accepted as a personal message Christ's analysis and appeal to the Laodiceans. (Rev. 3:14–22)
2. Leaders and people are in some ways disobedient to divine directives, both in personal experience and in the conduct of the Church's commission.
3. Leaders and people have not yet finished the Church's task."

In order to place the finger on the source of the problem, the gathered church leaders quoted from other writings of God's servant:

> Those who come up to every point, and stand every test, and overcome, be the price what it may, have heeded the counsel of the True Witness, and they will receive the latter rain, and thus be fitted for translation. (1*T* 187.)

So important was this appeal from the 1973 General Conference that we are constrained to present selections from the appeal, for it has stood as an awesome challenge to the Church of God.

> The message to Laodicea involved a personal relationship to Jesus Christ that will produce a quality people, a conquering people, a people who, in Christ's own words, will conquer "as I myself conquered." (Rev. 3:21 RSV) This message will produce a people whom God can set forth without embarrassment as exhibits of those who "keep the commandments of God and the faith of Jesus" (Rev. 14:12 RSV); a people who have learned through experience that all godliness is a result of being sustained by divine power. Such people can be entrusted with special power because they will use it the way Jesus used power; indeed, in all aspects of life they will reflect the character of Jesus.
>
> Becoming like Jesus in word and deed is the goal of the process called righteousness by faith.

The document then set forth another passage from the Spirit of Prophecy, which was anathema to those who had accepted the *new theology*. This passage stated:

> The righteousness of Christ is not a cloak to cover unconfessed and unforsaken sin; it is a principle of life that transforms the character and controls the conduct. Holiness is wholeness for God; it is the entire surrender of heart and life to the indwelling of the principles of heaven. (*DA* 555,556)

Such an analysis, which truly represents God's plan for His people, was far from music in the ears of Brinsmead, Ford and some Seventh-day Adventist theologians. They had absorbed the so-called Reformed Theology and were proclaiming that righteousness by faith included only the objective facts of Calvary, and that it was assuming a Catholic position to include the work of God in the believer (sanctification) as part of righteousness by faith. Indeed, it was from this point that the *new theology* gathered momentum in an effort to counter plain biblical and Spirit of Prophecy-oriented teachings sponsored by the church leadership.

Undaunted by this opposition to the truth, the world leaders, including the delegates from the Australasian Division, unanimously accepted this appeal which went on to leave no doubt that the very same message which Dr. Waggoner and Pastor Jones presented at the Minneapolis Conference of 1888 was still acceptable and was indeed imperative for today's Church.[1] The appeal of the Annual Council of 1973 went on to state:

> As delegates to this Autumn Council, we believe that this is the heart of the Church's need—understanding and experiencing all that is meant in the phrase, "righteousness by faith." Such righteousness is God's will lived out by continual faith in His power. God is waiting for a generation of Adventists who will

demonstrate that His way of life can truly be lived on earth, that Jesus did not set an example beyond the reach of His followers, that His grace "is able to keep you from falling and present you without blemish" (Jude 24 RSV).

Each member of the Laodicean church needs more than a theoretical knowledge or even a proof-text knowledge of the Word: he needs a genuine and complete surrender of the life and will to the divine authority of the Bible and of the Spirit of Prophecy—a surrender that may well call for revolutionary changes in personal life styles and in denominational policies and practices. Every member must recognize that he has a part in either hastening or delaying the coming of Christ. Says God's servant, "When the character of Christ shall be perfectly reproduced in His people, then He will come to claim them as His own." (*COL* 69)

After much prayer and study the delegates concluded that a number of factors had seriously reduced the work of the Church and hindered the return of our Lord, which they saw as our blessed hope. These factors they clearly set out in concluding that we as a people were insubordinate to God's clearest teachings.

It is recognized that in an age of growing social consciousness and change, Adventist institutions may become involved in worthy endeavors in which the world also participates, while neglecting the work which only the Church of the remnant can do. (See *Review and Herald*, Nov. 26, 1970).

One of the greatest threats to our institutions of higher learning is seen in the counterfeit philosophies and theologies that may be unconsciously absorbed in worldly institutions by our future teachers and brought back as the "wine" of Babylon to Adventist Schools (Rev. 14:8–10; 18:1–4).

It is recognized that a constant threat to spirituality grows out of increasing creature comforts, rising standards of living, and a desire for remuneration equal to that offered by the world. Wrote God's servant: "The cause of present truth was founded in self-denial and self-sacrifice. . . . We need to take heed lest we outgrow the simple, self-sacrificing spirit that marked our work in its early years." (*SM* Book 2, 197)

As the Annual Council has reviewed these and other aspects of the lives of God's people and the institutions of the church, it has raised the question as to whether much of this represents the insubordination to the authority and will of God so clearly expressed through His Word and the writings of the Spirit of Prophecy. Without attempting to pinpoint areas of insubordination, the council pleads with God's people everywhere to respond to the appeal for revival and reformation—to make whatever changes may be necessary to enable the church to represent Christ adequately and fulfill its unique mission.

Thus the leadership of the Church fearlessly threw down the gauntlet to those who would minimize the claims of God's sanctifying power within the lives of His people. There had been a number of years of uncertainty concerning some of these truths, but this statement left none in doubt that God's people need to follow—not the philosophies of men—but the clear truths of God. It was recognized that some of the problems which were quite evident at that time were brought into the Church by those who had studied in institutions which did not uphold the truths that had become precious to God's children. Such a forthright standard of faith quite naturally did not pass by unchallenged. Indeed, shortly the greatest challenge that our denomination has had on the principles of righteousness by faith and the associated doctrine of the Sanctuary was to be met.

It was this document which our mother read with such joy on Sabbath, May 4, 1974. She perceived that this call contained the kernel of that message which would finish God's work and bring Christ's coming which she so earnestly desired. A few hours later, in the early hours of Sunday morning, she died. In God's providence she had not been spared to live to that time which for her was truly the blessed hope. Over a decade has passed. The writers feel a deep sense of anguish that tens of thousands of church members still see no need to follow God's call to sanctified living so that His people can sally forth to complete the great task of taking God's last message to every nation, kindred, tongue and people. That some scoff at calls such as that of the 1973 Annual Council and further seek to pervert the plainest words of Scripture in order to validate their apostate views only deepens the crisis within God's Church. Worse still, it delays further that climactic event, which by our very denominational name should attest to a sincere desire for its occurrence at the earliest possible time.

There was eager expectation on the part of some that, following this 1973 challenge, the 1975 General Conference at Vienna would lead to an unprecedented revival of godliness, but tragically this expectation was not to be realized. That it did not happen was largely due to the counterattack on truth mounted by those espousing the *new theology,* and to the apathy of many church members.

Chapter 17 Endnote

1. Dr. Ford has publicly criticized the message of Waggoner and Jones. "Unfortunately neither man was clear on other important points such as the distinction between justification and sanctification . . . the nature of Christ (both men were inclined to make Christ altogether such a One as ourselves in nature rather than beholding Him 'that holy thing' 'separate from sinners,' 'without blemish and without spot,' 'who knew no sin.')" (*Signs of the Times*, Australasian Edition, Feb. 1978)

# 18    Opposition Surfaces

IT did not take long to see that the leadership of the Theology Department at Avondale College was not in harmony with the call of the 1973 Annual Council. A manuscript was produced entitled *The Soteriological Implications of the Human Nature of Christ*. This manuscript, written by Dr. Ford's second wife, Gillian, became prescribed material for students of theology at Avondale College and was sold in the college bookstore. It was also distributed to students in a number of Adventist high schools throughout Australia. In this manuscript Mrs. Ford stated that *"Adventists, in contrast to the New Testament*, have often used the expression Righteousness by Faith to include sanctification." (Gillian Ford, *The Soteriological Implications of the Human Nature of Christ*, 10) The doctrinal position which the 1973 Annual Council approved was referred to as a "false gospel" (*ibid.*, 8) and as "that other gospel (*ibid.*, 10). Of course the Annual Council's statement was not specifically mentioned. There was no room, however, to dispute that there was a direct challenge to the truth of such calls for sanctified living.

Robert Brinsmead's magazine *Present Truth*, also entered strongly into this controversy although refraining from mentioning the Seventh-day Adventist Church. The fierce attacks upon the Adventist views so powerfully set forth by the 1973 Annual Council can be dated to that time. It was then that the *new theology* became bolder in its opposition to truth. One matter is absolutely certain: when the truth of God is exalted there will always be a concurrent attack upon it.

About this time Robert Brinsmead stated that he had spent a decade or more bringing this message to the Seventh-day Adventist Church without overwhelming success. He vowed in the future that he would take his message to Christians outside the Seventh-day Adventist Church, for it was time for them to hear his message. Thus his magazine *Present Truth*[1] took on a new image and became Protestant rather than Seventh-day Adventist in character. It was shortly to become the most widely distributed theological journal in the world. It was circulated to forty thousand clergymen and found ready acceptance with a large number of them. It became well known on the campuses of the theological schools throughout the United States; indeed, the rapidity of its rise to prominence was nothing short of astounding. This fact further emphasized Brinsmead's gift of having his material read outside the

Adventist Church. Although *Present Truth* was not a subscription journal, nevertheless it was avidly sought and read in theological circles, and highly esteemed by many.

However, it need not be emphasized that *Present Truth* by then contained little of those doctrines which are distinctive to Seventh-day Adventists. Where these doctrines were mentioned the emphasis differed from that which Seventh-day Adventists would make. It became far less distinctive even than *Questions on Doctrine*. Had the precious Adventist truths been spread as freely as *Present Truth* there is little doubt that it would have been less well received but would have accomplished a task of a different order. The authors are not aware of a single person accepting the Seventh-day Adventist faith as a consequence of having read *Present Truth* after its change of direction.

Because of this new approach, Brinsmead made contact with a large number of Protestant ministers. Among these was a Queensland Anglican pastor, Geoffrey Paxton, who was principal of a small interdenominational Bible training college. In a short time Paxton had teamed with Brinsmead to present so-called "forums" throughout Australia. At these forums the two speakers presented their concept of the reformed theology to large gatherings of ministers and interested laity. Clearly Brinsmead was now working as much with Protestants as he was working for them— a most dangerous development.

Chapter 18 Endnote

1. The magazine's name was later changed to *Verdict* in order to avoid confusion with Herbert W. Armstrong's *Plain Truth*.

# 19 Old Errors Emphasized

UPON Ford's return from England, where he had acquired his second Ph.D., this time from the University of Manchester, he immediately launched into a series of articles for the Australasian *Signs of the Times* on the topic of the book of Daniel. Ford's Ph.D. thesis had been in this area and he was naturally keen to pass on his research. It was most unfortunate that this material was first aired in a magazine designed for those of other faiths. This fact highlighted one problem within the Australasian church at that time. Neither the Division president nor the editor of our church paper had had experience in evangelism. These men had been selected for other excellent qualities which made them suited for their tasks in so many other ways. This scarcity of doctrinal leadership facilitated the spreading of error by our publications, for the void in this aspect of the leadership was rapidly filled by the Avondale College theologians.

It was Ford's series of articles which soon alerted many of the experienced evangelists in the field. Men such as Pastors J. W. Kent, George Burnside and O. K. Anderson immediately detected that they contained error, and these men were deeply concerned. Another who was most upset by the articles was Pastor Andrew Stewart, a pioneer missionary to the South Seas and a former Division administrator. But it was Pastor Llewellyn Jones, a retired evangelist with long experience as a conference departmental director who took the trouble to compare Ford's reasoning with the Word of God and the Spirit of Prophecy and put down his thoughts on paper. The text, Daniel 9:27, and its interpretation was a matter of much comment. This text states:

> And he shall confirm the covenant with many for one week: and in the midst of the week he shall cause the sacrifice and the oblation to cease, and for the overspreading of abominations he shall make it desolate, even until the consummation, and that determined shall be poured upon the desolate. (Dan. 9:27)

Dr. Ford did not deny the Adventist interpretation of this prophecy. Seventh-day Adventists had properly seen that this text referred to the last week of the seventy, that is, the period of A.D. 27–34. They recognized that the midst of the week represented the date A.D. 31 and the reason that the sacrifice and oblation ceased was that Jesus died at that time, thus making these ceremonies obsolete. Dr. Ford, however, stated that this text had a further fulfillment which coincided with the Futurist interpretation of this text. This *apotelesmatic* or successive fulfillment principle soon became a trademark of Ford's teachings. Pastor Jones set forth precise evidence from Inspiration that Dan. 9:27 did not have a second fulfillment and that Dr. Ford's assertion that it would be fulfilled again at the end of the world was unscriptural.

This notion of the second fulfillment had, of course, a long history in the Futurist school of prophetic interpretation. It seemed to Pastor Jones and a goodly number of other experienced evangelists that Dr. Ford, in studying under a Plymouth Brethren theologian, had accepted "the counterfeit philosophies and theologies that may be unconsciously absorbed in worldly institutions by our future teachers and brought back as the 'wine' of Babylon to Adventist schools."[1]

Many lay people and pastors in Australia were soon reminded that error often enters together with truth. By this method Sunday solemnity gained acceptance—by joint worship on both Sabbath and Sunday. Soon the true day of worship was forgotten. It was felt too that the true interpretation of Dan. 9:27 would soon be lost as the false gained emphasis. Had Dr. Ford stated that the traditional Adventist interpretation was in error and the Futurist view correct, the vast majority of Adventists would have been alerted. By his still advocating the true position in addition to the false, some felt that this old error was indeed new and advanced light on our understanding of this prophecy. That this interpretation was not so was seen by Pastor Jones in quoting from the specific testimony of God's servant.

> The seventy weeks, or four hundred and ninety years, were to pertain especially to the Jews. All the preceding specifications of the prophecy had been unquestionably fulfilled at the time appointed. (*GC* 410)

To many true believers it seemed inconceivable, indeed almost blasphemous, to suggest that the pronoun *he* in Dan. 9:27 referred to Christ in A.D. 31 and to antichrist at the end of the world. Yet this was the position which Dr. Ford was upholding. Of course the seventy weeks prophecy is intimately associated with the Sanctuary doctrine, particularly as it provides a common commencement date for the 2300-year prophecy. As had been seen as early as 1965, there was detection of the changes incorporated into the Sanctuary doctrine by Dr. Ford, and these articles did nothing to allay the concern of the growing number of pastors and laymen who had been thus alerted.

Many also noted the increased emphasis of Dr. Ford and his theology department upon the notion of an exclusively objective gospel, one which excluded sanctification and any experiential aspects whatsoever. Thus the totality of the gospel was said to be confined to the objective facts surrounding Christ's death for our sins on Calvary in A.D. 31. Belief in this fact alone provided acceptance with God. Now the view that the atonement was completed on Calvary became tenable to those who were influenced by this opinion. The concerned ministers and laymen, who were later termed the Concerned Brethren, recognized, of course, that the sacrificial aspect of Christ's atonement on Calvary was complete, but they could not accept the inference that the whole process of atonement was completed. The entire Adventist doctrine of the work of Christ in the Most Holy Place of the heavenly Sanctuary and our concept of the final atonement seemed to be inconsequential if all was done at Calvary as Dr. Ford was now teaching. The Barnhouse-Martin episode, as we have seen, prepared the way for Ford's errors and the subsequent attacks upon the sanctuary doctrine.

It soon became evident that Dr. Ford was not the only one with new ideas about Adventist doctrinal thought. Another teacher in the college, who had also obtained his doctor of philosophy degree at the University of Manchester in the seventies, produced an article concerning the term *within the veil* as found in Hebrews 6:19.[2] In this article the theologian made it perfectly clear that in his opinion the antitypical day of atonement commenced in A.D. 31.

Thus many sincere pastors and laymen became deeply distressed by what they saw as a vicious attack upon the sanctuary doctrine. It would be correct to judge that the vast majority of these men did not at that time fully perceive just how significant the righteousness by faith issue was to become, but they were clear in their defense of the old sanctuary truths.

Chapter 19 Endnotes

1. An earnest appeal from the Annual Council, 1973
2. "Within the veil" is a figure of speech and means simply to be in the presence of God. One may well describe this as 'Fletcher's view,' and even Ballenger's. This is undoubtedly the correct view provided we do not lose sight of the fact that the figure of speech which the writer is using is the annual entrance of the high priest on the day of atonement into the holy if holies." (*The Checkered History of the Phrase 'Within the Veil'*) This was an admitted alliance with the views of two men whose concepts had been demonstrated to be in error. To claim that the term *within the veil* as used in Hebrews 6:19 represented the "annual entrance of the high priest on the day of atonement in the holy of holies" is to ignore the specific statements of the Spirit of Prophecy which indicate that the term refers to the daily sacrificial program. This theologian had used an indirect means of emphasizing his view that Jesus entered the most holy place at His ascension.

# 20  An Octogenarian Throws Down the Challenge

IN 1974 a group of retired ministers and a few lay people met in Sydney to discuss their growing fears concerning the turn of doctrinal events in Australia. The meeting was chaired by an octogenarian, Pastor J. W. Kent, who in earlier years held successively the posts of president of the North New South Wales, the Western Australian and South Australian Conferences. He was closely assisted by Pastor John Keith, a former Union president in Papua New Guinea and later president of the Trans-Australian Union. Eventually the group supported Pastor Kent's plan to write a letter to the Division president expressing their growing fears concerning the preparation of a ministry which did not preach the fundamentals of the faith. In his letter Pastor Kent referred to an anonymous letter concerning Dr. Ford's teaching. "However, it is not the gutless charge against Brother Ford's teaching that is giving me concern. Rather it is the product of his classes. Rightly or wrongly, these young people, some of them in denominational employ, cite the Doctor as saying that the Scriptures are not free from error. There is no real Sanctuary in heaven as we have believed and taught. Bible chronology is not reliable. Etc. etc. When questioned as to the origin of such ideas, the young men affectionately indicate Dr. Ford as their authority.

"Now these young men coming out of our College are they who will fill the pulpits of our churches in the future. The destiny of our work in Australia is largely in their hands. It is their testimony, if true, that disturbs me, and not that unsigned circular. Because of this, and paraphrasing Elihu's challenge to Job, my desire is that Dr. Ford be tried to the end for his answers. Such would clarify the atmosphere surrounding the Doctor's teaching at the College. It would certainly reassure and comfort my thinking if the dear Doctor would answer one question. It is this: Do you believe and teach with the Psalmist that 'Thy word is true from the beginning; and every one of thy righteous judgments endureth forever'? (Ps. 119:160) And I further believe, my dear Brother Frame, that as leader of God's work in this Division, it is your responsibility to be sure that every one in a similar position gives and carries out that assurance. Only in that way can our pulpits be sound and safe."[1]

Even from within the theology department itself came rumblings of concern. One of the lecturers, Pastor Aldred Jorgensen, who was later appointed field secretary of the Australasian Division, had published an article in the *Review and Herald* early in 1975. The sentiments of this article differed widely from Dr. Ford's teachings on righteousness by faith. In fact, this article had been written many years before by Pastor Jorgensen, but he had not sent it for publication in a vacuum. Having taught theology at Avondale College, Pastor Jorgensen was well aware of Dr. Ford's views of righteousness by faith. The article expressed the old Adventist faith in the most specific terms. It was entitled, "What Do I Understand by Righteousness by Faith?" In part, the article stated:

> Now how do I acquire this righteousness? There is only one way. I must have Him who is the righteousness of God personalized. For righteousness by faith is more than an abstract theological truth, a clearly formulated doctrine, a confessing of an abiding conviction. Righteousness by faith is in the possession of a Person. It is the glorious reality, the thrilling wonder, the ecstatic experience when Jesus Christ apprehends me for Himself, when HE regenerates my heart through the life-changing power of His transforming Spirit. (*Review and Herald*, Jan. 23, 1975)

Others also expressed their concern from within the theology department. So persuasive were Dr. Ford's arguments, however, that some men who had formerly opposed his teachings, themselves radically changed their long-held beliefs to conform with those of Ford. One minister who had strongly denounced Ford's teachings made such a turn-about in his views that Dr. Ford was able to state that the pastor "has told me times without number that his theological stance is the same as my own . . . on matters such as the Law, the Covenant, the Nature of Christ, and Righteousness by Faith, etc. In his home just a month ago he told me how he understood Paul's usage of 'Righteousness by Faith' identically with my own position."[2] Dr. Ford sent copies of this letter to the minister concerned, the General Conference president and the Australasian Division president. It seems that Dr. Ford himself may have doubted the constancy of the individual and used this opportunity to cement him into his (Ford's) views. It became apparent that the minister took no measures to correct Dr. Ford's statement.

Thus the Concerned Brethren faced a most perplexing situation, finding a number of men who shifted ground quite significantly and others who held to the truth of God but could not see the least danger in what was taking place. Many of the Concerned Brethren had been involved in the matters relating to Pastors Fletcher and Greive and knew how speedily their errors had been detected and the matter remedied. Initially, they had not doubted that this problem, even more acute than that with the other two pastors, would be remedied with equal decisiveness. In possessing this expectation, the Concerned Brethren had not recognized the special circumstances prevailing within the Division. It was these circumstances which caused much hesitation in dealing with the doctrinal problem that was now growing to massive proportions. For the Concerned Brethren, one of the most galling facts was that when visitors came to the Division from the General Conference, they always left with an impression that the problem which had now begun to be made known beyond the shores of Australia was indeed a very minor one and that apart from a "few disgruntled pastors and some misinformed lay people," the situation in Australia was very stable. It was this situation which caused the Concerned Brethren subsequently to seek to provide a more accurate picture of the growing problem to those leaders, particularly in the General Conference.

These men, who have since been greatly maligned, were very dedicated believers. While they have been represented as men and women bent upon causing division and uproar in God's Church, this assertion is totally out of harmony with fact. As this history unfolds, it will be seen that these men cautiously approached the Division leadership with their concerns according to church policy. They trusted the church leaders to redress the do ctrinal impurity entering the Church. Initially every effort was made to spare the flock from a knowledge of the problems they were confronting. Had their wise counsel been heeded, the conflict so evident in the Church today would scarcely have made a ripple on the surface. It will be seen that right from the beginning the motives of the Concerned Brethren were greatly misunderstood. Scant attention was paid to their input and indeed they were castigated by some for their fidelity to the truth. As ministers of the gospel, commissioned to cry aloud against the prevailing errors, these distinguished men with fine reputations in church leadership were presented with but two alternatives—to be unfaithful to their ordination vow and remain silent in the face of a telling apostasy, or to earnestly warn God's flock of its peril in accepting the *new theology*. That these men made the decision to stand true to their vows is now a matter of historic documentation.

Chapter 20 Endnotes

1. Letter to Pastor R. R. Frame, president of the Australasian Division, from Pastor Kent, dated July 17, 1974)
2. Letter from Dr. Ford to Dr. Russell Standish, Feb. 9, 1976

# 21

## Division in Quandary

To the consternation of many of the Concerned Brethren, the Division leadership appeared to throw its authority behind the teachings of the theology department at Avondale College under Dr. Ford. Why this situation developed when only a little over a decade earlier Pastor Greive's efforts to introduce the same errors had met with prompt action and his dismissal from the ministry is mere speculation. However, a number of perfectly explicable circumstances undoubtedly contributed. As has been pointed out, Dr. Ford had earlier been seen as a great defender of the Seventh-day Adventist faith when it was confronted by the earlier view of Robert Brinsmead. There was naturally a good deal of gratitude which was felt due to him for the way in which he had loyally supported the administration of the Church through that crisis.

Further, the Australasian Division had recently contributed a large sum of money ($14,000) toward Dr. Ford's attainment of a second doctorate. Among the Concerned Brethren there was a sentiment that objected to the provision of this money. They believed that it was ill spent because Dr. Ford had returned with concepts foreign to the Seventh-day Adventist faith, although well accepted within Plymouth Brethrenism. (One of the Concerned Brethren, Pastor John Keith, had as a young man been a member of the Plymouth Brethren faith, and from this position he early detected Dr. Ford's emphasis.) It would be quite understandable for the Division to see this line of concern as an indirect questioning of their judgment in sponsoring Dr. Ford to Manchester University.

Further, Dr. Ford had been a most popular speaker at camp meetings and many other large meetings within Australasia. His writings appeared regularly in the Australasian Division periodicals. If these sermons and articles contained error (and most assuredly they did), then it would be natural for the Division leadership to feel that they, themselves, would be open to valid criticism from far and wide for sponsoring Dr. Ford.

Not only was Dr. Ford a much admired speaker throughout the Australasian Division, but now a huge number of his students were pastors, preaching in the same vein as he. To call a halt almost certainly would have been schismatic. This factor too may have influenced the Division decision.

Compounding these facts was the dilemma of a Division president, Pastor Robert Frame, an excellent and kindly administrator who undoubtedly had an earnest desire to promote the progress of God's work in the Division. Because of his lack of evangelistic background, he leaned heavily on others in doctrinal matters. Unfortunately, some of the advice he received from the men in whom he had faith encouraged him to overlook Ford's errors and to believe that the senior pastors were misunderstanding his position.

Thus it was easy for leaders to see the concerned pastors as dear old men[1] who perhaps had a personal objection to Dr. Ford and saw his influence as far too great. Even the clearest statements to the contrary did not allay this opinion at headquarters.

Pastor Kent had concluded his letter as follows: "In conclusion, be it known that I am not an adversary of Dr. Ford. Far from it. On the meager occasions I have heard him preach, he had cheered and blessed this old heart of mine. My sincere wish for him is that he might ever abide in the confidence of his brethren, and with us all, he may 'Never be wise above that which is written.'"[2]

In addition, the concerned brethren and others still felt a deep respect for Pastor Frame and his associates. There was in no sense a desire to put the leadership of the Division in an awkward position; rather the Concerned Brethren felt they could rejoice if decided steps were taken to remedy the catastrophe which they foresaw all too clearly.

In early 1975 Pastors Kent and Keith were selected to approach Pastor Frame with the request that they, along with six others, be permitted to present to the church leadership the bases of their concern. Pastor Frame replied in writing. Two paragraphs from this letter do give considerable insight into the pressures felt by the Division administration at that time and the types of matters which weighed heavily upon the minds of its leaders. "Let me say at the outset that I much appreciated your visit to my office, and I would emphasize that the leadership of the denomination welcomes an alert on anything that concerns the cause we all love. Having said that, I must inform you brethren that the representative group with whom I discussed your letter, Brother Kent, expressed concern over the way these matters about which you wrote were drawn to our attention. They agreed unanimously that it is a dangerous departure from time honoured organizational procedure to study a report from a self-appointed group which met without the knowledge and counsel of leadership. We must be careful we do not encourage pressure groups or individuals with personal or doctrinal bias in their attempts to gain their objectives. All individuals who are concerned about any matter always have the right to express their concern through proper organizational procedures and channels.

"The brethren are concerned,[3] too, about the personal campaign of some of these individuals with whom you met against Dr. Ford in particular and the college in general. When some individuals by mail, telephone, and direct word of mouth start a critical campaign against any brother who holds a responsible position within the cause without confronting the person they criticize, and also denominational leadership, relative to the problem as they see it, the brethren feel that this is unfortunate in the extreme. Irreparable damage can be done to the cause we love when men act independently without seeking counsel from responsible brethren. You two men who have carried heavy responsibilities as conference presidents do not need to be reminded of the damage that can be done by self-appointed individuals and committees who may apply pressure to gain their objectives. I am sure that this is offensive to God, and I say again it can lead to disruption, disunity and confusion."[4]

As a sincere leader, Pastor Frame naturally expressed concern for the unity of God's Church. It was no doubt this concern which led administration to advise this group of people "that rather than have groups meet together to discuss a series of papers we use denominational machinery already established, i.e. the Biblical Research Committee to hear any individual who may have a burden regarding the teachings on a given subject." (*Ibid*.) The matter of unity was emphasized twice in Pastor Frame's letter, indicating just how significant a role the desire for unity played in the actions of the Division. "We must not divide our workers or our churches by pressing our personal opinions in private or public." (*Ibid*.) Pastor Frame seemed to harbor not a little anxiety lest the group of Concerned Brethren would act precipitously. He urged Pastors Kent and Keith to circumvent this possibility. " I say again that you brethren who have occupied senior administrative positions within the church know how important it is to deal with such matters along proper organizational lines, and I know we can count on you both to counsel the brethren on right procedures." (*Ibid*.)

The concern of the Division administration was entirely unfounded, for the men with whom they were dealing were "dyed-in-the-wool" Seventh-day Adventists anxious for unity, but not at the expense of obvious error. The greatest concern of these men, however, was the fact that Pastor Frame's letter indicated that he had totally misunderstood the motives of the group. Pastor Kent's reply emphasized their displeasure. The accusation that the group was a pressure group was denied as follows: "Whether your representative group intended it or not, we take that as an offensive judgment, so undeserved by a humble request for enlightenment and help from our leaders. The guidelines left with you which were intended only for our gathering, contradict that judgment. I quote therefrom: 'And further, we must remember that we are enquiring from men whom God has through the vote of His church, entrusted with the safeguarding of the faith once delivered to the saints. Therefore our inquiries should be fraught with LOYAL COURTEOUS SINCERITY' (Emphasis this letter only). Surely this does not sound like a pressure group! As a matter of fact we had not the remotest intention of exerting any pressure. Not an impulse of such even rippled through our gathering."[5]

In his reply Pastor Kent also expressed concern over Pastor Frame's complaint concerning the way these matters were originally drawn to their attention. "I would to the dear Lord that this were really so; for I obtained my information from eye-catching display articles in the *Signs of the Times*, and from the *Ministry*. Like a trumpet blast of invasion on our doctrinal heritage, these articles roused me from my retirement bed. I rubbed my aging eyes in astonishment as I read." (*Ibid.*)

The accusation that they were an unauthorized group also raised Pastor Kent to further eloquence: "May I ask, where is the law or directive that we have infringed? I know of none, and I used to be rather familiar with conference procedures and the Church's by-laws. God forbid that we should ever come to the time when erstwhile trusted ministers cannot come together to study the old sacred paths trodden by their once youthful feet without engendering suspicion from current leadership. Surely, Brother Frame, your Council is not afraid of its retired ministry to whom under God, they owe so much. 'A self-appointed group which met without the knowledge and counsel of leadership,' you write. In answer we would say, we met, it is true, but we acquainted you with our meeting which was convened to ask counsel of our leaders and what did we get? Misunderstanding and offensive direction. I speak as a man, but nevertheless kindly." (*Ibid.*)

Pastor Kent did not take kindly however to the suggestion that the group was exerting a personal or doctrinal bias. As an evangelist and administrator he had been known as a prince of orators. His comments show that although then eighty-five years of age he had lost none of his gift in employing the English language. "Brother Frame, such a judgment as that imposed is a real strain on good will and charity. It is so utterly wrong. We are not pressure people, and we had no intention of exerting any. No doctrinal bias, save for the doctrine of God contained in the revelation of The Word, and emphasized by the Spirit of Prophecy and our church fathers. We are not agitators, neither are we schismatics nor heresy hunters. Just a body of troubled men standing by the old pillars of our faith, seeking from our leaders whether there is any change of what is written thereon. Thankful of heart as we met together that we are not under a Papal Flag, and neither in Russia where permission for such gatherings must be sought, only to be denied." (*Ibid.*)

Once again Pastor Kent expressed his Christian love for Dr. Ford although his comment was tinged with a trace of concern. "Our guidelines plainly told them that 'we are not here to downgrade anyone.' Personally, we love Brother Ford. But with apologies to Shakespeare, We do not love Ford the less, but Truth the more. We know the important position he holds, and we pray that he may ever fill it with the approval of his God. Nevertheless, it is not the brand on a horse that makes him travel, but rather the stuff of which he is made. More to the point is the warning of the servant of the Lord that many a star which we have admired for its brilliance will go out in utter darkness." (*Ibid.*)

Tragically, these words were not appreciated as being prophetic at the time. Pastor Kent's protest at being advised to go before the Biblical Research Institute was also significant. Subsequent events were to prove his concern all too well founded. He continued, "There is something else that perplexed me in your letter. Instead of going to you, as our leader, and your officers, together with other representative leaders to clarify our troubled thinking, which was our expressed request made to you, the leading brethren advised us to go to the Biblical Research Committee. Now, if I mistake not this committee is the former New Light Committee with which in my day I was quite familiar. This Committee set up to take care of instruction given to us by the beloved Servant of the Lord was, as its name suggests, for those who had new or additional ideas or disseminate them in any way among the Flock. They were to bring them to a committee composed of leadership and experienced ministers. The verdict of such a committee was final. To this every loyal Truth lover must agree. And rightly so. It was mandatory.

"But, my dear Brother Frame, this does not apply to us. We are advancing no new theories. We are standing by the old Pillars of our Faith, which we have taught to hundreds, yes, thousands of our converts. The Faith once delivered wholly possesses us. If it does not sound irritable, I would exclaim, What in the world are the brethren thinking about when they render us such advice! I ask this with kindly concern. Those who are allowing a passing cloud of Futurism to obscure what is written into the Pillars of our Faith—these are the ones that need to do that. Had they done so, and had the Biblical Research Committee done its duty, then I would not be 'burning the midnight oil' in order to write this letter to my beloved Leader tonight.

"There is no doubt that Brother Ford has presented something entirely new to Adventist teaching in his articles in the *Signs of the Times* and *The Ministry*. As a result, the Editorial Department of *The Ministry* screened him in order to ascertain whether he was still a Fundamentalist (*The Ministry*, Oct. 1974). The said department says also: 'Dr. Ford is emphasizing a new application of verses 24–27 of Dan. 9' In the light of what I have written above on the New Light Committee, why did not Brother Ford submit his new application to the Biblical Research Committee for examination and decision? I look for an answer to this from your panel of advisors. That is why we asked for a meeting with our leaders. This is part of our problem. There are other problems to which the representative leaders may have a satisfactory answer that would set our minds at rest. Historicism's teachings of the 70th week and related doctrines, based on complete fulfillment at the time of the cross taught and supported by the Spirit of Prophecy and the founding Fathers of the Advent Faith, permits no variation whatsoever in its confrontation with Brethrenism's Futuristic teaching of the 70th week. Is this still right?

"Strange it is that those who are content with the light as it was from the beginning are requested to go with fettered hands before the New Light Committee, while those who are bringing in darkness are left at large." (*Ibid.*)

The authors have quoted extensively from this correspondence of 1975 for a number of reasons. First, it shows that instead of tackling the problem at hand, those involved became concerned with mere technicalities while the error proceeded unabated. Further, we believe that it provides an insight into the pattern of response from the leadership that became entrenched in the Australasian Division and was then unique to that Division.

The authors, who have worked in a number of Divisions, have never found such reluctance on the part of those in leadership in other Divisions to listen with open minds to the concern of members and pastors of the church. God's leaders worldwide need to examine this example lest they too fall into a similar style of leadership. As can be readily gauged, there seemed at that time to be a distinct barrier between the Division leadership and even men who had held positions of great responsibility in former years. This barrier possibly was one of the great factors which prevented the Australasian Division solving the problem of the *new theology*. It was the absence of such a barrier which made it so much easier for the General Conference to do so within two years of Dr. Ford's transfer to the United States. Perhaps another reason for the General Conference's prompt handling of the problem, which the Australasian Division had steadfastly refused to acknowledge, was that the world leadership had not felt that they could be validly cited as having promoted Dr. Ford's cause in the face of repeated warnings. Thus their actions created no need for an explanation of previous support.

Pastor Kent's work did much to arouse an alertness in Australia. That the Division repeatedly refused to answer his questions or comment upon his concerns greatly troubled many who believed that the church leaders as servants of the flock had an obligation to render frank replies to genuine concerns. Indeed many of God's people, rightly or wrongly, interpreted the silence of leadership as indicating an absence of satisfactory answers. Pastor Kent had been a giant in God's cause, as were many of those supporting his enquiries. He was without peer in the Adventist Church in Australia as a speaker, and it is most doubtful that any Adventist in the world field matched his eloquence. His power of writing may be accurately judged by his letter (quoted above) written at eighty-five years of age with mind undimmed and firm hand.[6]

Throughout the controversy in Australia the Biblical Research Institute (B.R.I.) had been used in a most inappropriate fashion—to examine those who were standing for the old truth. Never once was Dr. Ford or any of his associates requested or obliged to bring their views before the B.R.I., thus leaving them free to preach them. The only occasion on which Dr. Ford was present at the B.R.I. was at the time the Division finally convened a meeting on February 3 and 4, 1976, and Pastor Kent, despite his former protest, advised that his group of Concerned Brethren accept the Division offer to appear before it. However, before we can present an account of this significant meeting, two important phenomena must receive mention in order to fill in the background.

## Chapter 21 Endnotes

1. Later this kinder, although erroneous, assessment was discarded and replaced by much harsher assessments.
2. Letter from Pastor J. W. Kent to Pastor R. R. Frame dated July 17, 1974
3. Here we see that there was a second group of "concerned brethren"!
4. Letter from Pastor R. R. Frame to Pastors J. W. Kent and J. B. Keith, April 21, 1975
5. Letter written by Pastor Kent to Pastor Frame dated May 7, 1975
6. Pastor Kent was to live until May 5, 1983, when he died at the age of 93. His love for God's Church was maintained, and in some ways he was able to do a greater work in the final few years of his life than he accomplished even as a highly successful front-line evangelist and church administrator. Nothing perhaps was more important in his life than his defense of the truths of God. He lived to see vindicated that for which he stood, and he died rejoicing in the truths of the Adventist faith, unshaken in faith and belief. As Pastor Kent approached his ninetieth, Pastor A. C. Needham, a long-time evangelist, assumed the mantle as unofficial leader of the Concerned Brethren.

# 22    Learning from History

IF we are to learn the valuable lessons present in the history of Ford's successful insertion of error into the doctrines of the Church in Australia, it is essential that we examine the precise reasons why this development was permitted by a Division which had so ably met the identical problem in the Fletcher case (1920s and 1930s), the Greive case (1950s) and even in the Moulds situation (1960s). This clarification is essential since here is a whole Division which in less than two decades moved from the position of our faith, to one bedeviled by doubt in the Spirit of Prophecy, the Sanctuary truth and God's power to provide obedience to His law in the Spirit-filled Christian. It was a ministry which became decimated by these doubts with the loss of over seventy from its ranks in a mere four years. The documented evidence to this point would indicate that the following factors played a part in this most unhappy situation.

    1. The appointment to top administrative leadership posts of men unsure of the doctrines of the faith and untrained in its defense. This factor needs much consideration, for more and more there are calls, usually from laymen, for conference administrators to be selected from trained administrators rather than evangelists. Such a view totally overlooks that the greatest work that any president can do is to preserve and promote the purity of the faith. All else depends on this. The failure of leadership to perceive the subtle intrusion of error has caused the perilous situation now present in Australasia. It is no surprise that those who early saw through much of the subtlety of the *new theology* were evangelists and missionaries, men well acquainted with the scriptural truths.

    2. The subtle techniques utilized unquestionably aided the successful presentation of the *new theology* on this occasion. The use of phrases with double meaning, the preaching of truth while insinuating error in the classroom, the denial of responsibility by teachers for the views of their students, all these techniques and more made the situation a most difficult one.

    3. The fact that the Church became so engrossed in defending itself against one "enemy," Robert Brinsmead, blinded many to the errors entering from a second source. Thus it is essential that each message be tested by the law and the testimony. The folly of accepting a view as truth simply because it opposed another error is now plain for all to see.

*87*

4. Emphasis upon a person's apparent dedication as a criterion of the truth of his message also demonstrated the weakness of overlooking the law and the testimony as the lone criterion of truth. To use unscriptural criteria predisposes one to accept Satan as Christ, for,

> Disguised as an angel of light, he [Satan] will walk the earth as a wonder worker. In beautiful language he will present lofty sentiments. Good words will be spoken by him, and good deeds performed. Christ will be personified. (*FE* 471)

Thus we need to be aware of charisma. Many of God's men lacked this quality, for God used men who would direct minds to Himself rather than to themselves.

5. An untoward desire for church unity, despite the fact that only upon truth can that desired unity be truly established, certainly played its role. Unity based upon factors other than truth promotes union but not unity. In this case the desire led to a harboring of error.

6. Administrative sensitivity to criticism of its actions, for example, in sponsoring Ford for a second doctorate which unquestionably did not help him or the Church, undoubtedly played a minor role. God's people do not think less of their leaders when an honest error of judgment is admitted. But many leaders appear to fear a loss of influence should such an admission be made.

7. Another factor which assisted Ford, as we have seen, was the fear that he was in fact promoting ideas held by our theologians in the United States. The history of this controversy, however, has demonstrated that the theologians within the Church were, as a group, far slower than the evangelists, missionaries and many lay people in citing the error. Indeed, that no group within the Church offered, and continues to offer, greater support for Ford than this group, should surely caution against reliance on theologians ungrounded in the faith, in conferences evaluating truth.

8. It is now unquestioned that Ford, permitted to graduate so many students schooled in his errors, formed a body of ministers, now in a large majority in Australasia, who could support and ably promote not only his errors, but also his position. A prompt response to error is thus mandatory.

9. As will be seen, a situation developed whereby loyalty to God's Church and to its leaders was measured by acceptance of Ford's errors. This factor led to many true men muting their concerns, fearing that they would be maligned as disloyal to the Church and to its leaders. Never should such a situation be permitted to develop.

There were no doubt other factors, but this selection serves to highlight some of the most significant. They should serve as a warning to all leaders and believers who truly love the faith. If lessons have been learned from the tragedy of the *new theology*, then the episode will not have been entirely detrimental.

# 23
## The Review and Herald Special — an Adventist Landmark

THE deep sense of responsibility which was evidenced in Pastor Robert Pierson's approach to his awesome responsibilities as leader of God's Church and his evident desire to promote those church activities consistent with hastening the Lord's return was reflected in the publications of the Church. The *Review and Herald*, in 1974, was edited by three men who were like-minded with their leader. Kenneth H. Wood, editor, Don F. Neufeld and Herbert D. Douglass, associate editors, clearly saw God's truths for these days and proceeded fearlessly to present them despite opposition from some church academics. There was also a rapidly growing group of Seventh-day Adventists influenced by the *new theology* who took exception to that which was printed in the *Review and Herald*.

Indeed many of the *Review and Herald* articles were specifically designed to stand against this surge of acceptance of error, evident in trends which had commenced following the publication of the book *Questions on Doctrine*. Accordingly the plain Adventist truth on righteousness by faith was set forth in the *Review and Herald Special*, Vol. 151, No. 20, 1974. This special edition was distributed worldwide and was even provided for those who were not regular subscribers. This is evidence of just how serious the matter was felt to be at General Conference headquarters.

The articles of course engendered interest of the first order. Even omissions were seen to be significant. On page 26 of the publication there appeared a list of books which were recommended for further reading. Since the publication had spoken at some length concerning the Minneapolis General Conference of 1888, some noted that three important books dealing with this topic were not listed among the recommended reading. These books were written by Norvel Pease (*By Faith Alone*), A. V. Olsen (*From Crisis to Victory*), and LeRoy Froom (*Movement of Destiny*). Since each of these books had attempted to play down the rejection of God's message by the Church in 1888 and present the final outcome as a victory for God's Church, many assumed (whether correctly or not we cannot tell) that these books had presented a far too optimistic historical assessment of that period. While each contained some excellent historical data, each had fallen short of showing the dismal consequences of our failure to accept the great message presented by Waggoner and Jones. These books had received ready acceptance in the 1960s, but with the greater distribution of *1888 Re-Examined* by Wieland and Short it became evident to many that these assessments did not stand up to the in-depth analysis of the facts as presented by these authors. On the other hand, it was seen as being significant that Pastor Robert Wieland's book, *In Search of the Cross*, was recommended in this list of reading. This recommendation was indeed a great breakthrough, for during the decades of the '50s and '60s Wieland and Short, while still continuing their valuable ministerial work, received scant support for the views that they had presented. Indeed, Froom's book had specifically attacked their presentation. It was further noted that two books written by Waggoner and Jones who presented the 1888 message were also recommended. Thus it was perceived that our leaders were directing their attention toward a reexamination of that important message which, had it been accepted in 1888, would have taken God's people Home. That we were still—in 1974—attempting to complete the commission that God had given to us was proof beyond rebuttal that the message of 1888 had not been accepted.

Perhaps the theme of the whole special issue was to be found on its penultimate page where Mervin R. Thurber presented thirty-one direct quotations from the Spirit of Prophecy entitled "Gems for a Month of Meditation on Righteousness by Faith." Four of the quotations are cited to indicate Thurber's emphasis and also the teaching of the Spirit of Prophecy on these matters.

> The sacrifice that Christ made in order that He might impart to us His righteousness—this is the theme upon which we may dwell with deeper and still deeper enthusiasm. (*SD* 124)
>
> Righteousness is right-doing, and it is by their deeds that all will be judged. Our characters are revealed by what we do. The works show whether the faith is genuine. (*COL* 312)
>
> The religion of Christ means more than the forgiveness of sin; it means taking away our sins, and filling the vacuum with the graces of the Holy Spirit. . . . When Christ reigns in the soul, there is purity, freedom from sin. The glory, the fullness, the completeness of the gospel plan is fulfilled in the life. (*COL* 419, 420)
>
> Jesus revealed no qualities, and exercised no powers, that men may not have through faith in Him. His perfect humanity is that which all His followers may possess, if they will be in subjection to God as He was. (*DA* 664)

Pastor Pierson's concluding sentiments for the righteousness-by-faith issue specifically set forth the balanced and embracing theme of the publication. He stated, "As Jesus enters your life He will bring full salvation, forgiveness, victory and eternal life. (1 John 5:11, 12) This is good news. It is the best news sinful man ever heard! It is God's special message to you NOW."[1]

Dr. C. Mervyn Maxwell, professor of Church History at Andrews University, took up the theme "Christ and Minneapolis, 1888." Maxwell saw the theme of the conference as "God wants to remove sin from the life and make Christians Christlike."

(*Ibid*. 18) He further summed up the direction of the speakers at the Minneapolis Conference as follows: "Mrs. White spoke some twenty times in Minneapolis 1888. Like Elders Waggoner and Jones, she too spoke of Christ in appealing terms as One who both forgives and offers victory." (*Ibid*. 18)

The editors of the *Review and Herald* also contributed to this special publication. Dr. Douglass set forth the reasons "Why God Is Urgent—and Yet Waits." He based his conclusions on Inspiration and summed them up in a very few words—"God waits for a people who truly reflect His way of life." (*Ibid*. 23) Pastor Wood directed his study to Christ's parables. Much care was taken to present God's inspired commentary on these parables in the book, *Christ's Object Lessons*. Among others, the crucial parable of the wedding garment received attention. Wood quoted from *Christ's Object Lessons*, 307–310, reminding the readers that "In the parable the wedding garment represents the character which all must possess who shall be accounted fit guests for the wedding. . . . It is the righteousness of Christ, His own unblemished character, that through faith is imparted to all who receive Him as their personal Saviour." (*Ibid*., 15) Pastor Neufeld discussed the question "Righteousness by Faith—Is It Biblical?" Neufeld stated that "the death of Christ assures men that the debt for their sins has been paid, that forgiveness full and free is offered, provided they choose to forsake their sin and follow God's way." (*Ibid*., 7) Speaking about the Old Testament era, Neufeld asserted that "God was not asking of the ancients the impossible. Divine power was available for man to live a righteous life." (*Ibid*., 6) Other writers such as Pastor George Vandeman, Charles Bradford, H.M.S. Richards, Sr., Jonathan Butler, Richard Lesher and Mrs. Betty Holbrook made their contributions.

The opposition to this *Review and Herald Special* mounted almost immediately. Those promoting the *new theology* were prominent in their attacks upon it. The most common political ploy was to suggest that the *Review and Herald* editors had acted independently of the world leaders in printing this Special and had embarrassed them. One, asked if he accepted the *Review and Herald* Special, replied "Not at all. Not at all. You ought to have shame if you knew the background of it. Our brethren at the G.C. were most upset when this came out. It came out in the middle of the meetings with Wieland and Short. The brethren at G.C. were most disturbed when one or two men at the Review went ahead with their own personal views and put it in print. That has been said and I think some of you heard it from our men from G.C. And I certainly have heard it. And that is the background of it. This is not the official church paper any longer, according to Pastor Pierson, Pastor Froom, Brother Dower, et cetera. That may be hard to take. The fact is, we used to have it on the cover . . . that it was the official church paper. Now we use expressions like general, and so on. It's no longer official, why? Because what goes in here depends on a few brethren's minds. And it's mainly good. But none of it's perfect."[2]

It will be seen that this line of argument also claimed that the *Review and Herald* was no longer the official church paper. The implication was that its contents could be ignored with impunity. Such attacks lacked veracity. It had taken weeks for the *Special Edition* to reach Australia. If the magazine had caused so much upset at headquarters, it was difficult to understand why it was still distributed freely in Australia when the General Conference had ample time to recall it. Further, the president of the General Conference himself wrote an article in the issue as did an associate secretary of the General Conference (Pastor Charles Bradford), and an associate secretary of the Sabbath School Department (Pastor Richard Lesher).

That both of these statements were based upon false information was clearly established. In a letter dated November 5, 1976 Pastor Wood set forth the facts: "For several years the editors of the REVIEW felt that the Church needed a piece of literature that would present under one cover the beautiful truth of righteousness by faith. As they prepared to implement their plans, a committee was set up by the General Conference to spend several days studying questions raised by Brethren Wieland and Short. When one of the sub-committees was in session preparing for the meeting of the larger committee, I asked whether the brethren would advise me to hold up on publication of the special issue of the REVIEW. Unanimously the committee said 'Don't hold up; go right ahead.' So we did.

More important, however, is the fact that when the magazine was in page form I sent xeroxed copies of all the pages to our consulting editors who, as you know, include the president of the General Conference and all the vice-presidents. These pages were read carefully and were OK'd. In some cases the consulting editors actually initialled each page to indicate approval.

"Now, as you know, the material produced by our publishing houses is never voted by the General Conference Committee. The only publications that are truly official are the policy books and the *Church Manual*. We believe this is wise, for it gives our publishing houses both freedom and responsibility to produce that which they believe is in the best interest of the denomination. It avoids the appearance of 'censorship.' But the righteousness by faith issue was as thoroughly endorsed and supported as any piece of literature in modern times.

"I am sorry that until now apparently the discussion about the righteousness by faith issue has been proceeding in Australia without the facts. So far as I know, no one has ever written to us to get the truth of the matter. It is too bad that misinformation is disseminated when for the cost of a telephone call or a postage stamp the truth might be obtained."[3]

The second attack was also ably answered by Pastor Wood, this time in one of his editorials in the *Review and Herald* entitled "F.Y.I." (For Your Information). Pastor Wood pointed out that for only six years (1961–7) in its one hundred and twenty-six year history had the *Review and Herald* been referred to as the "Official Organ of the Seventh-day Adventist Church." The care with which articles are prepared was set forth.

## The Review and Herald Special

> The in-house editors (who incidentally, are elected by the publishing-house board, and approved by the General Conference Committee) examine and edit carefully all manuscripts. On sensitive matters, they ask that manuscripts be read also by some or all of the consulting editors (who are the president and vice-presidents of the General Conference). And all manuscripts are checked word by word by the copy editors. (*Review and Herald*, Feb. 17, 1977)

In conclusion Pastor Wood made a modest but strong appeal for faith in the periodical he edited:

> We recognize, of course, that that which makes any religious magazine effective is the Holy Spirit speaking through its pages to the hearts of readers. Words are important, but they are only agencies that the Spirit may use to lead minds to Christ and truth. In 1881 Ellen G. White wrote, "Those who consent to do without the *Review and Herald* lose much. Through its pages Christ may speak to them in warnings, in reproofs and counsel, which would change the current of their thoughts and be to them as the bread of life." (*Testimonies* Vol. 4, 599) Think of it! Jesus, our Saviour, may speak to us through the REVIEW.
>
> For Your Information, the editors will continue to do all they can to enable the voice of Christ to be heard through the REVIEW. They will do their best to retain the trust and confidence the worldwide body of Adventists has placed in it for more than 126 years. The REVIEW may not be labeled "Official Organ of the Church," but it is the nearest thing to an official organ that the Church has. (*Ibid.*)

The attack upon the *Review and Herald Special* was not based only on political considerations but also upon theological matters. Undoubtedly the most widely distributed objection was an article supported by the *Present Truth* organization written by an American, Robert A. McCurdy, Jr. entitled "An Examination of the Teaching of Righteousness by Faith as Presented in the Special Issue of the REVIEW AND HERALD. Vol. 151, No. 20, 1974."

McCurdy pulled no punches in his rebuke directed at the editors. He concentrated on what had become the hallmark of the *new theology*—a return to so-called 'Protestantism.'

> The publication of this issue of the REVIEW is a terrible tragedy. We do not care to judge the men who are responsible for it—we believe they acted sincerely and from the highest motives—but in the light of God's Word we must judge the doctrines they have presented. These the Word of God shows to be false. The voice of Protestantism for four and a half centuries has declared them to be false. We can only wonder that they have found their way into the official church paper of the people whom God has specially raised up to finish what the Reformers began? (*Ibid.*, 15)

McCurdy went even further and made his appeal for an official retraction explicit.

> We therefore appeal to these men and to the church leaders everywhere to retract the positions taken in this REVIEW and to bring the teaching of righteousness by faith among Seventh-day Adventists into harmony with genuine Protestantism. (*Ibid.*, 15, 16)

McCurdy went on to make dire predictions should his appeal be rejected and the old Adventist stand upheld.

> Unless the special issue of the REVIEW is retracted, sad and dangerous times are ahead for the people of God. We can only hope that it does not achieve a wide circulation among those not of our faith. Among the fallen churches are many individuals who have a clear grasp of the fundamentals of the reformed religion. The material in this issue of the REVIEW can only repel them. They will rightly reject this teaching as non-Biblical and non-Protestant. To them it can only serve as further proof that Adventism is a legalistic religion.
>
> A second consequence of a failure to retract will be to bring about the greatest crisis ever to shake Adventism. It is possible, even commendable, to hold one's peace regarding errors in administration and life in the church, for we are all sinners and all fall short of God's ideal. But when the gospel is perverted, silence is no longer a virtue. The honor of God is at stake, and souls of men are at stake. God demands that those who understand the issue make it clear where they stand. Everything that can be done must be done so that the people may not remain in ignorance of the issues.
>
> The issues have been clearly presented over a period of several years. Now the lines have been drawn. But strife may yet be averted by a clear-cut retraction of the errors presented in the REVIEW. There is nothing more urgently or desperately needed now. Would to God that we may all unite on the solid platform of the gospel, and use as our watchword;
>
> > 'Thy righteousness is in heaven!' (*Ibid.* 16)

In his article McCurdy echoed the strong revulsion felt by those who had accepted the *new theology* and were in open opposition to the truths of our Church.

> But to turn justification and righteousness by faith into something which takes place on earth in the believer is to say that in the end God will point to the saints "on earth" and say "without embarrassment," "Here are those who keep the commandment of God and the faith of Jesus." (*Ibid.* 22) This is to pervert the Scriptures and "to cast the truth to the ground." It is "the transgression of desolation." It is to "pollute the sanctuary of strength . . . take away the daily and . . . [put in its] place the abomination that maketh desolate." Dan. 11:31. Where such a doctrine is accepted today it will bear the same fruit that it bore in the early church and in the dark ages." (*Ibid.* 14)

# Chapter 23 Endnotes

1. *Review & Herald* Special on Righteousness by Faith, 1974
2. Dr. D. Ford, *An Answer to Dr. Russell Standish* 19: a tape transcription of a meeting held in Sydney, Oct. 2, 1976. The transcription was made by supporters of Dr. Ford on the staff of the Sydney Adventist High School.
3. Letter written by Pastor Kenneth Wood to Dr. John Clifford with copies to Pastors Pierson, Eva, Frame, Jorgensen and Dr. Ford, dated Nov. 5, 1976

# 24 The Committee of Concerned Laymen

AT the Victorian camp meeting of 1975 the president of the Australasian Division, Pastor Robert Frame, possibly acting upon the advice of his predecessor, Pastor L. C. Naden, and that of Dr. Ford, stated to the conference workers that Robert Brinsmead's views were now acceptable to the Seventh-day Adventists. This announcement led to forty-one lay people forming a committee of concerned laymen on March 1, 1975. Many of these people were believers from the Croydon Church located in an eastern suburb of Melbourne, although there were numbers from other churches within the metropolitan area. The committee elected Brother Harold Reid as its chairman and Dr. John Clifford as its secretary. The committee then passed the following motion which it sent to the Division leadership: "That as a committee of concerned laymen we ask the Division Executive Committee for clarification of a reported recent decision by some leaders in this field, that the current teachings of R. D. Brinsmead are now no longer unacceptable to the Australasian Division of Seventh-day Adventists. Further, that the Executive Committee be asked to clarify specifically if we are now free to believe and teach

"(1) that the Gospel of Jesus Christ consists only of the historic and objective acts of Christ.

(2) that Christ at the right-hand of God, and not Christ in the human heart, is the great focal point of the apostolic proclamation of the Gospel: that the Gospel reveals that righteousness of faith in Christ is imputed only in heaven: but not imparted, nor personal, nor experiential to the believer.

(3) that Justification by Faith and salvation are freely available and are not contingent upon or preceded by the work of the Holy Spirit in the regeneration and transformation of the sinner by the new birth.

(4) that the crucifixion of 'self' is unscriptural, and the only Biblical crucifixion of the believer is that crucifixion which has already taken place in the crucifixion of Christ on Calvary.

(5) that sanctification is not an integral part of righteousness by faith, and if this concept of sanctification is believed and taught, it is accepting and teaching the theology of anti-Christ.

"That the Executive Committee be informed that the reason this committee is seeking urgent and early specific clarification on the above points is that they seem to be in conflict with the views expressed by the General Conference in the special issue of the REVIEW AND HERALD, Vol. 151, No. 20., 1974."

It can be seen that this enquiry was phrased in terms of Christian courtesy and openness. It was a most reasonable query and merited a frank and courteous reply.

A spokesman for the Australasian Division replied to this motion: "Let me assure you that it is perfectly proper for any member of the Seventh-day Adventist Church, or any group of members, to approach the Division Executive Committee concerning any matter concerning which they desire counsel, guidance, clarification, assessment or action."[1] The spokesman then went on to list the route through which the request must travel—local conference to union conference to division. He assured the group "that in offering this counsel, there is no ulterior motivation whatsoever, no playing for time, no trying to 'pass the buck' or to shelve responsibility." (*Ibid.*)

The Division spokesman tried, however, to allay the fears of the committee members by telling them informally what he felt the Division Executive Committee would tell them formally. In summary, the Division spokesman stated:

(1) that no formal action had ever been taken by the Division in respect of Robert Brinsmead's teachings.

(2) that the Division cooperates in upholding the *Review and Herald* as the general church paper and that unless the special issue of the *Review and Herald* was refuted by the Biblical Research Institute of the General Conference and this refutation upheld by the General Conference Executive Committee, "The Australasian Division is prepared to cite it as representing the current teaching of the Seventh-day Adventist Church." (*Ibid.*)

He did not specifically answer the questions put to him. Simply he stated, "The answers then to the specific questions you ask are readily ascertainable. If they conflict with the clear teachings of the Bible and the Spirit of Prophecy and with the known position of the Church, place a cross in the appropriate box!" (*Ibid.*)

After this outline, the Committee of Concerned Laymen was asked, "Do I really need to say any more?" (*Ibid.*) The earnest group of believers felt that he did. In answering the first point, the Division spokesman had carefully avoided expressing the view of whether individual leaders of the Australasian Church were claiming that Brinsmead's concepts were now acceptable. There was much evidence and a good deal of hearsay indicating that Pastors Frame, Naden and Ford[2] had expressed such a point of view. On the second point no explanation was given of Dr. Ford's open objections to the *Review and Herald Special* in the light of the Australasian Division's assertion that it represented "the current teaching of the Seventh-day Adventist Church." It seemed as if the Division was prepared to permit the ministerial students at Avondale to be taught that the church's doctrines were incorrect. The reply concerning the specific doctrinal questions was a patent effort to avoid an answer. This evasiveness was to set the whole pattern of letters on the doctrinal issue emanating from this spokesman's office. Indeed, deliberate efforts to avoid frank answers to questions seems to have been a definite policy. This policy was shown when this church leader, speaking to the Victorian church workers on March 5, 1977, at The Basin, stated that Geoffrey Paxton, the Anglican pastor associated with Robert Brinsmead, had requested the Australasian Division to make a statement on its doctrinal position. This spokesman stated that he saw this duty as a problem. "Now my problem is to handle this situation in such a way that we will not commit the Church at all."[3]

Nevertheless the concerned lay people accepted the advice given and wrote to Pastor Clive Barritt, president of the Victorian Conference on March 14, 1975, requesting that their queries be passed on to the Biblical Research Institute. The executive committee of the Victorian Conference acted promptly four days later in agreeing to pass this request to the Trans-Australian Union.[4] Pastor S. M. Uttley, president of the Trans-Australian Union Conference, discussed the request with the Division officers and it was suggested that Brother Reid meet with Pastors Uttley, Barritt and Kingston, the church pastor of the Croydon congregation. Brother Reid agreed to this request on the condition that the group's secretary, Doctor John Clifford, accompany him. This condition was accepted. The meeting took place on May 29, 1975.

Reid and Clifford presented a formal request to the meeting in which they stated in part that this meeting was not regarded as a substitute for a clear reply from the Executive Committee of the Australasian Division to the five questions originally submitted. Reid and Clifford then asked the same five questions of the brethren gathered.

The Committee of Concerned Laymen was encouraged by the report that they received from that meeting. This fact is clear in Reid's letter to Pastor Uttley. Referring to the Committee of Concerned Laymen, Reid wrote, "Appreciation was expressed for the keen reception given to the facts presented by Dr. A. J. Clifford and myself on behalf of our committee. It is apparent that you and Pastor Barritt as presidents of the Trans-Commonwealth (now called the Trans-Australia) Union and the Victorian Conferences share our deep concern.

"This is further evidenced by your official answers in the negative to the five doctrinal positions of R. D. Brinsmead and *Present Truth*."[5] Reid's letter went on to state, "The views of the General Conference expressed in the *Review and Herald* extract 'Righteousness by Faith' Vol. 151, No. 20, 1974, substantiate your unequivocal statement that we are NOT free to believe and teach such liberal Protestant doctrines in these conferences. We now anticipate receiving the official Denominational clarification from the Australasian Division, promised by you at the meeting." (*Ibid.*)

Whether Reid and Clifford misunderstood the sentiments of the meeting or the president of the Victorian Conference subsequently changed his view, it is impossible to decide since no record of that meeting was made. What is certain is that much of the apparent progress made was nullified by the Victorian president's reply to Harold Reid following his receipt of a copy of the letter to the union conference president. In his reply the conference president stated, "In all fairness, however, I must inform you that I regard the wording of certain statements in paragraphs 2 & 3[6] of your letter to Pastor Uttley, as being subjectively coloured, inaccurate and consequently unacceptable."[7]

Five days later Reid visited the conference president in his home to discuss his objections to what Reid had written in his letter to the union president. Following that personal meeting Reid again wrote to the Victorian president. In that letter he stated, "You will recall the following question was asked after discussion on *each point* 'Are we all in agreement in answering "No?"' In each case there was not one dissenting voice in that room. To the contrary, agreement was expressed by all in replying 'No' to these questions. The fact that for some reason you now disassociate yourself from the agreed reply does not make us guilty of misrepresentation."

Another thread of communication had simultaneously been progressing with the Australasian Division. We cite the almost trivial details in order to demonstrate that either there was great fear on the part of some to make their position clear or there was a feeling that the laity should not be privy to the thinking of God's leaders.

Whatever the reasoning behind the following set of communications, one thing is certain: it is difficult to believe that it could have been engendered in any other division. In his original reply to the request of the Concerned Laymen the Division spokesman had forewarned that "If your petition in its present form is formally brought to the attention of this office, you will be requested to name the persons whom you nominate as 'some of the leaders in this field.'"[8] In that letter he had stated, "Let me assure you that it is perfectly proper for any member of the Seventh-day Adventist Church, or any group of members, to approach the Division Executive Committee concerning any matter concerning which they desire counsel, guidance, clarification, assessment or action. (*Ibid.*) Despite this generous acknowledgment of rights it did seem as if there was a great reluctance to fulfill the promise contained therein.

To the request that the names of those involved be revealed, Reid replied, "Whilst we are prepared to do so, we would like to make it clear that we do not believe this should be necessary. It is possible that at least some who made these statements may have done so in ignorance of the true nature of the Brinsmead teachings. Revealing their names, therefore, may cause hurt to those whom we believe to be sincere Christians." However, the Division spokesman, perhaps sensing a loophole, was uncompromising in his reply. "I must inform you, however, that we will be of no mind whatever to undertake a consideration of this petition unless, as I intimated in an earlier letter to you, your committee is prepared to disclose the sources of the information on which the petition is based."[9] Any fair-minded person would assess this request as both unfair and unnecessary.

This demand concerned many of the committee members who were kindly souls and did not wish to imperil Dr. Ford in particular. Since the vast majority of the committee had no real connection with the Division 600 miles away, they could not have known that in reality the Division was not in any way ignorant that Dr. Ford, for one, had made such statements at the North New South Wales camp meeting. The committee's information had been based on a rather small meeting conducted by Dr. Ford in the Hawthorn High School on September 9, 1974. At that meeting he had spoken at the invitation of the Melbourne University Seventh-day Adventist Students' Society. Dr. Ford was asked the following question: "What stand does the Church take today on Brinsmead's theology as it has changed over the last few years?" Dr. Ford's reply was recorded as follows: "I can quote you men in high places in our work that all of you would respect greatly, who would say that there is nothing now wrong with Brinsmead's theology. Though at first we were inclined to think he put too much emphasis on one area. That's what many men amongst us would say.... I can assure you that men at Andrews University and elsewhere would say that in essence the Brinsmead theology is now back to where it should have been years ago. There'd have been no Brinsmead movement if they'd had that emphasis. It's in Scripture, and it's in Ellen White."

The second source of information was that the Division president, apparently on the advice of others including Dr. Ford, was the one who had spoken at the 1975 Victorian camp meeting expressing a similar view. Perhaps the Division president was the person "in high places" to whom Dr. Ford alluded. The members of the Committee of Concerned Laymen had an affectionate loyalty toward their church leader and were well aware that he was relying upon others for counsel on doctrinal matters. Thus they were hesitant to sound harsh and judgmental by naming him. So once more Harold Reid expressed the thinking of the committee: "The major issue is whether the teachings of R. D. Brinsmead are unopposed by, and in harmony with the teachings of the Australasian Division of the Seventh-day Adventist Church. The major issue is NOT 'who said what' or 'who told whom.'"[10] Despite this plea, the Division spokesman again pressed his request in his reply: "We cannot proceed further with this matter until this information is disclosed."[11] Further along in the letter the writer stated: "I must, therefore, make it crystal clear to you that we cannot proceed further with the petition until such time as your Committee discloses to us the above-sought information." (*Ibid.*) He also stated: "We recognize that this is a capital issue and we plan to give it capital treatment." (*Ibid.*)

The committee's reply to this letter was brief: "We thank you for your letter of the 22nd of April, 1975. My committee feels disappointed that as Chairman of the Biblical Research Committee you do not appear to share our concern. We thank you for your time."[12] Eventually Reid requested a suitable time for him and Clifford to meet with them to discuss the matter. This meeting was not arranged until the Victorian camp meeting of January, 1976, when they met with two Division leaders and the president of the Victorian Conference.[13] At that meeting Reid and Clifford provided the promised revelation of the names and sources. Circumstances had greatly changed, however, by that time. The Palmdale Conference, which will be discussed a little later, had been mooted and the Division spokesman used this fact to refuse to answer any doctrinal questions on the grounds that these were *sub judice* since they were to be discussed at Palmdale. Thus the entire meeting was fruitless and it became evident that there was more than one way of circumventing the provision of a clear answer to the request that had been placed.

One of the saddest aspects of this issue was that these very good lay people who sincerely wished to protect the good names of the pastors of the Church and were pressed so hard to reveal these names, were subsequently cruelly accused by those who had pressed for this information of using smear tactics against Dr. Ford because they named him in supporting Brinsmead's views. The documented facts of the case as presented are clear. Surely few concerned groups have so patiently pursued their concerns through the approved channels. If doing this is ascribed to disloyalty, as it was, then surely our system for standing for the truth of God had broken down.

## Chapter 24 Endnotes

1. Letter written by an Australasian Division spokesman to the committee of Concerned Laymen, dated March 6, 1975
2. "Now Dr. Ford hands out PRESENT TRUTH to his students—recommends it. I've got a tape of his at home, where he got up in the chapel in front of all the students and faculty—told them that Robert Brinsmead was teaching the truth of the gospel." (Ray Martin at Croydon Church, July 7, 1974)
3. From taped record of the Division spokesman's meeting with church workers in Victoria, March 4, 1977
4. This name is used throughout as it is the correct name of the Union. It was formerly titled The Trans-Commonwealth Union Conference. This territory includes the states of South Australia, Tasmania, Victoria, Western Australia and the southern and western areas of New South Wales.
5. Letter of Harold Reid to the president of the Trans-Australia Union Conference dated June 30, 1975
6. These were the two paragraphs quoted above.
7. Letter from Victorian Conference president to Harold Reid, dated July 15, 1975
8. Letter from the Division spokesman to Harold Reid dated March 6, 1975
9. Letter from Division spokesman to Harold Reid, dated March 25, 1975
10. Letter written by Harold Reid to the Australasian Division, April 4, 1975
11. Letter from Division spokesman to Harold Reid dated April 22, 1975
12. Letter written by Harold Reid to the Division spokesman dated April 29, 1975
13. The Division spokesman was accompanied by the late Pastor Graham Miller, Director of the Youth Department of the Division. Pastor Miller appeared to stand by God's precious truths. Pastor Clive Barritt was the Victorian Conference president.

# 25

# Before the Biblical Research Institute

MEANWHILE with the conclusion of the 1975 General Conference Quinquennial meetings in Vienna and a return to normality in the Australasian Division, a meeting was arranged for the Concerned Brethren to present their objections to the teachings at Avondale College, to the Biblical Research Institute (B.R.I.) of the Australasian Division. Eventually sixteen brethren presented their concerns to twenty church leaders selected Division-wide. This meeting was of such significance and yet so little known that it seems appropriate to list the names of the brethren who were present. The personnel representing the Australasian Division were as follows:

1. Pastor Cyrus Adams, president, Tasmanian Conference
2. Pastor Donald Bain, Australasian Division health director
3. Pastor Clive Barritt, president, Victorian Conference
4. Pastor Clem Christian, president, South New Zealand Conference
5. Dr. Desmond Ford, Chairman, theology dept. Avondale College
6. Pastor Robert Frame, Australasian Division president
7. Pastor Alfred Jorgensen, Australasian Division field secretary
8. Pastor Claude Judd, president, Trans-Tasman Union Conference
9. Dr. Eric Magnusson, president, Avondale College
10. Pastor Rex Moe, president, Western Australian Conference
11. Pastor Lawrence Naden, retired Australasian Division president
12. Pastor Keith Parmenter, Australasian Division secretary
13. Pastor Robert Parr, editor, Australasian *Signs of the Times*
14. Pastor Arthur Patrick, theology dept., Avondale College
15. Dr. Alwyn Salomon, pastor, Wahroonga Church
16. Pastor Raymond Stanley, ministerial secretary, Australasian Division
17. Pastor Athal Tolhurst, president, North New South Wales Conference
18. Pastor Leonard Tolhurst, theology dept., Avondale College
19. Pastor Stewart Uttley, president, Trans-Australian Union Conference
20. Dr. Norman Young, theology dept., Avondale College

The sixteen Concerned Brethren who were present were as follows:
1. Pastor Ormond Anderson, retired evangelist, departmental director, college Bible teacher and missionary to the Middle East
2. Pastor Frank Basham, retired pastor and evangelist
3. Pastor Frank Breaden, retired pastor and evangelist
4. Pastor George Burnside, retired evangelist and former Australasian Division ministerial secretary
5. Dr. John Clifford, Melbourne physician; secretary, Committee of Concerned Laymen
6. Pastor Ronald Heggie, retired Mission president and church pastor
7. Pastor Arthur Jacobson, retired pastor and Mission president
8. Pastor Llewellyn Jones, retired evangelist and Conference Departmental director
9. Pastor John Keith, retired Union Conference president and Mission president
10. Pastor James Kent, retired Conference president and leading evangelist
11. Pastor Arthur Knight, retired evangelist, youth leader and hospital chaplain
12. Brother Raglan Marks, Cooranbong businessman
13. Pastor Elwyn Martin, retired evangelist and missionary
14. Brother Harold Reid, Melbourne engineer, chairman of the Committee of Concerned Laymen
15. Dr. Russell Standish, Melbourne physician
16. Brother Fred Williams, retired Sydney businessman

The meeting convened at Avondale College on February 3, 1976. The Division president was in the chair, and within the limitations of time gave a very fair opportunity for the issues to be aired. Only one tape recording was permitted on the understanding that a copy would be made available to the Concerned Brethren, but in fact this was not to be, for the tape was kept subsequently under stringent control at the Australasian Division headquarters. This tactic meant that a number of false rumors circulated concerning the meeting. The facts of that meeting would have been more accurately understood if free access to the tape recording had been permitted. Perhaps now with the passage of a number of years it may be possible for that tape recording to be de-restricted.

Pastor Kent, chairman of the Concerned Brethren, introduced the discussion. He stated that he had never heard anything from Dr. Ford's mouth which had not stirred his old heart. He did express his concern, however, over that which Avondale theology graduates were preaching.

The initial paper of the session was presented by Pastor Burnside who dealt with those concerns on the topic of the sanctuary previously mentioned in this book. It was a simple Bible and Spirit of Prophecy presentation in the inimitable Burnside style. Dr. Ford was given a full opportunity to reply. Despite prayer, there were tensions very evident on both sides. Dr. Ford, in fairness, was given the difficult task of speaking successively to four different papers on that one day. He called on all his undoubted speaking gifts and his superb memory to the full. Yet the strain of this extraordinary meeting was clearly evident.

Pastor Martin presented a small paper setting out some of the problems he had encountered with young pastors he had received as ministerial interns from Avondale. He stated, "On occasions I spoke to another young minister concerning his being so unsettled in his work. I found he was confused concerning the age of the earth and the two apartments of the heavenly Sanctuary, et cetera." Pastor Martin mentioned four other young ministers with various serious doubts on subjects such as the inspiration of the Bible and the Spirit of Prophecy.

The second major paper was presented by Pastor Frank Basham on the topic of righteousness by faith. Those presenting papers had been warned that they must produce undeniable evidence of the teachings of the Avondale College Theology Department. This Pastor Basham did most thoroughly. He then set out the objections to these teachings using the Bible and the Spirit of Prophecy. Once again Dr. Ford replied. As he had done with Pastor Burnside's objection, Dr. Ford relied extremely heavily upon the fact that he was able to show that some other Adventists had held his views. On a number of occasions he adopted a defensive stance and asserted, "If I am a heretic, so are these men." Naturally Dr. Ford used the Bible and the Spirit of Prophecy in addition, but his overwhelming use of other men's views was not conducive to convincing men who had spent a lifetime basing their views upon a plain Thus saith the Lord.

Many of the senior men were deeply disturbed as they heard long-held pillars of our faith rejected. Pastor Kent at last could stand it no longer. He stood up a few feet from Dr. Ford and clenching the Word of God in his outstretched hand exclaimed, "I'd *die* for the certainties of this Book! But I wouldn't shed a corpuscle of my blood for all the if's, but's and maybe's I've heard here today." It was a moment of high drama. The 86-year-old champion for truth had lost none of his lust for the defense of God's message in the heat of the battle.

Pastor Arthur Knight listened intently. He had been closely associated with Pastor W. W. Fletcher who himself had been chairman of the Avondale College Bible department in the late twenties. Pastor Knight detected very similar conclusions being put forth by Dr. Ford, to those he had known to be held by Pastor Fletcher prior to his dismissal from the ministry. In fact, Pastor Knight had typed Pastor Fletcher's defense of his views, and this defense Pastor Fletcher had subsequently presented, first to the Division in 1928, and later to the General Conference. Pastor Knight detected only one significant difference. Whereas Pastor Fletcher openly admitted that his views were incompatible with the teachings of the Spirit of Prophecy, Dr. Ford asserted full confidence in the writings of Sister White and insisted that his views were in harmony with her writings.

A not inconsiderable number of pastors appeared to sympathize with Pastor Kent, who later in the day stood up and expressed the following sentiments: "I've spent a lifetime defending our faith against such ideas as Dr. Ford expressed today. But while I defended our faith on these issues against ministers of various faiths, I never believed that the day would ever arrive when I would have to defend them against a Seventh-day Adventist minister."

Pastor John Keith, normally a man of quiet demeanor and firmly in control of his emotions, was almost brought to tears as he listened. As a former Plymouth Brethren follower, he found the expression of some of the concepts he had rejected for the light of Adventism almost too much for him.

All these sentiments created a high level of tension in the meeting and some of the Division-appointed men at times felt compelled to rise strongly to Dr. Ford's defense. Undoubtedly the most heated speech of the day issued from the lips of one of the conference presidents in defense of Dr. Ford. It was refreshing to see two of the men appointed by the Australasian Division, however, express their concerns. Both Pastor Stanley and Pastor Athal Tolhurst indicated that they had serious reservations about what Dr. Ford was teaching. Pastor Athal Tolhurst expressed concern that the students at Avondale College were now reticent to pray for victory over sin lest they be accused of legalism.

The day was not without its lighter moments, although perhaps those could have been a little more frequent. Toward the end of the day Pastor Kent, visibly disturbed by what he had heard of Dr. Ford's defense of the *new theology*, exploded: "Well, today I've heard a man who could talk his way out of jail!" Dr. Ford fairly bristled as he commenced his reply: "I regard that as an affront to my character. . . ." Pastor Frame perhaps reached the highest point as chairman of that meeting when he smoothly defused the heat by interrupting: "Don't worry, Des. You're looking into the eyes of a man who could do as well." The spontaneous laughter of those gathered including Pastor Kent and Dr. Ford, showed that all humor had not departed the scene. For here were two men from two entirely different generations, one virtually twice the age of the other, both princes in their own right in the use of the English language, one who had led hundreds upon hundreds of non-Adventists to accept God's truth and the other who had convinced a whole generation of Adventist young people that his understanding of the gospel was biblical.

The afternoon session was given over to Russell's presentation of a paper on the age of the earth. That one of the Division-appointed members (Pastor Raymond Stanley) came to him privately prior to the presentation and assured him of his prayers and support was a matter of great encouragement. At the conclusion of his paper, Russell addressed himself to those representing the Division who had been fellow college students at Avondale—Pastor Clem Christian, Dr. Desmond Ford, Dr. Eric Magnusson, Pastor Rex Moe, Dr. Arthur Patrick and Pastor Len Tolhurst—and challenged them to uplift the truths they had learned under Pastors Burns and Kranz during their student days.

Perhaps it was during the reply to this paper that Dr. Ford's verbal skills were seen at their best. Russell had pointed out that in answering a question at a youth camp in 1974 Dr. Ford had stated that Sister White, in the book *Patriarchs and Prophets*, in the chapter entitled "The Call of Abraham," had stated that all Abraham's ancestors were idolators. This statement was used as an argument in defense of the view that the period between the flood and Abraham was vastly extended from that which seems clear in Chapter 11 of the book of Genesis. Russell had read Sister White's account and found that in no place did she make this assertion, and this misquotation Russell mentioned in his presentation.

Dr. Ford did not take kindly to having his words called into question. He immediately held the floor and questioned in an accusatory manner, "Russell, have you read all there is in the Bible on this topic?" Russell stated that he had attempted to, but he could not give any full assurance on this matter. Quickly Ford said, "Well, what about Joshua 24:2?" Russell had to admit that without reading the passage he was unaware of the contents cited and requested that Dr. Ford read it aloud. This Dr. Ford did in an incredibly speedy fashion. In fact the text stated:

> And Joshua said unto all the people, Thus saith the LORD God of Israel, Your fathers dwelt on the other side of the flood in old time, even Terah, the father of Abraham, and the father of Nachor: and they served other gods. (Joshua 24:2) [1]

Even with a lightning reading it did not sound as if the text made the point that Dr. Ford was claiming. So Russell asked him to re-read the text more slowly. After this was done Russell stated, "Well, I'm afraid Des, this just does not support the point that you are making." Dr. Ford's reply was again effortless, "Well, Russell, I'm afraid you and I are both biased. We would have to find a third person to arbitrate." This rather minor episode alerted Russell for the first time to the fact that Dr. Ford commonly used texts and quotations which, although with a quick and superficial reading seemed to have some relevance to the point he was making, were in reality unhelpful in supporting his statements. Further, Russell found how easy it was for him to direct a person's attention away from his error. He had stated, of course, that the Spirit of Prophecy had made a certain statement concerning Abraham's ancestors. Knowing that he could not produce such a statement, he immediately turned everyone's attention to a passage of Scripture which, although still not supporting the claim that he had made, may have been accepted by some who did not stop to read it carefully. Obviously all Joshua 24:2 states is that *some* of Abraham's family members were idolators; it makes no statement at all about all of Abraham's ancestors. Thirdly, Russell found that when Dr. Ford's second line of defense was thwarted his mental ability was such that he was able to throw in a red herring of bias and quickly move away from the topic,[2] thus leaving many with the impression that perhaps after all Dr. Ford had ably defended himself. Such techniques certainly display first-class debating skills, but they are not conducive to deciphering Bible truth.

Chapter 25 Endnotes

1. The New International Version translates the conclusion of this passage as "worshiped other gods."
2. See Appendix E for a similar circumstance.

# 26
## The Biblical Research Institute —Second Day

THE one-day meeting of the Biblical Research Institute was of necessity extended to two days to accommodate all the papers. The meetings on the second day, February 4, 1976, were convened at the Australasian Division offices at Wahroonga, Sydney. Most of the morning session was devoted to the presentation and examination of the paper prepared by Pastor Frank Breaden, defending the infallibility of the Bible. Pastor Breaden had studied at Avondale during two periods, 1934 to 1940 under Pastor Alfred Kranz, and 1965 and 1966 under Dr. Desmond Ford. Pastor Breaden asserted that during the second period the class was told "that the leading scholars of the Adventist denomination had now abandoned the earlier view of unqualified infallibility, and that many of the simple 'peripheral details' of Holy Scripture—the 'trivia' and 'minutiae,' as they were called—were demonstrably errant." Pastor Breaden stated that virtually all Dr. Ford's students accepted this false claim.

There was another matter which caused Pastor Burnside considerable concern. As a previous ministerial secretary of the Australasian Division he had drawn to his attention the case of a brother of one of our pastors. This man was a humanist but subsequently, much to the delight of his ordained brother, accepted the truth. Once hearing the Adventist message and accepting it, this young man was content with nothing less than training for the gospel ministry. He later stated, however, that he had been taught that while the Scriptures are an infallible guide for salvation they were not infallible in matters such as science and history. He reasoned that if the Bible erred in the things he could verify, he could feel no assurance that it did not also err in matters of faith, which he could not prove. Rapidly he lost faith and returned to his former agnostic persuasion.

It was during the discussion upon this paper that Dr. Ford's position was seriously misunderstood. He had asserted that there were millions of mistakes in the Bible. This statement was made with rapidity during a somewhat heated exchange. Thus most men present thought Dr. Ford was asserting an even grosser standpoint on scriptural fallibility than he was prepared to propose. In a book containing approximately 750,000 words, millions of errors seemed incredible. The real problem, of course, was the unavailability of the tapes for subsequent study. When permission was finally granted for a transcript to be made of this particular portion of the recording, Dr. Ford's meaning became perfectly clear. Speaking to Pastor

Breaden's claim that there were only a few copyists' errors in the Bible, Dr. Ford had stated, "I think he said a few, in the matter of copyists' errors, but they run into millions! Millions! And my point isn't that the original men made these mistakes. I'm not saying that at all, but I'm saying that God has permitted the Bible to come to us with these, most of which we can eradicate by textual criticism." [1]

Pastor Ronald Heggie also spoke for a period of time concerning various matters which he saw as highly significant.

The final session was intended for Pastor Llewellyn Jones to present his paper objecting to Dr. Ford's interpretation of the seventieth week of Daniel 9. However, Pastor Jones graciously suggested that Dr. John Clifford be given the time to present his paper on righteousness by faith. Incidentally, Dr. Clifford's had been the only paper given to Dr. Ford for preview. He and Dr. Salom had carefully analyzed it the previous evening. Thus Dr. Ford had an advantage with this paper which he did not enjoy with the others. In reality the advantage was not great, for Dr. Ford was fully conversant with the established Adventist beliefs and the papers presented defended only these. Later extravagant statements were made to the effect that Dr. Clifford's paper was extreme, but the simple fact is that if this was so, neither Dr. Ford nor Dr. Salom showed any enthusiasm to demonstrate it, for they urged Pastor Frame to encourage Pastor Jones to present his paper and forbid Dr. Clifford's presentation.

It was only Pastor Jones' insistence that decided the chairman to proceed with Dr. Clifford's paper. Even then the two pastors selected by the Division seated themselves on either side of Pastor Kent and repeatedly during the presentation of the paper advised him in hushed tones to withdraw Dr. Clifford's paper. It seemed that they were more concerned about the matter of righteousness by faith than any other of the matters presented. There was, clearly, material in that paper which was extraordinarily upsetting to Dr. Ford and some others who were listening, yet it presented only the basic biblical truth of righteousness by faith and confirmed the 1974 *Review and Herald Special* on that topic.

During an interval Pastor kent called the Concerned Brethren together. He had perceived that the topic of righteousness by faith was of such stature that the brief period allotted to it could not do it justice. He told the Concerned Brethren that he fully endorsed what he had heard of Dr. Clifford's paper. With this opinion the others concurred. However, in order to obtain decisions on the Sanctuary, the age of the earth and inspiration, he suggested the topic of righteousness by faith be withdrawn. In this he included Pastor Basham's paper with Dr. Clifford's suggesting they present this topic independently at a separate meeting. Only Pastor Basham demurred at this decision.

The strength of the arguments presented, of course, produced judgments which were greatly subjective. One man had this to say, "The *Get Rid of Ford* faction met and discussed doctrine with Ford who trounced them." (A teacher at Sydney Adventist High School in a letter dated April 24, 1977) This person was of course not privy to the details of the meeting. Whoever communicated such a view to him was, we believe, very wide of the mark. What is clear is that around Avondale College within days there were numerous assessments being made. One student stated that Ford's brilliant mind made fools of the "wicked old pastors." Such an assessment was sheer fantasy. Men who have known the joy of entering the baptismal font with numerous souls won from the world could not be so easily defeated in their faith. The great pity is that a transcript of that meeting is not available for the study of God's people. One fact needs to be stressed. The concerned men present all urged free access to the tapes. It surely is doubtful they would have done so if these false rumors were true. Equally factual is the matter that it was the Division which consistently refused an open review of the tapes. A few who were present at the meeting were permitted to re-listen to certain portions of the tapes, but only under surveillance.

Russell's own conclusions concerning the meeting were recorded the day the meetings finished. "I want to say, Brother Pierson, that I was proud of the men with whom I associated myself in these meetings. They presented the Truth of God with conviction, power and certainty. Indeed, perhaps a single positive consequence of this meeting was the wonderful and obvious Spirit-filled presentation of God's sure Word by men whose lives had been dedicated to the cause of God." (Letter written by Dr. Russell Standish to Pastor Pierson dated Feb. 4, 1976)

For those who attended the meetings, that which they had heard only deepened their concerns. Russell had this to say, "Truly we are in deep crisis. We have heard doubts expressed as never before save those expressed by the acknowledged enemies of God's Church. Brother Kent, pray as never before that somehow the Lord will take hold of His work once more in this country. I believe He will continue to encourage the hearts of those who are perplexed. May God bless you as never before in your years of ministry. He has preserved you well past your three score and ten allocation for such a time as this." (Letter written by Dr. Russell Standish to J. W. Kent, Feb. 7, 1976)

In his reply Pastor Kent stated, "Des, I consider, skidded around our objections in theological shoes. I was endeavouring to bring about unity as an anticipated result of a tightening up of supervision at the College. But as I told Pastor Parmenter, his closing remarks made that an impossibility." (Letter written by Pastor J. W. Kent to Dr. Russell Standish, Feb. 23, 1976) Indeed, in the same letter Pastor Kent referred to these remarks as "A thinly veiled insult to us." (*Ibid.*) Another man who was in attendance added to the Concerned Brethren's apprehension by asserting during the meeting that the whole concern was really simply a personal attack upon Dr. Ford. Although he speedily withdrew this opinion when aroused men insisted, it nevertheless seemed to mark a dramatic turning point in the meeting. It led to a growing fear within those men who presented papers that now there was a distinct possibility that the Biblical Research Institute was looking at this whole matter from a political stance rather than one of doctrinal fidelity. This attitude sorely troubled the Concerned Brethren, for up to that point they had never doubted that the old truths would be vindicated. Now, however, serious doubts that this result would be the outcome were entertained. The passage of time was to reveal that these doubts were all too realistic.

## Chapter 26 Endnote

1. Obviously, however, Dr. Ford's statement was a gross exaggeration. Statements such as these do little to bolster the faith of our youth in the words of Scripture.

# 27 The Findings of the Biblical Research Institute

THE doubts of the Concerned Brethren were not removed by the subsequent actions of the Biblical Research Institute in that it refused to make known its findings to those who had presented the papers. Only Pastor George Burnside, himself a member of the Biblical Research Institute, was privy to the decision. Members were advised to keep this decision secret. Thus in loyalty Pastor Burnside kept this counsel, and other Concerned Brethren remained ignorant of this matter. This state of affairs was a most curious development. Perhaps the situation would have remained this way had it not been the fact that one of the Avondale College members of the B.R.I. had felt it profitable to photostat these findings and have them distributed all over the campus. The authors received their copies from someone who found them lying around the college premises. The text of the findings confirmed the worst fears of the Concerned Brethren. It was little wonder that Pastor Kent was constrained to write that the Avondale College students were gleefully proclaiming "that Des came through with colours flying." But as Pastor Kent perceptively observed, "I do not think that he could stand another such victory."

The full text of the B.R.I.'s findings is worthy of record: "WHEREAS: The Biblical Research Institute has on two occasions, February 3, 1976, at Avondale College, and February 4, 1976, at the office of the Australasian Division, heard a plea of a number of senior ministers[1] who have expressed their concern about the teaching of theology at Avondale College, particularly in the area of the Sanctuary, the Age of the Earth, and Inspiration, it now desires to present its findings to the administration of the Australasian Division as follows:

"1. That the Theology Department at Avondale is committed to generally accepted, moderate Seventh-day Adventist doctrinal positions and that Dr. Desmond Ford ably demonstrated that such stances as he takes which appear to diverge from what some senior men hold as 'Present Truth' can be justified by reference to majority positions taken by current Seventh-day Adventist authors and scholars.

"2. The senior ministers (as represented by their speakers) were somewhat unaware of the movements in Adventist thought and the style of doctrinal presentation in recent years, a fact which explains their reaction to some contemporary expositions.

3. That it expresses its sustained confidence in Avondale College and its Theological Faculty, but it is of the view that certain counsel should be appropriately tendered to the College administration:
a. That the Theological Department and the ministry in the field communicate actively on the exposition of Adventist doctrine in terms which can be understood by the Church generally.
b. That an even stronger and positive emphasis in the classroom on the fundamental truths of the Church be maintained.
c. That all College lecturers continue to be careful to emphasize the Bible as the inspired Word of God and the source of all truth and be ever mindful that the students they teach are working at undergraduate level.
4. That it draws attention to and reaffirms the guidelines already established that all material prepared by the ministry or by members of the Avondale College faculty which may be of a controversial nature theologically (other than material normally used within the College for regular instruction) should not be distributed unless approved by the Institute."

That the Concerned Brethren were alarmed by these conclusions scarcely requires reporting. As far as has been ascertained, this occasion was the very first time in the whole history of the Seventh-day Adventist Church that it had been found necessary to validate a man's doctrinal position on the basis of "majority positions taken by current Seventh-day Adventist authors and scholars." While it was true that Dr. Ford did not prove his doctrines from the Bible nor from the Spirit of Prophecy, and while it is equally true that in most cases he was able to point to a *minority* of Seventh-day Adventists who had held his aberrant positions, the Concerned Brethren little imagined that this latter fact would satisfy the B.R.I.[2]

Second, the Concerned Brethren were not a little dismayed by the assertion that there had been "movements in Adventist thought" and the inference that these "movements" were acceptable. It was clear that the members of the B.R.I. fully recognized that changes had come into our Church, yet as far as is known none of these were ever accepted by the General Conference in session. It had thus been a "backdoor" method of entry quite out of harmony with church policy. That Dr. Ford was subsequently dismissed from the ministry for some of the material which he presented on that occasion (that which related to the Sanctuary doctrine) demonstrates beyond all dispute that the Church had not moved away from the truth of this doctrine, as was the conclusion of the Australasian Division Biblical Research Institute. Indeed in the light of Dr. Ford's later history within the Church there can be little argument with the view that the B.R.I. seriously erred in its findings. A review of the findings would be in order.

That Dr. Ford could validly point to some Adventist authors and scholars who also promoted similar unscriptural errors to his own revealed the insidious changes which had been wrought by the Barnhouse-Martin dialogue and the publication of *Questions on Doctrine*. Obviously an unofficial departure from truth had been taking place for some years. This shift, of course, explains why Ford's views met such a ready audience in the United States.

These incidents indicate just how careful we should be in guarding the faith from "back-door" changes. Even when the General Conference meets in session, care should be taken to make no precipitous changes even in the wording of our statement of faith since such changes usually do not clarify basic truth but rather obscure it. A reasoned case could be made out for a five-year period of review and examination after a new statement of belief is given its first discussion at a General Conference in full session. The precious obligation we have to preserve the faith in its purity demands no less care than this.

Chapter 27 Endnote

1. For some curious reason the contribution of the five laymen was ignored.
2. When this fact was pointed out to the Committee Chairman, the minutes were amended on March 23, 1976 to add "the Bible and the Spirit of Prophecy" as bases of Ford's stand. However in truth he had utilized these sources very sparingly and had been able to support none of his propositions from them.

# 28 The Palmdale Meeting Mooted

PALMDALE is a small town in Southern California which became the site of a little reported but nevertheless historic meeting. It is true that the *Adventist Review* and the *Australasian Record* did provide brief reports of this meeting. Many people at the time were quite unacquainted with the nature of the problems discussed and the long term implications of these matters and thus quickly dismissed them from mind.

The General Conference had received many complaints from brethren and sisters in the Australasian Division concerning the doctrinal trends at Avondale College and within the Australasian Division. Despite the assurances which they were persistently given by Division leaders indicating that there was no major problem in this area, it nevertheless became evident to the General Conference men that there must be matters which did required their attention.

When they reached Australia, some General Conference men made themselves available to listen to the perceived problems of the Concerned Brethren, and no doubt their findings also influenced the General Conference to provide a meeting of a delegation from the Australasian Division and one from the General Conference. When it became known that this meeting was to be arranged, it was natural that the composition of the Australasian delegation would be viewed with great interest.

It soon became evident that the Australasian Division intended to select their eight delegates from men of their own choice, completely ignoring those men whose concern had engendered the Palmdale meeting. The Concerned Brethren suggested that two delegates be included from their group, and the names of Pastors Burnside and Keith were put forth. However, the Australasian Division refused to add either of these names to the list of delegates.

Many letters were sent to the General Conference leaders asking them to arbitrate in the dispute. Russell sent one which stated: "Following the meeting in Cooranbong, our concern has grown over the composition of the representative group from Australia. At the meeting only one of these men stood for Truth as the General Conference, and far more important, Inspiration sets forth. Some actively supported erroneous views, while others made no contribution whatsoever. Neither we, nor, I am sure, you brethren whom we value so highly, and to whom we look as the spiritual leaders of God's church around the world, would be satisfied that the chosen delegation truly reflects the spectrum of feeling and views in this country, should these eight men alone be our representatives. We would urge most earnestly that prayerful consideration be given to enlarging the Australasian Division delegation to include a representative group of pastors and laymen who are contending so forcibly for the Truth of God. Only in this way can a balanced view be presented by this Division." [1]

Pastors Kent and Burnside even offered to attend at their own expense, but the Australasian Division rejected this offer. Pastor Pierson, apparently feeling that the request made by the Concerned Brethren had some validity, gave his advice to the Australasian Division that they include two of the senior Concerned Brethren, but even this advice did not prevail. In these circumstances it was felt that there was only a single avenue remaining for the presentation of a fuller picture of the doctrinal crisis in Australia to those gathered at the Palmdale meeting. This avenue was the presentation of a manuscript detailing the problem. This purpose the manuscript, *Conflicting Concepts of Righteousness by Faith in the Seventh-day Adventist Church—Australasian Division*, set out to fulfill. Had a fair representation been accorded within the Australasian Division, it is certain that this manuscript would never have been written.

Chapter 28 Endnote

1. By consistently ignoring the contribution which the laity could make, the Australasian Division leadership not only appeared to alienate their most loyal supporters, but they also left themselves open to a charge of clericalism. (See "Clericalism in the Church," *Landmarks*, June 1983.)

# 29 Conflicting Concepts

RUSSELL and Dr. Clifford first met in 1961 in connection with matters concerning the Sydney and Adelaide University Seventh-day Adventists Student's Societies, respectively. Both were medical students at the respective universities situated one thousand miles apart. They did not meet again for twelve years, and then their meetings were few and brief. At the end of 1975 Dr. Clifford and Russell met once again quite by accident. A conversation lasting several hours ensued. Each was somewhat surprised to find that the other had an understanding of truth which was virtually identical with his own. Further, each had begun to feel great concern over the attacks which he noted on the pillars of our faith. The two men also shared a common friendship with, and admiration for, Pastor O. K. Anderson. They both owed him a deep spiritual debt. Pastor Anderson had been one of the early chaplains of the Adelaide University Seventh-day Adventist Students' Society and had taken a great interest in Dr. Clifford and his wife, Dr. Wilvene Hill. Russell's contact with Pastor Anderson was even of longer standing, for he (with Colin) had as a lad assisted Pastor Anderson's large evangelistic effort in the Newcastle Town Hall by distributing announcements of the meeting, and he was greatly indebted to Pastor Anderson as the pastor who had baptized his grandfather after many years of bitter antagonism toward the truth of God. Both physicians had discussed their views independently with Pastor Anderson, who was now living in retirement at Avondale. He full well understood medical men since his twin brother, Dr. Clifford Anderson, was well known to Adventists around the world as "Your Radio Doctor."

Following the B.R.I. meeting in February, 1976, and the abortive efforts to have the Australasian delegation increased to include representatives of the Concerned Brethren, Dr. Clifford approached Russell with a suggestion that they co-author a manuscript which would fully set forth their concern, to be sent to the Palmdale Conference and later to be presented before the General Conference Biblical Research Institute. At that time there was no thought given to a wide circulation of the manuscript, although it was considered that a final polished version might in years to come be suitable for such a purpose. In the brief period of time available, the authors knew they could not write a fully edited copy. They had no secretaries, no typists, no proof readers—just themselves and the assistance of John's wife, Dr. Hill, who performed a Herculean task in typing the manuscript.

Yet it was the Palmdale deadline which spurred on their effort. Where the time came for writing and editing the manuscript no one knows, but it did come. Dr. Clifford was forced at one stage to employ a locum tenens in his busy medical practice in order that he and Dr. Hill could complete the task. Russell had to fit his writing in between his duties as deputy medical superintendent of Melbourne University's Austin Hospital and the pursuance of his private practice in the evenings. It was truly a combined effort. Both had previously written papers for scientific journals, but neither had written a manuscript concerning doctrine. Only eleven copies were photostated. These were rapidly bound by Brother Llewellyn Jones Jr., a Melbourne printer. The three copies earmarked for Palmdale were rushed to the Melbourne general post office in order to meet the 10 A.M. deadline for airmail to the United States.

These three copies were addressed to Pastor Duncan Eva, chairman of the General Conference, Pastor Robert Pierson, the world leader of the Church, and Pastor Kenneth Wood, editor of the *Review and Herald*.

It is likely that the manuscripts made little impact at Palmdale. While they were certainly received there, and at least Pastors Pierson and Wood read some or all of the contents during the conference, it is certain that any real discussion of the contents was confined to times when the conference was not in session. The authors had in reality expected no more than this. It had been somewhat of a symbolic gesture with a faint hope that it was then not too late to alert our American brethren to the serious doctrinal controversy in Australia. We received the following letter in reply: "A few days ago I received from you and Doctor Standish copies of the results of research on the subject of Righteousness by Faith which you two brethren had undertaken. You had prepared some very good material, and we appreciated its input." (Letter written by Pastor Pierson to Dr. John Clifford dated May 6, 1976)

In his reply Pastor Wood indicated that "While at Palmdale I examined it [*Conflicting Concepts*] carefully and since returning to Washington I have given it further study." (Letter written by Pastor Kenneth Wood to Dr. Russell Standish dated June 7, 1976) Pastor Wood then proceeded to give the authors his opinion: "From the brief overview of your document I would say that it presents the historic view on righteousness by faith as proclaimed by Adventists for many decades. In saying this I do not mean to either endorse everything exactly as it has been expressed in the booklet, or to affirm that there are not other ways in which the subject of righteousness by faith may be presented. I feel, however, that anyone reading your booklet with an open mind and a prayerful spirit would find it helpful and would be led to a desire for a closer walk with the Lord. The purpose of righteousness by faith is not merely to change our standing before God, but to change our hearts and bring them into harmony with His will." (*Ibid.*)

The major aim of the authors, however, was to have the manuscript, when finalized, presented before the General Conference Biblical Research Institute. This purpose was never to be realized. In the limitations of time (the manuscript was prepared within a period of six weeks) it was quite impossible to construct more than a preliminary draft which contained a number of typographical and editorial errors. Of the eleven original copies, three had been sent to Palmdale and two were preserved by the authors. Two of the remaining six copies were sent to Robert Brinsmead and Desmond Ford "since we are anxious to set before these men frankly our objections to their views and also to correct any unintended misrepresentation of their positions should such be found in this paper." (*Conflicting Concepts*—distribution)

We had left with us the remaining four copies to share with "men and women of experience, both in the ministry and among the laity." (*Ibid.*) We stated: "We would have no objection to recipients of the paper sharing it, for the purpose of counsel, with other experienced Seventh-day Adventist men and women. However, we would genuinely request that the paper be preserved within the Seventh-day Adventist family." (*Ibid.*) The manuscript was carefully read by the four brethren—three pastors and one layman to whom we distributed it. These men in discussion with others felt that erroneous views of righteousness by faith were so widespread then in Australia that the Seventh-day Adventist Church needed to be alerted. Error, they felt, seemed to have a free rein while truth was greatly muted. In view of this conviction they suggested distribution of the paper on a far wider scale than the authors had envisaged. They expressed the view that time was short, for already error was being passed off in the pulpits of the Church as truth. They seemed to feel that the few editorial errors present were inconsequential. Thus one thousand copies of the manuscript were printed.

One humorous sidelight to this episode was the report of one young Avondale theology student who visited the Standish home to request a copy of *Conflicting Concepts*. He later reported that Enid, Russell's wife, had shown him three thousand copies in the garage. If only this were true! At least that would have meant that the Standishes had the luxury of a garage. Since at the time there were fewer than thirty copies in the home, that young man had more than the eye of faith.

In one area the authors felt considerable apprehension. Each knew full well that there were a host of other men, true to the pillars of our faith, who were not only more able in presentation but were also more deeply conversant with the truth of God. There was no doubt that in the sense of Bible study and understanding the authors felt as pygmies among giants. Yet it was these very giants who encouraged and urged them on. Over and over again, the view was expressed that men who were not dependent upon denominational financial support were freer to express their views within the Church. The book had been prepared with much prayer and Bible and Spirit of Prophecy study. Daily each had gleaned gems from God's Word, sometimes unknown texts and at other times texts previously well known but poorly comprehended.

The most persistent attack which was to come upon *Conflicting Concepts* was that it was unscholarly. How often we have heard that attack subsequently! It seems that there are a number of theologians who believe that only theologians are aware of scholarship. Both the authors knew full well what scholarly presentation involved, for they had had papers accepted by prestigious scientific journals, but both viewed Bible truths in an entirely different perspective. In the face of a clear challenge to the truth of God neither wished to be—

> ... dumb dogs, that would not bark. (*5T* 211)

Each was aware that—

> While those who have yielding temperaments, who have not courage to condemn wrong, but keep silent when their influence is needed to stand in defense of the right against any pressure, may avoid many heartaches and escape many perplexities, they will also lose a very rich reward, if not their own souls. (*3T* 302)

# 30 The Palmdale Conference

THE Palmdale Conference was held April 23–30, 1976. The General Conference delegates consisted of the following:

    Dr. Raoul Dederen, Andrews University
    Pastor N. R. Dower, ministerial secretary, General Conference
    Pastor Duncan Eva, vice-president, General Conference and chairman, General Conference Biblical Research Institute
    Pastor Willis J. Hackett, vice-president, General Conference
    Pastor Gordon M. Hyde, secretary, General Conference Biblical Research Institute
    Pastor Hans LaRondelle, Andrews University
    Pastor Don F. Neufeld, associate editor, *Review and Herald*
    Pastor Robert W. Olsen, chairman of Ellen G. White Estate
    Pastor Robert H. Pierson, president, General Conference
    Pastor Kenneth H. Wood, editor, *Review and Herald*

The Australasian Division delegation consisted of

    Dr. Desmond Ford, chairman, theology department, Avondale College
    Pastor R. R. Frame, president, Australasian Division
    Pastor A. S. Jorgensen, field secretary, Australasian Division
    Pastor C. D. Judd, president, Trans-Tasman Union Conference
    Pastor L. C. Naden, retired president, Australasian Conference
    Pastor R. H. Parr, editor, *Signs of the Times*
    Dr. A. P. Salom, pastor, Wahroonga Church
    Pastor C. R. Stanley, ministerial secretary, Australasian Division
    Pastor S. M. Uttley, president, Trans-Australian Union Conference

While, as in the meetings in Australia two and a half months previously, there were moments of high tension and striking disagreement, eventually it was possible to issue a consensus statement. This statement was published in the *Review and Herald* dated May 31, 1976. Its preamble stated that the participants "studied and prayed together, shared sweet fellowship, and gained in unity of spirit and viewpoint as the days passed." (*Review and Herald*, May 27, 1976) The final statement was made "not as a formal presentation of doctrine, nor as an official pronouncement by church leaders. Rather it is offered as a statement of consensus of their understanding on this vital issue of doctrine and experience." (*Ibid.*) The statement consisted of about two and a half pages of relatively fine print. It was the first sentence, however, that attracted the greatest attention. "We agree that when the words RIGHTEOUSNESS and FAITH are connected (by 'of,' 'by,' et cetera) in Scripture, reference is to the experience of justification by faith." (*Ibid.*)

If a simple statement is made on the roots of the controversy in Australia concerning the doctrine of righteousness by faith, it could be summed up in a single sentence. Those accepting the *new theology* proclaim that it is impossible to keep God's law fully, even for a Christian filled with the Holy Spirit, while those holding to the old Adventist beliefs assert that it is not only possible but mandatory.

Now these two positions have certain undeniable implications. One of these is that, if one believes the *new theology*, it naturally follows that righteousness by faith cannot encompass the process of sanctification. Rather it is confined to justification by faith alone. If a totally obedient life is not possible, then obedience, sanctification, victory, or any other synonym for the process of sanctification surely cannot be a requirement of acceptance with God. The *new theology* loudly proclaimed this view. For example, the fifth form (grade eleven) students at the Lilydale Academy in Melbourne in April, 1977, were given a sheet of paper in their Bible class. This paper asserted the following: "There are two aspects of Christ's work—that which He did for us which brings complete acceptance with God for every believer, and the work He does in us—which has nothing to do with our acceptance by God." (Dr. D. Ford, *The Good News*) A corollary of this idea is the view that our salvation is based entirely upon the objective facts of Christ's death on Calvary, and that to include experience within the confines of righteousness by faith is to accept a Roman Catholic concept. In order to bolster this position, the assertion is made that sanctification is not entirely of faith or even of God, but partly involves the input of the individual.[1]

Thus when the first sentence of the Palmdale consensus was read it provided a most tantalizing problem for those accepting the *new theology* in Australia. Superficially it looked so close to their pet theory and yet there were just two problems. Initially the followers of this view swept these problems aside. In the initial flush after the Palmdale Conference, one of the Australians who attended, along with others, claimed a great victory for Dr. Ford and "the defeat of the *Review and Herald* men." Of course the claim to victory or to inflict defeat was not the purpose of the meeting. Pastor Frame had emphasized in a letter distributed to the Australasian Ministry that no one was on trial at Palmdale. Nevertheless in the four-week period which intervened between the conclusion of the conference and the publication of the results, such rumors swept Australia. One of the members of the Australian party[2] soon passed on to Robert Brinsmead the news that the initial sentence of the Palmdale statement read: "We agree that when the words righteousness and faith are connected, by 'of,' 'by,' etc., Scriptural reference is to justification by faith only."

The astute reader will soon note the subtle difference between this report and the actual report as printed. This version became widespread throughout Australasia during the period of waiting, preceding the presentation of the consensus. Naturally those supporting the Adventist faith were absolutely dismayed by what they heard, for they full well knew that Scripture teaches that

> ... he that feareth him, and worketh righteousness, is accepted with him. (Acts 10:35)

Thus there was fear that at a high level an unscriptural statement had been made.

It was with no little relief that these people read the statement as finally printed, comparing the correct statement with the bogus report. It can be seen that the two differed in two vital ways: (i) The word *experience* was omitted in the bogus report. Naturally for those who did not believe that justification has any experiential aspects it was an embarrassing intrusion into the sentence. (ii) The word *only* was added. Interestingly, these modifications or similar ones continued to be used by the advocates of the *new theology* even after all could see the changes for themselves. In point of fact the modifications became so incorporated into the discussions on the Palmdale statement that many still may be unaware of the true version.

Other examples of modifying the first sentence of the Palmdale statement are easy to document. Three are cited below.

1. "Where the word righteousness occurs in the New Testament with the words faith, 'of' or 'by,' righteousness of faith or righteousness by faith—it always means justification" (Dr. D. Ford, a chapel talk at Avondale College entitled *Sanctification*, presented May 8, 1976, as a preview to the college students of the Palmdale Statement)
2. "It [the Palmdale Statement] clearly says that when 'righteousness' is linked with faith in any phrase such as 'righteousness by faith' or 'righteousness of faith'—it means justification only." (Dr. D. Ford letter to Dr. R. Standish dated June 7, 1976)
3. "The Palmdale Group did assent to the fact that in the Pauline writings the term 'righteousness' when linked with 'faith' by the preposition 'of' or 'by' means justification, and justification *only*." (Dr. D. Ford, letter published in the *Review and Herald*, Dec. 23, 1976. The italicized word was not in the original.)

Thus it can be seen that Dr. Ford made a habit of changing the Palmdale Statement in order to suit his view.

Being somewhat less ego-involved in claiming denominational support for their views, those who were following Robert Brinsmead recognized that the omission of the word *only* did seriously weaken the claim of Dr. Ford that the Palmdale consensus supported the *new theology*. Thus Ray Martin, who led the Sanctuary Awakening Fellowship in the state of Victoria, wrote: "Maybe Ford failed to sew up his case at Palmdale when he did not include the word *only* in the vital paragraph of the biblical meaning of righteousness by faith." (Ray Martin, *Objective Digest Report, What is Happening in Australia?* Italics in the original)

Chapter 30 Endnotes

1. For an exposition of the biblical principles of the gospel see *Adventism Vindicated* and *Adventism Unveiled* by the authors of this book.
2. Dr. Ford

# 31 The Controversy Continues

IT was perfectly plain that the Palmdale Statement did not in its unmodified form present support for Dr. Ford's position as he would have wished. For this outcome there can be only two possibilities. Either Dr. Ford, who has stated that he was prominent in framing the Palmdale Consensus Statement, failed to grasp the fact that this statement did not faithfully reflect his position, or the majority of other members at the Palmdale meeting refused to allow his viewpoint expression in the final statement, believing that the *new theology* was incompatible with the Bible and the Spirit of Prophecy. It is very likely that the second possibility was closer to the truth.

It should be stated here that the framings of consensus statements have not been entirely satisfactory. By their very nature these statements attempt to cover two incompatible positions with a statement acceptable to both parties. This procedure is not the way in which truth should be presented. Although it is obvious that the Palmdale Consensus did uphold the old Adventist teaching, it did so in such a way as to leave an escape for those who wished to continue in their false beliefs. The authors believe that the time has come to abandon this form of consensus statement. What we need are plain, precise, unequivocal statements of truth, statements which cannot in any way be misinterpreted by those who would wish to uphold a position divergent from that of Scripture. In this respect the Palmdale Statement fell short of the mark.

The fact that the consensus statement did not appear for one month led to the circulation of many wild rumors during this period. So bizarre and persistent were these rumors that those standing for truth felt perplexed by the delay of the General Conference in announcing its findings. They felt that the General Conference report would clear the misunderstandings perpetrated by those who had returned from the conference. Some even sent a cable to Pastor Pierson stating "Wild rumours in Australia re California meetings. Widely circulated by Ford's colleagues that there was complete vindication of Ford's view and *Review and Herald* position overthrown—Dr. Raoul Dederen reported by Brinsmead to have stated via telephone that he completely supports Ford. Think facts urgently required in Australia. Only immediate disclosure of results can save deteriorating doctrinal situation."

This period of uncertainty highlighted the tragic error of judgment in omitting representatives of the Concerned Brethren from Palmdale. Had men of this view been present at the meetings, they would have been in a position to present a balanced view of the Conference and to prevent the rapid spread of false information. As it was, by the time the church leadership recognized that some had seen the Palmdale Conference not as a session of deep Bible and Spirit of Prophecy investigation but as a political base from which to assert victory for their ideas, much damage had been done by the spread of rumor. These rumors had caused a level of complacency among many good people who fully accepted the view that the Palmdale meeting confirmed the truth of the *new theology* and the defeat of the long-held Adventist position.

Many people now contented themselves with this knowledge, as they believed that the *new theology* had General Conference support. This belief emboldened many of these people to take a more open stance in attacking the characters of the silver-haired pastors standing for truth—even to forbid at least one of them from using the pulpit, and to give credence to Geoffrey Paxton's attacks on the old Adventist position.

Of course as the statement was read in published form, it became very evident that the "doctored" first sentence of the Palmdale statement was in total error, and that those who wished to interpret it that way were failing to read the statement in its entirety, for the statement went on to say subsequently, "Righteousness is concerned with both God's gifts and His requirement, with justification and sanctification, with both imputed righteousness and repentance, and imparted righteousness by faith and obedience, with both the title and the fitness for heaven." (*Review and Herald*, May 27, 1976.) So inventive had become the minds of some of the holders of the *new theology* that they tried to minimize even this clear statement by contending that it simply mentioned *righteousness* and not *righteousness by faith*. One example of this distortion is cited, "When 'righteousness' is used on its own it can mean either justification or sanctification." (Letter written by Dr. Ford to Dr. Russell Standish, June 7, 1976) The reader must surely be led to wonder whether there is some form of righteousness which is not of faith.

So persistent were the misrepresentations of the Palmdale Consensus in Australia that eventually the editor of the *Review and Herald*, who himself attended Palmdale, had little option but to express the true conclusions of the conference in a series of four editorials entitled F.Y.I (For Your Information). In the first of these articles it was stated: "Historically Seventh-day Adventists have used 'righteousness by faith' to mean the whole process of God's saving grace—both justification and sanctification. . . . The Palmdale Statement concurs with this view." (Pastor Kenneth Wood, *Review and Herald*, Oct. 21, 1976) This statement, expressed in the clearest and most unequivocal terms, left no doubt that the Palmdale Statement meant that which it stated. It easily refuted the assertion—"It's a wonderful thing that recently in America (at Palmdale) we could make a statement like this for the first time in our history—a wonderful thing." (Dr. D. Ford, a chapel talk at Avondale on the Palmdale Statement entitled *Sanctification*, delivered May 18, 1976) Incidentally, this statement unquestionably shows that Dr. Ford fully knew at that time that the *new theology* was indeed new to Seventh-day Adventists ("for the first time"). And so it would have been if his modification of the statement had been accepted, but God's people can rejoice that it was not.

Naturally the topic of the nature of Christ received attention, for it is so closely bound to the doctrine of righteousness by faith. The statement quite properly stood for the biblical principles as accepted by the Seventh-day Adventist Church. However, the statement fell short of specifically stating that Christ came with the nature of fallen humanity, even though it implied the same. Once again this omission was no doubt due to this document's being a consensus statement, and this fact does underline once more the urgent need to be more precise in our statements. Nevertheless it is a most interesting presentation and demands record—

> When Paul noted that Jesus was "tempted like as we are, yet without sin," [1] he was proclaiming the good news that sin is neither necessary nor inevitable. Because Jesus took upon Himself man's nature and denied Himself access to special advantages not available to "His brethren" His secret of victory is ours too: He came into this world "not to reveal what God could do, but what a man could do through faith in God's power to help in every emergency. [2]
>
> He is simultaneously our Substitute, our Redeemer, and our Example. As He overcame with His Father's help, [3] He invites us to overcome, "even as I also overcame," [4] living by faith as He Himself did. Divine power was not given Him in a way different from the way it may be given to us. [5] "His imputed grace and power," specifies Ellen White, "He gives to all who receive Him by faith." [6] "Jesus our Lord not only delivers us from the condemnation of sin but also from its power. Forgiveness of sin and victory over sin is the promise to everyone who chooses to trust and obey God. In Christ, we are brought into a position of victory over sin, over deliberate acts of rebellion against God as well as over hereditary and cultivated tendencies to evil." [7] Over men and women of faith sin no longer has dominion. [8] Having surrendered to Christ, renewed in the spirit of our mind, [9] we put on "the new nature, created after the likeness of God in true righteousness and holiness." [10] (*Review and Herald*, May 27, 1976)

Another important feature of the Palmdale consensus was the review of the 1888 message. Not only did it uplift the presentation of that message but it also supported "all who may have faithfully presented it in the years since." (*Ibid.*) Since the 1888 message is such a key to the correct view of righteousness by faith, the report of the Palmdale meeting is worth recording.

> In reviewing the history of the 1888 era, we are led to the conclusion that it was a time of unparalleled opportunity for the Seventh-day Adventist Church. The

Lord actually gave His people the "beginning" of the latter rain and the loud cry in "the revelation of the righteousness of Christ, the sin-pardoning Redeemer." The attitudes and spirit manifested by too many at that time made it necessary for God to withdraw this special blessing.

While nothing is gained by disputing over the actual number of those who accepted or rejected this blessing in 1888, we recognize that those who then heard the message of righteousness by faith were divided in their response. It is clear that the fullness of the marvelous blessing God wanted to bestow upon the church was not received at that time nor subsequently. In the light of these facts of history, our special concern now must be to remove every barrier that holds back the promised power, and by repentance, faith, revival, and reformation clear the way so that the Lord can do His special work for us and through us. We recognize that a primary responsibility in this respect lies with the leadership of the church.

We take our stand not only with the messengers whom the Lord used in 1888 to proclaim the most precious message of the righteousness of Christ, but with all who may have faithfully presented it in the years since. We desire to benefit from the mistakes of the past so that rebellion, stubbornness, insubordination, suspicion, and envy shall not be found among us. This is a day of emphasis on revival and reformation on the part of the leadership of the church, and we join with our faithful members in an earnest desire to embrace the full truth that will allow us to enter into the genuine experience of righteousness by faith, receive the resulting outpouring of the latter rain, and see the earth lighted with the glory of God. (*Ibid.*)

What has been the impact of the Palmdale Statement on the Church? Possibly the impact has been rather slight, since most have forgotten its existence and many were scarcely ever aware of it. The great weakness of the Palmdale Statement was that it was a consensus of two diametrically opposed series of doctrines, indeed of truth and error. That the old Adventist view dominated is perfectly obvious. The chief input of the proponents of the *new theology* was to prevent a fuller and more precise statement of truth. This fact was particularly noticeable in the failure to be more specific on the topic of the fallen nature of Christ. However, not one of the errors of the *new theology* was permitted a voice in the statement.

In summary it could be said that the Palmdale Statement was free of doctrinal error, but that it was vague in one place (the first sentence) and fell short of a full statement in another (Christ's human nature). The *F.Y.I.* statements which appeared six months later in the *Review and Herald* corrected these two defects in unequivocal terms. Had the Palmdale Statement been as clear on these matters as it undoubtedly should have been, there would have been no need for these explanatory and follow-up statements in the *Review and Herald*; and the vital six months in which the errors of the *new theology* found fertile ground for propagation based upon these defects would not have gone by.

Chapter 31 Endnotes

1. The references given here were placed as footnotes in the original statement and were numbered consecutively, 42–51. Heb. 4:15
2. *SDA Bible Commentary*, Comments on Heb. 4:15, 929.
3. See John 6:38–40; 7:16; 8:26–28; 12:48.
4. Revelation 3:21.
5. Manuscript 1, 1892.
6. *Ibid*.
7. *COL* 420.
8. Romans 6:14
9. Ephesians 4:23
10. Ephesians 4:24

# 32 An Emotive Reaction to Old Truths

CONFLICTING *Concepts* soon caused an emotive reaction throughout the Australasian Division. The authors were truly amazed at the ire which was generated against a manuscript which had merely set out the well-established Seventh-day Adventist position. They had noticed that when Mrs. Gillian Ford's manuscript, *The Soteriological Implications of the Human Nature of Christ* had been published the previous year, there was virtually no reaction to it despite the fact that it boldly proclaimed the Seventh-day Adventist position to be false. Indeed, it was sold at Avondale College bookstore and was recommended in classes in the college.

The authors have recorded the reaction to *Conflicting Concepts* and the furor which it engendered in considerable detail in order to give exposure to the manner in which Ford's errors were supported with full ecclesiastical authority, and the methods adopted to silence the presentation of God's truth.

When the same views which were expressed in Mrs. Ford's manuscript had been enunciated by W. W. Fletcher in the 1920s, Robert Greive in the 1950s and Len Moulds in the 1960s, the Church itself had strongly opposed the views and had provided the biblical reasons for this opposition. Indeed, the Australasian Division in the late 1950s published an excellent book on righteousness by faith. It stated:

> Righteousness by faith, then, starts at conversion. It commences with a sinful soul being born again, transformed by the Holy Spirit, and made a new creature in Christ Jesus. When the sinner, drawn by the cords of God's love, confesses his sins and turns from his evil way, he is justified. He can say with confidence, "through the merits of Christ Jesus our Lord, I am now in the sight of God just as if I had never sinned." That is what the word "justified" means. (*Righteousness by Faith*, published by action of the Australasian Division Executive Committee, 7)

It is instructive to look at one type of reaction to the publication of the book, *Conflicting Concepts*. Although these reactions were very emotional, looking at the correspondence which followed, now having the benefit of the passage of a number of years, we must admit that on both sides correspondence had its defects. Nevertheless it did become standard procedure to make no effort to deny the doctrinal accuracy of *Conflicting Concepts*. Such would have been rather difficult since it was merely a simple presentation of that which was well-known to be confirmed Seventh-day Adventist belief. Thus some found it necessary to level attacks upon the book from another point of view. Since the manuscript had been sent to the meetings at Palmdale it had been labeled a Biblical Research Institute paper. Further, the authors' aim was to present this paper to a full meeting of the General Conference Biblical Research Institute. Thus the use of this term, in the view of the authors, was quite proper. It was this triviality, however, which was seized upon to bring a heavy attack upon the manuscript and to discredit it before God's people in Australia.

The authors were told that the use of the term *Biblical Research Institute Paper* should not have been made "until it had been approved by the Biblical Research Institute Committee" (Letter written to Drs. John Clifford and Russell Standish dated June 28, 1976, by Division spokesman) The writer further stated that "to present your material as a 'Biblical Institute Paper' is to tacitly claim our consideration and approval of it. Which, I repeat, you well know is not the case! I reiterate, therefore, 'I marvel at your audacity.'" (*Ibid.*) This reply was a clear case of overreaction and misrepresentation.

No doubt the obvious anger displayed in the letter had little to do with the use of the term. This reaction was rather seen as an objection which could be exploited in order to discredit the entire manuscript without the necessity of answering the difficult questions that were posed.

Dr. Clifford and Russell replied to this letter. Undoubtedly in a calmer environment they would have replied in a different way. It is a matter of record, however, that the following reply was given, and we do not wish to be selective in presenting both sides of the picture. Thus in fairness the letter as written is presented, warts and all:

"We, because of our professional commitments, are conversant with the procedures of presentation of unpublished manuscripts for comment by colleagues. The procedure we have followed is considered courteous and correct.

"We would be pleased for the reference in our paper upon which you base your assertion that the paper claims to have been considered and approved by the Australasian Division Biblical Research Institute. If such a quotation exists, then we will freely correct the error. If you cannot find such a statement we feel sure that as a servant of God, you will openly disassociate yourself from this false conclusion.

"This paper, which was freely offered to the Australasian Division (our letter and Pastor Frame's reply are in our files) prior to the Palmdale meetings, was never, as you somehow carelessly assumed, prepared for the Australasian Division Biblical Research Institute. It is a matter of record that it was sent for the consideration of the *General Conference* Biblical Research Institute's Special Committee, at Palmdale, and we have on file two expressions of appreciation for the input of the material, from two very senior American members of that Committee. . . . We had distributed a letter with each copy of the manuscript, which inexplicably your informant, it appears, did not pass on to you. As a courtesy, we enclose a copy with this letter.

Had you received this letter we believe you would have been saved much subsequent embarrassment, since it clearly states the aim we had was to present the corrected, final draft to the General Conference Biblical Research Institute, and not to the Australasian Institute.

"The reason we did emphasize the truth that the manuscript was a Biblical Research Institute paper was to avoid following the unprecedented action of Doctor Ford in freely distributing, as a matter of final truth, his wife's document and several of his own, without going through the Denominational procedures. Since the manuscripts asserted that the old Adventist faith is contrary to the New Testament and a false gospel, there is no doubt that the Denomination could never approve them. We have no doubt that the Division has taken firm measures to prevent the escalation of these actions of Dr. Ford's which have caused such a schism in our beloved Church. We have, on the other hand, been most anxious to follow approved denominational procedures.

"However, we can put your mind at rest. Numerous pastors and laymen, have given us unexpected encouragement by their kind remarks and by the relief they have expressed in hearing the Bible-based Seventh-day Adventist position on this topic once more uplifted. Among those, not one has confused our intent, nor misunderstood that the Australasian Division Biblical Research Institute has considered or sponsored the paper. This should bring you much assurance."[1]

Unfortunately the matter was not concluded at this point. It was decided to call together a limited number of the Biblical Research Institute Committee (those residing within the 100-mile strip from Sydney to Newcastle). Since this area included the Avondale College representatives, they were represented out of all proposition to their numbers on the total committee. This meeting met at the Australasian Division office on July 6, 1976, and passed the following resolution:

> VOTED: That because of the nature and tone of the document, "Conflicting Concepts of Righteousness by Faith," including its attempt to discredit Avondale College, its use of the Biblical Research Institute's name, its attacks on workers, its misleading use of quotations, its circulation to church and non-church members here and overseas, R.R. Standish and A.J. Clifford be requested to withdraw the publication and to agree to abide by the accepted policy of the church on unauthorized publications.

This motion caused the authors much heartburning. They felt a deep sense of loyalty to God's Church and felt pained to be so forcibly accused of an issue and of such a large number of ecclesiastical misdemeanors. Some of these matters seemed to the authors to lack any foundation in fact whatsoever. There were many other perplexities and these were brought out in the letter of reply to the Biblical Research Institute motion.

"Thank you for your letter dated July 15, and particularly for the advice you so kindly offered us. We assure you that we have given and will continue to give careful and prayerful consideration to your views. Perhaps you could be so good as to provide us with a little additional information for your study. Firstly, we would greatly appreciate a photostatic copy of the relevant General Conference policy alluded to as 'accepted policy on unauthorized manuscripts.' Apart from restrictions on the sale of independent publications through Book and Bible Houses, we are unaware of any documented denominational policy in the terms you have used.

"Secondly, having not seen a copy of the terms of reference of the Australasian Division Biblical Research Institute, we would appreciate a copy of these so that we can be assured that they give the Biblical Research Institute power to stop the printing by church members of manuscripts which support the General Conference leadership and the traditional Seventh-day Adventist position. Our concern is that if such a prerogative existed it would be in apparent opposition to the principle and inspired counsel of the servant of the Lord given at Battle Creek in 1896. 'Shall we, uninspired men, take the responsibility of placing our stakes, and saying, This shall not appear in print? . . . Will we ever learn the lessons which God designs we should learn? Will we ever realize that the consciences of men are not given into our command? If you have appointed committees to do the work which has been going on for years in Battle Creek, dismiss them, and remember that God, the infinite God has not placed men in any such positions as they occupied at Minneapolis and have occupied since then.'—TM 295. Further, we are interested to know if all committee members appointed to your Committee were invited to be present at the meeting you called at the Division offices on the morning of Tuesday, July 6th, 1976.

"Since our document deals with matters concerning the current theology disseminated through Avondale College (which, as you know is strongly represented on your committee) you would recognize no doubt that failure to call in the men from outlying fields would leave this particular committee largely unrepresentative in its position and views. This does appear to have been the case.

"We have yet another concern with which you could assist us. It would be most helpful if you could advise us just how many of the members of the Australasian Division Biblical Research Institute you know had a copy and had read our manuscript in its entirety and in addition given deep study to its contents prior to the Biblical Research Institute meeting which passed the motion you sent to us. I'm sure you recognize that it would reflect little credit on your chairmanship of the committee if you entertained a motion such as the one enclosed in your letter to us, unless you had ascertained that all the men voting had given time and prayerful consideration to the many aspects of the document. Our concern is heightened by the knowledge that prominent members of the Australasian Division Biblical Research Institute Committee requested copies of our document subsequent to your Committee Meeting and stated that they had not even read a copy at that time.

"Indeed one member of the Australasian Division Biblical Research Institute confessed that as late as the 25th July—nineteen days after he supposedly voted on the motion stated in your letter of the 15th July (and subsequently amended in our letter of the 21st)—that he *still* had not read our manuscript, nor indeed did he have one. This is understandable, for with one exception, we have not given copies of our manuscript to any member of your committee to study. We respectfully ask if the above-mentioned men were typical of those who voted in favour of your motion?

"Could we remind you that we published but eleven copies of the manuscript, and as previously stated only one of these was passed to a member of the Australasian Division Biblical Research Institute for comment? He is a man[2] whose spiritual guidance we greatly value. All other advice from your Committee was uninvited—although we hasten to add, highly valued. However, we do prefer advice based upon careful study rather than hearsay. Further, we anticipate comment from individual thinkers at this time, rather than the stated consensus of your men, as the document is not yet ready for us to present to any committee.

"Could you inform us if you sent us an invitation to be present at your discussion of our manuscript? Neither of us did receive one. We would find it hard to conceive that you, as chairman, would proceed to take a decision on any manuscript without its authors being invited to be present.

"Now, no one who had carefully read our manuscript could have accused us of making an attack on Avondale College or an attack on workers as you suggest. God forbid! Should our hearts be so directed we would be denying the very faith we are striving under God's blessing to uphold. It is obvious that we are protecting Avondale against the false doctrine soiling its image among the church folk. Nor would it be charitable or correct to suggest that we have misused quotations. We feel certain that you will ensure that the Australasian Division Biblical Research Institute promptly withdraws this section of the motion, and in fact we ask you to do so. I know that you with us will regard it less than common justice, let alone Christian rectitude, to condemn our document without appropriate and full consideration. To all evidence available to us, this latter situation appears to have been the case."[3]

The authors were very much disappointed with the reply they received. Instead of frankly relieving their expressed concerns, perhaps for reasons which may be obvious to the reader, none of the questions put were dealt with. The reply contained simply a series of counter questions.

## Chapter 32 Endnote

1. Letter written by Dr. Russell Standish and Dr. John Clifford to Division spokesman dated July 1, 1976
2. Pastor George Burnside
3. Letter written by Dr. R. Standish and Dr. A. J. Clifford, dated July 29, 1976

# 33 Curious Questions

IN order to present a fully-documented account of the type of correspondence which took place while error continued to be preached and little was done to cause its abeyance, the ten questions which were put to Dr. Clifford and Russell will be set forth. To the recipients of these questions, they were an obvious effort to avoid the provision of necessary answers to difficult questions. Nevertheless each question was answered and the answer given is provided.

**Question 1:** "Am I right in concluding that the 'eleven copies of the manuscript' to which you refer on page 2 denotes what I understand was the first edition of *Conflicting Concepts*—the 'edition' (or duplication or however else one may appropriately denominate it) which has been described to me as spiral-bound, of which copies were sent to Elder Pierson and one other General Conference and/or Review and Herald personnel?"
**Answer:** "No."

**Question 2:** "Did the copy which you presented to Elder Pierson contain the section, *Part Seven, SUMMARY*, in which you set what 'Ford-Brinsmead Say' over against what 'God Says'—the section which constitutes pages 142–154 of the centrally stapled 'edition' of which mine is a copy? (By the way, for your information: I understand that in Victoria copies of *Conflicting Concepts* are available gratis. My informant thus secured one. Here in New South Wales they appear to be retailing for one dollar—the price I actually paid.")
**Answer:** "No."

**Question 3:** "If the answer to Question (2) is No, have you informed Elder Pierson that the later edition (which in this case it would be) had had such a section added? In fact, have you sent him a copy of the added material (i.e. if material had been added in the centrally stapled edition to that which appeared in the spiral-bound edition)?"
**Answer:** "Yes."

**Question 4:** "Reverting to your letter: On page 3, paragraph 1, are you referring to the letter which Dr. Ford wrote to you on June 7, 1976?"
**Answer:** "No."

**Question 5:** "In the same paragraph you refer to a letter written to you by a certain correspondent. You mention his 'honest assessment' of *Conflicting Concepts*. Would you care to share this assessment with me? For the way I read the paragraph, it could be construed that the correspondent approves of *Conflicting Concepts*, which, of course, he would be perfectly entitled to do if it represented his conviction. (Incidentally, I have not overlooked your statement that this correspondent wrote you principally concerning 'the issue of motive.' However, you do indicate that he gave you his 'honest assessment' as well.)"
**Answer:** "We would be most happy to do this."

**Question 6:** "Would you care to indicate who are the 'at least three members of the Australasian Division Biblical Research Institute [who] have publicly expressed substantial support for the manuscript, *Conflicting Concepts*, as well as the 'a number of General Conference men' who you claim have given some form of approval? Furthermore, have the General Conference men indicated whether they had read your manuscript through at the time of their writing to you? (I'm sure you will recognize that I am entitled to ask these questions, seeing you mention these matters in evidence against the decision taken by our Biblical Research Institute.)"
**Answer:** "We understand that the time is near when these men will express this matter to you."

**Question 7:** "Would you also please indicate the names of 'the Committee, consisting of highly respected pastors and church elders, which copied our document'? (I am sure that again you will recognize the appropriateness of my asking this question, as neither I, nor our brethren, here propose to deal with any self-appointed committee of 'faceless men.')"
**Answer:** "We have passed on your request to the Chairman of the Committee for its consideration."

**Question 8:** "You write as though you possess 'inside' information concerning a meeting which we held at the Division office on Tuesday, July 6, 1976. May I ask: Did you receive this information directly from a member of the Biblical Research Institute or did you come by it indirectly?"
**Answer:** "Could you please advise as to the specific information you refer to?"

**Question 9:** "Am I justified in concluding from the last paragraph that anyone who does not acknowledge your particular theological perspective on righteousness by faith is to be considered as not strongly supporting 'the Bible-based doctrines of our Church'?"

**Answer:** "We are disappointed that such a question should emanate from one in such high office. We are sure you have read page 157 of our manuscript: 'Neither view is correct because it is held by good men. . . . A doctrine is true by one criterion alone—the law and the testimony.' We feel it is dangerous for anyone to fix his gaze upon one man's view. I am sure that you will agree that only God's perspective carries validity."

**Question 10:** "In this final paragraph you write *concerning me*:—'the knowledge that we still have men in leadership positions who strongly support the Bible-based doctrines of our Church will no doubt warm your heart. We say this since you yourself have on many occasions in the past—both privately and in print—supported the doctrines upheld in our manuscript. Indeed, on many occasions in private you have, like us, condemned as being unscriptural the current Avondale College Theology Department doctrines under question.' Will you please *itemize* and *identify*:—

"A. The current Avondale College Theology Department doctrines you claim as 'unscriptural' which you affirm I have 'on many occasions in *private* condemned? I want you to be entirely specific. State the *persons*, the *occasions*, and the *statements* I allegedly made. (In view of the fact that you used the phrase, 'on many occasions,' I shall expect that there will be a considerable list.)

"B. The articles I have written in which I support the doctrines you uphold in *Conflicting Concepts*? You might also wish to add to this any sermons or addresses you have heard me give, in which such support has been given."

**Answer:** A one and a half page answer was provided which set forth four specific instances with dates where the writer had stated the matters which had been mentioned in the letter. It is interesting that although this letter was sent to a number of influential people the writer did not subsequently persist with this matter, for clearly he recognized that he had no grounds on which to complain that he was misrepresented.[1]

These letters have been quoted rather fully to demonstrate that, sadly, the discussion on both sides degenerated to points of technicalities, and the one purpose of *Conflicting Concepts*, to express the old Adventist faith on the topic of righteousness by faith, once more was overlooked. Had the writers of these various letters settled down to examine God's Word much would have been achieved. In the light of this long correspondence it is very obvious that the whole strategy seemed to be point-scoring rather than a true determination of where truth lay. If the matter had been a football match the considerable effort involved would have lead to a 0–0 result. The tragedy was that the terrible problem in Australia was allowed to progress virtually unchallenged while these letters passed back and forth achieving absolutely nothing in defense of the great truths of God.

Chapter 33 Endnote

1. See Appendix D for full reply.

# 34 A Secret Letter

THAT the publication of the manuscript, *Conflicting Concepts*, caused so much concern within the Australasian Division may seem to be little short of amazing. However, in the situation which existed in Australia at the time, it appeared to many absolutely essential that Dr. Ford's doctrinal position be supported irrespective of what he was teaching, and every effort no matter how bizarre, had to be taken in order to ensure that his doctrinal stance was not questioned by God's people in Australia. Unbeknown to Dr. Clifford and Russell, an eleven-page letter was sent to the leaders of the Church in Australia. It was addressed to the following:

The Australasian Division officers
The presidents of both homeland unions
The presidents of all local conferences
The directors of all departments of the Australasian Division
The managers and directors of all division and union institutions
Dr. Ford

No copy of this letter was sent to either Dr. Clifford or Russell. Indeed, each would have remained totally ignorant of the secret communication if it had not been that some of the recipients felt it proper to supply them with a photostat copy in the interests of fairness. Later when Dr. Ford's own answer to *Conflicting Concepts* was produced, it seems that virtually every point raised in this letter was the result of research by Dr. Ford and probably did not reflect the writer's own insights.

The letter made every effort to portray *Conflicting Concepts* as a subtle effort to deceive. One quotation in *Conflicting Concepts* was emphasized in every attack upon it. This quotation was from Manuscript 43, 197. The authors were totally unaware that the same quotation occurs in the *SDA Bible Commentary,* Vol. 1, p. 1118. In the *SDA Bible Commentary* the quotation is prefaced by a heading which is not part of the quotation. This heading is as follows: "Obedience by Faith is Righteousness by Faith." (*1BC* 1118) In citing this reference, the authors had included this particular statement as part of the quotation which followed from the Spirit of Prophecy. This error was seized upon as an example of the "sinister" endeavors of the authors to deceive those who read the book. Perhaps one of the lighthearted aspects of this matter was the number of people who suddenly had such a wide knowledge of the *Bible Commentary* that they detected this "mistake." In no

*141*

time the authors received four written appraisals, each of which gave the impression that the writer had independently detected the error. None thought to check with the authors before levelling their accusations of deceit. It was also significant that none of these writers cared to mention the fact that the Preamble "Obedience by Faith is Righteousness by Faith" had been inserted by one of the many church leaders who contributed to that volume, and therefore indicated that this statement was their interpretation of the words which followed in Sister White's quotation.

In reality, however, there was no sinister plot. Truth would only be hurt by such a tactical approach. Truth can stand on its own two feet. It requires no assistance. Had the authors been questioned concerning this matter they would have been able to explain how the heading came to be included in the quotation. As mentioned earlier, the authors were totally unaware that the statement was repeated in the first volume of the *Bible Commentary*. They had found it in Pastor Collier's book, *The Early and Latter Rain of the Holy Spirit*. This book was recommended reading by *The Ministry* magazine. The statement in question was quoted on page 149 of Collier's book. There were four other minor errors in the statement, and these had also been pointed out. Most were just punctuation errors and three of these were also in Collier's quotation. Only one, the substitution of the preposition *into* in place of *to* was not taken from Collier and was simply a trivial typographical error. How different the many harsh insinuations which were made would have been had the source of the quotation been ascertained from the authors! Had the authors had the time to properly edit the manuscript, it is likely that Collier's book would have been listed as the source of the quotation. As it was, simply the manuscript number was published. Those reading the material must have been aware that it was not obtained from the *Bible Commentary*, for the authors gave no *Bible Commentary* reference.

As has become the custom, virtually no effort was made to examine the doctrinal position. The letter consisted of insignificant and, in many cases unfounded accusations against the authors. It was never considered that the authors may have been sincere in their desire to stand by that which had become precious in their lives.

The secret letter just briefly looked at the matter of doctrine. "Incidentally they [Drs. Clifford and Standish] rightly state that Dr. Ford believes that justification is not contingent upon regeneration."[1] It was strange that the writer of this letter should criticize the authors of *Conflicting Concepts* for objecting to this theology since eighteen months earlier he had stated, "Righteousness by faith is a possession of a Person. It is the glorious reality, the thrilling wonder, the ecstatic experience of what takes place when Jesus Christ apprehends me for Himself, and when He *regenerates* my heart through the life-changing power of the transforming spirit, when He cleanses my soul with His precious blood, and covers me with the garments of grace wrought in the loom of Heaven." (*Review and Herald*, Jan. 23, 1975) Since Dr. Ford equated righteousness by faith with justification by faith, and clearly the writer's term "the garments of grace" refers to justification, it can be seen that eighteen months earlier he had shared the same convictions as the authors of *Conflicting Concepts* in suggesting that justification necessitates a transformation.

The letter also accused Dr. Clifford and Russell of conducting a personal attack upon Dr. Ford. The book *Conflicting Concepts* is now a matter of public record for all who wish to read.[2] Upon doing so, they will find absolutely no personal attack on Dr. Ford. Indeed, Dr. Ford himself recognized this in his communication with Russell. "I assure you, Russell, if the time ever comes when you ever hit me over the head with a crowbar, I will still be prepared to believe it dropped from your hand, rather than it was willingly inflicted. Both you and Colin have the amiable ability to disagree without being disagreeable."[3]

That some of the leaders in the Australasian Division were having difficulty with the *Review and Herald Special* on righteousness by faith can be gauged by one paragraph in the secret letter. Referring to the special issue of the *Review and Herald* the letter stated, "The authors are certainly misinformed if they imagine that this issue of the *Review* was prepared at the instance of, or voted by, the Executive Committee of the General Conference and may thus be cited as 'the true Seventh-day Adventist position on Righteousness by Faith, *as presented by the General Conference leadership*."[4]

Toward the end of the letter the true concern of the writer came to the fore. "Now the point I want to make is that, putting all theological consideration to one side, not only is this document an affront to the leadership of this Division; it is potentially divisive." (*Ibid.*) It seemed that any effort to uphold the proven Adventist position was, at that stage, regarded as an affront to the leadership of the Australasian Division. This conclusion was very sad indeed. It was felt that those who attempted to support traditional beliefs were disloyal to the Division leadership. However, the most loyal members of the Australasian Division were those who were upholding the standard of truth. Those who were supporting the Church most diligently with their means, with their prayers, and with their talents were not those who were accepting the *new theology*. Time has shown that many of the latter have long since left the Church, and have ceased to support it with either their means or their talents.

It is true that the group of Concerned Brethren were disappointed on a number of occasions with some of the actions of the Division leadership, but to continue loyalty in the face of such disappointments surely is more difficult than when this emotion is absent. It is in time of disappointment that the believer's true loyalty is tested. The senior pastors and lay people who constituted the bulk of Concerned Brethren never paused to spare themselves in doing all that the Church had asked them to do. In some cases, particularly with physicians, those demands had been great, for they had been asked to assist in many of the health education programs of the Church and had given unstintingly and tirelessly of their knowledge in these areas.

The accusation of divisiveness was of course only to be expected. But God's people have to ask themselves the question, Who is causing the division? Is it those who wish to remain steadfast to the pillars of their faith, or is the division the result of the actions of those who would destroy those pillars? How different the situation could have been if the manuscript had been read as it was written! Quite interestingly, the vast majority of God's believers in the field did just that. The letters objecting to the manuscript were surprisingly few; indeed the authors received only thirteen letters of complaint. Seven of these were from pastors and two from theology students at Avondale College; thus only four lay people wrote expressing their complaints.

This situation has been a feature of the doctrinal controversy in Australia. By and large the lay people have remained true to the Advent message. Although we published only a thousand copies, letters of support poured in at an astounding rate. Naturally the majority were from believers in Australia, but others wrote from every continent other than South America. We were amazed to find that one copy had somehow gotten beyond the Arctic Circle to Finland. Others reached to various areas of Africa and Asia, and many different countries in Europe. Naturally there were many letters from the United States, even though at that time Dr. Ford was barely known. What was clear was that by 1976 and 1977 many persons were starting to see the spread of the *new theology* in their areas. [5]

Chapter 34 Endnotes

1. Letter from Division spokesmen to the leaders of the Church in the Australasian Division dated July 19, 1976
2. Copies are being held in the General Conference archives and in the E. G. White Research Center of Andrews University, among other libraries.
3. Letter written by Dr. Ford to Russell Standish, dated June 22, 1976
4. Letter from the Division spokesman to the leaders of the Australasian Division, dated July 19, 1976
5. See Appendix A and Appendix B.

# 35    A Four-Pronged Attack

IN a short time four documents were produced specifically for the purpose of refuting *Conflicting Concepts*. The first of these was the circular letter written by an Australasian Division spokesman and sent secretly to leaders throughout Australia and New Zealand. This letter was a rather limited analysis, but its circulation was somewhat increased beyond that which was intended, for one of the departmental leaders in the Trans-Australian Union Conference passed a copy on to one of Robert Brinsmead's supporters.

The second document was written by a third-year theology student attending Avondale College[1] and was entitled *The Biblical Concept of Righteousness by Faith*. It also contained a sub-title, *A Critical Analysis of the Recent Publication Conflicting Concepts of Righteous by Faith in the Seventh-day Adventist Church—Australasian Division* (Drs. A. J. Clifford and R. R. Standish), along with a presentation of various basic Christian beliefs. The theology student was merely the mouthpiece for his mentor. For some time Dr. Ford, who was anxious to reply to *Conflicting Concepts*, was prevented from doing so by the Australasian Division. Ford even prepared an article for publication in the *Australasian Record* as a refutation. This article was even typeset ready for printing, later put on standby and finally abandoned at the Division's insistence. Thus at this stage Ford's views could only be made known by the use of a mouthpiece. This need the third-year theology student supplied.

Ford's subsequently published arguments were naturally very similar in numerous places. It is truthful to say that this booklet made very little impact on the doctrinal situation. Later Dr. Ford's forty-nine page reply, *Observations on Conflicting Concepts of Righteousness by Faith* appeared with a preface written by the chairman of the Australasian Division Biblical Research Institute. The first eleven pages consisted of an evaluation of the attitudes of the writers. It surprised many readers that over twenty-two percent of the space should be devoted to factors which in all charity could not be described as anything but the surmisings of one man. Absolutely false statements were made, such as, "the attitude of the authors to the General Conference is best revealed by their rejection of the Palmdale Statement."[2]

The second section of the book, consisting of well over twenty percent of its content, dealt with research and literary procedures. This section also examined heavily the subject of attitudes and motives, thus indicating that almost fifty percent (23 of 49 pages) of Dr. Ford's book was confined to discrediting the integrity of the authors of *Conflicting Concepts*. This section of the book commenced with a rather harsh personal judgment: "That which is most serious in *C.C.* to any investigating scholar is its devastating lack of either care or honesty in dealing with original sources." (*Ibid.*, 12) The great emphasis on scholarship continued in Dr. Ford's manuscript. This same argument, of course, was to surface years later when Attorney Lewis Walton published his book *Omega*. There seemed to be certain theologians who believe that people trained in medicine, law and other disciplines are somewhat inferior to theologians in their use of scholastic methods. Indeed, sometimes one could wonder if scholarship isn't advanced as a basic guide to truth rather than the infilling of the Holy Spirit.

On one such occasion Dr. Ford wrote: "I plead that heaven may cause medical men such as yourself to refrain from rushing into the theological arena till all necessary training has been fulfilled. These topics under discussion require up to thousands of hours of study in some cases, study of every nuance in Scripture and the Spirit of Prophecy."[3] In the same letter Dr. Ford suggested it was also necessary to have the additional gleanings from Greek and Hebrew. If by thousands of hours Dr. Ford meant even two thousand hours, this amount of time would total eight months of full-time study of eight hours per day, seven days per week. If such lengthy periods of study are required for even a small number of doctrines in order to perceive truth, then understandably truth is not the province of the lay person. Such would be left in a situation comparable to that of the Middle Ages where men were required to look to their theologians for an understanding of Scripture, and the priesthood of all believers so dear to Protestants was thought to be an unattainable and undesirable concept.

Some of the letters received by the authors of *Conflicting Concepts* led them to wonder whether others felt that it would be desirable to return to this situation of the Middle Ages, where the theologians had free rein in interpreting and presenting Scripture, and lay people were expected to have no personal understanding whatsoever. It should not be forgotten that God had promised that—

> the wayfaring men, though fools shall not err therein. (Isaiah 35:8)

The servant of the Lord has told us,

> As the time comes for it [the third angel's message] to be given with greatest power, the Lord will work through humble instruments, leading the minds of those who consecrate themselves to His service. The laborers will be qualified rather by the unction of His Spirit than by the training of literary institutions. Men of faith and prayer will be constrained to go forth with holy zeal, declaring the words which God gives them. (*GC* 606)
>
> The Bible with its precious gems of truth was not written for the scholar alone. On the contrary, it was designed for the common people; and the interpretation

given by the common people, when aided by the Holy Spirit, accords best with the truth as it is in Jesus. (*5T* 331)

This latter statement has been verified over and over again in the present doctrinal crisis.

One has to set a high level of personal scholarly standard indeed in order to use this criterion as a major attack on another's work. The authors themselves could have spent endless hours searching for imperfections of scholarship in the works which were written in opposition to the truths of *Conflicting Concepts*. But such would have been a wasteful, though perhaps revealing search. Just to give the reader a single example of this type of foolishness, the authors could not miss the footnote on page 13 of *Observations on Conflicting Concepts of Righteousness by Faith*, where a 1900 article from the *Review and Herald* is stated to have been one which was classified as 'our official church paper.' In point of fact this term was used for only six years in relationship to the *Review and Herald*, from 1961 to 1967. Thus it was "poor scholarship" to state that a 1900 article came from our official church paper. But of course the authors did not make a point of this, for they recognized it was an unintentional error of scholarship, and of no consequence to the point Dr. Ford was making.

Of the four systematic analyses of *Conflicting Concepts*, only one, An *Answer to Conflicting Concepts of Righteousness by Faith in the Seventh-day Adventist Church*, by Robert Brinsmead made a plausible effort to examine the doctrines presented. This book was an edited transcript of Brinsmead's Melbourne talk of the same title. Yet this book too spent twenty percent of its effort on examining so-called scholarship, although at least this author had the insight to acknowledge that poor scholarship (as he saw it) did not necessarily invalidate the truth of the position. Brinsmead set forth the ideal that in order to evaluate another man's theology, his theology should be placed in its best rather than its worst light. This most certainly is a fine ideal, seldom if ever achieved. The fault is probably twofold. It is most difficult for someone opposing another's views, particularly in such an emotive area as doctrine, to do total justice to the other's concept. Second, it seems very difficult for the one whose views are under the microscope to concede that justice has been done.

One matter seemed blatantly clear so far as *Conflicting Concepts* was concerned: that virtually without exception every point of the *new theology* which was challenged was stoutly defended by Ford and Brinsmead. Men surely do not defend a position which is not dear to them, simply because someone else asserts it to be their belief.

Brinsmead himself, however, could be found at times placing Adventism in its worst light. He appeared incensed when a paper written by Brother

Roy Davies was assessed by Pastor Willis Hackett, then vice-president of the General Conference, as balanced. Using heavy sarcasm Brinsmead stated, "All sensible people are balanced—like the Laodiceans, neither cold nor hot—50/50. Our works are balanced with fear, and inward righteousness is made to have as much saving merit as His, and the moon and its brightness is balanced with the sun and its brightness. This is tradition, typical Adventism, and it is a revolting, Christ-denying insult to the grace of God in Jesus Christ—it is a doctrine that is wretched, miserable, poor, blind, and naked, and we who have been enlightened by the gospel will declare war on it and shall overcome it by the blood of the Lamb and our testimony thereto. This old Adventism is dead, and those who are trying to get a revival going with their Laodicean balance might just as well try to resuscitate a corpse. It's bad religion because experience cannot rise higher than this miserable doctrine of Laodicean righteousness by faith. For us the darkness is past and the true light now shineth . . . half law and half gospel is neither law nor gospel."[4] It seems that it is easy to uphold an ideal of putting another's views in their best light, but very difficult to practice it consistently. Few informed readers would regard the above assessment as a really fair evaluation of "old Adventism" and its position on righteousness by faith, even if one used only minimal criteria of fairness.

The strange matter was that while in his unguarded moments Robert Brinsmead, like Desmond Ford, was declaring his rejection of the old Adventist stand, there were thousands of their followers who in 1976 firmly believed that they were upholding the old pillars of the Church. No evidence seemed sufficient to dissuade these people from this erroneous view. That Brinsmead, even in 1976, detested the Adventist faith was clearly to be seen in this same letter. "Wake up, my brother! There is no future in trying to warm over that old Laodicean religion. We've heard it for 100 years and it's running out of our ears and it stinks." (*Ibid.*)

Brinsmead was not here speaking of some recent phenomenon. He was speaking of the faith held by Seventh-day Adventists for the previous century. It is little wonder that he now makes no pretense of having any relationship with the Seventh-day Adventist Church. So despising of the truth was Brinsmead that he swore an oath against it. "I swear on the altar of God, eternal hostility to it [the old Adventist beliefs], so help me God."[5] (*Ibid.*) Such statements have a persecuting ring to them. Are we reaching the stage where the holders of the *new theology* would be prepared to persecute those who remain true? Sister White has told us that those without our Church who prove false will indeed become our most intense persecutors.

Thus it was of little importance that Brinsmead took great exception to *Conflicting Concepts*. In the major section of his book he demonstrated very ably that many theologians disagree with the proven Adventist stand. This Dr. Clifford and Russell freely acknowledged. No fewer than forty-five theologians and writers on biblical topics were quoted by Brinsmead and many pages were given over to verbatim statements from these theologians. If these sections, based upon sources which were in no way inspired, were removed from Brinsmead's book, it would be very short indeed.

Surely there needed to be a proper balance between the use of Scripture and the Spirit of Prophecy and the works of even good but fallible men. Brinsmead's heavy emphasis upon theologians did indicate a dangerous trend among a number of those espousing the *new theology*. Early in his book Brinsmead had demonstrated poor taste in attacking what he termed "mother's knee theology," but perhaps we would all do well to heed a little of our mother's knee theology. After all, was it not Jesus who said,

> Except ye . . . become as little children, ye shall not enter into the kingdom of heaven. (Matthew 18:3)

### Chapter 35 Endnotes

1. Sadly this young man did not complete his course.
2. (D. Ford, *Observations on Conflicting Concepts of Righteousness by Faith*, 2) The sincerity of this unfortunate barb may be judged by Des' attitude to the counsel of the General Conference brethren at Glacier View.
3. Letter from Dr. Ford to Dr. R. Standish, Feb. 17, 1976
4. Brinsmead letter to Roy Davies dated December 18, 1976
5. It is interesting to note the proclivity of believers in the *new theology* to desecrate the third commandment. It will be recalled that Barnhouse in 1959 had stated, "In the name of Jesus Christ, I curse the seventh-day Sabbath."

# 36    The Victorian Conference Targeted

IN 1976 it seemed as if the Victorian Conference became the battleground for the doctrinal controversy. From every conceivable angle the *new theology* was promoted. Dr. Ford was invited to Melbourne and spoke in three churches—Glenhuntly, Hughesdale, and Oakleigh—promoting the *new theology*. Leaflets were distributed throughout the other churches in the metropolitan area urging members to attend these meetings. The youth leader of the Conference, Pastor Allen, was invited to sponsor these meetings. To his credit he displayed sufficient courage in the prevailing doctrinal climate resolutely to refuse. Later Dr. Ford was sent to the rural area of Gippsland, in the east of the state of Victoria, where he again presented his concept of righteousness to a combined meeting of the Seventh-day Adventist Churches in that area.

At successive Victorian camp meetings the evening services were dominated by speakers from the younger group of the ministry. Two of these were given opportunity to speak at prime times at consecutive camp meetings (1976 and 1977) despite the fact that some of the senior ministers had not been invited to speak at such meetings for a number of years.

Robert Brinsmead traveled down to Victoria and spoke on two occasions in the Croydon Church of Christ. Many Adventist ministers attended these meetings, the majority expressing their support for that which was spoken. Brinsmead was followed a few months later by Geoffrey Paxton, who presented his view of the Seventh-day Adventist Church at the same venue. Between 150 and 200 Seventh-day Adventists attended that meeting. Paxton took this opportunity to attack the *Sabbath School Quarterly* prepared for the second quarter of 1977.

Throughout the conference it seemed that Sabbath after Sabbath the only topic which was preached was that of righteousness by faith, and in most cases the *new theology* was that which was proclaimed. The Nunawading Church, during one month of five Sabbaths, (April, 1977) was listed to have divine service speakers on each occasion from those who had attended and supported the Paxton meetings. That arrangement seemed to be less than coincidental since four separate speakers were involved.

In the church schools the children were pressed to believe the *new theology* from the lips of teachers who were largely recent Avondale graduates. The book *The*

*Soteriological Implications of the Human Nature of Christ* was freely loaned to senior pupils. Even some student teachers from Avondale saw it as their beholden duty to evangelize these pupils in the Melbourne schools with the *new theology*. In at least one of these Melbourne Adventist high schools, the Lilydale Academy, a short summary of Dr. Ford's concept of the gospel was distributed to the fifth-form (eleventh grade) pupils by their Bible teacher. However, in the three high schools the Lord did have His restraining influences. At the Lilydale Academy Pastor Horace Watts, the school's resident chaplain until December 1976, quietly guided the bewildered pupils toward the truth. He was a real bulwark. At the Hawthorn Adventist High School Pastor Malcolm Allen, the conference youth secretary, was part-time chaplain and he, too exerted a modifying influence in the dispersion of false theology. At the third Adventist high school, Nunawading, the headmaster, Mr. David Chesney, steered a level doctrinal course.

There was little help from the denominational publications. The *new theology* was expressed indeed with ever increasing volume. *The Australasian Record* championed its cause to the exclusion of the Adventist position on righteousness by faith. A series of five articles by the chaplain of the Aukland Adventist Hospital made no secret of the proclamation of this new view. These articles were published in March and April, 1976. Attacking those who believed the truth of God and presenting their beliefs in a most unflattering manner, the author of this article stated:

> And so this striving after ethical betterment in itself is the evidence of trying to achieve righteousness not so much by works alone, but by a strange, almost unconscious admixture of faith plus works. This is the undergirding characteristic of Babylon in the Revelation. While I am not saying that many Adventists can be just as much in Babylon sitting in church every Sabbath as those actually in Babylon openly. (*Australasian Record*, April 12, 1976)

Such statements were in line with the flood of uncomplimentary descriptions heaped upon the established Adventist faith by followers of the *new theology*. Thus it was described at that time by various derogatory titles such as Contrary to the New Testament, A False Gospel, Another Gospel, the Spirit of Anti-Christ, Legalistic, Babylonish, together with many other tragic assessments. Dr. Ford's articles found frequent outlet in the *Australasian Record* and almost without exception these articles dealt with sensitive doctrinal issues. The old position of the Church speedily faded from the pages of this publication until one could hardly believe the *Review and Herald* and the *Australasian Record* were sponsored by the same Christian body. Other series dealing with the controverted topics included one by a Victorian layman who was an engineer.

The Australasian *Signs of the Times* also became a forum for the *new theology*. In Dr. Ford's two-page question and answer spread there developed a most surprising number of questions dealing with the very points under dispute. Quite expectedly, these were all answered from the viewpoint of the *new theology* and did not reflect faithfully the Adventist message. When believers, concerned at the proclamation of error in our magazines, wrote gentle protests to the editor, they were often rewarded with particularly rude replies. Thus protests were found not only to be of little avail but also to be most unwelcome.[1]

Meanwhile the issues were spread far and wide. In quick succession Dr. Ford was presented as the chief guest speaker at the South Queensland Conference camp meeting, the Trans-Australian Union Youth Congress, the South New Zealand Conference camp meeting and the Tasmanian Conference camp meeting. This series of appearances was most decidedly a case of overexposure. In the South Queensland camp meeting alone Dr. Ford presented fifteen services. This series was supplemented by a talk by a Division officer to the conference workers condemning *Conflicting Concepts*. The president of the North New South Wales Conference also called his workers together for a similar condemnation. Both of these talks simply accepted Dr. Ford's assessment of the book and presented his views to the assembled workers. Neither speaker made the least attempt to verify Dr. Ford's contentions.

Despite the evangelical fervor accompanying the spread of the *new theology* throughout Australia and New Zealand, those maintaining the accepted Seventh-day Adventist position in seeking to maintain church harmony as far as was feasible, deliberately chose to follow a course of least confrontation. The wise counsel of such pastors as J. W. Kent, George Burnside, John Keith, Frank Breaden, Austin Cooke, Llewellyn Jones, Arthur Knight, and Ronald Heggie was to this effect, and their views prevailed.

Thus in Victoria, despite the repeated open proclamations of error, not a single meeting was called to present the historic view of the Seventh-day Adventist Church despite the great provocation. It was well known that had such a meeting been called it would have attracted a large audience consisting of those believing a wide spectrum of doctrinal belief. Some strongly urged such a course, but the majority of those standing for the historic Adventist truths recognized that the battle was the Lord's and had absolute faith in the final triumph of His truth. It will be seen from these simple facts that those provoking the controversy were not God's people. Rather it was provoked by leaders, false to the faith, who sought to promote that which they full well knew was in direct opposition to Adventist truths proclaimed for a century or more. The leading of the General Conference was a great comfort to those true to the fundamentals of the faith.

It is possible that a charge could be leveled against those believing the truth, claiming that they were guilty of fulfilling the prediction that error prevails when true men keep silence. Such a charge should, however, be modified to some extent by the knowledge that there was no silencing of the expression of concern to those in leadership, for it was felt proper that the approved channels should be used in preference to stirring up God's people. Nevertheless, the continual presentations of the *new theology* itself stirred many members to commence their own inquiries.

None who asked was refused a frank statement of truth. Thus many sincere pastors and lay people grew in strength and knowledge of the truth of the Adventist faith.

Eventually, worn out by the persistent refusal of many church administrators to promote speakers who would present historic Adventism, sincere Adventist laymen responded by introducing weekend seminars at which these precious truths were presented. (See chapters entitled "Australian Laymen's Fellowship" and "American Leader in Australia.")

Chapter 36 Endnote

1. See Appendix C for one example of this type of correspondence.

# 37 Victorian Pastors Disunited

THE printing of *Conflicting Concepts* seemed to cause a totally unnecessary panic in the Australasian Church. Apparently a raw nerve had been touched. No incident better illustrated this fact than a Victorian Conference workers' meeting at which the matter was the sole topic of discussion. A representative of the Australasian Division was present and it was stated that there was a need to demonstrate unity among the ministry. This unity was to be based upon the curious proposition that the ministers unitedly accepted the doctrine as outlined in Dr. Ford's Avondale College lecture entitled "Sanctification," together with the united rejection of the doctrines contained in *Conflicting Concepts*. The incredible fact was that a number of pastors spoke favorably to this motion which blatantly looked to men's words rather than to God's.

It was not until Pastor Wallace Hammond, who had recently been transferred from his post as pastor to the Nunawading Church where Russell was an elder, called the first halt to this absurd situation and spoke in kindly terms of his association with Russell, that the one-sided comments began to change. Pastor Malcolm Allen, who had seen the appalling effects of the *new theology* on the lives of the conference young people, spoke strongly against the motion. Others to do so were the conference Sabbath School and Temperance Director, Pastor George Drinkall, Pastor Charles Lowe, conference evangelist Pastor Needham, Pastor Lyn Burns and Colac Church pastor, Maurice Peterson. These pastors showed they were quite unprepared to stand by the errors of the *new theology*.

Yet it would give an unfair picture of the meeting to suggest that the majority of the pastors present opposed the *new theology*. The Victorian Conference contained a large number of recent graduates from Avondale, and of these Pastor Peterson alone indicated his acceptance of the old Adventist faith. Perhaps the fact that he was mature when he studied for the ministry was a vital reason why he was not influenced by the errors of his mentor.[1] Had a vote been taken on the motion, there is little doubt that the proposed motion would have received a majority. A majority vote, however, would hardly have achieved the aim of the motion—an expression of unity among the ministry in Victoria. Undoubtedly the Lord's hand was present to prevent such a tragedy.

Pastor Raymond Stanley, Division ministerial secretary—a man full of zeal for the old Adventist faith—was providentially present. His calm direction and counsel did much to lead away from the path which surely could not have brought God's blessing. Eventually the meeting achieved nothing other than to show that there was complete disunity among the ministry of Victoria Conference, and the motion was quietly withdrawn.

Despite the enormous interest and controversy which *Conflicting Concepts* had caused, only two meetings were held in relation to its publication. In July 1976 Russell was invited by the Greater Sydney Conference youth department to speak at a conference-wide meeting on drugs. While he was in Sydney for this meeting, Dr. Peter Martin, a Sydney psychiatrist, stated that quite a number of members of the Dundas Church were vitally interested in the current theological discussion. He requested that Russell speak to a group of these people at the home of Brother Wesley Searle, one of the elders of the church. Since Russell's family was planning a vacation with relatives in Sydney, this request was agreed to and the meeting was convened on August 28, 1976.

In the meeting members from the Dundas Church were in the minority. About sixty or seventy people attended, many being Avondale college theology students who had somehow learned of the meeting, while other supporters of the *new theology* attended in full. In the sixty-minute address Russell confined himself to the central issue of the controversy—Can man, when filled with the power of the Holy Spirit, keep God's holy law? Emphasis was laid upon the innumerable times that God demands obedience, and those listening were asked to decide whether God is mocking us when He makes this request. Is God commanding the impossible? Is it possible to be a saint since the three angels' messages define a saint as one who keeps the commandments of God? A few quotations from the Spirit of Prophecy are included to illustrate the type of quotation used from that source:

> The holy life of Abel testified against Satan's claim that it is impossible for man to keep God's law. (*PP* 77)

> Entire conformity to the will of our Father which is in heaven is alone sanctification.... The keeping of all the commandments of God is sanctification. Proving yourselves obedient servants to God's Word, is sanctification. (*Review and Herald*, March 25, 1902)

The first epistle of John was used freely.[2] At the conclusion of the talk, pastor J. W. Kent, who was present stated, "I need not say just where I am, for what Russell said today I have preached for sixty-five years. And I believe it just as he believes it today." Pastor Frank Basham stated, "I believe this cannot be refuted, that the traditional view of righteousness by faith has ever been, until 1976 and including 1976, that righteousness by faith includes together justification and sanctification."

Much discussion time was spent on a question from the deputy headmaster of the Sydney Adventist High School who asked among other things whether or not we should be searching for new light. His question, in support of Dr. Ford's position, was based on the oft-expressed view that Dr. Ford had brought new light to the Seventh-day Adventist Church. Those supporting the *new theology* were anxious to see their doctrine in this light. However, Brother Reglan Marks of Cooranbong presented the alternative view when he stated with force,

> And when men arise bringing in false doctrines that attack the foundations of this church and attack the truths that were proclaimed by Sister White and Daniells and Jones and those which were recognized as the light from God, then they are doing the work of the devil.

As usual, the meeting had its lighter moments. It seemed that every one of the numerous attempts to answer the questions posed by the deputy headmaster of the Sydney Adventist High School failed because he repeatedly claimed that not a single person understood his question. In exasperation he eventually stated, "The point that I have asked has been completely lost, and lost again." Pastor O. K. Anderson, ever a quick wit, interjected, "He lost it before he started."

One pastor present, supporting the *new theology*, stated that he was concerned because when he became a Seventh-day Adventist he read the book *Questions on Doctrine*, and also Walter Martin's *The Truth About Seventh-day Adventism*. He asserted that it was on the basis of these books which taught the unfallen nature of Christ that he became a Seventh-day Adventist. He further asserted that he had sat in a recent seminary extension school where the professor from Andrews University had taught that which was in accordance with Dr. Ford's teachings.

The second meeting was arranged at the same venue on October 2, 1976. The format of this meeting was slightly different. Brother Searle arranged that Dr. Ford should make a sixty-minute reply, after which Russell would be permitted to ask questions but not reply. Dr. Ford's talk commenced in ominous fashion. Quoting two texts of Scripture his tone left no one in doubt that he intended for those present to see his view as the true gospel and the view of those still persuaded by the historic Adventist position as that so roundly condemned in Scripture. First he quoted,

> ... but there be some that trouble you, and would pervert the gospel of Christ. But though we, or an angel from heaven, preach any other gospel unto you than that which we have preached unto you, let him be accursed. (Galatians 1:7,8)

Commenting upon this text, Dr. Ford stated, "In the same gospel he [Paul] says, 'I would they were . . . cut off. (Gal. 5:12) Who would wish the death of even his enemy? But Paul was so excited over the gospel of the grace of God, he could say, 'I wish they were dead.' No light issue, apparently."

Such an introduction set a vastly different tone for the October meeting from that which had been set in the previous meeting in August. Dr. Ford continued to assert that those opposed to his doctrine stated falsely that he did not believe in sanctification. Significantly he quoted no evidence for this allegation. It is always easier to bring up a red herring and to use this as evidence of false reporting. In fact, what was believed was not that Ford did not advocate sanctification but that he advocated a false sanctification, one which did not include full obedience to the law of God as set out in Inspiration.

Prior to this meeting it had been stated: "Of course the Ford-Brinsmead adherents claim that they have a definite place for sanctification in their view . . . basically sanctification is the result of Christ's justification and if you do not have sanctification, they say it indicates that you do not have justification." (*Conflicting Concepts*, 87) Doctor Ford completed his discourse with the catch-cry, "Brethren, the righteousness of justification is perfect, but not inherent. The righteousness of sanctification is inherent, but not perfect. The righteousness of glorification is both perfect and inherent."

In the time given to Russell to question Dr. Ford he felt that this opportunity could best be used by pointing out very clearly that Dr. Ford was in opposition to the Seventh-day Adventist beliefs. This approach was essential, for the vast majority of believers in Australia at that time had been led to believe the Dr. Ford was perfectly fundamental and that anyone opposing his view was opposing the truth as espoused by the Seventh-day Adventist Church.

Russell commenced by quoting from the *S.D.A. Bible Commentary* on Romans 12:1 which states, "Righteousness by faith means not only forgiveness of sin but also newness of life. It includes sanctification as well as justification, transformation as well as reconciliation." Dr. Ford skirted this quotation in his reply, "Yes, the brethren have said, it is not a technical exegesis of Paul to do so. That is quite incorrect as the professors of exegesis of Andrews University admitted at Palmdale. That is not correct. That is our official position, that to make that a technical exegesis is erroneous. But if we are only saying in the passage which is suggested here that the brethren have meant, OK. If they are saying, 'You cannot have righteousness by faith without holiness coming into it,' agreed. It is always there— as the fruits." (Dr. D. Ford, *An Answer to Dr. Russell Standish*, 17)

Dr. Ford did imply that he was taking a stance different from the past Adventist views when it was pointed out to him that Robert Brinsmead had stated in the meeting he held in Croydon that he full well knew that *Conflicting Concepts* represented the past Adventist view on righteousness by faith in essence. Replying to this statement Dr. Ford said, "I agree wholeheartedly to this. This is the way Adventists have viewed it. But so what?" (*Ibid.*) Russell then mentioned that he felt it was important to demonstrate that what Des was stating was basically new to Seventh-day Adventism. To this Dr. Ford replied, "What you are saying is true." (*Ibid.* 18)

Russell next turned to the definition of righteousness by faith found in the S.D.A. Encyclopedia, 1085. This volume states: "In S.D.A. terminology, the instantaneous experience of conversion through faith in Christ often spoken of as justification by faith and the lifelong experience of Christian living also is through faith in Christ." Dr. Ford replied, "Russell, you're entirely right in saying this is the way most Adventists regard it."

Since many of those who had accepted the *new theology* were asserting that Pastor Pierson had changed his views on the topic following the hearing of Dr. Ford's presentations at Palmdale, Russell read a letter written by Pastor Pierson several months after Palmdale. "My position on the subject [referring to righteousness by faith] has not changed. It is in harmony with the *S.D.A. Encyclopedia*, 1085." (Letter written by Pastor Robert Pierson to Brother Victor Christiansen, dated Sept. 7, 1976) This definition, of course, has been quoted above. That this statement was not an isolated comment by Pastor Pierson is demonstrated by the fact that later, in an article entitled, "What is Righteousness by Faith?" Pastor Pierson quoted this definition from the *S.D.A. Encyclopedia*, and then went on to comment, "From these words it is clear the Seventh-day Adventist Church accepts the two phases or steps in the experience of righteousness by faith. One is the 'instantaneous experience' known as justification . . . the second phase is a 'lifelong experience of Christian living' . . . we dare not minimize either justification or sanctification." (*Ministry*, Feb. 1977)

When Dr. Ford was confronted with Pastor Pierson's letter as quoted above, the following comments ensued. Dr. D. Ford: "So let me tell you a few more words from the writer of that letter as said to me. 'Des, I am not a theologian. I am a Sabbath School student.'" Dr. R. Standish: "I thank God for Sabbath School students." Dr. D. Ford: "Amen. [audience amusement] But I do not want them all writing pamphlets." [4] (*Ibid.*, 18, 19)

Still attempting to continue to have Dr. Ford demonstrate that he was far from the Seventh-day Adventist standpoint, Russell stated, "I want to say, I stand unashamedly by what is written in this document [indicating the 1974 *Review and Herald Special* on Righteousness by Faith]. And I wonder if you [referring to Dr. Ford] can stand by me and hold it up and say the same thing?" Dr. Ford's reply was unequivocal. "Not at all. Not at all. You ought to have shame if you knew the background of it."

Perhaps the only value which came out of these two meetings was the fact that publicly Dr. Ford had virtually for the first time acknowledged that he had departed from the old Adventist position. To those reading this book, it may not seem to have been any great admission, for this fact is now well known, but in 1976 it caused a wave of surprise to a number of godly people who had felt fully assured that Dr. Ford was simply echoing the past Adventist faith.

## Chapter 37 Endnotes

1. See Appendix E.
2. The type of materials used is illustrated in the book, *Adventism Vindicated*, which may be obtained from Historic Truth Publications, Inc., Box 1, Rapidan, Virginia 22733 USA or Adventist Laymen's Fellowship, P.O. Box 83, Windsor, NSW, 2756, Australia.
3. It is true, however, that Pastor Morris Venden, then pastor of the Pacific Union College Church, did state publicly at the 1976 Trans-Australian Union Youth Congress that after listening to Dr. Ford's talk it seemed to him that when Dr. Ford spoke about sanctification it was like giving birth to barbed wire.
4. The word "pamphlet" is used in Australia as a synonym for *Sabbath School Quarterly*.

# 38 The Clippard-Slandish Brochure

To illustrate how far the matter of *Conflicting Concepts* spurred persons in Australia, this ludicrous episode in the doctrinal issue is cited. It does at least add a little humor to the history. The Clippard-Slandish Brochure was designed to caricature Pastor George Burnside, Dr. John Clifford and Russell. While no one claimed responsibility for its publication, it was known to be printed in the United States, almost certainly by the *Present Truth* organization. It was printed in sepia on top-quality thick glossy paper. Whoever designed the set of cartoons had certainly been filled in on personal data.

The cartoon entitled "The Joust" showed the two physicians riding on a hobbyhorse, both decidedly rotund and carrying rough wooden swords. One had a box covering his head entitled "Ignorance," while the other was crowned by one which was entitled "Prejudice." The hobbyhorse was entitled "Conflicting Concepts," and was being pushed by Pastor Burnside who was labeled "The Burntside Finance Corporation, Limited." [1] A tattered flag held on a crude twig had the insignia, "Out of context, innuendo, insinuation, misquote, error, misrepresentation, confusion" upon it.

By contrast the trim figure of Dr. Ford was seen seated on a superb and speedy steed named "Justification Alone." The horse's feet were all off the ground, indicating great speed. Dr. Ford was attired in the traditional knight's armor: his cloak entitled "Sir Phorde, Knight of the Lord," was flying in the breeze from its attachment to his shoulders. In his right hand Phorde carried a steel sword and in his left a fearsome lance from which an elegant flag entitled "The Gospel" flowed. Undoubtedly the challenge was totally unequal.

A second cartoon depicted a chasm which the physicians and Dr. Ford were compelled to traverse in order to reach safety on the other side—Paradise. With great gymnastic skill Dr. Ford was seen swinging by a rope across the gulf. The rope was entitled "Justification by Faith Alone." Dr. Ford generously shouted back, "Grab a cord quickly, Doctahs, it is your only chance." The physicians, whose faces were now revealed, compared rather unfavorably with Ford's 'all Australian boy' appearance. One was totally bald and the other little better endowed with any crowning glory. Both had mean noses and the sort of expressions one would not wish on his worst enemy. While grasping a large tome entitled *Conflicting Concepts of Righ-*

*teousness by Faith in the S.D.A. Church*, or "How We Rewrote the Council of Trent," one physician replied to Dr. Ford's 'kind' suggestion: "Heresy! With Christ's help I have developed enough perfection in myself to make the leap." One matter in this cartoon continued to intrigue the authors of *Conflicting Concepts*. On the side of Paradise is a salivating vulture awaiting the inevitable fall of the physicians. Could that really be true of Paradise? Or was it some fatal Freudian slip indicated that Ford had crossed to a false Paradise? Even the animal awaiting his arrival looked somewhat like a cross between a half-starved, wide-eyed wolf and a doe.

The last cartoon entitled "The Ambush" depicted the physicians as witch doctors appropriately attired with wild headdresses and rather revealing grass skirts. This attire permitted an ample revelation of the physicians' massively protuberant abdomens together with a somewhat unanatomical positioning of the umbilicus of each. With the help of a third witch doctor, the Burntside Finance Co., Drs. Clippard and Slandish were depicted mixing a large portion in a cannibal's bowl. Skulls, a pig's head and poison were being put into the brew under the titles of "slander, character assassination, and warped facts"—to make the "Burntside Brew." The clear purpose of the brew was to throw it over Dr. Ford as he athletically did his daily jogging. The second scene showed a lookout, Burntside Finance Corp. Ltd., warning of Dr. Ford's approach.

Scene three depicted the physicians waiting in ambush, both carrying buckets full of the Burntside brew.

As the action moved on to the fourth scene, Dr. Ford was seen to deftly avoid the physicians' aim, permitting the brew to be thrown over each other. The final scene showed a delighted and sarcastic Dr. Ford exclaiming, "Deah, deah, let us not quarrel, Doctahs; come to my Bible classes and I will show you how to deodorize—free!" The two physicians, however, appeared to be too irate with one another to take advantage of the clear generosity of this offer. One physician shouted, "You—You—fat pig! You missed!" The other meanwhile retorted, "Me? I ought to throw you in the stewpot!" The two physicians were left with "smell" and "stink" over them.

While the authors of *Conflicting Concepts* have to admit to the generous physiques depicted in the cartoon, they would have felt happier had their cranial hirsutism been given full credit and the umbilicus of each been placed where their embryological development had determined.

While the Clippard-Slandish Brochure once more interjected a lighter side into the very serious matter of the discussion of God's truth, it caused very little impact upon the whole matter. It did leave, however, one intriguing puzzle unsolved. In a clear parody on a statement written by Drs. Clifford and Russell in a private letter to a Division worker, the brochure stated: "Not copyrighted. No permission necessary for further reproduction." Just how the authors' letter got from the private files in the Australasian Division to the *Present Truth* organization remains one of the unsolved, but not altogether unimportant, questions surrounding the history of this whole problem in Australia.

Chapter 38 Endnote

1.  This caption referred to the totally false surmisings of many that Pastor Burnside was financing the printing of the manuscript, *Conflicting Concepts*.

# 39 Anglicans and Adventists — The Twofold Union

GEOFFREY Paxton, a Queensland Anglican minister, was seen about this time to gradually emerge from the shadows and present himself as a friend of the Seventh-day Adventists seeking to present their views in the best light. Apparently Robert Brinsmead and Geoffrey Paxton had struck up a friendship through Brinsmead's health outreach, and also through Brinsmead's interest in taking his views to the evangelical churches. In a way, Brinsmead needed Paxton in the early seventies to give him credibility with the Evangelical Protestants in his thrust toward them. For some unclear reason Paxton apparently had some reciprocal need of Brinsmead.

Paxton was, at the time of their meeting, the principal of a small interdenominational evangelical Bible training college in Brisbane. Geographically he was situated within a hundred miles of the Brinsmead farm, located just south of the border of Queensland with New South Wales. Shortly, Paxton's articles began to appear on a regular basis in *Present Truth*, and Brinsmead seemed to see a clear advantage in emphasizing the byline—*Anglican Clergyman*. Shortly, Paxton and Brinsmead teamed up to present Bible Institutes all over Australia. Through his contact with Brinsmead, and to a lesser extent with Ford, Paxton planned to write a thesis for his Master of Arts degree at the University of Queensland on the topic, *The Reformation and Contemporary Seventh-day Adventism*.

In order to enlarge his body of background data, Paxton, at the expense of the *Present Truth* organization, made a trip to the United States early in 1976. Perhaps through the by now well established Ford-Brinsmead-Paxton network, Paxton managed to concentrate his interviews on most of the Americans who subsequently attended the Palmdale Conference. At the time that Paxton was in the United States, the names of these Americans were not known to the members of the Adventist Church in general. Therefore, the fact that he could ferret out so many of these men indicated a source of information rather close to the highest church administration in Australia. Paxton subsequently reported on his trip to a group of Queenslanders supporting the *new theology*. His report was presented on March 13, 1976. Men whom Paxton claimed to have spoken to included Pastor Robert Wieland, Dr. Raymond Cottrell, Dr. Herbert Douglass, Pastor Kenneth Wood, Dr. Siegfried Horn, Dr. Raoul Dederen, Dr. Hans LaRondelle, Dr. James Cox, Pastor Ivan Blazen, Dr. Gerhard Hasel, Dr. Edward Heppenstall, Pastor Willis Hackett, Pastor Gordon Hyde, and Pastor Don Neufeld. Paxton reported to the meeting that he had found no unanimity "in the area of the meaning of the essence of Christianity" within the Adventist Church. He asserted that he had found three more or less distinct views within the Church—he termed those holding them the liberals, the traditionalists, and the reformationists. He cited members of the theological faculty at Loma Linda University as belonging to the group which he would classify as liberal, and named Drs. Graham Maxwell and Jack Provonsha as leaders in this postulated wing of Adventism. Paxton asserted further that "the dominant representation in Washington D.C. seems to be in the second area of the traditionalist mentality." On the other hand, he stated that he found the reformationist school dominant at Andrews University. It was this latter group which found favor with him and who were, in his view, following the true tradition of the Reformation.

Paxton went on to suggest that "the central conflict in the Adventist Church today is unquestionably the conflict over the meaning of the expression 'righteousness by faith.'" Paxton was perfectly correct when he stated that his research indicated to him that in "the literature from around about just prior to 1888 right down to a special issue on righteousness by faith put out by the *Review and Herald* looking over the span of time down to this issue put out in 1975 [actually the issue was dated 1974], I found that the prominent tendency of the Adventist Church has been to see righteousness by faith as that which means justification and sanctification . . . and that is what I mean by traditionalist." Making his meaning even more specific, Paxton described this position as believing that righteousness by faith means "the work of God in us as well as the work of God for us."

On the other hand, Paxton asserted that "the reformationist school, as represented by Andrews University, wishes to stress, I say, that righteousness by faith equals justification, period." The speaker then postulated "that the issue facing the Adventist Church today is the same issue that faced Luther in the 16th century . . . It is the Reformation all over again." It was quite obvious that Geoffrey Paxton saw the issue as the Catholic versus the Protestant stance of the 16th century. Pathetically, he saw the reformationists in the Church as being compatible with the Protestant teachings and those whom he called the traditionalists as supporting the Catholic point of view. This conclusion was a rather serious charge upon those who believe the well-established Seventh-day Adventist position. It seemed almost inconceivable that anyone could be so clouded in his thinking, for the whole mark of Catholicism is that it would change the law, and thus make it of none effect. That those in the Adventist Church who firmly believed that God empowered obedience to the law should be classed as Catholic seemed to many to indicate a great paucity of thought.

Paxton was quite specific in his condemnation. He set out a list of examples of books and publications which showed the type of traditional Adventist thinking which he deplored. In commenting on Pastor Thomas Davis' book *How to Live a Victorious Christian Life*, he described it as "a terrible book in this respect, that his holiness-movement type of zombiism is creeping into Adventist thinking." He further went on to criticize Dr. E. J. Waggoner's book *The Power of Forgiveness*, A. G. Daniells' book *Christ Our Righteousness*, A. W. Spaulding's book *Origin and History of Seventh-day Adventists*, together with a number of others, including manuscripts by Steinwig and Pease, and a sermon delivered on May 10, 1975 at the Campus Hill Church by J. W. Lehman.

Having falsely contended that these authors confused justification with sanctification, Paxton formed the judgment that "there is no excuse for that. If the Adventist Church thinks that she is going to be God's remnant or selected few people with God-given purity and such, that type of theological and doctrinal confusion right at the heart of its movement, then all I can say is that it is more mistaken than I ever thought. This is sheer Romanism to confuse justification and sanctification. . . . Look, if we Evangelical Babylonians have to wait on you Adventists to bring the coming of the Lord, and that is the sort of thing you go on with, I am very pessimistic about His coming."

It became plain that what Paxton asserted as being a friendly attitude toward the Seventh-day Adventists and their faith fell somewhat short of that assertion. Paxton spent a considerable period of time upholding the views expressed in the *Soteriological Implications of the Human Nature of Christ*, and suggested that the manuscript represented the true position on the gospel, and contrasted it with the *Review and Herald* Special of 1974 which he claimed "downgrades justification."

Another finding which Paxton said he had made during his tour of the United States was "that the professors at Andrews University in the theology department and in the biblical studies department at least, if I may use a colloquialism, would not have a bit of the sinful nature of Christ approach. I find that at the *Review and Herald* Publishing House, the predominant approach is that Jesus had a sinful human nature."

Perhaps one of Paxton's most disquieting assertions concerned one of the professors in the theology department at Andrews University. He stated, "One of the happiest times that I had was with Dr. LaRondelle because some time ago Dr. LaRondelle wrote a paper on the Seventh-day Adventist statement of righteousness by faith which I, as a Babylonian, challenged. I wrote quite an extensive reply to Dr. LaRondelle on this paper, so naturally I had not received a reply and I was sort of wondering what I would encounter. Like a truly great man, Dr. LaRondelle said he believed my reply was correct. I was right. He had not been as clear as he should have been, and I spoke to him how I heard on the grapevine that Dr. Desmond Ford was in hot water in Australia for propounding what I believe to be the biblical gospel and where he would stand. Dr. LaRondelle himself, I am happy to say, sent me back to Dr. Ford to tell Dr. Ford personally that he intends to stand with Dr. Ford in the front row in this issue."

Whether Paxton represented his meeting with this Andrews University professor in its right light or not the authors do not know. What is known is that Paxton and the holders of the *new theology* were far less joyous over LaRondelle in 1977 than they had been in 1976, for he published an article in the *Review and Herald* which beautifully expounded what Paxton condemned as the traditional view. Further, he later wrote an article in a Dutch denominational paper condemning Paxton. Naturally someone soon spotted the article and sent it speedily to Robert Brinsmead's desk.

Paxton further stated that many of the Seminary students at Andrews University "treat the *Review and Herald* as a bit of a joke . . . they do not place much store by it. They say, 'Well, *Ministry* magazine is better and you ought to read it more than the *Review and Herald*.'" He quoted one Andrews University student as expressing the view of others when he stated, "I read the *Review and Herald* to keep informed on what's happening in the Church, and I read *Present Truth* for my spiritual comfort."

One interesting fact was that when Colin visited Andrews University some time later, he was surprised to find just how few of the University's leadership had any idea that their campus had been graced by the presence of Geoffrey Paxton; thus it seems that he was very selective in those he interviewed.

Geoffrey Paxton's assessment of Sister White was that she had a wax nose. By this he meant that her material could be used to support various positions. Sometimes he asserted it pointed in the direction of the teachings of *Present Truth*, and other times the nose was looking in the direction of the *Review and Herald*, and sometimes looking in the direction of the liberal position. This attitude suggested that Paxton had made little more than the most superficial attempt to study the writings of Sister White.

Some time later, during a Sabbath morning service at the Avondale Memorial Church, it was announced that the afternoon service was to be conducted by a mysterious speaker. This news caused considerable speculation, the more so when the program was cancelled at the last minute and a substitute program presented. Subsequent investigation revealed that the mystery speaker was to have been Geoffrey Paxton. Two college students had arranged, presumably with the cooperation of senior Avondale College staff members, for Paxton's visit. Paxton stayed on the college premises. When the church pastor of the Avondale Memorial Church, Pastor Les Coombe, discovered the identity of the mystery speaker he took speedy action to cancel the meeting. His lead could well have been taken by a number of our churches in the United States, which showed less than wisdom in this respect during the year 1978 when Paxton made yet another visit to America.

The college group responsible for Paxton's visit, however, was not content to be hindered in its aim and substituted a walk through the bush with a large number of theology students and some faculty members to a rural house where Paxton presented his meeting. The fact that an Anglican pastor, actively engaged in opposing God's church, was permitted freedom to speak to our young people caused no little stir among those of God's children standing for the old truth.

Paxton even received mention in the *Australasian Record* when he performed a marriage ceremony between one of Robert Brinsmead's relatives and the daughter of a senior faculty member at Avondale College in an Anglican church. The reception to this wedding was held in the Avondale College dining room. In fairness it must be pointed out that the young couple chose Paxton as their celebrant when they were denied the services of a Seventh-day Adventist pastor. No doubt this is the first time that a wedding conducted by an Anglican pastor in an Anglican church was recorded in the *Australasian Record*.

What is certain was that from 1976 there was a growing fusion of Paxton and those members of the Seventh-day Adventist Church espousing the *new theology*, yet on no occasion did Paxton give the slightest indication that he was interested in accepting the unique truths of the Seventh-day Adventist Church. This situation was a very disturbing state of affairs and should have warned many, many people that the *new theology* was something not sent from God.

# 40    Truth Mixed with Error

IN the meantime the differing views of perfection within the Church were curiously highlighted by the Southern Publishing Association in a book entitled *Perfection: The Impossible Possibility*. This book was written by four authors, two of whom (Dr. Edward Heppenstall and Dr. Hans LaRondelle) adopted a doctrinal position similar to that of the *new theology* and two (Dr. Herbert Douglass and Dr. Mervyn Maxwell) who put forward the Scripture-based Seventh-day Adventist view. The very fact that such a book was published was a matter of great concern. Both views cannot be truth, for they are incompatible and in conflict. Thus they were both wrong or one view was truth and the other error. There is no place in God's plan for error to be printed on our presses, except for the purpose of refutation. But in this book both viewpoints on the central issue of truth were given equal weight.

Sister White spoke strongly against the printing of conflicting materials in our publications. In the early 1890s Uriah Smith and Alonzo Jones wrote articles in the *Review and Herald* on the topic of the image of the beast. These articles were in obvious conflict. One brother wrote to Sister White expressing his confusion. Sister White, referring to this incident, wrote to church leaders and ministers:

> The zeal that leads to this kind of work is not inspired of God. (Manuscript 1, 1893, quoted in Arthur White's biography of Sister White, Vol. 4, 65)

The printing of this book illustrated most graphically a trend which had been developing within our Church. This trend took a casual view of doctrine, indicating that both sides of the issue should be presented with equal emphasis so that each reader could make up his own mind on which view was truth and which was error, or maybe take a little from each point of view. The proclamation of truth has never been strengthened by such a weak attitude. Doctrine is precious, for it is divinely inspired. Thus there is no ground to confuse error with truth as if either alternative were acceptable.

The two authors whose views were close to the *new theology* had been invited to Australia in order to speak at ministerial institutes. It seemed that the American speakers invited were much more likely to come from that group which was close to the *new theology* than from those believing the fundamental Adventist message. Numbers of pastors in Australia asserted that they believed in the *new theology*, not because of what they had heard from Dr. Ford, but from what they had heard from these men.[1] Surely there is a great need for those in responsible positions to take a greater interest in this matter, for error can thus easily spread around the world. It is tragic when men sent to increase the knowledge of our ministry in fact produce the opposite result. The greatest care must be exercised in selecting representatives of the Church to visit other lands, for these almost automatically are assumed to carry the Church's approval upon their utterances. In the past too little care has been exercised in this matter. Dr. Heppenstall, in supporting the *new theology* in the book, *Perfection: The Impossible Possibility*, made the statement, "If Christian perfection means restoration here and now to Adam's sinless state . . . then the Bible knows nothing about it." This assertion contradicts the plain statement of Scripture itself:

> Now unto him that is able to keep you from falling, and to present you faultless before the presence of his glory with exceeding joy. (Jude 24)

> Forasmuch then as Christ hath suffered for us in the flesh, arm yourselves likewise with the same mind: for he that hath suffered in the flesh hath ceased from sin; that he no longer should live the rest of his time in the flesh to the lusts of men, but to the will of God. (1 Peter 4:1,2)

> We know that whosoever is born of God sinneth not; but he that is begotten of God keepeth himself, and that wicked one toucheth him not. (1 John 5:18)

Sister White further denied the words of Heppenstall most specifically:

> Those only who through faith in Christ obey all of God's commandments, will reach the condition of sinlessness in which Adam lived before his transgression. (*6BC* 1118)

Presumably the author was well acquainted with this statement. Certainly one of the other authors felt quite justified in including it in his contribution. Why, in the light of such unequivocal evidence, the author would choose to make a statement that could only lead the reader to believe the direct converse remains a mystery. Such statements certainly weaken the faith of God's children. Never do the proponents of the *new theology* feel comfortable in accepting the conclusions of the Spirit of Prophecy. Perhaps the Spirit of Prophecy is too direct, and not having required translation from Greek or Hebrew, the question cannot be utilized to overcome the objections of those less learned in biblical languages.

## Chapter 40 Endnote

1. For example Pastor George Conley stated that he learned his views from Dr. Heppenstall. A former pastor, Jim Johanson, stated his concept of the *new theology* came from the Seminary Extension School held by Dr. LaRondelle.

# 41

# Jesus, The Model Man

THE publication of the *Sabbath School Quarterly* for the second quarter of 1977 was bound to raise controversy. That the controversy, however, should reach the level of bitterness that it did could not have been anticipated. The *Quarterly* was written by Dr. Herbert Douglass and set forth the old Adventist position of the nature of Christ. The nature of Christ is a matter of central importance to our understanding of righteousness by faith. If Christ had a nature different from ours, then those exploiting the views of the *new theology* would be totally correct in their assumption that man in fallen nature could not obey the law of God. But every relevant text of Scripture and every related text in the Spirit of Prophecy indicate that Christ did have our nature and with our nature obeyed every one of God's commandments. This fact leaves man without an excuse, a situation abhorrent to those believing the *new theology*. Douglass summarized the whole significance of Christ's human nature thus: "When God asks men and women to obey him and to live above sinning, He is not asking the impossible or merely tantalizing them. Jesus proved what a man or woman can do." (*Jesus, the Model Man*, 21)

As the quarter's lessons were studied, they showed full biblical and Spirit of Prophecy proof for this contention. This fact only raised the animosity of some to a higher level.

The Australasian Division had two readers on the *Sabbath School Quarterly* committee. Both made strenuous efforts to have modifications made to this particular set of lessons, without significant success. The weight of the 140 readers[1] of the *Sabbath School Quarterly* throughout the world fell on the side of the old Adventist position. This bent led to a brisk correspondence across the Pacific, for the Australasian Division leadership knew full well that Dr. Ford had been teaching contrary to this doctrine at Avondale College. It was partially due to this reason that this *Lesson Quarterly* was an acute embarrassment to the Australasian Division, possibly because it highlighted the fact that the doctrines being taught at Avondale were not in accord with the beliefs of the Church.

Naturally many of the younger pastors who knew little of the potent biblical and Spirit of Prophecy evidences for the Adventist stand on the nature of Christ were alarmed at the arrival of this Church-sponsored publication. It struck at the basis of all they had been taught at Avondale College as being the truth of the gospel. The

## Jesus, the Model Man 171

quarter's theme was very clearly observed in the last lesson, entitled "The Model Waiting to be Reproduced." Some of the quotations from that particular lesson merit reprinting, for they typify the author's theme:

> Adventists also believe that God will bring an end to the sin problems at the second coming of Jesus, and that this momentous event has been delayed not because God has changed His plan, but because His followers have not yet fulfilled His plan." (*Adult Sabbath School Lessons*, Second Quarter, 1977, 105)

> We are living in the time when the world needs a very clear demonstration of God's will for men and women of His grace and love by which men and women can be changed into the likeness of their Lord." (*Ibid.*)

> The separation and the line of demarcation will become obvious; philosophies, theologies, and life-styles will be judged on one basis—how faithfully is the character of Jesus being reproduced." (*Ibid.*, 106)

> Jesus overcame temptation the same way we must—by faith, by the trusting, obedient relationship with the Father that says Yes to whatever God says is best. The faith of Jesus develops the character of Jesus. Such will be the experience of His people in the last days. (*Ibid.*)

> Neither is ready to harvest unless the grain has matured. Even as the farmer waits for the grain to mature, so Jesus waits until the gospel seed has produced a sizeable and significant group of mature Christians. (*Ibid.* 107)

> One of the reasons why Jesus came to earth was to give men and women a model of what the truly human was like; He showed us that the sanctified life simply means that God has full ownership—mentally, physically, socially and spiritually. (*Ibid.*109)

All of these statements, of course, were the words of the editor and, true as they were, they pale into insignificance compared with the powerful words of Inspiration quoted. These words left no doubt concerning the veracity of the theme of the Quarterly.

> To him that overcometh will I grant to sit with me in my throne, even as I also overcame. (Revelation 3:21)

At a time when total victory over sin in the believer was stated to be merely vicarious, this text stood as a forcible rebuke to those who would so misrepresent the plain truth of Scripture. Dr. Douglass also quoted:

> Consider the life of Christ. Standing at the head of humanity, serving His Father, He is an example of what every Son should . . . be. (*COL* 282)

Of course Dr. Douglass did not omit the two words which have been omitted deliberately by the authors from this passage. With the omission of these two words, this is how the statement is so often read by those who are blind to its message. As rendered above, those believing the *new theology* have no objection to its message. They fully believe that Christ's perfect obedience should, under the power of God, be our aim. They assert, however, that such victory is not possible prior to glorification, apart from vicariously accepting Christ's life in our place.[2] It is instructive to read the quotation in its entirety:

> Consider the life of Christ. Standing at the head of humanity, serving His Father, He is an example of what every Son should *and may* be. The obedience that Christ rendered God requires from human beings *today*. (*Ibid.*, emphasis added)

It was little wonder that this *Quarterly* caused such consternation in the hearts of those believing the *new theology* when it contained statements of this nature. These statements so utterly destroyed that which was being preached that the only options open to those reading them were to either accept the truth or condemn the author, lest anyone detect that what he was saying was the truth of God. That the *new theology* has the least credibility in the face of such statements of Inspiration can only be attributable to man's long-cherished desire for the title of heaven in the absence of his fitness for it. It also emphasizes just how much the majority are looking to themselves rather than to Christ as the source of their obedience.

Since the *Signs* Publishing Company employed a number who were avid followers of the *new theology*, and further since the publishing house printed the *Lesson Quarterlies* for the Australasian Division, these men were prematurely alerted to its contents. Whatever their motives, some early circulated the *Quarterly* to the supporters of the *Present Truth* organization and to young pastors known to be most active in support of the *new theology*. This action had the effect of arousing antagonism and organized opposition to the *Sabbath School Quarterly*. For example, at the Victorian Conference camp meeting held in mid-January, 1977, two and a half months prior to the introduction of this *Quarterly*, one pastor at the meeting of conference workers suggested that the *Quarterly* be banned entirely from the conference. This suggestion led to a lively discussion during which he received inordinate support from some of the younger pastors and from some who were more senior.

The Conference president, taking his cue from these pastors, discussed the matter with the president of the Trans-Australian Union and went so far as to write Pastor Pierson personally expressing concern over the effect of the *Quarterly* in Australia. At the Ballarat Church, situated approximately seventy miles west of Melbourne, the church treasurer reported to the incoming pastor that his predecessor had requested that the treasurer refrain from ordering the *Lesson Quarterlies* for the church. Meanwhile the editor of the *Australasian Record* offered to print a series of "helps" for the study of the lesson. It was thought in this way the readers of the *Australasian Record* could be oriented away from the clear teachings of the *Lesson Quarterly*.

## Chapter 41 Endnotes

1. This figure was stated by one of the Australasian Division readers. Other inquiries indicate fewer readers.
2. That this position is taken, despite Sister White's clearest statements, even by some men in high posts within the Church, was shown by a response to a sermon on the subject of perfection, preached by Dr. David Pennington in the North New South Wales Conference. The Conference president sent a copy of the sermon to the Division spokesman who cast doubt upon the statement of Sister White which assures us that, "Everyone who by faith obeys God's commandments will reach the condition of sinlessness in which Adam lived before his transgression. (*ST* July 23, 1902) The Division spokesman's comment upon that was, "Thank God for that, but . . . when?" (*An Assessment of an Untitled Sermon on Christian Perfection*, Division spokesman, circa June 1981) As the full quotation cited in the text demonstrates, the Division spokesman was in error in his inference that this situation would not prevail until the second coming. The answer to his question is, "Today!"

# 42 Australasian Division Responds

A retired Australasian Division leader informed Pastor Keith Parmenter, Division president, that the *Lesson Quarterlies* would tend to split the membership of the Division. Shortly Robert Brinsmead produced a critique of the *Quarterly*. He stated that he did so at the request of this former Division leader. Brinsmead's critique was entitled *An Appraisal of Jesus, the Model Man*. Whether the former Division leader had requested him, as Brinsmead asserted, to make an appraisal of the *Sabbath School Quarterly* is not certain. What is certain is that apparently Pastor Max Townend, Australasian Division Sabbath School secretary, was not informed of such a background to Brinsmead's article, for he wrote to all Conference presidents: "Before we received our final print of the *Quarterly*, one Robert Brinsmead, apparently received an advance copy of the *Quarterly* and wrote a critique which was not flattering to the content of the *Quarterly*. . . . I do not think we should unduly disturb ourselves about criticism of Adventist publications by those who choose not to be members of the Seventh-day Adventist Church."[1]

One matter which is again highlighted was the ease with which Robert Brinsmead and his organization were able to obtain private letters from the Division and Conference files. Clearly sympathizers were in high places.

While Pastor Townend was perfectly proper in his statement that there was no cause to be alarmed at the criticism from a non-Adventist, there certainly was much greater cause for alarm when vitriolic attacks upon the *Quarterly* were made by ordained ministers. Two ministers, one in the Western Australian Conference and the other in the Greater Sydney Conference, published their attacks upon the *Sabbath School Quarterly* in further editions of the *Adventist News Service* printed by the Present Truth organization.

Brinsmead's critique was not one of his best thought-out papers. For instance, in an argument which could influence only the gullible, he stated: "*What is true of the nature is true of the person.* That is a fact that cannot be controverted because there is of necessity a communion of the nature with the person. If Christ's human nature was sinful it would have to be said, 'He was sinful.'" (*An Appraisal of Jesus, the Model Man*, 16) The examination of a single quotation from the Spirit of Prophecy completely shattered Brinsmead's particularly weak argument.

That he should take man's fallen nature, and His strength would not be even equal with theirs [the angels']. (*1SG* 25)

Using Brinsmead's logic on this particular passage we would have to say that because Christ had a fallen nature He must Himself have fallen, yet all Scripture and all evidence of the Spirit of Prophecy, of course, deny any such fall.

Throughout his critique, Brinsmead uses terms such as "the orthodox Christian message" and "the orthodox Christian faith." Such terms are meaningless. In the Dark Ages Catholicism was the orthodox Christian faith. Rarely has orthodoxy been reliable. That the *Quarterly* was said to oppose such orthodoxy is a prima facie case for thinking it may at least have avoided the usual errors of Christendom. Nevertheless, Brinsmead concluded that "the Douglass theory is an old heresy." (*An Appraisal of Jesus, the Model Man*, 19) To brand the truth of God as "the Douglass theory" is to demean and belittle it.

Although not directly accusing Dr. Douglass of believing or teaching these facts, Brinsmead thought it prudent to state, "Some are saying that the death of Jesus was only an exhibition to propitiate man's wrath towards God." (*Ibid.* 22) Further, he said, "That sort of picture of the final generation is a lot different to what rather appears like the 144,000 Laodiceans strutting about like replicas of Jesus, and who have got past sinning, justification, imputed righteousness, forgiveness, mercy and all that 'elementary stuff.'" (*Ibid.* 23) Since no one upholding the truth of God had been heard to support such absurdities, Brinsmead was rather wasting his ink on such nonsense.

Later Brinsmead published a modified version of his critique which made no mention of the *Lesson Quarterly* nor of Dr. Douglass. This publication was entitled *The Theology of Imitation*, and bore the subtitle "*Is Salvation by Imitation or by Grace?*" This subtitle, of course, indicated an inexcusable misconception of the true Adventist stand on this important subject. It is difficult to believe that this tactic was not an attempt to bias the reader against the truth. The question, "imitation or grace?" has never been posed. Imitation of Christ's character *is* by grace alone—a very different position from the impression Brinsmead left. By adopting this open stance of failing to name the Church or its servants in his work, Robert Brinsmead had adopted a new tack. Many wondered why this change had occurred. It was almost certainly related to the meeting held at the General Conference office in the summer of 1971, when Robert and John Brinsmead and Dr. Jack Zwemer met with General Conference leaders, including Pastor Neal Wilson, then vice-president for the North American Division. At that meeting it was suggested and agreed that Brinsmead would direct his literature to those outside the Church. Speaking of this change of direction, Ray Martin, Brinsmead's leader in Victoria, perceptively stated that *Present Truth*'s impact outside of Adventism has had a very decided influence inside Adventism. Instead of dying out, as the G. C. brethren had assumed it would, it soon became apparent that thousands of Adventists were reading *P.T.* It seemed that out of the ashes of what remained of the old 'Awakening,' the influence of *P.T.* within the Church had actually grown several times over." (*Objective Digest Report*, 2)

Quite clearly Brinsmead had no desire to upset the success he was achieving by returning to methods which had proved less successful in earlier years. One serious fact, however, was the growing evidence that Brinsmead continued his attacks vicariously through his Anglican mouthpiece, Geoffrey Paxton. Paxton had no qualms about openly attacking both the Church and its publications. One of Robert Brinsmead's associates, Alan Starkey, stated: "What was presented by Paxton was not his own findings. Bob researched all of this and handed it over to prove that Adventists were not Protestant, but Catholic." (Letter written by Pastor Mervyn Ball to Dr. R. Standish, dated June 14, 1977) Perhaps Robert Brinsmead also deserved a Queensland University Master of Arts degree similar to that which was awarded to Geoffrey Paxton.

So heated did the situation in Australia become concerning the *Sabbath School Quarterly* that Pastor Pierson, the president of the General Conference, found it necessary to virtually direct the Australasian Division to study it. He wrote in a letter to Pastor Max Townend, "I have checked carefully with Brother Rampton [Sabbath School director of the General Conference, and incidentally an Australian] about the routing of this manuscript [Jesus, the Model Man], and I discovered it was processed through the regular channels. First it was evaluated by the Sabbath School Lessons sub-committee. Then it was passed along to the Adult Sabbath School Lessons Committee, which is composed of some fifty representative scholars, administrators, departmental directors, etc. These were all given opportunity to check the manuscript. While not all responded and provided input on the manuscript, all had opportunity to do so. When in your [Pastor Max Townend's] letter of May 3, addressed to Dr. Lesher, you raised some questions regarding the manuscript, I was not in the office, but it was arranged for Elders Nigri, Eva, Hyde, Lesher, Rampton, and Dower to consider the questions you raised. The brethren went through the problem areas and were under the impression that after this they had dealt with these matters satisfactorily and so the manuscript has been published, and, as you know, is already in the field. I have personally gone through the lessons within the last few days and I received a blessing from the thoughts presented."

Even such support as this was not sufficient for many of the ministers in Australia, particularly in the Victorian Conference. So great did the agitation become there that the Division spokesman was sent down to talk to the Victorian Conference workers at a meeting held on March 5, 1977. This meeting was meant to be kept a secret, presumably so that the laity would be unaware of the problem which was apparently confronting the ministry. The Division spokesman stated, "Now it would be most regrettable if what I am saying this afternoon should ever be relayed outside this room." He was quite unaware that one pastor, enamored with the *new theology*, was secretly recording the meeting, and within one or two hours of its completion that tape recording was in the hands of Ray Martin, Brinsmead's leader in Victoria, who speedily sent it on to Brinsmead and Paxton.

Since the statements of that meeting are no longer secret, outside the Church let alone within it, there is no virtue in excluding some of its detail from this discourse. The Division spokesman, who was one of the two who had reviewed the *Quarterly* for the Australasian Division, left little doubt concerning his own disappointment with the *Quarterly*, and at one point he associated himself ('numbers of us') with the critics but quickly corrected the slip to say simply 'numbers.' He also revealed that much correspondence went back and forth between the Australasian Division and the General Conference on this matter. A verbatim account of what the Division representative said is presented: "You are all aware by this time the Sabbath School pamphlet for the third [he meant second] quarter is a fait accompli. There is the pamphlet and in a week or so's time this will be distributed in all our Sabbath Schools. I know with long discussions I've already had with workers on this—I was going to say Campus—on this ground, that there are numbers of us—numbers—who are concerned about the emphasis that is given in this pamphlet and some of its theological implications. The original manuscript, the initial manuscript, was written by Douglass. Dr. Douglass, who until some months ago was a sub-editor [actually he was an associate editor] of the *Review and Herald*. Dr. Douglass has now relinquished his position in the *Review and Herald* and is privately employed. When Dr. Douglass had written his manuscript, it was sent out to the world field for an initial vetting. Now there are two persons in the Australasian Division who have been appointed to the Sabbath School Reading Committee, Dr. Alwyn Salom and your present speaker, and we read through the pamphlet and we made our comments. I would point out that altogether there are some 140 persons[2]—reporting on the Sabbath School Pamphlet, so our two voices don't necessarily carry the day on any issue, and in due course the pamphlet was prepared in the form it is now presented to us. I'm well aware that there are those who will have their concerns as to the theological implications of this pamphlet. I would like to share with you therefore the counsel we have received from our General Conference president. It is not my purpose this afternoon to fill in any detail with the correspondence that has gone back and forth between Wahroonga [Australasian Division headquarters, situated in the Sydney suburb of Wahroonga] and Washington, but I would like to share with you a final statement or two from a letter which Elder Pierson wrote to me. The suggestion has been raised by certain people that perhaps subsidiary material could be published regarding the lesson pamphlet. But the opinion of the brethren is expressed by Elder Pierson in these words, 'If you in Australia and we in the General Conference should attempt to put out some subsidiary material, we feel that this would accentuate the problem and make it worse than it is at present. In fact we do not feel that there will be any stir in most parts of the world over the *Quarterly* and we hope that it will be minimal there in Australasia.' Our counsel from the Division to our workers is that where we ourselves happen to be the teachers of the lessons for any given Sabbath that we present the truth as we have known and taught it through the years, and if there are any problems, that we do not accentuate these but that rather we [one word was too soft here to hear] the teaching and remember that it is our task as a working force to remain loyal and united in our adhesion to the Church and to its leadership but also to use our influence wherever we are to prevent anything which would introduce unnecessary controversy. Now it's no secret that ever since the 1870s, perhaps 1880s, right through to the present time there has been a considerable amount of variant thinking amongst our people regarding the person of Christ and it would be quite impossible for any one person to write a pamphlet which would suit everybody. Now our counsel therefore, is that whatever may be our personal predilection concerning matters that appear in the pamphlet, when it comes to presenting the lessons in our Sabbath Schools, we ourselves present the truth positively and that we do all in our power to prevent any kind of unfortunate controversial discussion."

The speaker did not make his intent perfectly clear. Many of the younger pastors saw his statement as a carefully worded piece of advice to push the *new theology* contrary to the clear teaching of the *Quarterly* so long as they refrained from mentioning that they were so doing. In effect this is what occurred in some churches. In others, the pastors disdained the advice given and publicly, either in church board meetings or during the service itself, condemned the *Lesson Quarterly* openly. One young pastor[3] caused dissension, for example, in both North Fitzroy (Australia's oldest church) and Preston Churches, when he openly condemned the *Quarterly*. Another pastor caused a similar situation at Springvale Church when he spoke to the church board of his objections. In another church, East Prahran, the class teachers followed the lead of their pastor and spent valuable lesson study time objecting to the *Quarterly*.

Wahroonga Church, situated across from the Division headquarter, was a critical area. The church pastor prominently supported the *new theology*, attended the Palmdale meetings and was one of the two readers of the Sabbath School lessons nominated by the Division. Thus he had early unsuccessfully objected to its theme. A combined Sabbath School class was held in the church during the Sabbath of Easter. A layman, Brother Neil Foxcroft, led out. The lesson topic for the week concerned was "God With *Us*," one of the most sensitive topics of the quarter. Foxcroft, an astute Bible student, perfectly understood the import of the lesson and its divergence from the *new theology*. Accepting the true Seventh-day Adventist position, he set forth the powerful evidences supplied in the *Quarterly* and other sources concerning Christ's nature when on earth. So intense was his concern over the error taught on this point at Avondale College that he felt constrained to mention that our young people at the college were being taught a different doctrine.

It must have taken great courage for him to speak in the manner in which he did, but as could be anticipated, a number took umbrage at what was said. Later Brother Foxcroft received a visit from the church pastor who informed him he intended to place a rejoinder in the church bulletin. This rejoinder was printed in the Wahroonga church bulletin dated April 23, 1977, and was signed by the church pastor. It stated, "In the Sabbath school lesson of two weeks ago [April 9, 1977] some statements were made concerning what is taught by the theology department at Avondale College. These statements were inaccurate and misleading. As a former member of the faculty, and of that department, I am fully aware of what I and my colleagues taught then, and what those same men are still teaching. Contrary to what was stated, the college does not now, and never has, taught that Christ did not come in the flesh; nor has it taught the immaculate conception and thus that Christ could not have sinned. Neither does it assert that the law of heredity only affected Christ's outward form. The inferences made on the above occasion with respect to these subjects were false. These matters have been discussed with the person concerned. Like our church leaders from Division level down, we may safely give our full support to Avondale."

This statement sadly did far less than justice to Brother Foxcroft's presentation. Foxcroft's assertion was that Avondale College was teaching differently from the theme of the *Sabbath School Quarterly*. No one could rightly have denied this assertion. The church pastor, it will be noted, referred to "inferences" which he had made. It is likely that the majority of those who heard Brother Foxcroft's presentation (including Russell) did not make the same inferences as the church pastor.

Chapter 42 Endnotes

1. Quoted in *Adventist News Service*, Ray Martin, 1, printed by Jack B. Walker for the *Present Truth* organization
2. It will be noted that Pastor Pierson gave the number as 50.
3. This man is no longer a credentialed pastor.

# 43 The Lesson Quarterly Outside Australia

THE activities of the *Present Truth* organization ensured that objections to the *Lesson Quarterly* of the second quarter of 1977 would arise also within the United States. In fact, this did lead to a flood of letters reaching the General Conference objecting to the contents of the *Quarterly*. One state from which the objection seemed to be particularly strong was Ohio, although objections came from many states. This constrained Kenneth Wood to write a forthright editorial in the *Review and Herald*. It was entitled "Jesus—the God-Man." In this editorial Wood wrote:

> But Christ lived on earth, not only to show us *what* we may become but also to show us *how* we may live victoriously. Little has been said about this in recent years. This is regrettable. (Review and Herald, May 3, 1977)

Speaking of Christ's example of how to live the sanctified life, Pastor Wood suggested:

> From this standpoint the lessons being studied by the world church in the Sabbath School this quarter have exceptional value. (*Ibid.*)

Pastor Wood further expressed his conviction that Seventh-day Adventists—

> are to present to the world Christ and His righteousness, both for justification and for sanctification. Are they doing this? Not as fully as they should. And perhaps one reason is that for a number of years too many members and ministers have feared to discuss the humanity of Christ lest they appear irreverent and seem to make Christ "altogether human" (which He was not; He was also divine). They have been disturbed when some church members and leaders have preached the Christ of historic Adventism, the Christ who lived as we must live, who was tempted as we are tempted, who overcame as we must overcome, and who has promised to live in us by His Holy Spirit (uniting our human nature with His divine nature). (*Ibid.*)

While Pastor Wood expressed his concern that in recent years the humanity of Christ had become reduced in prominence within the Adventist Church, this trend was certainly not the case during Sister White's lifetime. The authors possess copies of old *Lesson Quarterlies*. The writers in those days appeared to be fearless in their proclamation of this Bible truth. It surely is not without significance that Sister

White did not go on record in opposition to such truth as year after year the same theme was expressed.

Some examples follow:

> Christ in His humanity, subject to all the conditions and limitations of humanity, obeyed perfectly that law which He in His divinity had proclaimed with His own voice from Sinai, and thus was for us a life of obedience, which as our High Priest, He ministers to all who yield themselves to Him. (*Sabbath School Quarterly*, fourth quarter, 1896, 12)

> Divinity tabernacled in the flesh of humanity, not the flesh of sinless man, but such flesh as the children of earth possess. That was the glory of it. The divine Seed could manifest the glory of God in sinful flesh, even in absolute and perfect victory over any tendency of the flesh. (*Sabbath School Quarterly*, second quarter, 1909, 8)

> In order to establish this relation between God and sinful flesh, it was necessary for the Son of God to take sinful flesh; and thus was bridged the gulf which separated sinful man from God. (*Sabbath School Quarterly*, first quarter, 1913, 14)

> By assuming sinful flesh, and voluntarily making Himself dependent upon His Father to keep Him from sin while He was in the world, Jesus not only set the example for all Christians, but also made it possible for Him to minister to sinful flesh the gift of His own Spirit and power for obedience to the will of God. (*Sabbath School Quarterly*, first quarter, 1913, 15)

> He was the same flesh as the seed of David, in and through which for generations had flowed the blood of sinful humanity—Solomon, and Rehoboam, and Ahaz, and Manasseh, and Amon, and Jeconiah, and others. (*Sabbath School Quarterly*, fourth quarter, 1914, 6)

> The Son took the flesh of sinful man, and overcame where man failed, overthrew sin in the flesh; and so He can come into the flesh of those who will open their hearts to receive Him, with the same power and conquer sin there. (*Sabbath School Quarterly*, first quarter, 1914, 16)

Thus in the early part of this century the authors of the Sabbath School lessons perceived the truth of the nature of Christ. That men have gone to the institutions of error and have not been sufficiently perceptive to discern this error, should not discourage those who have the enormous body of truth from which to understand the significant implications of the nature of Christ. For churches which refuse to keep the fourth commandment and insist that any or all cannot be kept it is mandatory that they find an excuse for their disobedience, and this excuse they find by suggesting that Christ had a nature superior to their own. This was Augustine's excuse for his disobedience to God's law. But for Seventh-day Adventists called specifically to uphold the sanctity of the law of God, it is inexcusable to misunderstand the nature of Christ and the doctrine that man, under the power of the Holy Spirit, must obey as Jesus obeyed.

# 44 Adventism Attacked

ON January 28–29, 1977, Geoffrey Paxton came to Melbourne to speak on his theme—"Adventism and the Reformation." The two meetings were held in the Croydon Church of Christ. The first meeting, conducted on Friday evening under the chairmanship of Ray Martin, was confined to showing that Adventists claimed to be the true successors of the Reformation. Since no Adventist could rightly disagree with such an assessment, the first meeting engendered little interest.

The meeting held on Sabbath afternoon, January 29, however, was of a different order. The church was packed with Seventh-day Adventists, some even having to sit in the vestry. In his disarming manner, Paxton delivered one of the most vitriolic attacks on God's Church ever heard. For someone asserting that he was a friend of Adventists, his tone was remarkably critical.

Eight extracts from the two-hour discourse will give the reader an insight into Paxton's aims. "And [I] find in the Adventist stream a terrific attempt—like this book of Douglass' [holding up the *Sabbath School Quarterly* of the second quarter of 1977] to show that Jesus Himself was a sinner in order to make it more possible for you and me to meet His standard." "This book, *If It's So Easy, Why Is It So Hard?* [recently published by the *Review and Herald*] I must classify as little better than utter nonsense." "I consider it [April–June *Sabbath School Quarterly*, 1977] to be less than orthodox. In fact, it is downright heretical." "I regard the Sabbath School Lessons heretical and not-mostly-of-the-best of Adventism." "I see the general testimony meeting of Evangelicalism and Adventism to be nothing other than the counterpart of the Catholic teaching of the veneration of the saints." Speaking of Dr. Douglass' recent *Review and Herald* publication, The *Medium and the Message*: "May I say, God help us, Dr. Douglass, if you are right." "If the Lord's return depends upon Adventists becoming perfect in themselves, then I am very sad to hear it and I think it will go on indefinitely." (This statement was accompanied by raucous laughter from most of the Adventists present.) "What Dr. Douglass does in this book—it's heretical. Several years ago he would have been tried for heresy. And not only that, but Dr. Douglass enters into philosophical nonsense when he seeks to posit a sinful nature apart from sinful deeds."

Seventh-day Adventists are quite used to pastors of other faiths totally misunderstanding their Bible-based presentation. There is a long tradition of this, but the response of the 150–200 Seventh-day Adventist lay people and eight Seventh-day Adventist ministers present was less to be expected. Ray Martin stated after the meeting that all pastors, and 90–95% of the lay people present, totally supported Paxton's demeaning attack upon our Church! Martin asserted that "One minister present told a fellow minister that the only thing wrong with the Rev. Paxton was that he was telling the truth." (*Adventist News Service*, 2)

The pastor of the Nunawading Seventh-day Adventist Church prefaced a question to Paxton by stating, "Well, Brother Paxton, I'll express my appreciation for what you have presented, for coming all this way to talk to us. I think it has stimulated our thinking beyond measure."

The senior elder of the same church, taking courage from his pastor, asserted, "I have been present at both of your addresses and I must admit that reluctantly I have to agree with much of what you have said." Some of those present held positions of high trust in the Seventh-day Adventist Church. One held a Division appointment and another a Union appointment, one was attached to the Warburton Health Care Centre, yet not one of these offered a single word of protest and were among those whom Martin claimed supported Paxton's attack on our Church. Nevertheless throughout the entire four hours occupied by Paxton's two discourses, not once did he open the Word of God. It is a simple matter to destroy Adventism if the criterion of truth is the word of theologians. But what a difference it is when the law and the testimony are substituted as the criteria for truth. It is little wonder that the concerned brethren in Australia were crying and sighing for the abominations in the Church.

Paxton even resorted to direct untruths in order to disparage the *Quarterly*. He maintained that Douglass attempted to show in the lesson that "Jesus was a sinner." Since no sane Seventh-day Adventist has ever made such a blasphemous claim, Paxton's failure to cite proof was perfectly understandable. In the *Quarterly* Douglass had stated, "We can never say it often enough—Jesus never sinned in thought or deed." (*Sabbath School Quarterly*, second quarter, 1977). Yet not a single pastor corrected this pathetic falsehood which was inexcusable since, as we have seen, Douglass specifically stated the converse.

Unlike Paxton's message, the Adventist faith is founded firmly on the Word of God. His near-blasphemous attack on Seventh-day Adventist testimony meetings as being equivalent to the veneration of the saints is once again without scriptural backing.

> Oh that men would praise the LORD for his goodness, and for his wonderful works to the children of men! Let them exalt him also in the congregation of the people, and praise him in the assembly of the elders. (Psalm 107:31,32)

It is this command of the Lord which Adventists humbly and faithfully follow in their testimony meetings. Let theologians pontificate as they please, but loyal Adventists will continue to follow a plain "Thus saith the Lord." As with Ford and

Brinsmead, Paxton did not offer a single text of Scripture to support his contention that a belief in sanctification as part of the gospel, and part of righteousness by faith, is Catholic. Once again the reason for this missing text was perfectly explicable. It is as difficult to find that text as it is to find the one enjoining Sunday sanctity. The Bible clearly distinguishes between what God sees as Catholic and the faith of His true followers. Speaking of the little-horn power (Roman Catholicism) God states:

> And he shall speak great words against the most High, and shall wear out the saints of the most High, and think to change times and laws; and they shall be given into his hand until a time and times and the dividing of time. (Daniel 7:25)

Here is God's elucidation of what He sees as evil in Catholicism. Is it not strange that one facet of Catholicism God specifies is the changing of His law, yet those upholding God's law were termed "Catholic" by one who subscribed to that major change in the law. Far more tragic was the pitiful gullibility of certain Seventh-day Adventist pastors and lay people who, failing to request the plain "Thus saith the Lord," accepted such errors. Such men and women need our earnest prayers.

Somewhat ironic was the fact that the week prior to Paxton's meeting, his own Anglican Archbishop, Dr. Felix Arnott, Archbishop of Brisbane, returned from England where he had been part of a working party of the Anglican Church which had declared that it was not opposed to a union of the Anglican Church with the Roman Catholic Church. This group said that it was fully prepared to accept the pope as supreme head of this united church. Perhaps Paxton would have been better employed trying to help his own people with their genuine Catholic problems. When Dr. Arnott's statement was mentioned to Paxton following his meeting, Paxton merely replied that he had the same respect for Dr. Arnott as he had for many Adventist pastors such as Dr. Douglass and Pastor Wood.

It could have been anticipated that the actions of these Seventh-day Adventist pastors and laymen in supporting Paxton's vicious and largely unfounded attacks upon our Church would have led to the deepest soul-searching by responsible leadership and correction of this public support. Yet when the Conference president received a copy of the letter of protest sent to Pastor Pierson concerning the incident, he was quite caustic in his defense of those who had so let down the Church. It was a strange attitude indeed.

Fortunately the Division president saw the tragedy of the situation and sent a message to the workers in Victoria through Pastor Alfred Jorgensen, field secretary in the Australasian Division. In part Pastor Jorgensen said, "I understand that the Rev. Paxton visited Melbourne a few weeks ago and that a meeting was held at which a number of workers and members were present.... Now Pastor Parmenter [Australasian Division president] told me, authorized me, to say today at this meeting that he felt that we as workers should not patronize meetings of this order where the Adventist Church is likely to come under negative criticism. So I pass this on to the workers' group this afternoon, and Pastor Parmenter will hear what I am saying in due course. I pass on to this workers' group the recommendation of our president that we do not by our presence attend any meetings that are going to undermine in one way or another the confidence of our people in the main. After all, it is only understandable that if our members see us present at meetings of this kind, they will naturally conclude that what is being presented is worthy of their support, and as the Bible said, our Lord Himself said, offences must necessarily come but woe to the man by whom they come. I would hate to be in the shoes of any man who in the Day of Judgment must give account of himself for having been instrumental in any way, even through the influence he has exerted, of turning the feet of any of our dear people out of the way. Our business is to establish them in the faith, not to undermine it. So our counsel to you would be—if meetings of this order should be held in the future that we restrain our presence as an encouragement to our own people not to conclude that we give our support to what is presented on such occasions."

While it was clear that the Australasian Division saw Paxton as a real embarrassment, the mild counsel given to the Victorian workers in private, even failing to mention the fact that some had openly supported Paxton, fell far short of the open condemnation essential to undo the immeasurable harm done by these men. Unfortunately this course of action was in line with the soft words of counsel handed on in private to ministers openly denying the truth of God and giving support to those who attacked these truths on other occasions. This procedure often contrasted with the harsh condemnation at times made public, of the Concerned Brethren.

# 45 General Conference Youth Leader Condemned

PASTOR Dick Barron, associate youth leader at the General Conference, spent three months in Australia during the early part of 1977. He was a guest speaker along with Dr. Ford and Pastor Morris Venden, pastor of Pacific Union College Church, at the Trans-Tasman Union Youth Congress in New Zealand. Pastor Barron had ample opportunity to listen to Dr. Ford's preaching. Further, he used his spare time speaking to the youth and thus was able to gauge the effect of the *new theology* upon the youth of the Australasian Division. It is perhaps sufficient to record that Pastor Barron made a most perceptive analysis of the serious doctrinal situation in Australasia and reported his findings to Pastor Pierson on his return to the United States.

Undoubtedly nothing served more to bring matters to a head than Pastor Barron's disgraceful reception at the Victorian Conference camp meeting held in January, 1977. He preached a most powerful sermon on Christian standards to the youth on the final Friday evening of the camp. Among other matters, he appealed for true Sabbath observance and dress reform. At the conclusion of the service Russell sought out Pastor Barron in order to make himself known since Colin, then president of Columbia Union College, was well known to Pastor Barron and had referred to him in his correspondence with Russell. There was no need for introduction, for having sighted Russell Pastor Barron immediately recognized him. Such are the advantages of being an identical twin. Russell expressed appreciation of the message presented. However, within a few minutes Pastor Barron was completely surprised to be surrounded by a group of irate young people protesting against the them of his message. One described it to him as "ninety-eight percent Catholic" (a strange comment on a service inviting greater care in Sabbath observance), another charged that he was "legalistic," and yet a third offered the opinion that "It wasn't the gospel."

To describe Pastor Barron's response as one of amazement is to minimize his reaction. Simultaneously five or six groups of young people, each containing about fifteen or twenty persons, were standing outside the youth tent analyzing the contents of the service in less than complimentary terms. One girl, while still happily claiming to be a born-again Christian, used profane language to present her opinion of Pastor Barron. Pastor Barron, of course, was more than equal to the onslaught. He pointed out that the message he had given he believed was given to him of God.

Eventually one asked of Pastor Barron in sarcastic tone, "Do you think *you're* perfect?"

Russell, who had been standing in silence feeling deep shame that young Australian Seventh-day Adventists would be so downright discourteous to an overseas visitor, felt it was time to speak. He pointed out the improper nature of such a question and suggested that the young people look to the one perfect Man rather than to men. This counsel met with the rude retort, "We're not speaking to you!" Pastor Barron quickly corrected that false claim. When Pastor Barron concluded that nothing he could say would alter the opinion of the young people, he drew himself up to his full six-foot seven-inches height—converting the young people to pygmies by comparison—and commanded the young people to go away since no good purpose could be served in continuing the discussion, and he had to rest for his Sabbath service.

Rest for him, however, was still far off. So disturbed was Pastor Barron over the serious situation evident among the youth that he stayed up until 1:00 a.m. discussing his deep concern with Pastor Malcolm Allen, youth leader of the Victorian Conference. When this sad episode was pointed out to one church leader, he expressed less than deep concern by stating, "If anything less than Christian courtesy was extended to Pastor Barron, it would have been from 'a group' who are, as it were, fringe dwellers as far as the Youth Department and the Church are concerned, and who lack judgment and maturity in both conduct and theology." (Letter written to Dr. Standish dated Feb. 10, 1977) While one cannot deny that this analysis of the young people concerned was correct, it should be pointed out that a number of these were Avondale College theology students and at least one was an Adventist high school teacher.

Pastor Barron's receipt of abuse was not confined to the Victorian Conference. For instance, in Sydney one young minister told him that he had done immeasurable harm to the young people by his preaching. Fortunately in the Greater Sydney Conference stronger action was taken and the Conference president, Pastor Bullock, at least rebuked the young worker.

On Pastor Barron's return to Washington, the General Conference did not view the rudeness as benignly as some had done in Australis. A request for clarification was sent to the Australasian Division, and leaders scurried around for tape recordings of Pastor Barron's sermons in Australia. That Pastor Barron had preached sermons which he had already preached in other parts of the world, to the great blessing of those who listened, only emphasized the pernicious nature of the *new theology*. Little by little the Lord was showing the fruits of the *new theology* to those who wished to know the truth.

# 46 Secret Papers Published

No doubt Robert Brinsmead would have desired to enter directly into the doctrinal controversy within the Church. It appeared, however, that he wished to keep the letter of his undertaking to the General Conference made in 1971 that he would not enter into Adventist Church affairs or attack its leadership. The agreement did not preclude Brinsmead's attack on *Conflicting Concepts* since he saw himself as at least supporting the Australasian Division's cause in this respect, and thus found himself on a popular bandwagon. This situation would have been inconceivable for Brinsmead a decade earlier.

The *Present Truth* organization, however, seemed very anxious to capitalize on the current controversy within the Church. With his promise to leave the Church alone, no doubt another way had to be found. A gentleman by the name of Jack D. Walker from a town incredibly bearing the name of Goodlettsville in Tennessee filled the breach. The *Present Truth* organization had a scoop which it was eager to publish—Dr. Ford's three Palmdale papers together with Dr. Alwyn Salom's Palmdale paper. Walker wrote a letter advertising his desire to spread these papers far and wide. This letter was not posted from Tennessee, but from the *Present Truth* headquarters in Fallbrook, California. The use of Walker, who in all probability was unknown both to Ford and Salom, as a front man, made it possible for him to write in strict honesty, "I want to make it clear that I am publishing these papers without the author's permission, knowledge or consent, and I thereby take full responsibility for doing this. The papers were not obtained from Australia, but they are already in limited circulation in North America."

This disclaimer was yet another of the little word games devised to cover up the fact that Ford had given a copy of his presentation to Brinsmead prior to the Palmdale meeting. Since Brinsmead had assisted Ford in the preparation, it was not unexpected that he should be provided with a copy. Somehow the Australasian Division wished to enter into this game of words, for when the Division spokesman was instructing the ministry in Victoria concerning the approach they should take to the *Sabbath School Quarterly*, he stated, "Well, Walker has since decided that he's going to publish the Palmdale papers. Now, fortunately in his advertising he pointed out that he didn't get them from Australia. Oh, I was so delighted to read that. So I wrote over to the General Conference president and asked him what he knew about it and he assures me that there has been no release of Palmdale papers in the United States. I wrote to my good friend, Des Ford, and asked him what he knew about it. Had he seen the present papers in Australia and he said, "Yes," and he told me they were not complete, and then he went on to point out—Dr. Ford went on to point out—what he used of mine was indeed written by me some considerable time before Palmdale itself and certainly well before we gave any promise about not distributing any of the materials. Some of my materials were out both here and in America before we were ever required to give that consent regarding restraint." (Meeting held in Victoria, March 5, 1977) It would have been far simpler and clearer had the speaker simply stated the fact that Dr. Ford made the papers available to the *Present Truth* organization prior to Palmdale. It is obvious that Dr. Ford joined the others at Palmdale in giving assurances that there would be no distribution of the papers presented. Surprisingly he failed to mention that at the time of his promise the papers were already in the hands of some not privy to the Palmdale discussions.

The wisdom of refusing to provide all papers presented at Palmdale for serious study by God's people must be questioned. Obviously it was felt that this action was necessary to prevent an escalation of the division coming into the Church. In reality it simply meant that some of those papers promoting error were widely read, while, to our knowledge, the papers of men protecting the truth have still not been released. This incident again illustrated the oft-demonstrated fact that only truth was silenced while error was proclaimed virtually unchallenged.

Walker continued to print material concerning the doctrinal controversy. His next pamphlet was written by Ray Martin[1] and was entitled, *Objective Digest Report* and subtitled *What Is Happening in Australia?* While this paper was clearly slanted to the *new theology*, its basic fairness could not be denied. Of course Martin did include some statements worthy of denial. For example, he stated that "Dr. Ford . . . is widely acknowledged by friends and foes as perhaps the most outstanding scholar in Adventism today." (*Objective Digest Report*, 1) While the term "foe" was far too strong a term, those disturbed by Dr. Ford's theology saw far too many easily demonstrable weaknesses in it to concur with such a standing among Adventist theologians. A man who time after time has been demonstrated to have misrepresented the clearest words of Scripture could hardly be afforded such a stature.

Another piece of information in the manuscript was Martin's referral to a K.F.O. (Kick Ford Out) Committee. (*Ibid.*, 3) No such committee existed. Martin also used considerable hyperbole when he stated, referring to John Clifford and Russell, "The two doctors are triumphantly waving two letters of endorsement from America—a very favourable one from *Review* editor, Kenneth Wood, and a cautiously favourable one from G. C. President Robert Pierson." (*Ibid.*, 6) In fact, the authors never entertained the possibility of anything less than support from these leaders in God's Church, for they were perfectly well aware of their strong stand for truth.

Nevertheless in most areas Martin's reports were correct. The whole crux of the situation was nicely expressed by Martin, "One thing is clear, a new Adventism is emerging from Australia, and its shape is now quickly visible. Some see it as the destruction of all that Adventism has stood for and as the omega of apostasy, while others see it as the beginning of that truth which will lighten the earth with the glory of God and believe that at least Adventism has come of age." (*Ibid.* 7).[2]

Perhaps the greatest matter of concern to those standing for truth was the often expressed, but never previously written, thought, "Some of the young ministers in Australia are becoming impatient and often repeat Froom's famous saying, "We need more funerals to get Adventism going." (*Ibid.*, 8) As one very much alive pastor[3] commented, "We old fellows must be a great disappointment. We're just too dense to catch on to their desires." Perhaps another pastor summed up the feelings of most when he wrote that Martin's statement was "dreadful."

Shortly following the *Objective Digest Report* Walker published another short paper by Ray Martin entitled, *Adventist News Service*. This paper dealt with the controverted *Sabbath School Quarterly* and the ugly reaction to it in Australia. Martin's major complaint stated that "At the Palmdale concord the leaders of the Church appealed for unity and requested that differences on righteousness by faith not be agitated in such a way as to cause division in the Church. But it now appears that the brethren have ignored their own advice, for in publishing the Douglass *Lesson Quarterly*, they have shown that their sympathies are with those who advocate perfectionism and the sinful nature of Christ. They are doing this in spite of the opposition of their leading theologians in Australia and at Andrews University and the opposition of many ministers and lay people." (*Adventist News Service*, 2)

Once again an altogether undue emphasis was being placed upon the opinion of theologians as if that were the last word on truth. It was quite evident from the abundant material provided by this manuscript that the theologians mentioned above had introduced considerable error and provided little light.

### Chapter 46 Endnotes

1. Of course no relation to Dr. Walter Martin; Ray Martin is an Australian.
2. The passage of time has certainly shown which view was correct.
3. Pastor George Burnside

# 47 The Gathering Storm

"DO not suppose that this is the end. This is only the beginning of the reckoning. This is only the first sip, the first foretaste of a bitter cup which will be proffered to us year by year unless by a supreme recovery of moral health and martial vigour, we arise again and take our stand for freedom as in the olden times." (Winston Churchill, *Into Battle*, 53) So stated Britain's wartime leader on October 5, 1938, just eleven months prior to the commencement of hostilities in the Second World War.

For Europe, the 1930s was a time of crisis. Appeasement was the policy of the day. Undoubtedly Adolph Hitler could have been turned aside if decisive action had been taken the moment he reoccupied the Ruhr without allied consent. Europe should have braced itself also at the time of his conquest of the southern Germans of Austria and prevented aged Jews from scrubbing the wintered roadways of Vienna. Many of these poor souls were overtaken by the chilly exposure, the burden of years, the torment of mind, and the crippling infirmities of the body. Large numbers found death the only solace in a life so utterly miserable that death alone gave promise of hope. If Hitler had been challenged even at that time, the pernicious thrust toward global conflict could have been stayed. But Europe claimed peace as its inheritance and even injustice, genocide, and the unlawful expansion by armed might did not arouse in most people the awareness that such acts were inimical to their delusions of peace and security.

Churchill, of course, was expressing his assessment of the series of appeasement conferences held at Berchtesgaden, Godesberg, and finally Munich. The passage of time was to fully justify Churchill's prophecy, for this truly was "only the beginning of reckoning" for Europe. Yet those who perceptively weighed the obvious evidence at hand were subjected to criticism of the most malicious nature. Their very motives were challenged, as if their detractors had access to the inner recesses of their consciousness. It was an unpopular stand, but it was right. Only six months prior to the war an opinion poll found only seven percent of Churchill's fellow Britons regarded him as a suitable successor to Mr. Neville Chamberlain as the holder of the highest office of the crown in the United Kingdom (H. Cantril, *Public Opinion*, 1935–46, 195) [1]

In the Seventh-day Adventist Church of the sixties and the seventies we faced an era Churchillian in its qualities. The majority of members had so valued peace and unity that it had been felt prudent to ignore or minimize the gathering storm. Many church members had been cognizant of an enemy within. They disliked it, but had not summoned either the "moral health" or the "martial vigour" to venture forth in battle. It was inexpedient and unpopular to do so. The "peace party" had been in power, and to cry aloud making a call to arms had been a sure-fire method of attracting ecclesiastical ostracism.

But now is the day to hold aloft the sword of the Spirit rather than Munich-like treaties of consensus. We have had our Munichs which have only led to the emboldening of those intent on increasing their territorial grip upon the Church. "The bitter cup" has been "proffered to us year by year." Just as the latter half of the 1930s saw the Ruhr takeover accepted, the enforced union of Austria with Germany condoned, the acquisition of Sudetenland exonerated, and the military occupation of Bohemia meekly countenanced, so Seventh-day Adventists, alert to the ruthless destruction of one doctrinal province after another, have found their earnest cries to halt the insatiable onslaught given interpretations entirely alien to their motives.

Had decisive action been taken after "the first sip," how few then would have been the casualties. Make no mistake, men of courage moved by the Holy Spirit will call forth the armies of the Lord and will stand firm where their predecessors have retreated. But where once there might have been rescue of all but the weakest of the weak, then will be salvaged none but the strongest of the strong.

This ever-thrusting evil will not be stayed by assurances that all is well, that the situation is not grave, or by attempts to find non-existent common grounds, such as calls for unity among the irrevocably disunited. Such calls only encourage the advance of error which shows no hesitancy in its steady onslaught against truth. It advances from the Ruhr to Austria, to Sudetenland, to Bohemia, while the cries of "Halt!" are lost on the ears of those who could, and should act decisively to stem a tide of evil, which will place no limitations upon its own encroachments. Must God's people await a climactic Polish invasion before a full-blown effort to throw back this wave after wave of error is initiated? Each delay, each accommodation of those bent on replacing firmly established doctrinal positions with those of an alien character involves human losses. Not loss of life as in a battlefield, but loss of everlasting life. Can we dare to trade the eternal destinies of our college-aged youth while carefully skirting the advances of those whose loyalties are most certainly foreign to Seventh-day Adventists? Will such an awful price be justified in hindsight?

Each erroneous doctrine condoned has proved to be "only the beginning of the reckoning." The purveyors of the *new theology* have not halted with each doctrinal defection. They have taken those whom they have conquered step by step along the road of error. There has been no cessation of hostilities since they have established their beachhead on the date of creation week. They have advanced relentlessly in attacking the doctrine of the sanctuary, in weakening the defenses of scriptural and

Spirit of Prophecy inerrancy, in placing smoke screens over biblical prophetic interpretations, and finally, in encouraging a complete loss of the will to resist temptation by disdaining obedience to the law of the Almighty. And so this army continues to attack from within, creating an effective fifth column within the ranks of those claiming to be citizens of heaven. Such attacks, when from without, have been nobly and effectively countered in the past with little loss of life.

Having established subversive elements within, the leaders of this group have formed unholy alliances with the emissaries of other churches, churches long known to be at enmity with the truth of God. Yet so beguiled have some become that they retain no sense of the mortal dangers of such federations, and have even hailed them as if God Himself would approve.

No longer can an indulgent Church slumber on in Laodicean complacency. The call is to arms. The King calls out for volunteers. There will not be a single conscript in this army. All volunteers must pass a stringent medical test to determine the presence of "moral health and martial vigour." Their leaders must meet this advancing evil alliance head on. First, present positions must be held, and then lost ground reclaimed until there is unconditional surrender of the "enemy." Then it will be said that we have taken "our stand for freedom as in the olden times."

# ADVENTISM CHALLENGED

Book Two

# The Storm Bursts

Russell R. Standish
Founder, Remnant Ministry

Colin D. Standish
President, Hartland Institute

Published and Distributed by
Hartland Publications
Box 1
Rapidan, Virginia 22733, U.S.A.

# 48 Nineteen Fifty-Six Revisited

IN August, 1977, Geoffrey Paxton published his book entitled *The Shaking of Adventism*. Before reviewing its contents, the authors wish to insert a statement which was written by Russell fifteen months prior to the publication of Paxton's book. This statement was not published at the time, but it does reflect Russell's thinking then.

In 1976, Paxton's influence in the doctrinal crisis was far less important than it subsequently became. Before we quote from this paper, it should be noted that Ray Martin announced that Paxton's book was read by Ford prior to its publication and that Ford gave advice. Further, some of the material was researched by Brinsmead. Thus, the fact that the private doctrinal dispute in the Church was distributed for all to read, was not the fault of Paxton alone. This fact disturbed many.

Russell's paper shared the same title as this chapter: "Several years ago, I was appointed as a physician to Penang Adventist Hospital in Malaysia. On one occasion my family and I entertained a doctor and his wife,[1] who had previously spent eleven years at the hospital in similar service. It was obviously a time of nostalgia for the visiting couple. We were entertaining them in *our* home, but it had been *theirs* three years before. We were bringing up three sons; so had they. We discussed many of the joys and a few of the problems we were encountering. Suddenly, as we lazed in the tropical splendor of Penang, the doctor exclaimed, "I see it all! I've been through it all before. The plots are the same, Russ, only the actors on the stage change."

"In 1976, there is a repeat of the 1956 'play.' True, most of the principal actors have changed, but the plot is strikingly similar. The 1956 'play' to which I refer is the Barnhouse-Martin episode which so destroyed our Church's purpose that it has taken twenty years to recover. In that year a young man decided to write a thesis on Adventist doctrines. He planned to submit it for a higher degree. That man was Walter Martin. He was an evangelical theologian and was sponsored by the editor of one of the most influential evangelical magazines in the United States—*Eternity* magazine. The editor was the late Donald Barnhouse.

"Martin met a receptive Church. Two factors dominated this situation. Firstly, the church leadership and many of the laity were proud of the newly established scholarship of our theologians at our universities and colleges. It was easy for them to accept the advice of these men of learning as they struggled to redefine our faith. Secondly, these theologians had, almost without exception, obtained their scholastic achievements at evangelical institutions and many were thus partial to theologians and theologies of that section of the Christian church.

"Perhaps a third factor, permeating the Church as a whole, should be emphasized. This was the desire of large sections of our membership for approval from the evangelical wing of Protestantism.

"The sum total of these factors was a decided masking of a number of our distinctive doctrines and an emphasizing of those doctrines which we held in common with the evangelicals. In return, Barnhouse proclaimed in his magazine that we were no longer a cult but 'part of the body of Christ.' Far from causing the alarm this statement should have caused to Seventh-day Adventists, it produced a period of euphoria, punctuated only by the godly voices of men like the late Pastor M. L. Andreasen, who stood up boldly for the truth once delivered to the saints. Oh, that the Church had heeded his God-inspired concern!

"It has taken two decades for the 1956 apostasy to be reversed.[2] It has taken a whole new administration in the General Conference and a fresh editorship of the *Review and Herald* and *Ministry* magazines. The *Review and Herald Special* on Righteousness by Faith was a real milestone in the reversal of the Church's drift towards evangelical Protestantism. The Sabbath School Lessons have been written by dedicated men, directing the hearts of the believers back to the distinctive doctrines of the old Adventist faith.

"In the present revival of truth, it would be anticipated that the arch-opponent of God's last message to sinners would wish to reverse the trend. How better than by the device so effective in 1956?

"Thus, a young theologian has again been brought to the stage— Geoffrey Paxton, an Australian Anglican pastor. He, too, is writing a thesis on Seventh-day Adventists, and he, too, has gone to Andrews University and the General Conference, in order to gather material for his thesis. He, too, is backed by the editor of one of the most influential evangelical magazines in the United States—*Present Truth*. The editor of this magazine is Robert Brinsmead. Paxton, too, intends to publish his findings. He, too, has found a ready reception of his un-biblical views by some church theologians. He proudly quotes some of these as accepting a similar view to his own. These men, significantly, have all received their training in the schools of evangelical Protestantism.

"The plot of the 1976 'play' is uncanny in its exactitude of the 1956 plot. But today there are marked differences in the audience and the producers. In 1956, virtually the total Church slept through the performance and only awoke to applaud at the end. In 1956, the producers of the 'play' were so enamoured with the skills of the actors, the applause of the audience and the favourable write-ups received, that they failed to examine the reliability of the script.

"Today, in the General Conference leadership, we have men who have taken time to read the 1956 script and compare it with the original. They have noted marked deviations. Today, these leaders are less interested in the applause of the laity and more concerned with awakening the laity to hear the original and verified version. Today, we have a ministry and laity which, while still a minority voice, are not prepared to accept the new version.

"This has become evident in the new leading man—Geoffrey Paxton. He is now constrained to state that he found the theologians receptive to his false doctrine, but found that the present General Conference leadership was not. He was prepared to state that our theologians were in conflict with pioneers of the Adventist faith, such as Waggoner, Daniells and Spicer.

"The Lord, in His mercy, has once again set His Church at the crossroads. The same false elements are present within the Church. But the Lord has given us more evidence. For example, Dr. Ford's open apostasy on such significant doctrines as the inspiration of Scripture, the Sanctuary, the age of the earth and prophetic interpretation, has placed him in a position where any true Adventist should at least suspect his false stand on Righteousness by Faith. The continuous error which has flowed from some of our colleges and universities over the last two decades in such magazines as *Spectrum*, though somewhat reversed by wiser selection of academic personnel, has alerted our people to the fact that the criterion of truth is the law and the testimony—not the thinking of Adventist theologians.

"But there are dangers nevertheless. Many ministers and even some in leading positions are favouring the present departure from the faith. Further, this whole matter is about to be discussed in the United States [this was a reference to the Palmdale Conference of 1976]. A number of the men who have been called to this Conference have muted their concern for the inroads of the *new theology*, and some have actively supported Dr. Ford's position. There has been a repeated refusal to include the very men whose concern has led to these meetings. Further, even two of the delegates selected by the General Conference to this meet, it has been asserted by Geoffrey Paxton, confided to him that they are in harmony with the present views of Dr. Ford on Righteousness by Faith.

"Surely this is a time of great crisis. Once again the Lord has brought His message forcibly before us. The question is: Whither shall we go— back to 1956, or on to Glory?"

Chapter 48 Endnotes

1. Dr. and Mrs. Brian Hammond
2. This has subsequently proved to be an all-too-optimistic assessment.

# 49
## The Shaking of Adventism

A very few airmailed copies of Geoffrey Paxton's book, *The Shaking of Adventism*, reached Australia in early October, 1977. The book was a published version of Paxton's Master of Arts thesis, which was submitted to the University of Queensland Department of Religion.

It was quite obvious to both the cursory and careful readers of Paxton's book that much of the material must have been fed to him by persons close to the center of Adventism. It was most unlikely that any non-Adventist could have without this assistance been privy to some of the details presented. Presumably those assisting Paxton saw him as a useful vehicle for casting doubt upon Adventist doctrine.

A reading of this book left an inescapable impression upon many. The conviction grew that Geoffrey Paxton had set himself up to sit in judgment upon the doctrines of the Seventh-day Adventist Church, particularly in respect to righteousness by faith, by himself imposing a premise upon the Church. His premise was stated in a few words:

"The hallmark of the Protestant Reformation doctrine of Righteousness by Faith" is "no perfection in the believer until the second advent of Christ." (*The Shaking of Adventism*, 105)

This dangerous thesis, which has its foundation in the religion of Babylon and most other pagan religions and which was introduced into the Christian church by a "converted" pagan—Augustine—in the fifth century of the Christian era, has no foundation in the Bible whatsoever. Despite this fact, Paxton asserted that when Dr. Edward Heppenstall became "the first [Seventh-day Adventist] to openly advocate" (*ibid*.) the anti-perfection view, he was making doctrinal progress for the Seventh-day Adventist Church and assisting in fulfilling its claim to be the inheritors of the Reformation. However, in Paxton's view, when "Herbert Douglass . . . emerged in the 1970s as the one who is seeking to make the Andreasen-Branson perfectionism dominate in Adventist thinking" (*ibid*. 126), and when, in addition, this theme was taken up by Kenneth Wood, editor of the *Review*, and Robert Pierson, president of the General Conference, they were beating a retreat from the Reformation faith.

One would hope that a Christian would not put forth such a premise as Paxton's, without providing a plain "thus saith the Lord." If Paxton had found such a text in Holy Writ, he certainly did not divulge it to his readers. Rather, he somewhat naively assumed that his readers would accept his criterion on the basis of his personal assurance that "The Reformers contended that *the believer is righteous in this life only by faith.*" (*Ibid.* 46, italics in original) On the other hand, the author claimed that "Perfectionism in this life is a major aspect of the gospel of the church of Rome." (*Ibid.*, 47)

Interestingly, Paxton attempted to confirm this assertion by quoting from the conclusions of the Council of Trent. "If anyone denies, that, by the grace of our Lord Jesus Christ, which is conferred in baptism, the guilt of original sin is remitted, or says that the whole of that which has the true and proper nature of sin is not taken away . . . let him be anathema." (Leith, *Creeds of the Churches*, 407, quoted in *The Shaking of Adventism*, 47) Since Paxton in his book accuses Seventh-day Adventists of a disbelief in the doctrine of original sin (and he is quite correct in this assertion), it is curious that he uses the Roman Catholic concept that the guilt of original sin is remitted at baptism (thus necessitating infant baptism), to prove that Adventists accept other Roman Catholic concepts. This example is typical of Paxton's fuzzy thinking in this area. It is rather surprising that one of his University examiners did not notice the irony of this faulty type of "proof-texting."

Paxton's effort to align Adventist teachings with the edicts of the Council of Trent failed for lack of evidence. The Council of Trent spent a major portion of its time debating sacramentalism. The question of whether or not the so-called "sacred sacraments," seven in number, of the Roman Catholic Church were essential to salvation was heatedly discussed. The final conclusion of the Council was in the affirmative. To link the biblical concept of sanctification accepted by Seventh-day Adventists with the Roman Catholic doctrine of the sacraments, displays a shallow, indeed false, reasoning.

Paxton's book attempted to stress the dichotomy that Reformational Protestantism believes perfection will not occur until the Second Coming of Christ, while Roman Catholicism teaches the need for perfection now. Noting that the Seventh-day Adventist Church early proclaimed that commandment-keeping was possible under the power of the Holy Spirit and that indeed it was an essential condition of salvation, Paxton sees our Church as "Off to an Inauspicious Start." (*Ibid.*, Title of Chapter 3) On the other hand, when the Church, following the Barnhouse-Martin dialogue, commenced the path of rejection of this Bible-based concept, Paxton visualized the Seventh-day Adventist Church as "Off to an Auspicious Start." (*Ibid.*, Title to Chapter 5) How Paxton could overlook the almost inexhaustible number of direct testimonies of Scripture demanding obedience to God's law, one cannot imagine. At one point he rather unnecessarily admonishes that "we must beware of being holier than Paul." (*Ibid.*, 47) Rather, he should be exhorting us to be no less holy than Paul; but even more to the point, he should have directed his readers to the one true example—Christ; as Paul himself did:

> Husbands, love your wives, even as Christ also loved the church, and gave himself for it; that he might sanctify and cleanse it with the washing of water by the word, that he might present it to himself a glorious church, not having spot, or wrinkle, or any such thing; but that it should be holy and without blemish. (Ephesians 5:25–27)

Here, Paul is not speaking of imputed holiness. The term *sanctify*[1] excluded that. This text is a beautiful illustration of perfection in God's people. Geoffrey Paxton may not wish to include Paul among his category of Roman Catholics, but unless he does, it would seem to be discriminatory to have designated Seventh-day Adventists as such for accepting Paul's teaching, as it so clearly reads. The truth is, that there is absolutely no biblical basis for the Paxton premise, nor for the dichotomy he postulates. It was at this very point that the total structure of his thesis collapsed.

This assessment is not to suggest that Paxton's work was entirely worthless. The authors have viewed his book from two perspectives—first, as Seventh-day Adventists jealous of the reputation of their Church; and second, as Seventh-day Adventists deeply concerned over the drift toward the *new theology* within their Church. From the first standpoint, we are saddened that so much of the Church's doctrinal discord has been aired outside of church ranks. Most Seventh-day Adventists, loyal to their Church, have not been afraid to discuss their concerns with their brethren and sisters, but have stopped short of informing their good friends outside the Church of what is essentially an internal problem. Such members, true to the Adventist faith, believe that the Seventh-day Adventist Church has the most significant message ever given to sinful man, and that this message must be taken worldwide. It seems that such a message supported only by a portion of its adherents would lose a great deal of its dynamism. Yet we do not underestimate God's power to turn evil to good. It may be that He will use this growing awareness of His truth, among those of other doctrinal persuasions, as one significant way to bring the issue before the world.

From the second standpoint, Geoffrey Paxton has made some telling observations. It has been fascinating for the authors to read some of these in relation to material that is presented in Book One of this volume.[2]

Because of what has been written in the first book, it is interesting to note that Paxton suggested (in the authors' view quite correctly), "It may be that the conflict with Brinsmead [in the 1960s] was so fierce, that Dr. Heppenstall's radical deviation from traditional Adventism was able to pass unchallenged." (*The Shaking of Adventism*, 106) He went on to say, "Dr. Desmond Ford and Pastor L. C. Naden [3] were among others who adopted the new approach to perfectionism against the Brinsmead teaching." (*Ibid.*)

A second point made by Paxton is well taken. Those loyal church members who noticed the tragic doctrinal swing of the 1950s and 1960s toward what is now termed the *new theology* were greatly encouraged by the reversal of the leadership of the

Seventh-day Adventist Church in the 1970s, in adopting the return to the Bible-based doctrines of the Church.

However, just as the Church of the 1950s steadfastly refused to acknowledge to its members that a major doctrinal change was being foisted upon them, so, too, there had been a reticence on the part of many to acknowledge, in public, either by writing or by word of mouth, that there was a return toward the Adventist truth of the 1970s. Of course, in private, much has been acknowledged, but public representations have been accompanied by a deafening silence. This fact has caused much confusion in the Church. It is surely time that our brethren in positions of responsibility wrested the initiative from the theologians and from those who would attack our Church, and admitted quite plainly that in the last quarter of a century, there have been some quite violent doctrinal movements within our Church.

Unfortunately, today many good members have become so confused that they now throw up their hands in despair and offer their ignorance of God's truth as a virtue, for it removes them from the arena of doctrinal controversy. Others, including ministers, have adopted as a means of self preservation, the posture of following the current view as accepted by the majority of those around them. This attitude has meant that they have had to change their doctrinal beliefs from time to time, but this need has been less disturbing to them than having to defend the truth of God when it has been under attack. For them the scorn of their peers is more to be avoided than the wrath of God.[4] Thus Paxton could truthfully state, "*Not one word of public acknowledgment concerning this about-face has come from the leadership of the church.* There is only astounding silence about the fact that what was opposed in the 1960s is now embraced. Why the lack of candor? Is the leadership *able* to truly repent?" (*Ibid.*, 153. Italics in original)

These questions are perfectly fair. They are matters to which those of us within the ranks of workers of God must address ourselves. It may be that because of this silence there has been a tendency for many in the eighties to drift back to the position of the 1950s and 1960s. Perhaps the reason for this silence is that there is a fear some will lose faith in the Church if such an admission is made. But, in reality, it would only strengthen confidence in the leaders of God's Church. Another reason for this failure to speak clearly of the changes is that there is so much pressure, particularly from one segment of our theologians, that many feel they do not wish to create a storm within the Church. However, the record of silence in settling controversies is a very poor one indeed.

Over eighteen months before Paxton's book appeared, Russell wrote to Pastor Pierson the following: "One matter greatly concerns me. As you will hear as you listen to the tapes (of the February 3 and 4, 1976, Australian Biblical Research Institute meetings), over and over again Dr. Ford was able, as we knew he would be, to state with truth that other denominational writers have previously presented the errors he espoused. With one or two exceptions, all these writers appeared in denominational literature after the Barnhouse-Martin episode in 1956. Brother Pierson, we are fully aware that your administration has taken great pains to rectify the compromise with evangelical Protestantism, which led to many serious errors creeping into our denominational literature. This fact is widely known and well understood in this country [Australia]. However, many men, of whom I am one, believe that the General Conference will only be successful in its aims of restoring the truth, if its leadership takes the unprecedented step of acknowledging the reforms which it is instituting and has instituted in the past. Only then will it be impossible to pass off unscriptural errors as standard Adventist belief."[5]

When Paxton laid these doctrinal charges there for all, both within and without God's Church, to see, there should have been no further grounds for reluctance in declaring truth to be truth and error to be error, admitting our past mistakes and pressing forward with the presentation of truth. We did deny some of our basic truths in the 1950s and 1960s and we must be sufficiently forthright and honest to admit it. We have now, under God's mercy, acknowledged truth once more and our people deserve to know why. The steady drift away from truth, which is becoming evident again in the 1980s, will be halted only if such acknowledgments are made. If Paxton's book had led to the Church becoming more open concerning the doctrinal variations, his work would have accomplished some good, despite all the error and unfounded charges it contained.

Paxton, himself, had not been perfectly balanced in his evaluation of his source material. To say as he does, "When justification and sanctification are synthesized . . . *sanctification becomes the predominant emphasis over justification*," (*The Shaking of Adventism*, 135, italics in original) is just plain wrong. This relationship is not an automatic cause and effect as he asserted. To quote two or three Adventist writers, who have taken an extreme view of sanctification, in no wise proves Paxton's point. The vast majority of Seventh-day Adventists believe both justification and sanctification to be mandatory conditions of salvation. Neither is of value without the other. Indeed, neither is in the least possible without the other. The authors of this book would be considerably disturbed if any chose to interpret their belief that sanctification is an integral part of the gospel and of righteousness by faith, as in any way underestimating the significance of justification. Let it be repeated again, lest any should so misinterpret us: justification by faith is essential to salvation at the commencement of one's Christian experience and throughout the Christian life. It is never subjugated to sanctification, nor, on the other hand, is it ever of greater significance than sanctification. Justification and sanctification are of equal relevance, simply because a lack of sanctification (obedience to God's law) cancels the saving effect of justification. Further, a lack of confession and repentance (the prerequisites for God's justification of a person) never permits sanctification to occur and equally leads to loss of eternal life.

Paxton clearly revealed that the leading exponents of the *new theology* have introduced doctrines contrary to those of the Seventh-day Adventist Church. He stated: "It is obvious that, while there are some encouraging aspects in Adventism's

## The Shaking of Adventism

articulation of the Reformation gospel in the 1960s, the real theological gains of the decade are to be found in the affirmation of original sin and the repudiation of perfection in this life. This significant advance appears in the theology of such men as Edward Heppenstall, Desmond Ford and H. K. LaRondelle." (*Ibid.*, 119) It is more than significant that not only did Ford lead the theology department at Australia's only senior college, but also that both the other named men were sent to conduct Summer Schools of Theology in Australia. In such a small denominational environment, it is little wonder that so many began to "see green when they were shown purple." With no other theology departments in the country, it was clear that much greater care was required to ensure that error was not brought to Australia. This statement applies also to many other countries.

Many who have read Paxton's book wish to know why much greater care was not taken to preserve the faith once given to the saints. They want to know why Ford was so avidly sponsored to preach his views contrary to those of the Seventh-day Adventist Church, and why his errors were so widely printed in our publications, including those which were prepared for believers of other faiths. Naturally, many want to know why such changed views were introduced without a single word of acknowledgment, without consultation with any church body, nor with the approval of the General Conference in session. Surely there is a need to make much more effort to see that devious errors are not introduced into the Church by back-door techniques. No longer do the holders of the new theology conceal the fact that they wish to destroy the old faith and supersede it with their theology. Ford made this aim clear after Palmdale. "For a time after Palmdale, it was not clear to what extent the representatives from the *Review and Herald* supported Ford's position that righteousness by faith equals justification alone. But Ford was confident that this was the predominant concession at Palmdale, and he said it was a 'first' in the history of the Seventh-day Adventists." (*Ibid.*, 130, 131)

Paxton paid some attention to the teachings of the book *Conflicting Concepts*. He stated: "This teaching of Douglass and *Conflicting Concepts* is an unprecedented high in Adventist perfectionism." (*Ibid.*, 144) Upon what basis he formed this judgment, Paxton did not enlighten the reader. It will be noted that he used the emotive term *perfectionism* over and over again. His usage of this false term was in order to disparage that which was written. It seems necessary to distinguish once more between the biblical doctrine of *perfection* and the erroneous doctrine of perfection*ism*, which no true Seventh-day Adventist espouses. Perfectionism teaches that a person reaches obedience to the infinite will of God at the moment of his conversion and that for all future time, he is incapable of sinning. Paxton knew that no sane Seventh-day Adventist has ever put forward such an absurd and nonscriptural doctrine. Thus, his use of the term *perfectionism* was inexcusable. Either it reflected poorly on his understanding of the matter, or, alternatively, it was a deliberate "straw man" tactic.

On the other hand, the Adventist view of perfection is that God empowers men to obey all that He has revealed to them. This revelation increases as the Christian grows in his faith. Of course, it is possible to become a backslider and even to lose eternity. Others will sincerely repent and salvation will be theirs. This is Christian perfection, the doctrine taught by Scripture. Yet, virtually, every person cited by Paxton as upholding the Seventh-day Adventist doctrine of perfection was labeled as teaching *perfectionism*. It was a remarkably unfortunate choice of terms.

In a number of areas in his book, Paxton's treatment was quite superficial and consequently misleading. His dealing with the view of the carnal nature in *Conflicting Concepts* amply illustrated this fact. Paxton stated the manuscript teaches that "the carnal nature is eradicated at regeneration." (*Ibid*., 144) If the term *totally subjugated* were used in place of *eradicated*, no one could quarrel with this statement. However, Paxton's failure to set out the authors' distinction between a carnal nature subjugated at conversion and a sinful nature retained until glorification left many readers imagining that *Conflicting Concepts* teaches that at regeneration the carnal nature is exchanged for a sinless nature. This concept is not the teaching of the book.

In the concluding chapter of his book, Paxton cited what he asserted were four "perplexing aspects of Adventism" (*ibid*. 150); *viz*. (1) Adventist isolationism; (ii) Adventist triumphalism; (iii) Adventist fear of antinomianism; (iv) Adventist use of Ellen G. White. Two of these deserve a little comment. In one sense, Adventists must, of necessity, be isolationists[6] when dealing with these distinctive doctrines. We should not be defensive about this point. It is indeed proper. Elijah did not accept the false views of those about him in presenting the first Elijah message, nor did John the Baptist in preaching the second. Likewise, the Seventh-day Adventist Church must remain doctrinally aloof from the errors of today's Christendom in presenting the third Elijah message. As has been mentioned previously in this volume, we, as Seventh-day Adventists, can never work doctrinally *with* members of other faiths, but we most certainly can and must work *for* them. But in another real sense, Seventh-day Adventists are not doctrinally isolationists. We take our doctrines straight from the Bible, and in doing this, are in no wise isolated from the pure stream of Christianity.

Paxton repeated the usual verbiage of those accepting the *new theology* on the nature of Sister White's writings. He repeated his metaphor: "She [Sister White] has a wax nose." (*Ibid*., 146) It seemed strange that he was concerned that Sister White's writings are used to settle doctrinal differences in the Church. "If Adventists wish to bring Mrs. White to the place where she has no authority at all in their movement, then let them keep using her writings as a source for point-scoring in their intra-church squabbles." (*Ibid*., 146) Ignoring the cutting tone of this sentence, readers may be excused if they wondered whether Paxton had the same view of using the Bible as a means of settling points of doctrinal difference. His consistent lack of appeal to the Scriptures as a basis for his views might imply that he did have similar fears in that direction.

What was clear was that Paxton continued in his book to adopt the "hands off Sister White" policy, so evident in his lectures to Seventh-day Adventists. No doubt he did this to preserve credibility with Adventists, rather than from any conviction of her direct inspiration. It is much more damning, in reality, to plant the thought that perhaps Sister White's writings are capable of many and quite opposite interpretations. Nothing would more thoroughly rob the Testimonies of their value than such a belief. Further, Paxton did not miss any opportunity to score indirectly against Sister White's writings. Thus, in discussing the "errors" of *Conflicting Concepts* on the subject of the carnal nature, he stated the book asserted that "those who say the carnal nature remains are to be more pitied than blamed." (*Ibid.*, 144) Paxton cleverly omitted the fact that the authors were simply quoting God's servant:

> Those who are carnally minded will be found in the church. They are to be pitied more than blamed. (F.E. 294)

Paxton also avoided reference to the Sanctuary doctrine in his book. When asked concerning this omission at the Rockville Church, Maryland in 1978, he replied that he could not cover every topic. Some in attendance felt this reply to be less than convincing. At the time of publication, Desmond Ford's open attacks upon the Sanctuary doctrine had not been mounted. It is possible that Paxton, who was close to Ford and aware of his thinking, may have felt that he would have lost credibility with his Adventist readership had he introduced his views on the Sanctuary doctrine at that time.

Perhaps one of Paxton's most telling insights was the observation that the *new theology* breaks down sectarian barriers. "With the coming of the gospel of Paul and the reformers [to Brinsmead], sectarian mentality began to fade away." (*Ibid.*, 124) This insight is not surprising, since Brinsmead had merely accepted the views of other Protestant churches. The *new theology* had a compelling ecumenism about it, since it had long been the belief held by the fallen Protestant churches. But the truth of the Seventh-day Adventist Church will, by its very nature, build barriers between those true to the Lord and those unwilling to follow their Master fully.

In summary, it may be stated that Paxton has revealed an improper scriptural understanding of the distinction between Protestant and Roman Catholic doctrine. This deficiency invalidated most of his major conclusions. As in his lectures, he appeared to be more interested in a personal interpretation of the basic Protestant truths than in an examination of Bible truths. Having made these important criticisms, we must point out that there was merit in his unfolding, with some accuracy, of the doctrinal swings of the last three decades in the Seventh-day Adventist Church. Strangely, these doctrinal changes were virtually unrecognized by the vast majority of church members. He also accurately showed that the *new theology* was an innovation and diametrically opposed to the Bible-based Seventh-day Adventist faith.

This revelation no doubt alerted a few Seventh-day Adventists to recognize the nature of the *new theology*.

Paxton also clearly demonstrated that the General Conference leadership took a doctrinal position entirely opposed to that of the *new theology*. His implied call for a direct denominational statement on the Church's stand and its reason for rejecting the errors which crept into the Church in the decades of the fifties and sixties merited a positive response. He also deserved to be complimented for his choice of the title for his book. In seeing this conflict in terms of the Shaking, Paxton has demonstrated much more insight than those believers who insist that church unity is a more important aim than the proclamation and preservation of truth. Whether the dust cover of the book is correct in its assertion that "his [Paxton's] thoroughly documented account of the terrific tussle over justification by faith now going on in the Adventist community, is as exciting as an Agatha Christie mystery,"[7] only a devotee of that author could tell. What is certain is that Paxton's book, warts and all (and there are plenty), may well have jolted some Seventh-day Adventists out of their apathy. Sister White stated:

> Indifference and neutrality in a religious crisis is regarded of God as a grievous crime and equal to the very worst type of hostility against God. (*3T* 281)

Since the publication of Paxton's book, there was no longer any excuse to represent one's cowardice as if it were a virtue. Nor did any reason remain to refuse to take an open stand on the side of truth.

### Chapter 49 Endnotes

1. There is general agreement that the term *sanctify* in the New Testament means to cleanse, to set aside for a holy purpose. Perfection—both imputed and imparted—occurs at the moment of conversion. Thus: At every stage of development our life may be perfect; if God's purpose for us is fulfilled, there will be continual advancement. Sanctification is the work of a lifetime. As our opportunities multiply, our experience will enlarge, and our knowledge increase. (*COL* 65,66) This sanctification is a progressive work, and an advance from one stage of perfection to another. (*ML* 260)
2. It should be pointed out that, while this book had not been published until well into the 1980s, much of its detail referring to the period up to 1977 was written during 1976-77, prior to the appearance of Paxton's volume. Because it was written so close to the events that are described, we believe that this gives accuracy to the account presented. Thus, the authors had absolutely no idea what conclusions Paxton would draw in

his book, nor the thesis he would present at the time most of Book One was written.
3. President of the Australasian Division, 1962–1970. Pastor Naden was greatly influenced by Dr. Ford's reasoning and while he may not have agreed with every aspect of Ford's teaching, yet as Division leader, he actually supported and protected Dr. Ford. This was in spite of strong counsel from experienced administrators and ministers that he should do something about the errors emanating from Avondale College.
4. Psychologists have long observed this phenomenon of peer pressure. One classical experiment has been performed, in which a group of individuals have been asked to cooperate by declaring a piece of purple cloth to be green in color. A single individual unaware of the deception, is introduced to the group on some pretext. After some innocuous tests, the purple cloth is shown and one by one, those who cooperating with the experimenters, declare it to be green. The individual subject can clearly see that the cloth is purple, but rather than stand out against the weight of evidence of his peers, and somewhat doubting his own senses, also declares the cloth to be green. Today, far too many of our people are declaring purple cloths to be green. These people know the truth, but so many others seem to see it in such a different way that they fear to stand out against them. Thus, many men who saw the truth clearly before 1956, accepted error as truth just as clearly in the 1960s, only to return to the truth in the 1970s. Yet many of these would deny that they had ever changed or deviated from their original position. Rather than Sister White possessing a wax nose, it is surely these people who possess the putty probosci.
5. Letter written by Dr. R. Standish to Pastor R. Pierson, dated Feb. 4, 1976
6. This charge may be viewed in another way. In 1983, Walter Martin, on tape, complained to his non-Adventist audience that, in an evangelistic sense, Seventh-day Adventists were not isolationist enough! He based this charge on his observation that Seventh-day Adventists insist on entering mission areas already controlled by other denominations to disseminate their distinctive truths.
7. The late Dame Agatha Christie was a prominent English writer of mystery novels.

# 50 Personnel Changes

THE announcement at the end of 1976, that Pastor Robert Frame had accepted the position of Director of the Adventist Media Center in Thousand Oaks, California, naturally caused speculation as to the reason for this change of position. The *Present Truth* organization had its own reasons for proclaiming: "Australasian Division President, R. R. Frame, has recently been relieved of his position by General Conference action, because he feels he cannot cope with the theological issues of serious controversy in Australia." (R. Martin, *Objective Digest Report* 1) This statement induced Pastor Frame to write a stern letter to Ray Martin, protesting against this allegation. Martin, in return, asserted that his information originated from Dr. Ford, who had stated that Pastor Frame had confided in him. According to Martin, Ford had stated that the heat of the doctrinal controversy had caused Pastor Frame to accept the California position.

Whether this rumor was correct or not, one matter was certain and that was that Pastor and Mrs. Frame had greatly enjoyed living in Washington during the period that Pastor Frame had occupied the post of associate secretary of the General Conference from 1966–1970.

It is possible that Pastor Frame, who was not trained for the ministry, felt that he would like to return to the managerial sphere of the Lord's work. The fact that the most serious problems he faced in Australasia were doctrinal did not suit his background, as he was largely dependent on others for advice in this area. This circumstance was a burden to him, since he was a conscientious man with noble intentions. The implication that he was deliberately transferred because of poor performance in his office would not only constitute a harsh evaluation of the available facts, but is, in fact, false.

One matter that is worth reporting is that there was no rejoicing among the Concerned Brethren over Pastor Frame's resignation. Even though, at times, they felt Pastor Frame had leaned on poor advice, nevertheless they respected him as a wise chairman, a man of Christian dignity and basic fairness. We do not dare to judge God's decision in this matter, but perhaps Pastor Frame's complete reliance upon God's plan for his life could be the answer to the change in posts, for Pastor Frame had written, "If I am not effective in my work, then I am sure the Lord will soon see that I am removed and someone else elected in this chair. In these final days of earth's history, I doubt whether there would be very many making application for positions of leadership where one is confronted with such a wide variety of problems."[1]

Speculation was rife over the possible successor to Pastor Frame. Many felt wisdom dictated that an overseas man would be invited to replace him. It was felt that most men in Australia were much too close to the issue to be able to take an objective stand. Certainly there were a number of distinct advantages in the making of an overseas appointment. Most of the leading Australasian contenders for the post had sat in the Biblical Research Institute meetings and were parties to the endorsement of Dr. Ford's false views on the age of the earth, the Sanctuary, the inspiration of the Bible and Spirit of Prophecy. While it was true that most of the men in their personal convictions did not accept any of these views, it seemed that they felt impelled to support them as a sign of loyalty to Dr. Ford, fearing that to lose Dr. Ford's supporters would split the Church.

The action of these men in giving written approval to Dr. Ford's errors, did, however, cause enormous disappointment among God's people in Australasia. It was possible the men on the Biblical Research Institute Committee correctly judged that no matter what they did, the Concerned Brethren possessed such a depth of loyalty to God's Church, that even a major rebuff, such as that provided by the Biblical Research Institute, could not weaken their hold upon the Church. On the other hand, many who had accepted the *new theology* did not possess similar loyalties and thus a rebuff for them would have opened the door for them to leave the Church of God. That this assessment, which was made by not a few people long before Dr. Ford was dismissed from the Church, was correct is now a matter of history. As we look at the large numbers in the United States and Australia, New Zealand, South Africa, and several other countries who have departed from God's Church because of the rebuff given by the Glacier View Committee to Dr. Ford, we can see that those believing the *new theology* had a different attitude to God's Church than did the Concerned Brethren.

Thus, it may have been evaluated in the minds of some that in the aim of unity and maintaining the flock, the loyal Adventists and those following the *new theology* could not both be satisfied by the decision of the Biblical Research Institute. Therefore, the safer option in the minds of some may have been to support the *new theology* at the expense of fundamental Adventism.

In the event, Pastor Keith Parmenter, who was holding the post of Division secretary, was elected to the vacant position of president. As we have seen, Ray Martin and others in the *Present Truth* organization seemed to have a remarkably accurate source of information at the Division office. They were able to publish numbers of private documents from the Division files, thus giving credibility to some of the assessments which they made. Ray Martin asserted (*Objective Digest Report,* 8) that Pastor Parmenter was unfriendly to both Brinsmead and Paxton, but friendly to Ford. On the other hand, he also stated that Pastor Parmenter was not enamored with the work of the Concerned Brethren. This accusation to many seemed strange, for surely those who had early sensed the crucial danger to the Church of men like Paxton and who, using only the approved channels of the Church, earnestly warned of these dangers prior to the church administrators sensing it, merited the appreciation of leadership.

Pastor Parmenter did, indeed, send out signals that he would be far happier if the obvious ties between Ford, on the one hand, and Paxton and Brinsmead on the other, were broken. This suggestion did seem to many to represent the attitude of seeking to destroy a symptom rather than the disease. The disease was the common doctrinal error shared by all three. The symptom was their association one with the other. Dr. Ford surely could not be expected to break his ties with men with whom he shared a common belief.

On March 4, 1977, a group of Concerned Brethren, led by Pastor J. W. Kent, met with the new Division president in the presence of the Division, Union and local leaders and Dr. Ford. The Concerned Brethren protested against Dr. Ford's Sanctuary errors and his alleged intellectual dishonesty.

On this occasion, the Concerned Brethren were informed that this meeting would be the last time they could approach leadership as a group. In the meeting, Dr. Ford firmly maintained his erroneous position, in spite of clear statements read to him from the Spirit of Prophecy. At the conclusion, the Division president and chairman, in ending the meeting, declared himself for Dr. Ford, saying that never before had Dr. Ford stood so high in his estimation as the present. He also stated that he himself had problems in regard to our doctrine of the Sanctuary. Then turning his head slightly in the direction of Pastor Burnside, he warned in an intimidatory tone that if the attacks on Dr. Ford continued, he would have them (the Concerned Brethren) dealt with.

Pastor Kent immediately reacted and said: [Name deleted], are you threatening me?" The Division president replied: "No, I am not threatening you, Brother Kent," implying that he was directing his threat against others in the group. It was understood by the Concerned Brethren that the threat meant being disfellowshiped. The Division president also directed the Concerned Brethren to discontinue their gathering together in private cottage meetings.

In an earlier meeting the senior Concerned Brethren had been forcibly reminded by the Division president that Robert Brinsmead had been disfellowshiped, not for doctrinal deviation but for opposition to church authority.

The transfer of Dr. Ford from the chairmanship of the Avondale College department to the staff of Pacific Union College theology department in July, 1977, came as a surprise to many, but not to those who had been cognizant of the moves afoot to implement this transfer to the United States. Moves had been underway for the previous two years. A number of men in the United States, not fully conversant with Dr. Ford and his talents, believed that if he were sent there into an environment where there were many Adventist theologians, he would be dwarfed by such theologians.

As early as the General Conference Annual Council, held in October, 1975, Dr. John Cassell, President of Pacific Union College, had consulted Colin for advice regarding the possible appointment of Dr. Ford to the theology department at Pacific Union College. Dr. Cassell stated that the General Conference brethren felt it would help the situation in Australia for Dr. Ford to spend some time in an American college. Colin's simple answer was: "Jack, if you want to split your faculty, bring Des." In reply, Dr. Cassell stated that Dr. Ford was a good teacher and that the General Conference brethren felt it would work out all right.

In May, 1976, while presenting a series of lectures at the Lake Union Conference Quadrennial Session, Colin approached Pastor Willis Hackett, vice-president of the General Conference. At this time, the decision to transfer Dr. Ford to Pacific Union College had been taken. Colin expressed the view to Pastor Hackett that a serious mistake had been made. Pastor Hackett indicated the thinking was that, in Australia, Dr. Ford was a big fish in a little pool, but that in America he would be a little fish in a big pool. Pastor Hackett felt, at that time, the Australasian Division needed a little respite, so that the controversy could settle down. It was anticipated that, when Des was able to exchange views with the sharp minds of the American Adventist theologians, his own views would mellow.

This posture indicated a number of misunderstandings at Headquarters. First, the extent and danger of the Australian apostasy was completely underestimated. This fact was no doubt the result of the repeated assurances from the Australasian Division, indicating that all was well within the Division, apart from the presence of a few agitators. Second, Dr. Ford's ability and charisma were undervalued. Subsequent events have shown just how far the above estimates fell short of the reality. Within a few months of Dr. Ford's taking up the post at Pacific Union College, he was the most heralded theologian in the world field. Third, and of great significance, it cannot be doubted many leaders were completely unaware that numbers of our American scholars had imbibed the same errors of evangelical Protestantism as had Dr. Ford, and were also stealthily teaching them to their students. These men were ready for a rallying point, and Ford provided this. Had Ford delayed his October 27, 1979, speech one or two more years, his coup possibly would have been complete. But Providence chose otherwise.

Another matter which was not well assessed was the feverish efforts of Brinsmead and Paxton to prepare the way for Ford's advent to the United States. Within a month of Ford's arrival, both Brinsmead and Paxton had held a major weeklong seminar in Oakland, California, and had met with numerous members of the staff and students at Pacific Union College. From thence, they traveled to Chicago and later Philadelphia for similar meetings, each of one week's duration. The United States was saturated with copies of *Present Truth* and tapes of both Brinsmead and Ford.

Sad to relate, numerous pastors and church administrators supported these and similar meetings. One church administrator in the Oregon Conference attended the *Present Truth* meetings and gave the appearance that he favored the *new theology* put forth. Pastors in churches in California advertised these tapes of Brinsmead and Ford from their pulpits.

Meanwhile, in Australia, attempts were being made to suggest that Dr. Ford's transfer was merely a routine one. This stance defied the facts. As we have seen, it was well known in Australia and the United States, that at least eighteen months prior to the move, Pastor Willis Hackett, vice-president of the General Conference, had suggested this transfer as a solution to the division within the Church in Australia. It was also well known that Dr. Cassell, president of Pacific Union College, was well informed of these efforts to remove Dr. Ford to his college. At that time, Dr. Cassell[2] seemed to be quite undecided as to the course of action he should pursue. It was indeed a proper hesitancy, having regard to the controversy and questions surrounding Dr. Ford.

That the Pacific Union Conference accepted Dr. Ford primarily to ease the problems in Australia cannot be denied. Speaking of the issues in Australia, Pastor Cree Sandefur[3] wrote: "The Pacific Union has become somewhat involved in the issue, in the light of our invitation to Dr. Ford. We have voted to invite him to the campus at P.U.C. for a two-year term. We think it may be in the interest of the Church in Australia."[4]

The *Australasian Record* created confusion. Initially, it stated that Dr. Ford would retain his title as chairman of the Avondale College theology department during the two years of his absence. Later, it was announced that Dr. Gordon Balharrie, chairman of the department of theology at Walla Walla College, had been appointed to this position. No mention was made correcting the former announcement.

In all the moves which occurred about this time, the hand of God can be plainly seen. There were many good Seventh-day Adventists who refused to believe that Dr. Ford was in any way in error. Such stated that if he were in error, he would have been removed by responsible brethren. It was always the thought of the authors that Dr. Ford would be removed when God deemed this solution to be optimal for the Church. There were probably far too many good people in Australia who could not have understood such an action prior to 1977. It was necessary for Dr. Ford to be transferred from Australia, for men of experience in the United States to detect his error, and for the full extent of the *new theology* to become more evident, before God's plan could best be fulfilled. Although Dr. Ford could not have known it at that time, by accepting this call he was exposing himself to a situation which was going to completely change his relationship to the Seventh-day Adventist Church. It is quite possible that, had he not gone to the United States, even now he would still be leading the theology department at Avondale College, and being promoted in the way he had been for the previous fifteen years.

Chapter 50 Endnotes

1. Letter written by Pastor Frame to Dr. Russell Standish, date March 29, 1976
2. Dr. Jack Cassell's acceptance of Dr. Ford's appointment at Pacific Union College eventually so weakened his own position in the College that he found it necessary to resign his post in 1983.
3. President of the Pacific Union Conference and Chairman of the Board at Pacific Union College.
4. Letter written by Pastor Sandefur to Brother Roy Davies, Feb. 2, 1977. Years later, this fact was confirmed in the secular press. The article quoted was based upon an interview with Dr. Ford himself. It stated that in the mid-seventies, Dr. Ford "came under attack from strongly conservative elements for his views. As a result of their pressure, he was posted to the U.S." (Sydney *Daily Telegraph*, May 3, 1983)

# 51    Australian Pastors Attack the Truth

IN 1977, a New South Wales pastor, a convert from the Jehovah's Witnesses' faith, and a Western Australian pastor published their objections to the old Adventist position on the nature of Christ. Once again, the Brinsmead *Present Truth* organization was the medium used for publication. Jack D. Walker again appeared to use a flimsy device to give the impression that these men had no knowledge that their material was to be published. As if he were playing a record, he asserted that the material "is being distributed by me without the knowledge or consent of the writers." (*Adventist News Service* No. 4) This tactic again was in all possibility a little game playing in order to deceive the gullible. Was it just by sheer coincidence that the private correspondence between a man in the extreme west of Australia and another in the extreme east of that country should flutter, somehow, into the hands of the Brinsmead organization and be published by a man in Goodlettsville, Tennessee? That the N.S.W. pastor, who at that time was little known in his homeland, should write a thought paper which wended its way, as if by some guided missile programmed for Goodlettsville, into the hands of Jack D. Walker, and that the same person was able to press into the recesses of the Palmdale Conference and obtain not just one paper but indeed four, displays a detective skill which rivaled that of Sherlock Holmes. That the four papers from Palmdale were presented by men well known to be prominent supporters of the *new theology*, and not those of men standing for the old Adventist truths, certainly was a real bonus for the *Present Truth* organization. We wonder why people find it necessary to follow such deceptive practices if they have the truth to proclaim.

Unfortunately, these devices have been used on both sides of the doctrinal fence, since it seems to have been the safest way to present one's concept. For instance, if at Palmdale, when asked to keep his and other papers confidential, Dr. Ford had declared, "Brethren, I cannot give such an undertaking, for I have already given copies to Robert Brinsmead, who assisted me in the preparation, and he will be publishing my papers for all to read," he would have been frank, but probably would have come close to losing his credentials at that time. However, when he stood shoulder to shoulder with the other men present and gave the same undertaking as they did, to keep the papers confidential, few were concerned when subsequently his papers were published. They were prepared to accept that "somehow" his papers passed into the hands of the *Present Truth* organization prior to Palmdale. In other words, there were rewards for being less than frank, but there was punishment for frankness.

Whether the two Australian pastors were afraid to state the manner in which their material found its way into *Present Truth*, we do not know. If so, their fears, unfortunately, were not unfounded. In Australia, in particular, there seems to be far less freedom afforded God's people than is afforded our brethren and sisters in the United States. In Australia, however, there is a tendency to accept the type of little games that men like Jack D. Walker seem prepared to play. No doubt Walker did this with the best of intentions, in order to protect the authors. Perhaps the time has come for God's people to look at these tactics, which border upon deception, in order to decide if they wish to continue with this type of conduct. Should we continue to regard our readers as imperceptive, unintelligent human beings quite incapable of reading between the lines, or should we recognize that men and women other than the writers can fully perceive those matters which are being covered up? Of even greater importance—is it possible for all of us to put honesty and openness before self-interest? Perhaps it would help if honesty were rewarded and deceit condemned, rather than as appears to be the case at the present, that the reverse sometimes prevails.

The N.S.W. pastor may be forgiven for his false doctrinal position. He had been an Adventist for only twelve years. This period of time, of course, should have been ample for him to have mastered the truth, had he been taught it. But accepting the false views of *Questions on Doctrine* as Adventist belief, and studying theology under Dr. Ford, were hardly solid bases for a correct understanding of the Bible and Spirit of Prophecy. Thus it was only natural that he would accept a false view of the nature of Christ. It was most disappointing, however, to read such an apparent paucity of understanding by a man who had taken such an active interest in the doctrinal conflict within the Sydney Area. That he had taken the trouble to read material and listen to expositions on truth cannot be doubted. What was surprising was that he still favored a false position, despite the absence of biblical evidence to substantiate it.

A reading of the pastor's paper indicated the real poverty of understanding among the vast majority of those accepting the *new theology*. He apparently was unacquainted with the concept of God's ideal for His people:

> God's ideal for His children is higher than the highest human thought can reach. (*DA* 311)

If this fact had once been grasped, many of the pastor's misapprehensions would have been dismissed. The pastor continued to use one of the most misused statements of the Spirit of Prophecy:

> Do not set Him before the people as a man with the propensities of sin . . . not for one moment was there in Him an evil propensity. (5*BC* 1128)

By misusing such a statement, the pastor concluded that "we can see that Jesus did not have the passions, the evil propensities, the sinful nature we have." (*Adventist News Service* No. 3, 7) Was this conclusion justified? Now it is true that Christ did not possess evil propensities and passions.[1] It is just as true that every unregenerate human being does possess them. Thus there is a decided difference between Christ's nature and the unregenerate human nature. Sadly, the holders of the *new theology* continued to assert that this carnality of nature persists after regeneration and the new birth. "The old nature does not die, neither does it gradually disappear, until Christ comes and changes it at His return." (Gillian Ford, *The Soteriological Implications of the Human Nature of Christ*, 9) Here was the key to the pastor's error. In accepting this soul-destroying premise, he could not understand Christ's nature was that which He bestows (imparts) to every born-again Christian. Christ's freedom from sinful propensities in no way sets Him apart from regenerated Christians. Listen:

> We must learn of Christ. We must know what He is to those He has ransomed. We must realize that through belief in Him it is our privilege to be partakers of the divine nature, and so escape the corruption that is in the world through lust. Then we are cleansed from all sin, all defects of character. *We need not retain one sinful propensity.* (*7BC* 943, emphasis added)

If only the holders of the *new theology* could cease to minimize the power of Christ in the life of a man who gives himself in full submission to God, they would soon leave their doctrine with the fallen churches of Babylon from whence they have resurrected it. How pitifully weak such make the divine nature when they continue to assert that, in combination with the human nature, such human nature has total dominance, for it continues to have sinful passions and propensities. As seen above, this assertion is just not true. When at the new birth man receives the divine nature, it is the divine nature which takes control of his life. If this were not so, one could only conclude that the wiles of Satan were far more powerful than the love of God. This conclusion we refuse to accept. It is both unscriptural and blasphemous.

The pastor's incorrect concept of the born-again Christian had led him to feel that he had made point after point in favor of the difference between Christ's human nature and that of man. In reality, all he had demonstrated was that to which every Seventh-day Adventist would agree—that Christ's nature, with its combination of the human and the divine, was entirely different from that of the unregenerate man. However, when man accepts Christ, he, too, becomes a partaker of the divine nature:

> Whereby are given unto us exceeding great and precious promises; that by these ye might be partakers of the divine nature, having escaped the corruption that is in the world through lust. (2 Peter 1:4)

he, too, becomes holy:

... he that is holy, let him be holy still; (Revelation 22:11)

he becomes righteous as He is righteous:
> Little children, let no man deceive you: he that doeth righteousness is righteous, even as he is righteous; (1 John 3:7)

perfect, as He is perfect:
> Be ye therefore perfect, even as your Father which is in heaven is perfect; (Matthew 5:48)

pure, as He is pure:
> And every man that hath this ope in him purifieth himself, even as he is pure; (1 John 3:3)

and walks even as He walked:
> He that saith he abideth in him, ought himself also so to walk, even as he walked. (1 John 2:6)

The authors cannot comprehend such divine power, but we dare not deny that which God has promised.

Thus, when the pastor, in an effort to reduce the credibility of Dr. Douglass' *Sabbath School Quarterly*, promised to "prove from the Bible and the Spirit of Prophecy that Jesus did not give up these [attributes of divinity]" (*Adventist News Service* No. 3, 4), he pursues an argument which no one rightly wishes to contradict. Though Christ was fully God, He did not use His innate divinity upon earth, and thus He could not have lived above sin without the infilling of the Holy Spirit, any more than can the born-again Christian devoid of the divine nature. The pastor ignored those texts which showed quite clearly that Christ on earth was absolutely dependent upon His Father in the same way as is any overcoming Christian.

> Then answered Jesus and said unto them, Verily, verily I say unto you, The Son can do nothing of himself. (John 5:19)

> I can of mine own self do nothing. (John 5:30)

A few moments' reflection will permit the reader to recall a number of similar texts.

The pastor's futile search for the evidence that Christ had an advantage over the born-again sinner can be laid to rest:

> God was manifested in Him that He might be manifested in them. Jesus revealed no qualities, and exercised no powers, that men may not have through faith in Him. His perfect humanity is that which all His followers may possess, if they will be in subjection to God as He was. (*DA* 664)

Some, espousing the *new theology*, have attempted to emphasize that the true Seventh-day Adventist position sets out the depravity of Christ's human nature. This is in no way the purpose of the Seventh-day Adventist belief. Rather, it emphasizes just how elevated is the born-again Christian's divine nature. The only way in which the divine nature can be combined with the fallen human nature is by that divine nature being in total dominance, as was seen in the life of Christ. In point of fact, there was no depravity in Christ's life, no sinful passions, nor are there in the born-again Christian:

> Having taken our fallen nature, He showed what it might become, by accepting the ample provision He has made for it, and by becoming partakers of the divine nature. (7BC 657)

The whole import of this statement is that Christ took exactly the same nature as we have. To continue to contend that Christ here was referring to Adam's sinless nature would make Sister White's statement ludicrous. We can only assume that many have overlooked this and similar statements. It seems likely that some even overlook these passages deliberately, preferring error to truth.

In pressing the point that man cannot obey fully until the Second Coming of Christ, the pastor overlooked many of the great promises of God:

> When He comes, He is not to cleanse us from our sins. (2T 355)

Indeed, this statement alone destroys most of the *new theology*. It is little wonder that the Spirit of Prophecy is seen as an undesirable part of the Seventh-day Adventist faith by these people. Of course, the *new theology* asserts that to have a sinful nature is to have sin in the life. This both Scripture and the Spirit of Prophecy deny. A brief look at the statement just cited will prove this to us.

> When He comes, He is not to cleanse us from our sins. (2T 355)

If the cleansing from our sinful nature is essential for a cleansing from our sins, then one would be compelled to postulate that the sinful nature was also not cleansed at the Second Coming. But all Seventh-day Adventists are agreed that there is no eradication of the fallen nature,[2] until the Second Coming of Christ. Thus, it is perfectly evident that a person can be cleansed from sin prior to the eradication of his sinful nature. This truth is beautifully consistent with the doctrine held for so many years by our Church, but this position is directly antagonistic to the philosophy of the *new theology*. Once more the testimony of Inspiration leaves no grounds for anyone to accept this blatant error. No matter how we may seek to misconstrue passages from the Bible and the Spirit of Prophecy, no such technique can convince the student of God's Word that it is impossible to be sinless while in the possession of a fallen nature. Christ achieved this, and so must we, for Sister White states in the same paragraph:

> The Refiner does not then sit to pursue His refining process, and remove their sins and their corruption. This is all to be done in these hours of probation. It is *now* that this work is to be accomplished for us. (2T 355—italics in the original)

Fearing lest we overemphasize this point, we would like the reader, nevertheless, again to note: God declares that sin must be removed during the hours of probation.

Thus, sinning is not inextricably a consequence of the possession of a fallen human nature. Once that nature has been combined with the divine nature, victory over sin is a consequence. Therefore, there is no excuse for us to be blind to the fact that God is calling His people to total obedience now. This fact is inescapable. It is only as we accept Satan's 6,000-year-old delusion that man cannot obey the law of God, that we reject the clear words of our Lord and Saviour on this matter.

One of the authors had a man of great learning say to him, "Please don't destroy the security which Des Ford has given me. I used to worry that I had not reached the standard, but now I know that my failure to reach that standard doesn't matter, because Christ reached it for me. I accept that by faith, I will be carnal until the second coming, when my sinful nature will be removed." And then, almost as a desperate plea, he added, "Please don't take that assurance away from me!" [3]

That poor soul represents the experience of thousands of Seventh-day Adventists who claim full assurance, but, tragically, it is a false assurance. As Seventh-day Adventists, we must move every sinew in our being to take away such false assurance, for the eternal destinies of those who accept such error are at stake. It is *now* that we must reach the standard *in these hours of probation*. Our appeal to the ministers of God's flock is—Never, never give false security to those whom God has entrusted to you.

Perhaps it is worth recalling that the "loyal" Adventists at the end of time will consist of two basic groups. Both groups will have assurance, for they will possess lamps and both will have trimmed those lamps—that is, they will have studied deeply into God's Word. But the two groups will be distinct, in that one will receive eternal life and the other eternal death. What a gulf! What a distinction! What will cause this crucial difference? Every Sabbath School child knows that the difference will lie in the possession of oil. One group will possess the Holy Spirit in the life. One group will be sanctified. One group will be so filled with the power of the divine nature, that each member will have every sin removed during the hours of probation. The experience of the lost will be that they had "assurance" while continuing in sin. It is true that the second group will also be eager to have the infilling of the Holy Spirit. The members of that group, too, will desire to be cleansed from every sin, for they will seek the oil with diligence, and even beg some from their wise friends. But they sought it not *now*, not during these hours of probation, but after the close of probation and it will be forever too late. The hour even now is late. We can listen to the sweet words of fables, or we can rather turn to the plain promises of God. The decision is ours, but the consequences are eternal.

## Chapter 51 Endnotes

1. For an excellent discussion of Sister White's usage of these terms, see "Passions and Propensities in the Writings of E. G. White," by Dr. Ralph Larson, *Landmarks*, 1983.
2. For the distinction between the fallen nature and the carnal nature, see the chapter entitled "The New Birth" in *Adventism Vindicated*, by the same authors, obtainable from Hartland Publications, Box 1, Rapidan VA 22733, U.S.A. or from Adventist Laymen's Fellowship, P.O.Box 83, Windsor, N.S.W. 2756, Australia.
3. The tragedy of this plea was that it revealed the very lack of assurance the poor soul was craving, and to which he believed he was clinging. When Bible truths are brushed aside, insecurity always results. This insecurity even extends to an insecurity in the very assurance the person claims.

# 52  Further Attacks on Truth

THE Western Australian pastor's two letters to Pastor Kenneth Wood, editor of the *Adventist Review*, together with a reply to the first by Eugene Durand, assistant to Pastor Wood, were published by Jack D. Walker in *Adventist News Service*, No. 4. This pastor's attack was less understandable than that of his New South Wales colleague, for he had been honored with a knowledge of the truth from his earliest years and had been in ministerial work for almost thirty years. That he once accepted and knew the truth of Scripture is obvious, for he himself admitted: "I once believed in the sinful human nature of Christ."[1] It is doubtful, however, whether the pastor fully understood that message, for he appeared to have accepted errors equally as elementary as those accepted by the New South Wales pastor.

This pastor did not conceal his annoyance with Pastor Wood. This feeling was particularly noticeable in his second letter. A few extracts of this letter are quoted to show this emotion: "It concerned me that the Editor of the *Review and Herald*, occupying an official position in our organization, should use the opportunity afforded by his position to publish your own private opinions."[2] "Frankly, you give me the impression that you are taking advantage of your official capacity to urge your own opinions upon this movement, and you will find there will be a limit to how far the Lord will allow you to do such a thing." (*Ibid*.) "It did concern me very greatly to read that you there at the *Review and Herald* do not believe in original sin! Do you know what it sounded like to me, my dear brother? 'Thou knowest not that thou art wretched, and miserable, and poor, and blind, and naked.'" (*Ibid*., 5) "There is an alarmingly shallow and superficial definition and concept of sin among us, if we fail to perceive how profound the sin problem is in man, and we see this trend in such statements as we read in our current Sabbath School Lesson Pamphlet: 'The real Jesus was a real Man, *except He did not sin.*' (Emphasis Herbert Douglass) That is about as trite an analysis of the truth as anyone could put into print. The concept expressed in such a statement is Pelagian, essentially. I cannot but feel the same about the expressions in your own letter, when you direct your remarks to discussing sin." (*Ibid*.)

The pastor appeared to be quite agitated by one of Pastor Woods' statements. Pastor Wood had written, "As we see the situation, the chief danger in believing that Christ's humanity was different from ours is the use of this 'difference' as an excuse for sinning."³ In both of his letters and on more than one occasion, the pastor returned to this statement. He insisted, "I have not heard those, who do believe in the sinless human nature of Christ, say anything that could be suspected of having such danger."⁴

Since the pastor resided almost two thousand miles away from the State of Victoria, he could be excused for not having heard his fellow ministers in that state preaching to the young people that even with the Holy Spirit in their lives, they could not keep God's law. One could raise the question as to whether anyone should be concerned about sin, if one believed that "The Christian is always right with God.⁵ There is no condemnation to them that are in Christ Jesus."⁶ Also, one would, no doubt, continue to sin if one believed Dr. Ford's view that "'Likewise reckon ye also yourselves to be dead indeed unto sin, but alive unto God.' Now you wouldn't have to 'reckon' if it were so. 'Reckon' means 'count as though.' When he says 'reckon,' he's saying that sin isn't at all dead, it's very, very much alive. It's only legally dead."⁷ A little study of the word translated *reckon* would have shown Dr. Ford that, to the Greeks, it was related to something that had mathematical certainty. Thus, today, when we use a calculator to *reckon* some mathematical matter, we do not believe that it states one thing and means something else. This was the certainty that Paul was expressing over the death of the Christian to sin.

The pastor posed an interesting question: "Can anyone be sinful, either in word, or action, or thought, or nature, and not be a sinner?"⁸ Notice what has happened here. Acts of sin, i.e. words, actions, and thoughts which are always willed, are not distinguished in any qualitative way from the nature which is innate and which is the major predisposing factor to sin. Obviously, if we use sinful words, we are sinning. If we perform sinful acts, we are sinning. And if we cherish a sinful thought, we are sinning. All are acts of known disobedience to God's holy law. But what of the sinful nature? To possess a sinful nature is not to transgress God's law. It is possessed by an infant before he has the ability to will anything, before he can recognize right from wrong, before he can repent. To impute sin to an innocent babe has as much value as to baptize him as a sign of his regeneration at the same age.

Adventists have so properly and staunchly stood out against infant baptism that it would be perilous to take steps in accepting a faith that would necessitate the provision of infant baptism. After all, in this way infant baptism entered the Roman Catholic Church. The belief in original sin, which apparently this pastor espoused, was the doctrine which necessitated the introduction of infant baptism to preserve young children, in case they died, from eternal torment. If ministers believe that babies cannot accept Christ, then it is equally clear that they cannot accept the devil. We have already seen from the statement in the second volume of the *Testimonies*, page 355, that sin must be eradicated prior to the close of probation. Victory must occur now, while we still possess fallen natures. On the basis of God's infallible statements, we must emphatically declare that the answer to the pastor's question,

"Can anyone be sinful in nature and not be a sinner?" is a decided "Yes." Indeed Christ is the answer to such a question.

The pastor, following his own false reasoning, again asked Pastor Wood, "He was different in His humanity, in His sinless words, was He not? and in His sinless actions? and in His sinless thoughts? What makes you think that to carry the distinction just one step further makes for greater danger?"[9] The answer to the pastor's question from the Word of God is absolutely apparent. The dangers are enormous. To believe as did this pastor, that the possession of a sinful nature is, in itself, a sin, would lead to the notion that one is lost eternally, for as we have seen, all sin must be overcome prior to the close of probation. The fallen nature, however, remains until glorification. It was little wonder that the week prior to the writing of his reply, Pastor Wood received a letter from a church member, who openly admitted: "Always I had used Christ's 'different' nature as an excuse for my sins."[10] Yet it seemed that many believers in Australia were being coached by their pastors to do as that poor soul had done.

In his reply to the letter, Pastor Durand did not conceal the convictions of the editors. Three examples are cited: "We here at the *REVIEW* believe that Christ had a sinful, human nature because of such texts as Heb. 2:16,17; 4:15,16; and Rom. 8:3, as well as statements in the Spirit of Prophecy, such as the one in the *Desire of Ages*, p. 49. Over and over again Ellen White states that Christ had a sinful human nature. We have not been able to understand, therefore, how we could believe any differently." (*Ibid.*)

"At the same time, we understand that Christ was born of the Holy Spirit and hence had a nature at least like the totally converted human being. We are told in the Spirit of Prophecy that Jesus accepted all the liabilities to which we are heir. This would not be the nature that Adam had." (*Ibid.*)

"There is a danger then, of confusing the term 'sinful nature' with sin itself. It was possible for Christ to have a sinful nature without partaking of sin in any sense." (*Ibid.*)

The pastor's reply of April 5, 1977, was more forceful than his first letter—longer—and contained more errors. For example, he stated, referring to Romans 8:7: "Here is an explicit and forceful definition of sinful, human nature: THE CARNAL MAN—he is at enmity with God, he cannot obey God's law. This is no description of Jesus Christ! But it is a description of sinful human nature!" It will be noted that the pastor had written as if there were no change of nature at conversion. Pastor Wood had stated through his amanuensis that Christ's nature was that of a totally converted human being. Let us look at the text:

> Because the carnal mind is enmity against God; for it is not subject to the law of God, neither indeed can be. (Romans 8:7)

We can most assuredly agree with the pastor's claim that "That is no description of Jesus Christ!" But what the pastor had overlooked was, neither is it a description of a born-again Christian, as he had inferred. The following verses make this perfectly apparent:

> So then they that are in the flesh cannot please God. But ye are not in the flesh, but in the Spirit. (Romans 8:8,9)

Could anything be clearer? Here Paul tells us that Christians are not in the flesh, i.e., they are not carnal. Neither was Christ carnal. His true followers possess the impartation of His nature. Strangely, the pastor, commenting in his letter on Romans 8:8, states: "This verse describes man's propensity to sin"[11] Once again, we would have to agree wholeheartedly. Strangely, however, the pastor ends his comment at the conclusion of verse 8. Why? Why not continue to comment on verse 9?

> But ye are not in the flesh. (Romans 8:9)

By the pastor's own logic, the born-again Roman Christians quite obviously did not have the natural man's propensity to sin. This, too, is the clear testimony of the Spirit of Prophecy.[12] It was a sad reflection on the pastor's judgment that he recommended to Pastor Wood Gillian Ford's thesis on the *Soteriological Implications of the Human Nature of Christ* as "one of the finest and most carefully thought-through documents I have ever read on His sinless human nature." (*Ibid.*) He then questioned, "Why could not that material be published to be available to our people and indeed to the world, so that we could say to the world—this is what we believe about Jesus Christ?" (*Ibid.*) How grateful we should be that Pastor Wood displayed greater care than to accept such ill-founded advice! Believers in other lands will be astonished to know that, in a country so blessed with the long ministry of Sister White, even ministers of experience could have ignored her plain statements. For a minister of the gospel to advocate a book which so plainly stated that the firm platform of truth established in the Adventist Church, was contrary to the New Testament and a false gospel, was a matter of deep anguish and concern. That this man was subsequently appointed to the theology department of Avondale College again illustrates the concerns of God's people in Australia.

The authors know nothing of the background of the American pastor from Texas whose protest was also published by Jack Walker. While one notes a ring of sincere concern through his article, his purported aim to present "an appeal to withdraw and make a public confession for the *Sabbath School Quarterly*, entitled: '*Jesus, the Model Man*'—April–June, 1977" (*Adventist News Service* No. 4), is entirely ill-conceived. Once again we can but marvel that a man of the cloth should so confuse truth as to call it error.

By some strange process of reasoning, the American pastor was led to assert that "The Church of God, the appointed vessel to promulgate the truth in A.D. 33, cried: 'Crucify Him,' or being interpreted—'Crucify God, crucify Divinity.' Though the beloved Church of ours, the Seventh-day Adventist movement, is the appointed means of the Lord in this day and hour, she is now guilty of this very malediction." (*Ibid.*) It seems that no evil connotation was so severe that it could not be hurled by the holders of the *new theology* upon our beloved Church. It is hardly feasible that this pastor was studying the same Quarterly as the rest of the Church, for he proclaimed, "The *Sabbath School Quarterly* uses this great truth of restoration as a vehicle to reject the Greater Truth of Righteousness by Faith Alone." (*Ibid.*) Quite understandably, he presented absolutely no evidence for his curious assertion. Nor could the authors find any basis for another of the pastor's assertions, *viz.* "It [the *Quarterly* of the second quarter of 1977] implied right throughout, that Christ took on the propensities to sin when he took on sinful flesh."(*Ibid.*) True Adventism makes no such claim. If this American pastor and others of similar views would take the time to study their own faith and spend less time studying the views of the apostate churches, most of the problems which they have had would quickly disappear. He would not then have quoted Sister White's statement:

> No one ... could say that Christ was just like other children. (YI. Sept. 8, 1898)

to imply that Christ had a different nature from ours. One matter that does need to be said is that at least the pastor had the courage to present his convictions in an environment which was hostile to them. He full well knew that the North American Division had come out in favor of the *Sabbath School Quarterly*. It was much easier for the Australian men to present their objections, knowing that there was so much sentiment against the Sabbath School Lessons in Australia.

Of course, this fact also illustrated the greater freedom of discussion which prevails in the Church in the United States. This is perhaps well illustrated in the following experience. Some years ago, one of the authors wrote a very mild letter in opposition to the acceptance of State aid by our church schools in Australia. The editor of the *Australasian Record* replied: "It's not worth my job to print that." In reply, it was pointed out to the editor that a much more vitriolic letter on the subject had just been published by the *Review and Herald*. This letter compared our leaders to Eve envying the forbidden fruit, simply because they discussed the pros and cons of acceptance of State aid for education. The editor of the *Australasian Record* replied that our people in Australia were much less mature than those in the United States. That, of course, was as untrue as it was insulting to the believers in Australia. The difference, in fact, lay in the relative degree of freedom of speech within the Churches of the two countries.

There is a great need for open discussion within the Church of God. men like the American pastor should be entitled to have their positions evaluated. We cannot lose by adopting Gamaliel's counsel:

> If this counsel or this work be of men, it will come to nought: but if it be of God, ye cannot overthrow it; lest haply ye be found even to fight against God. (Acts 5:38,39)

Sister White adopts a similar attitude of tolerance:

> We should never refuse to examine the Scripture with those who, we have

reason to believe, desire to know what is truth. Suppose a brother held a view that differed from yours, and he should come to you, proposing that you sit down with him and make an investigation of that point in the Scriptures; should you rise up filled with prejudice, and condemn his ideas, while refusing to give him a candid hearing? The only right way would be to sit down as Christians, and investigate the position presented, in the light of God's word, which will reveal truth and unmask error. To ridicule his ideas would not weaken his position if it were true. If the pillars of our faith will not stand the test of investigation, it is time that we knew it. (*TM* 107)

Thus, while it is essential that only those who believe the truths of God should be committed to the teaching of our young, nevertheless, others should be afforded every opportunity to have their materials freely evaluated by their peers. Naturally, there is a dividing line which comes when men persistently refuse to accept the pillars of our faith, but this dividing line should be carefully placed in its proper perspective, so that men and women are not prematurely led from God's Church.

Chapter 52 Endnotes

1. Letter to Pastor Wood, dated January 28, 1977
2. Letter to Pastor Wood, dated April 5, 1977
3. *Review and Herald*, November 18, 1976
4. Letter to Pastor Wood, dated January 28, 1977
5. This statement reiterates the Calvinist view of predestination, a view which, like much of the error of the *new theology*, can be traced back to Augustine rather than to Scripture.
6. Dr. D. Ford, *The Gospel is Good News*
7. Dr. D. Ford, *Study in Romans* 4–8. Sermon preached at Sawtell, New South Wales Youth Camp, October, 1974
8. Letter to Pastor Wood, dated January 28, 1977
9. Letter to Pastor Wood, dated January 28, 1977
10. Letter written by Eugene Durand to the Western Australian pastor, dated March 1, 1977
11. Letter to Pastor Wood, April 5, 1977
12. See *Adventism Vindicated*, R. R. Standish, C. D. Standish.

# 53 Armidale Church

ARMIDALE is a city situated on the Northern Tablelands of New South Wales. Some years ago, a church was organized in this city, where the University of New England is located. The pastor of the church was Ormond K. Anderson.

In October 1977 some members, chiefly academics, invited Robert Brinsmead to preach in their church. Observing proper procedure, he declined in the absence of an official invitation from the Armidale Church Board. Such an invitation was soon forthcoming and Brinsmead duly accepted it. News of this unprecedented decision was speedily conveyed to the president of the North New South Wales Conference by those Board members dissenting from the decision. The president made a speedy, unscheduled visit to the city and called the Church Board together, in order to point out the dangers inherent in such a course. After the discussion, he called on the Church Board to declare its loyalty to his administration by reversing its former decision. The result staggered the church leadership in Australia, for the Board simply re-confirmed its invitation for Brinsmead to speak. In taking this action, in the face of opposition from the Conference president, the Church Board was perfectly within its rights, for within the Seventh-day Adventist Church the congregation has every right to make its own decision on such matters. Whether, in this case, the Church Board was prudent is quite another matter.

Robert Brinsmead arrived on the Sabbath and presented his lecture to the satisfaction of the greater part of the Armidale Church. In deference to the Conference Administration, Brinsmead spoke in a hall rather than in the church itself.

The Administration found itself in a perilous situation. Although the Conference president had at least twice publicly expressed concern over the teachings of Avondale College,[1] he had also given little support to those who had been the means of bringing the errors to the attention of God's people. Thus a virtual ban had been placed on Pastor O. K. Anderson, preventing him from occupying the pulpit.

Striking condemnations of *Conflicting Concepts* in somewhat intemperate and inaccurate terms were made before the gathered church workers. A tape recording of this denunciation reflected many unfortunate misrepresentations. Further, in opposition to the General Conference's support of the Sabbath School Lessons, the Conference president had encouraged one of his Conference workers, Pastor Frank Slade, to circulate a paper on the nature of Christ, quite contrary to the biblical and

Spirit of Prophecy statements concerning that doctrine. This paper attempted to counteract the truths found in the *Sabbath School Quarterly: Jesus, the Model Man*. Pastor Slade's paper was in entire accord with Robert Brinsmead's paper; *The Theology of Imitation*, although not as subtly reasoned. This paper was therefore a good reason for many of our believers to feel confused as to precisely where the Conference leadership stood on this doctrinal issue.

The believers at Armidale were quite incredulous that the church leadership should be exercised over their action in inviting Robert Brinsmead to speak. With indisputable logic they reasoned that if the Conference supported Brinsmead's views on these doctrines, there should be no hostility to hearing these views from the man himself, for he could present them with greater clarity and depth of understanding than the men whom the Conference leadership had supported. They argued that if Robert Brinsmead had the truth, as so many leaders in Australia were said to proclaim, they would prefer to hear it from the man himself, rather than from others far less gifted.

For instance, at about the same time as the controversy was occurring in Armidale, it had been stated, "He [Robert Brinsmead] has completely changed his view to the extent that it now accords with that taught by Avondale College." (Letter written by the president of the South New Zealand Conference to brother Alan Jackson, elder of the Timaru Church, dated November 4, 1977) If this Conference president's assessment was correct, and few could rightly dispute it, then the only ground possible for the Conference's concern could be fear of loss of influence. There could not possibly be the least concern that the believers would be doctrinally corrupted.

Looking for a man to set the situation straight, the Conference turned to Pastor Frank Breaden. There was no doubt that he was a most appropriate person to select, for few pastors have so carefully studied the *new theology* and produced irrefutable biblical evidence of its error. Yet, considering the theological climate in the North New South Wales Conference, it was a rather puzzling selection. Pastor Breaden was well known for his bold and most effective stand against the *new theology*. He was one of the sixteen men who openly stood against the errors presented by the Avondale Theology Department at the Biblical Research Institute on February 3 and 4, 1976. Indeed, he presented a very telling paper on that occasion concerning the inspiration of Scripture. After that time, he continued to make earnest submissions to our church leadership in declaring the *new theology* to be in error.

The extent of the concern of the Conference over its perceived loss of influence can be measured by its decision to turn to a man for help, who, it was full well known, believed the Seventh-day Adventist position they condemned. The tragedy of the situation was that it was only those men who were sometimes derogatively termed "Concerned Brethren," who could stand in a mighty way against the errors of Robert Brinsmead. It is almost certain that many sincere souls in the Armidale Church had not heard our special truths from the pulpit for some time. By hearing week after week the errors of the *new theology*, and having these errors confirmed by approval from some members of leadership, the situation within the Armidale Church was perfectly explicable. Indeed, the flagrant denunciation of men standing for God's truth only opened the doors to the solicitation of preachers who would declare soothing messages before their hearers.

This episode in the history of the Armidale Church illustrates most forcibly the dangers inherent in a vacillating attitude by the leadership. The time had surely come when strong and consistent stands for truth should have been made, irrespective of the popularity of such calls. Yet it needs to be recorded that in this Conference leader was a man who valued truth more than the majority of Conference presidents at that time. Further, he did have sufficient courage to exalt truth and condemn error from time to time. Perhaps the problem he faced was the derision he full well knew he would engender should he associate himself with those senior pastors who had risked their reputations in the defense of truth.

We must not feel compelled as leaders to support the errors of charismatic men within our Church, while believing that we are at liberty to condemn the views of those of lesser popularity, even when correct. Truth stands on a plain "thus saith the Lord." This lesson has yet to be learned by some of our people.

# 54 Persecution

ONE of the most puzzling aspects of the doctrinal controversy in Australasia has been the fact that a considerable number of pastors, formerly staunch in their proclamation of the Seventh-day Adventist faith, changed their views quite dramatically after their sons had studied theology at Avondale College. There are as many reasons for this perplexing state of affairs as there are pastors who have accepted the *new theology* as a replacement for the Seventh-day Adventist truths. The majority acknowledge their changed position; a few apparently seem to be more at ease in asserting that they have never believed or taught other than the *new theology*.

One pastor very frankly stated his reason for muting his concern and restraining his preaching of the Seventh-day Adventist position. He had early detected the errors of the *new theology* and had even formed part of the first delegation of concerned pastors and laymen proposing to see the Division president about their concern. As his own son neared graduation from the theology course, this pastor's ardor for his open stand for truth completely abated. He honestly revealed his reason—he was deeply concerned that his son would not be given an appointment if the father persisted in his open opposition to the *new theology*. Tragically, the son, in spite of his father's inaction (or maybe because of it), did not receive an appointment in God's work.

It is really quite sad that some pastors so little trusted the men in authority that they fear discrimination against their children because of their own doctrinal convictions. Even sadder is the belief that, should they proclaim the truth of God, their families will be penalized.

It may be that this basic reason is behind the doctrinal changes of other pastors, whose sons have studied theology at Avondale College, although it is more than likely that this reason would be too simplistic in most instances. What is certain is that all pastors are deeply concerned that their children remain members of God's remnant Church. They are in a position to see the results of apostasy in the lives of children of many of their flock, and all too frequently, those of their ministerial colleagues. This fact builds up a sense of anxiety over the fate of their growing families. Naturally, when one member of the family responds to a call to the gospel ministry, the pastor's heart overflows with joy, and not a little relief. No father would want, in any way, to discourage this decision of his son.

Thus when, as invariably happens, the young theology student becomes evangelical concerning the *new theology*, his father dares not weaken his faith in the views of the men conducting the course, lest he discourage the son in pursuing his training for the ministry. A powerful stimulus is therefore supplied for the pastor to look into his son's new concepts, in order to find as much truth in them as is possible. Many of the pastors also have another mitigating factor. Most of them took ministerial training courses far short of a degree level. Some have even labored, quite unnecessarily, under a sense of inferiority because of this fact. Thus they see their sons being educated to a higher level than they themselves were, and so defer to the apparent greater learning of these lads.

It seems a great pity that these pastors do not perceive that their sons in reality know far less about the Bible truths than they do themselves, because the sons have spent a great deal of their time studying the views of theologians, rather than the plain word of Scripture. Worthy of record is the fact that laymen of understanding have appeared to be far less influenced by their sons' acceptance of the *new theology* than are the clergy.[1]

Wherever the *new theology* has gone, it has led to well-documented ecclesiastical persecution. Ministers have been deprived of pulpits; laymen have been excluded from church office and occasionally threatened with disfellowshipment; church transfers have been rejected; others have been deprived of important positions in the church organization, while yet others have had their reputations unfairly damaged. Many examples of these breaches of Christian ethics could be cited. It says little for the *new theology* that, in order to spread its message, such actions appear essential to enforce convictions.

In order to illustrate the type of persecution which was employed in the Australasian Division, one well-documented example is often cited. The three principals in the incident were the president of the South New Zealand Conference,[2] Brother Alan Jackson, formerly an elder of the Timaru Church in New Zealand,[3] and lastly, the young pastor of the Timaru Church, trained under Dr. Ford.

Excerpts from Brother Jackson's letter, directed to the Conference president, clarified the background for the persecution. Brother Jackson mentioned that on the day of writing, his pastor "came to see me about a problem that had arisen in the nominating committee. Briefly, it concerned certain typed matter my wife had given to friends, and views I had expressed in sermons and Sabbath School class on Christian perfection. . . . Members of the nominating committee shared this view [the pastor's objection] and felt we should not be eligible for office into the Church. . . . He [the pastor] was concerned to discuss the matter with me because he was fearful of the consequences if we continued to work in the way we were. I asked what the consequences were and he told me it would eventually lead to disfellowshipping. . . . I pointed out the sermon consisted of large readings from the book, 'Why Jesus Waits,' by Dr. Herbert Douglass. He told me the author represented a fringe idea. However, I am holding a personal letter which Pastor Pierson of the General Conference directed his assistant, Pastor F. C. Webster, to write, stating that the General Conference fully supported the work of H. E. Douglass. I obtained this letter because it was widely reported in this Conference that this man had been disfellowshipped."[4]

This letter highlighted the perplexity of God's people in the Australasian Division. On the one hand, they received truth-filled literature from our Church Headquarters in the United States, yet when they dared to preach it, they were persecuted by those holding to the *new theology*. These brethren and sisters knew full well that the General Conference material was truth, for they had judged it, not by the thoughts of theologians, but by the infallible word of Inspiration. For similar reasons, they rejected the *new theology*, which was continually pressed upon God's people. These men recognized the *new theology* as patent error. It contained not a thread of support from the law and the testimony. It became quite impossible in some Conferences to be doctrinally loyal to both the General Conference and the local Conference. There is no doubt that if these men, who were persecuting God's loyal people in Australasia, had had the same control over many of our leaders and editors in Washington, they would have inflicted upon them similar persecutions.

Frequently, those ministers supporting the *new theology* stated that they wished to see the removal of men such as Robert Pierson and Kenneth Wood from their high offices. In view of the letter that Brother Jackson wrote, it would have been anticipated that the Conference president would have taken his young worker aside, and counseled him regarding his actions toward a brother of experience who had stated, "My views are quite settled, since I have maintained them all my life." (*Ibid.*)

However, the Conference president surprisingly saw fit to support the action of the Timaru Church pastor, and the threats of this minister of little experience. Thus the Conference president wrote that he felt the church's pastor's "caution in this matter is justified. . . . There is certainly no thought of disfellowshipping people who hold divergent views on righteousness by faith *at this moment*. However, constant opposition to that which the church supports may lead to this."[5]

The president's letter also expressed a number of most disturbing attitudes and a rather poor insight into the doctrinal controversy. Thus he saw the conflict as one between Avondale College and the authors of *Conflicting Concepts*. The authors of that manuscript held beliefs in no way novel to the Seventh-day Adventist Church, beliefs for which the Seventh-day Adventist Church has always stood. These beliefs were shared by the aged pastors standing for truth. Therefore, to promote the authors of *Conflicting Concepts* to the leadership of one doctrinal position was very demeaning to the senior pastors. It also placed the world leaders of this Church in a ridiculous position, for they supported these identical truths. But even more seriously, it degraded the precious Word of God, which alone is the source of true doctrine. Thus the president wrote, "Unfortunately, in Australia, there has been a certain amount of polarization among some of our ministry and laity over this issue, and a good deal of unofficial material has been circulated. The two camps involved in this issue seem to be those who support the message of Righteousness by Faith, as taught at Avondale College, and those who support the theories propounded by Drs. Standish and Clifford from Melbourne. Unfortunately, certain influential retired ministers have thrown their weight on the side of Drs. Standish and Clifford, but they do not have the support of our church in these views." (*Ibid*.)

The authors of *Conflicting Concepts* were absolutely dismayed by the thought that the presentation of the old and trusted faith of the Church was maligned by being classed merely as "the theories propounded by Drs. Standish and Clifford." (*Ibid*.) Furthermore, as the passage of time has proved, neither was the type of person who desired to lead any "camp." They simply supported that which the General Conference and the *Review and Herald* were proclaiming, because it concurred precisely with Scripture. These facts should have been sufficient to recommend the matter to the Conference president. The authors of *Conflicting Concepts* are Seventh-day Adventists in their innermost hearts and do not see themselves in any way as leaders of a doctrinal position. None of the other pastors and laymen standing for truth saw them in this light. Rather than decrying the witness of the old pastors, the Conference president should surely have rejoiced that these worthy men were standing solidly for those truths which he himself once so firmly believed. As a former Division youth leader, he had openly sorrowed over the trends among the youth of the Church. At that time, he seemed to understand the fearful consequences of at least some of the *new theology*.

The South New Zealand Conference president then attempted to brand the old Seventh-day Adventist position as being identical to the previous Brinsmead error. A careful reading of the early pages of this history will discount such a conclusion. However, referring to Robert Brinsmead, he quite correctly stated: "He has completely changed his view, to the extent that it now accords with that taught by Avondale College." (*Ibid*.) Some had criticized *Conflicting Concepts* for placing Ford and Brinsmead in the same doctrinal mold. Clearly the authors were not alone in making this linkage.

Perhaps the most debasing aspect of the Conference president's letter was his assertion on two occasions, that the standard Adventist belief on righteousness by faith was that taught at Avondale College. "The Australasian Division have thrown their weight behind the teaching of Righteousness by Faith as taught at Avondale College." (*Ibid*.) "The matter of Righteousness by Faith is under a lot of discussion by our leadership and until we have some indication that the matter has been resolved, I feel we should support that which is currently taught at Avondale." (*Ibid*.)

To the above two statements must be added a third, written in a subsequent letter. It stated that "the Division stands behind the teaching as it is presented to our ministerial students at Avondale College."[6] Surely it would have been far preferable to see the Australasian Division stand behind the Bible and the Spirit of Prophecy teaching on this important subject. The president's trio of statements were in accord with the Australasian Division Biblical Research Institute's support of Dr. Ford's errors on the age of the earth, the sanctuary, and Inspiration, solely on the basis of the thoughts and writings of current Adventist scholars and authors. It is little wonder that Sister White informs us that in the last days God will have a people who will accept the Bible and the Bible only as the standard of faith.

While in reality the Conference president referred to Dr. Ford's theology when he was discussing Avondale's teachings on righteousness by faith, the situation at the time was quite interesting. By November 1977, Dr. Ford had been replaced as chairman of the Avondale College theology department, following his appointment to Pacific Union College. Dr. Gordon Balharrie, a Bible teacher from Walla Walla College, was his replacement. In his personal teaching Dr. Balharrie desired to re-orient the teaching of that department toward the truths of the Bible.[7] If the South New Zealand Conference president sincerely accepted the Avondale theology as standard Adventism, then by the time he had written, he and the Timaru Church pastor were well out of line, and Brother Jackson was well within the fold. This simply highlights the folly of looking to men rather than to God for truth.

The Conference president also made another false assumption. The reader no doubt was surprised to observe that a Conference president had stated that the doctrine of righteousness by faith had not been resolved by our Church. It certainly was when he graduated from Avondale College, along with Dr. Ford in 1950. We have absolutely no right to regard ourselves as a Church if we do not know what the truth is concerning righteousness by faith. In reality, it was only following Dr. Ford's introduction of his alien theology that such doubts were expressed. One can be excused for wondering whether men who express doubts on such a cardinal doctrine hold any truths at all with certainty.

Brother Jackson, a school teacher, was sorely perplexed by his Conference president's letter, and this is reflected in his reply consisting of two major segments. The first expressed Brother Jackson's alarm that he and his wife had been disciplined without recourse to proper church order. The second reflected his amazement that he had received this discipline when he was teaching and preaching only the message which he found in the Bible and Spirit of Prophecy.

Brother Jackson's censure under these extraordinary conditions was becoming somewhat typical. Perhaps fearing that the full Church would not endorse their untoward actions, a number of pastors began to totally ignore the *Church Manual* and enforced discipline without calling the church body together, either to consider the matter or to give the accused an opportunity to speak in his defense. The *Church Manual* declares both these procedures to be obligatory. In a nation which prided itself as one of the world's bulwarks of democracy, where the term *fair play* is a byword, it was distressing to note that these elements of simple justice were not always followed in God's Church.

The Conference president's approach to this serious abrogation of the clear rights of Brother and Sister Jackson, was to deny that they were under church discipline. If being forbidden to hold office, to teach Sabbath School class and to preach, and further, to be threatened with disfellowshipment, are not acts of discipline, then we could rightly ask, What acts are?

The president suggested that this wrongful act by the Timaru pastor was less than discipline, because it was not offered by the duly designated means. "Firstly, Brother Jackson, I should point out that the action that is being taken by the Timaru Nominating Committee does not really amount to church discipline, for if that were the matter, then as you have indicated, this would have to go to the church and be handled by the church." (*Ibid.*)

What would the reader think of a country which hanged a man on a charge of murder without giving him a proper trial? Would the reader feel that justice had been served if the president announced that the one hanged was not really punished for his crime, since, to be punished, he would first require a legal trial, and this had not occurred in this case? Yet this was precisely the type of "logic" expressed in this letter. On many occasions the explicit laws of the Church have been set aside in order to bring actions against men and women whose only "breach" of ecclesiastical order has been to stand by the pillars of our faith. Men and women today, of course, are perfectly able to detect the falsity of such actions, and this injustice tragically weakens the esteem of God's precious Church.

Very alarming were the words of the young church pastor in his denunciation of the men associated with the *Review and Herald*. Brother Jackson revealed this matter in his letter: "Part of the objection to my Sabbath School teaching goes back to the lessons, *Jesus, the Model Man*, a pamphlet Pastor [name deleted] tells me the Australasian Division was reluctant to accept. Because I have taught these ideas, I am now to be disciplined. Concerning a sermon based on the book, *Why Jesus Waits*, by H. E. Douglass, to which Pastor [name deleted] objected, I have since checked my notes and discovered that all the quotations I read were from the Spirit of Prophecy, except in one instance. I can supply a copy of this sermon. Pastor [name deleted] also held to question the *Review and Herald*, mentioning Kenneth Wood and T. A. Davis, in particular, as men who had deflected in the direction of a former Bob Brinsmead heresy. If this is the case, it puts you in the position of selling books in your Conference Office as fully supported by the Church, but if used in the construction of a sermon, the person concerned comes under discipline."[8]

Brother Jackson was unknown to the vast majority of the men and women upholding the truth in Australia. He had truly written, "I have never publicly denounced the teaching of Righteousness by Faith as taught at Avondale College, nor have I had any contact, nor received any communication with Drs. Standish or Clifford, whom you mention in your letter."[9]

However, when the news of the unjust treatment meted out to him became known, his Australian brethren and sisters in truth felt that no longer could they, in silence, countenance such persecution of a brother and his wife. There is much talk about unity today, but only one thing will bring that long-desired condition, and that is the truth of God. This these brethren and sisters shared with Brother and Sister Jackson across the Tasman Sea.

Thus a petition was devised, signed by a representative group of the ministry and laity, requesting that the General Conference leadership directly intervene in the case of Brother Jackson in order to ensure a speedy overruling of the Timaru Church pastor's quite arbitrary decision and failure to follow church order. It was felt that here was a man standing staunchly for the very same truths proclaimed by the leadership of God's Church, against men who were openly undermining these truths and criticizing those in Washington who had so wonderfully dared to proclaim them.

## Chapter 54 Endnotes

1. Today many lay people do not send their children to Avondale College, lest they accept the *new theology*, which is greatly taught there.
2. It is worth noting that this president's son studied the *new theology* under Dr. Ford at Avondale College.
3. Brother Jackson's son also studied under Dr. Ford at Avondale College and illustrates a common feature among laymen, in that Brother Jackson did not, as a result, accept the *new theology*.
4. Letter from Alan F. Jackson to the president of the South New Zealand Conference, dated Nov. 1, 1977
5. Letter written by the president of the South New Zealand Conference to Brother A. Jackson, dated Nov. 4, 1977, italics supplied
6. Letter written by the president of the South New Zealand Conference to Brother A. Jackson, dated Nov. 15, 1977
7. Upon his arrival, the Division leadership instructed Dr. Balharrie not to become involved in the controversial theological issues at Avondale College, and so he was greatly hindered in altering the direction of the Theology Department of the college back toward truth.
8. Letter written by Brother Alan Jackson to the president of the South New Zealand Conference, dated Nov. 6, 1977
9. *Ibid.*

# 55 Pastors Deprived of the Pulpit

IT has already been mentioned that certain pastors were removed from the pulpit by somewhat unofficial methods. It was felt that their voices of protest against the error of the *new theology* were causing dissent and troubling the Church. Yet the pronouncements that these men made, in their capacity as shepherds of the flock, were very mild indeed, compared with those of the prophets of old, and indeed as compared with Christ's pointed denunciations in His day. Nevertheless, the history of Christ's Church has shown that over and over again efforts have been made to seal the lips of those who would render a ministry of reproof.

Today we are in no different situation from that of previous generations—speak smooth matters in the pulpit, lull the congregation into a sense of security while in a carnal state, and all is well. But preach repentance and the specific truths of God and very shortly opposition will arise and efforts will be made to silence such voices. It will be remembered that God's word came to Jeremiah compelling him to—

> Stand in the gate of the LORD's house, and proclaim there this word, and say, Hear the word of the LORD, all ye of Judah, that enter in at these gates to worship the LORD. Thus saith the LORD of hosts, the God of Israel, Amend your ways and your doings, and I will cause you to dwell in this place. Trust ye not in lying words, saying, The temple of the LORD, The temple of the LORD, The temple of the LORD are these. For if ye throughly amend your ways and your doings; if ye throughly execute judgment between a man and his neighbor; if ye oppress not the stranger, the fatherless, and the widow, and shed not innocent blood in this place, neither walk after other gods to your hurt: then will I cause you to dwell in this place, in the land that I gave to your fathers, for ever and ever. Behold, ye trust in lying words, that cannot profit. Will ye steal, murder, commit adultery, and swear falsely, and burn incense unto Baal, and walk after other gods whom ye know not; and come and stand before me in this house, which is called by my name, and say, We are delivered to do all these abominations? (Jeremiah 7:2–10)

Naturally, the words of Jeremiah were not music to the ears of those he condemned. They were not meant to cause rejoicing. Rather, God explicitly inspired these words to encourage true repentance. Unfortunately, rather than to heed the God-given message sent with such wonderful love, the hearers turned on the speaker and cast him into a dungeon.

Fortunately, in this age, no such form of persecution is acceptable. Nevertheless, the effort to stem the voice of concern is still made. With some, this pressure does produce the desired effect. Many men, fearing the contempt of their peers, will mute their concern rather than stand boldly for the truth. This reaction is no different from that in Christ's day, for we are told:

> Nevertheless among the chief rulers also many believed on him; but because of the Pharisees they did not confess him, lest they should be put out of the synagogue: for they loved the praise of men more than the praise of God. (John 12:42,43)

But God has always had men who not only believed the truth but who also proclaimed it with boldness. Among these were two who have been mentioned previously: Pastor George Burnside and the late Pastor J. W. Kent. These men had read Dr. Ford's thesis submitted to the University of Manchester, and they had noted that what Dr. Ford had written was in direct contradiction to the Spirit of Prophecy on the matter of the man of sin. Thus they published a paper entitled, *Dr. D. Ford Versus E. G. White on the Vital Subject of the Man of Sin*. These men stated, "May God give every lover of the Advent Message grace to continually lift voice, pen, means and influence, in combating this enemy of truth."

In his thesis Dr. Ford had asserted that the anti-Christ would "appear only at the end of time." He also stated that the anti-Christ "belongs to the future and not to history." (Both of these quotations appeared in *Dr. D. Ford Versus E. G. White on the Vital Subject of the Man of Sin*.) Clearly, Dr. Ford was in gross error, having succumbed to the Plymouth Brethren[1] and Jesuit Futuristic interpretation of prophecy, and therefore, having discounted the inspiration-based, historical interpretation of prophecy as confirmed by the Spirit of Prophecy. Ford also had clearly stated that the papal succession did not represent the power of anti-Christ.

For warning God's people concerning this matter, Pastors Kent and Burnside were banned from the pulpit. The ministers of the Greater Sydney Conference received the following letter: "Considerable anguish has been caused in the Conference by the circulation of an anonymous document entitled, 'The Man of Sin.' Pastor J. W. Kent states that he and Pastor Burnside are responsible for the document. It has apparently been placed in the hands of some retired ministers and possibly some laymen at Cooranbong, who have assisted in its circulation. The document is unscholarly,[2] unethical and seriously misrepresents Dr. Desmond Ford.[3] The conclusions drawn in the document are totally invalid and the spirit of it certainly not good. We consider that while this document is in circulation, Pastors J. W. Kent and G. Burnside should not occupy the pulpit in our Conference churches, and we are therefore asking you not to list them for preaching appointments."[4]

No act could have more clearly demonstrated the dangers of the *new theology* than the banning of an 86-year-old pastor, who had been one of the leading evangelists in the Australasian Division and three times Conference president; and another man in his seventies, who had been one of the most successful evangelists this denomination has known within the Australasian Division. So many people in Australia rise up and call these men blessed that it was inevitable that this action left good men and women aghast.

The Conference leadership was deluged with protests, and very shortly the president telephoned the two men concerned and suggested that the ban on their preaching had been lifted. However, Pastor Kent very properly stated that the ban had been placed in writing and distributed to the ministry of the Conference, and he believed that the only proper course for its lifting was to follow a similar procedure. This request was never implemented.

Sadly, the spirit which motivated that most unfortunate decision did not teach some leaders the lesson that it should have, for another renowned retired evangelist, Pastor Austin Cooke, was treated in a similar fashion five years later.

In 1979, Pastor Cooke began to warn believers in the Greater Sydney Conference of the dangers of the *new theology* in the Adventist Church. He and his wife were soon visited by the Union and local Conference presidents[5] and warned that if he mentioned the errors being taught in the churches, he would not be allowed to occupy any pulpit. Pastor Cooke replied that the situation was now so serious that he was under deep conviction our people must be warned and he would do so, no matter what. The presidents then stated that he would no longer be on the preaching plan.[6] After five years, Pastor Cooke is still banned from the Greater Sydney Conference Churches as are numbers of other faithful retired ministers.

In 1983, the following letter was sent to the ministers of the North New South Wales Conference: "Our committee have asked me to write, suggesting that at this time Pastor A. P. Cooke not be given preaching privileges until he undertakes not to publicly denounce Avondale College."

The president's concern would have been far better directed to placing his efforts behind correcting the teaching of the unscriptural errors at Avondale College, which were of such concern to Pastor Cooke.

These acts of persecution against God's retired servants, who have dared to call sin by its right name, indicate that all is not well in many areas of the Australasian Division. This course of action has led to devastating results as far as evangelistic acquisitions are concerned, for if we do not preach the message of God, then, quite obviously, we cannot win people to that message.

Even more disturbing was a statement contained in the same letter which attempted to dictate who could preach and who could not.

"Some time was spent on discussing the ethics of preachers who may become itinerant after they retire, and in one or two cases have used the pulpit as a forum for presenting their own views about Avondale College,[7] etc. At the recent Union Meetings, it was suggested that the Union president write to all retired brethren, stating that, if they are invited to preach in their local area, this is acceptable and according to ethics, but should they be invited to another area, district or Conference, then the invitation should be extended to them through the local Conference or Union, wherever personnel cross boundaries. These are the normal ethics that we have for our licensed and credentialed ministers, who are currently on the payroll, and the Union is anxious that the conditions also apply to those who have retired." (*Ibid.*)

God has warned us over and over again concerning the centralization of authority;[8] yet this is the very mistake that is being made here. It now seems that, in the Trans-Tasman Union Conference, no congregation or church pastor has the right to invite another pastor from another area to speak in the church, without first receiving the approval of either the Conference or the Union authorities. Such decisions as these indicate the insecurity of some leadership over the stand they are taking concerning the error which has pervaded the Church of God. Had they been standing strongly for the truth and condemning the error, there would have been no need for measures such as these. The whole history of the Christian Church teaches us one thing: that tactics such as these are used only when the leadership of the Church feels that their stand for truth is insufficiently strong to withstand criticism from those who hear the truth of God preached in its purity.

In reference to the fictitious charge of a lack of scholarship leveled against those who oppose the *new theology*, it is a fact that, as theological "scholarship" is today, this evaluation is a supreme compliment. The apostasy in our beloved Church is due almost entirely to such "scholarship." In 1984, a television series entitled *Jesus—The Evidence*, was screened in the United Kingdom. It set Jesus forth as a very human individual, debasing His miracles and denying His resurrection. "The programme calls the four gospels fallible documents containing propaganda and myth." (The London *Sunday Times*, April 8, 1984) Yet the assertion, no doubt valid, was made that the series presented "the present state of the New Testament scholarship among Protestants," (*Ibid.*) and that it could "fairly claim to be more or less in line with the present balance of scholarly forces." (*Ibid.*) Biblical scholarship today merely uplifts blasphemous error. Adventists need to seek simple Bible truths and eschew such "scholarship."

Back in 1975, Pastor Ormond Anderson, brother of R. A. Anderson, was barred from preaching while visiting in the South Australian Conference. This order had come from the then Division president, as a result of a complaint from Dr. Ford. About the same time, Pastor Anderson was barred from occupying any pulpit in North New South Wales Conference, where he resided. This action was taken because Pastor Anderson was endeavoring to warn concerning the errors of Dr. Ford and Avondale College.

Excerpts from the following letter, written to him on December 22, 1976, by the then president of the North New South Wales Conference, reveal the naiveté of some church leaders at the time.

"What the Conference has done regarding you and the preaching plan is not a matter of gossip on our part. We do not go about sharing with other people that we have refused the pulpit to you over the last fifteen months, for we consider that it is no one else's business. But I would say to you, that in private conversation you have not manifested a very different spirit to that which you manifested in the Dora Creek and Charlestown Churches. You still insist that Des Ford is a rebel; that he must go; you still insist that he teaches heresy and you still become extremely wrought up if anyone should differ with you in these points which you make.

"Now, Brother Anderson, I wonder if you have taken the time to visit with Dr. Ford and to ask him whether he teaches the things which you claim he teaches, and which Doctors Clifford and Standish claim that he teaches? I have examined very carefully the publication of the Melbourne doctors and I have also read very carefully, material presented by Dr. Ford and I say there is no shadow of doubt but that he is being grossly misrepresented and that much of what he is represented as teaching, he does, in fact, not teach at all. Now I do not mind a man being exposed if he teaches error, but when a man is attacked for teaching something which, in fact, he does not teach, then I am not prepared to give my sanction or the sanction of the Conference to those attacks.

"I would like to state in conclusion that I will make recommendation for your name to be included in the preaching plans of this Conference, when I have evidence that you have dissociated yourself from the misrepresentation and subsequent attacks upon the Theology Department of Avondale College and upon Des Ford in particular. You see, Brother Anderson, you have been too wise a counsellor and too long a servant in the cause of God, to go down in these latter years of your life, as one who supports unscholarly research and misrepresentation. I appeal to you to endeavor, with all your might, to understand what Dr. Ford is endeavoring to say, without forming conclusions at every line and every sentence."[9]

In the light of the fact that Pastor Anderson has been proved so right by subsequent events, as have the other retired pastors who are being penalized, surely the time is well past when the leadership concerned should apologize for their injustices. Instead of continuing to bar these men from pulpits and even from Sabbath School teaching as the leaders are doing, justice demands that they be reinstated and publicly exonerated.

## Chapter 55 Endnotes

1. Dr. Ford studied in Manchester under Professor F. F. Bruce, member of the Plymouth Brethren. In the 1920s Baron Porcelli, son of an Italian nobleman and a Scottish mother, had written, speaking of the Church of England: "The interest, however, in prophetic studies, did not long continue to be a general characteristic of the High Church Party, but their prophetical views spread among the writers of the so-called Plymouth Brethren. Most of their leaders wrote on prophecy and more or less in support of the futuristic views." (Porcelli, *The Antichrist*, 81)
2. This was becoming a worn-out complaint. It surely cannot be unscholarly to point out blatant error and define clearest truth.
3. It seemed that no matter how correctly Dr. Ford's errors were pointed out, his defenders always felt it necessary to claim he was misrepresented.
4. Letter written by the president of the Greater Sydney Conference, dated Dec. 18, 1978
5. President of the Trans-Tasman Union Conference. President of the Greater Sydney Conference.
6. Reported to one of the authors by Pastor A. P. Cooke.
7. This implied accusation was merely a smokescreen. What was objected to was the positive preaching of truth contrary to the errors by recent Avondale College graduates, and many of the ministers in the churches.
8. See "The 1901 Plan for the General Conference," by Dr. Deone Hansen, *Landmarks*, June 1983.
9. Letter written to Pastor O. K. Anderson by the president of the North New South Wales Conference, dated Dec. 22, 1976

# 56 New Theology Spread by Old Apostate Protestant

IN April 1978, Geoffrey Paxton undertook a lecture tour of the United States. This lecture tour was planned to concentrate on Seventh-day Adventists, particularly in the locations of Adventist settlements and educational institutions. The tactics of the followers of the *new theology* were quite transparent. The triumvirate of Brinsmead, Ford and Paxton discerned that Geoffrey Paxton, being an Anglican clergyman, could do the work of destroying the old pillars of God's Church, while the other two members would find this impolitic.

Brinsmead had promised the church leaders early in the decade to put his energies into the non-Adventist realm, and Ford, the tightrope walker supreme, felt restrictions of another kind. He had continued to clothe his erroneous doctrines in the cloak of orthodoxy by shrewdly appealing to a select group of Seventh-day Adventist scholars and authors, whose words he could use as a boast that his doctrines were in accord with theirs. By skirting the impelling arguments of Scripture, which showed his false doctrines in their true light, and upholding the words of men, Ford had been able to convince thousands that his views were standard Seventh-day Adventism. Ford was placed, however, in a position where it was not prudent to make his opposition to the views of the leaders of God's Church apparent to all.

An Anglican could, in some circles within the Adventist church, even be honored when, using debating tactics, he belittled the church leadership. But for a Seventh-day Adventist theologian to do so openly would have been highly dangerous. Thus Paxton was the best suited of the three to take a tour, which was to attempt to undermine the faith and integrity of God's people, together with the firm doctrines they held.

That Paxton had not come as the friend of Seventh-day Adventists he claimed to be, was demonstrated in that he made every effort to spread discomfort in the Church, by attempting to find national magazines which would write up details of the doctrinal dispute within the Church for the information of those of other persuasions. Thus the editors respectively of *Time* and *Christianity Today* were both approached for this purpose.[1] It must have been somewhat of an anticlimax at that time, that neither of these magazines found Paxton's "revelations" sufficiently newsworthy to print.[2]

Further, Paxton used every opportunity afforded him to cast aspersions upon the leadership of God's Church, and to represent its actions and words in the most unflattering light. That many Seventh-day Adventists, particularly those swayed by the *new theology*, approved his sentiments, merely emphasizes the disloyalty of one element within our Church. Those who are indifferent to the church's doctrines show a similar disregard for their Church. If one fact was demonstrated above all others during his 1978 American tour, it was that Paxton was certainly no friend to our Church.

The incredible situation was that so many of our churches and colleges in the United States were willing to open their dedicated doors to his lectures. Even with the worst excesses of the doctrinal dispute in Australia, Paxton did not receive such treatment, although, as we have seen, he almost sneaked in the "back door" of the Avondale Memorial Church.[3]

The church leadership was faced with a major dilemma as it learned that churches and colleges were eagerly pressing to have him speak. Paxton's choice of so many colleges was perfectly understandable, since Dr. Ford had demonstrated that the persuading of college staff and students to follow new doctrines was the most efficient means of spreading these new views in the field. This technique produced a whole army of militant agitators for the changed doctrines. Educational institutions such as Andrews University, Loma Linda University, Pacific Union College and Southern Missionary College were making definite plans to receive Paxton.

In view of this dilemma, the General Conference leadership felt that guidance was necessary. This guidance took the form of a mild letter written by Pastor Neal Wilson, then the vice-president of the General Conference for the North American Division. This letter was written to the presidents of the various Union Conferences in North America. The letter was temperate in tone and contained no threats or coercive language. It is important to quote significant extracts from the letter, a copy of which Pastor Wilson presented to the authors. These extracts will indicate that the criticism which was provoked from the lips of Geoffrey Paxton was quite unjust. Pastor Wilson emphasized that "We understand that we cannot lay down a mandate or physically police this situation." (Pastor Neal Wilson, Letter to North American Division Union presidents, dated March 16, 1978) Nevertheless he put the view of the church leadership when he stated, "We feel that your brethren should counsel with our Conference presidents and institutional leaders and possibly our pastors, informing them that we should not invite him [Paxton] to speak or use our churches or denominational facilities." (*Ibid.*)

Pastor Wilson cited reasons for this recommendation. The reasons put forth, accurately and moderately, represented the true situation. Speaking of Geoffrey Paxton, it was stated, "There is little or nothing that he may do or say that will build the spiritual strength of the Seventh-day Adventist Church. It is evident from the way he has approached the writing of his book and the interviews he has had, that the book is designed to embarrass and divide the church."[4] (*Ibid.*) Pastor Wilson confirmed the intentions of some of our church institutions in the United States when he reported, "From information we have received, it would appear that institutions have officially or unofficially invited him [Paxton] to speak on their campuses." (*Ibid.*)

The authors are not aware of the responses from the various Union Conference presidents. However, one, Pastor Willis Quigley, president of the Columbia Union Conference, wrote to the eight Conference presidents in his Union, endorsing the General Conference suggestion. He stated, "The General Conference has given attention to this [the matter of Paxton's meetings] and are urgently requesting that no Seventh-day Adventist leader entertain the idea of a meeting before their people with this group." [5] No person can rightly question the judgment of the leadership in this matter. Our churches had been dedicated to the glory of God. Indeed, to open our churches to one bent on demeaning God's Church bordered on the sacrilegious, if indeed it did not fully traverse such a path. If men wish to berate God's Church, they have perfect freedom to do so in halls of their own choosing. Our people have every right to hear them in these unsanctified meeting places. Seventh-day Adventists do not fear their flock hearing or reading these false attacks on the truth, for those committed to the Lord are only more deeply confirmed in truth as it shines more brightly in the background darkness of error.

> Truth is eternal, and conflict with error will only make manifest its strength. (*TM* 107)

The decision taken by the General Conference did not reflect a fear of any revelations Paxton could make. The concern was for the preservation of God's Churches as houses of worship, rather than debating halls. In the events which followed, Paxton amply demonstrated by his own words that he was devoid of any worthwhile contributions to the Church. It is doubtful that he influenced a single church member who had not already been committed to the implications of the *new theology*.

Nevertheless, Paxton tried to make capital out of the counsel of the brethren. In a letter published in the Southern Missionary College student paper, entitled "Paxton Banned from S.D.A. Institutions," he wrote, "I am distressed that, since leaving Southern Missionary College, I have been banned from all S.D.A. churches and institutions. This puzzles me greatly and makes me somewhat fearful of the rising hierarchicalism that is increasingly evident in the S.D.A. Church. From my basic knowledge of Seventh-day Adventism, this appears to me to be quite alien to the true spirit of your Church and ultimately destructive. I cannot but feel that the increasing loss of Christian freedom is a direct result of the failure to grasp what Mrs. White called the third angel's message in verity." [6]

Wherever he went, Paxton made every effort to win personal sympathy by highlighting that the General Conference had "banned" him from speaking in churches and institutions. Paxton failed to mention that he had spoken at the Capitol Memorial Church, Washington, D.C., the Rockville Church, Maryland (twice), the Southern Missionary College and Loma Linda University Church, among others. Even the letter quoted does not truly reflect the situation, for he was not "banned" from all S.D.A. churches and institutions" (*ibid.*) after leaving Southern Missionary College. This is evidenced by the fact that he spoke at Loma Linda University Church, the largest in the U.S.A., *after* his visit to Southern Missionary College.

Chapter 56 Endnotes

1. Geoffrey Paxton openly stated this fact during his 1978 tour of the United States.
2. As will be seen later, publicity was very plentiful indeed at a later date.
3. When Paxton's meeting was cancelled in the Avondale Memorial Church, Dr. Ford arranged for the meeting to be held at the home of Brother Max MacDonald, a few miles from the church. Ford was seen leading a group of theology students to the meeting. When this was reported to the Division officers, they stated they had checked it out with Dr. Ford and found that the report was another false attack on Dr. Ford by the Concerned Brethren. However, Max MacDonald later confirmed that Dr. Ford was in attendance in his home for Paxton's meeting on that day.
4. Paxton produced his book at the home of Robert Brinsmead. The material from which he drew, in compiling his book, was located at Brinsmead's. It was divided into three shelves: One shelf was by R. Brinsmead. Another was material provided by Dr. Ford, and on the third shelf was Paxton's own material. Reported by Dr. Earles, an ex-Brinsmead supporter who was staying with Brinsmead while Paxton was compiling *The Shaking of Adventism*. Dr. Earles reported that Dr. Ford influenced Paxton to rewrite certain sections of the book.
5. Letter written by Pastor W. B. Quigley to the Conference presidents within the Columbia Union Conference, dated March 17, 1978
6. G. Paxton, *The Southern Accent*, April 20, 1978, 8

# 57 The Retirement of Pastor Robert Pierson

WHEN Pastor Robert Pierson was elected president of the General Conference in 1966, he ushered in a period in which much of the doctrinal ground which had been surrendered to the wooings of the Evangelicals was reclaimed. With the unfailing support of the then editor of the *Adventist Review*, great progress in reformation occurred. Inspired calls for reformation issued from the presidential office. The correct position on the nature of Christ was presented on a number of occasions in the *Adventist Review* and the biblical position of righteousness by faith upheld, particularly in the *Review and Herald* Special in 1974.

It was at the annual council on October 16, 1978 that Pastor Pierson announced he would relinquish his post in January, 1979. In doing so, he presented an earnest appeal to God's people. In this appeal he frankly set out some of the problems which he full well knew were plaguing God's Church.

> Already, brethren and sisters, there are subtle forces that are beginning to stir. Regrettably there are those in the Church who belittle the inspiration of the total Bible, who scorn the first eleven chapters of Genesis, who question the Spirit of Prophecy's short chronology of the earth, and who subtly and not so subtly attack the Spirit of Prophecy. There are some who point to the Reformers and contemporary theologians as a source and the norm for Seventh-day Adventist doctrine. There are those who allegedly are tired of the hackneyed phrases of Adventism. There are those who wish to forget the standards of the Church we love. There are those who covet and would court the favor of the Evangelicals; who would throw off the mantle of a peculiar people; and those who would go the way of the secular materialistic world. (*Adventist Review*, Oct. 26, 1978)

This was no cover-up of the problems besetting the Church, but a bold announcement for all to hear, that they were accurately perceived by our world leader. In a plaintive plea, pastor Pierson advised:

> Fellow leaders, beloved brethren and sisters—don't let it happen! I appeal to you as earnestly as I know how this morning—don't let it happen! I appeal to Andrews University, to the Seminary, to Loma Linda University—don't let it happen! We are not Seventh-day Anglicans, not Seventh-day Lutherans—we are Seventh-day Adventists! This is God's last Church with God's last message! (*Ibid.*)

Pastor Pierson referred to the work of Pastor and Mrs. Ralph Neal who had written a description of the typical evolution of religious sects through first, second, third and fourth generation processes. He stated,

> In the fourth generation there is much machinery; the number of administrators increases, while the number of workers at the grass-roots level becomes proportionately less. Great church councils are held to define doctrine. More schools, universities, and seminaries are established. These go to the world for accreditation and tend to become secularized. There's a re-examination of positions and modernizing of methods. Attention is given to contemporary culture, with an interest in the arts, music, architecture, literature. The movement seeks to become "relevant" to contemporary society by becoming involved in popular causes. Services become formal. The group enjoys complete acceptance by the world. The sect has become a church. (*Ibid.*)

Quite obviously, Pastor Pierson did not select this description without thought. It too well characterized the processes already far advanced within our beloved Church. We wonder how many filling that vast Takoma Park Church during the presentation of this impassioned address have since spent time considering the important nature of that plea. Have the presidents of Andrews University and Loma Linda University and of other educational institutions spent time considering the vital role that they are playing, either in establishing or destroying the Church of God? Are the lay people around the field standing as true as they need to do in the face of the terrible problems which have attacked our Church? These questions demand prayerful answers and appropriate responses.

No doubt when Pastor Pierson mentioned some of our educational institutions, he was influenced by an open letter which he had received from the editorial staff of the *Criterion*, the paper of the La Sierra Campus of the Loma Linda University. In that letter the editorial staff asserted, "Young Adventism is in almost total agreement that Ellen White has lost much influence in Adventist circles. She has been used to prove both sides of every issue, to repress creativity, to punish differing views, and to supersede the value of the Holy Bible." (*Criterion*, March, 1978, p. 8)

The same letter quoted, "Our samplings suggest a consensus that Adventists are altogether too legalistic in outlook. Young Adventism is finding it difficult to incorporate this perfectionist view into a positive, personal religion. Tragically, we have witnessed discouragement and apostasy that were caused by this feeling that perfection is required." (*Ibid.*)

One point is certain: the test of time has demonstrated that the *new theology* leads to gross apostasy and inevitably destroys the faith of the adherent. Thus it must be met in a positive way at every opportunity. As Pastor Pierson in his retirement speech said:

> And then I call attention to a vision the Lord's servant had, in which she saw a ship heading toward an iceberg. She said, "There, towering high above the

ship, was a gigantic iceberg. An authoritative voice cried out, 'Meet it!' There was not a moment's hesitation. It was time for instant action. The engineer put on full steam, and the man at the wheel steered the ship straight into the iceberg. With a crash she struck the ice. There was a fearful shock, and the iceberg broke into many pieces, falling with a noise like thunder to the deck. The passengers were violently shaken by the force of the collision, but no lives were lost. The vessel was injured, but not beyond repair. She rebounded from the contact, trembling from stem to stern, like a living creature. Then she moved forward on her way." . . . Fellow leaders, it may be that in the not-too-distant future you will have to meet it. I pray God will give you grace and courage and wisdom." (*Adventist Review*, Oct. 26, 1978)

# 58 Adventist Laymen's Fellowship

WHILE Colin was in Australia on furlough in early 1979, he discussed with an old school friend, Carl Branster, the problems that each perceived in the Church. Earnest discussion was given to the best method of effectively witnessing to the great truths of the Seventh-day Adventist Church which were being so modified in Australia. The two had met on the Central Coast of New South Wales, and as they strolled along the beautiful white sandy beach with the Pacific Ocean breaking upon it, they decided to call a meeting of a few sincere members, whose hearts were aching because of the degeneration in the doctrinal stance of the church in Australasia.

This meeting, which 103 Seventh-day Adventists from thirty-five churches of the South Queensland, North New South Wales, Greater Sydney, South New South Wales and Victorian Conferences attended, was held at Turramurra, a suburb of Sydney, on February 11, 1979.

The meeting commenced with a review of the history of the theological crisis in the Australasian Division, followed by an earnest season of prayer. Then ensued a discussion of the critical issues which were presently confusing and dividing God's Church in Australasia. It was agreed that it was by then perfectly evident that from the pulpits and in the high schools and colleges of the Australasian Division, the prevailing teachings were out of harmony with the fundamental Seventh-day Adventist faith. It was perceived there was a generation of Seventh-day Adventists arising who were not even aware of the old pillars of the faith and the landmarks of the remnant Church.

A grave fear that the Australasian Division was in danger of complete doctrinal separation from its brethren, worldwide, was also expressed. After separating into study groups, those attending passed a number of resolutions. These involved the upholding of the principles of the Adventist faith. They may be summarized as follows:

    1. Confirmation that the Bible and the Spirit of Prophecy are inspired of God and are utterly reliable, not only in terms of salvation, but also where they speak of history, science, and any other matter.

    2. That the historicist interpretation of prophecy, as followed by the Seventh-day Adventist Church, is the correct method of understanding the prophetic truth.

3. That there is a two-apartment Sanctuary in heaven and that Christ ministered in the first apartment upon His ascension in A.D. 31, and that he entered the most holy apartment in 1844 to commence the investigative judgment.

4. That only those who keep the commandments of God in the strength and power of Jesus Christ will make up God's remnant people.

5. That man inherits the fallen, sin-oriented nature of Adam and that this nature must be transformed by receiving the mind of Christ, if man is to be fitted for eternity.

6. That justification is not merely a judicial act by which we are freed from condemnation. It is not merely forgiveness for sin, but involves reclamation from sin.

7. That righteousness by faith is the central theme for the three angels' messages and that it involves the total salvation acts of man, including justification, sanctification and glorification.

8. That Christ took upon Himself fallen human nature, and in this nature He overcame sin in the flesh.

9. That creation week occurred approximately 6,000 years ago.

Following this affirmation of fundamental faith, six resolutions were taken. In summary these were:

1. To support and earnestly pray for the leadership of God's Church.

2. To exhibit care in the use of personal names, reserving this for formally constituted meetings or other forms of communication in the church, or in a formally and objectively written paper. It was also resolved to avoid references to inferred motives or personality characteristics.

3. To affirm the view that those who oppose or teach contrary to the Spirit of Prophecy should not be continued as salaried representatives of the Seventh-day Adventist Church.

4. To request leaders and pastors at all levels of God's Church to lift all bans on ministers and laity standing for and teaching the historic Adventist faith.

5. To earnestly request and pray that all the denominational publications produced by the Australasian Division fully reflect the Seventh-day Adventist historic faith, and that, in line with repeated Spirit of Prophecy counsel, the publications reflect specifically the distinctive doctrines surrounding the 2,300-day prophecy, the heavenly Sanctuary, the investigative judgment, the law of God, and the faith of Jesus.

6. To request urgently that the General Conference president seriously consider the appointment of a committee, committed to the historic Seventh-day Adventist faith, to investigate the serious allegations of widespread teaching and preaching inconsistent with the Seventh-day Adventist truth.

These resolutions were signed by Brother Walter Hansen of Melbourne, Brother Philip Harker of Brisbane, and Dr. Peter Martin of Sydney. Out of this meeting grew a loose organization known as the Adventist Laymen's Fellowship. This organization, sponsored, as its name implies, by lay people, concerned itself with getting the positive truth of God out to God's people at a time when little of this was being preached from pulpits or taught in our church schools.

In order to accomplish this aim, the group commenced the now-famous Vision Valley meetings. These meetings have proved to be an enormous success, for many people are hungering for the truths of God. Men brought from various places have made presentations. Most of the speakers have been from the United States, where the defense of the truth has been so much stronger. Among these have been Dr. Ralph Larson, Attorney Lewis Walton, Dr. LeRoy Moore, Pastor William May, brother Charles Wheeling, Pastor Morris Lewis, Dr. Mervyn Maxwell, Pastor Richard Lange, Colin, as well as Dr. Erwin Gane, who is an Australian domiciled in the United States. Pastor George Burnside and Pastor Austin Cooke have been the two resident Australians who have made significant presentations at the Vision Valley meetings.

From these meetings have gone forth many audio and video tapes which have compounded the influence of these vital meetings. The Adventist Laymen's Fellowship has also published a paper call *Landmarks*, first edited by a Sydney plastic surgeon, Dr. David Pennington. This magazine has developed a very good balance between presenting the positive truths of God, and presenting warnings to God's people. There is little doubt that the Adventist Laymen's Fellowship has been one of the most significant organizations holding before our people in Australia the great truths which many seem bent on destroying.

A more recent development has been the work of Maranatha Ministries, with Robert and Dorothy Wilson leading out. This organization has also brought out to Australia faithful ministers, including Pastors Ron Spear and Robert Wieland, to present the truth of God. The Maranatha Ministries has circulated much literature and many cassettes upholding truth. Much material is now being printed by the Elijah Press originally located at Cooranbong. Here, young men, including Pastor Jacobsen's three sons, have dedicated themselves to this work.

# 59 Righteousness by Faith Consultation

ON October 3 and 4, 1979, one hundred and fifty men and women met in Washington, D.C. to examine the Church's stand on the vital topic of righteousness by faith. The chairman of these meetings was Pastor Neal Wilson, president of the General Conference, and the secretary was Dr. W. R. Lesher. The delegates were divided into six groups presided over by vice-presidents of the General Conference—Pastors C. D. Henri, W. J. Hackett, C. E. Bradford, F. W. Wernick, G. R. Thompson, and W. D. Eva.

Colin was privileged to be invited to this consultation and sat in the committee presided over by Pastor Wernick. That it was necessary for such a meeting to be held, indicated the serious inroads made into the Church by the *new theology*. Some of the chief points which were examined at this particular meeting included:

1. The nature and means of justification and its relationship to the other steps in the plan of salvation.
2. How the believer throughout his life and in the judgment is accepted by God.
3. The relation of faith to justification and sanctification.
4. The characteristics of genuine faith in Jesus.
5. The nature and means of sanctification.

These matters were selected because—"In the meetings that have been held on the subject of righteousness by faith, there seems to have developed general agreement on some points which had been disputed.... This meeting will also provide an opportunity to reaffirm and/or refine those concepts previously endorsed." (Statement of Purpose presented to delegates at the Righteousness by Faith Consultation, October 3–4, 1979) Many attending the Consultation recognized the necessity of the power of the Holy Ghost to direct the minds of those present.

One group of delegates, composed of Pastor Tom Davis, a book editor of *Review and Herald*; Dr. Ralph Larson, pastor of the Campus Hill Church; Pastor Robert Wieland, pastor of the Chula Vista Church; Dr. LeRoy Moore, director of the Indian Ministries; Dr. Erwin Gane, professor of theology at Pacific Union College; Pastor Ronald Spear, *Review and Herald* evangelist; and Colin, all met in Tom Davis' office for fervent prayer. No doubt many others felt a similar need.

Dr. Lesher presented a paper, and on the second day, Pastor Wilson spoke for three-quarters of an hour. He left no doubt that he stood behind the old Seventh-day Adventist truths by stating, "If there are any here who are determined to change the Church, I want to tell you, you will not just be against me or the Church, but against God. And I want to tell you that you are doomed to failure."

In the group into which Colin was assigned, he noticed the pulling together by the Spirit of God. There had been some initial disagreements, but later, one after another of those who were present in this group made strong defenses of the truth. Olie Berg, the secretary of this group, brought things together in an introductory statement which put Romans 7 and 8 in their right perspective. Dr. E. Ludescher, president of the Euro-African Division, emphasized the veracity of the writings of the Spirit of Prophecy, while Pastor B. M. Wickwire, publishing director of the General Conference; Dr. W. R. Lesher from the General Conference Sabbath School Department; Dr. Wayne McFarland, General Conference Department of Health; Pastor Roger Coon, of the Takoma Park Church; and Mrs. Margaret Davis, wife of Pastor Tom Davis, all made strong contributions. Any predestinarian inferences were ruled out and free choice strongly supported.

At 11:15 a.m. on the second day, the various groups returned to present their reports. It then became apparent that the Spirit of God had worked in a mighty way to demonstrate His power. This was the consensus of many of the dedicated men there. Pastor Eva's group emphasized that Christ had no power to overcome sin that we do not have. Pastor Hackett's group stated that the gospel includes justification, restoration, sanctification and glorification. It involves all the most urgent features of our faith. Pastor Henri's group emphasized that the law of God can be perfectly obeyed by the Spirit-filled man. The group led by Pastor Ralph Thompson focused on the fact that justification is much more than a forensic act. It results from the work of the Holy Spirit and involves the transformation of human experience. Salvation is not only central to the cross but also to the Sanctuary ministry, for we are preparing a people who would rather die than break the commandment. Pastor Bradford's group emphasized the need of works with faith, while finally, the contribution of Pastor Wernick's group can be summarized as follows:

1. It was the wrong use of the will that lost the ability to choose in Eden.
2. The will became enslaved to Satan.
3. Divine intervention came with Genesis 3:15, to give us again the power to choose.

4. God imparts desire in the soul
5. God does not force the soul
6. Salvation comes when man chooses Christ.
7. Man's nature then comes under the control of the Holy Spirit.

There was time for much comment, and many spoke to the issues under consideration. Dr. Ford took the opportunity to emphasize the infinite nature of God's law, thus indicating that it cannot be obeyed. He cited Romans 7:14–25 and Galatians 5:17 as indicative of the mature Christian life. Over and over again there had been pointed out to him the non-validity of this understanding. Galatians 5:16 clearly indicates how wrong is such an analysis. He insisted that the Christian daily fails in speech and actions, and indicated that this failure would continue.

Such meetings, of course, are only of importance as they uphold the truths of God. It is a great pity that such meetings become necessary because of the working of persons against the truth of God. These matters should be so fixed within our knowledge, and so elementary to our understanding of the truths of God, that they are unnecessary. That such doctrines become contentious in the nineteen-seventies and -eighties simply indicates the terrible influence of the *new theology* within the hearts of many.

# 60 The Forum Revelation

ON Sabbath, October 27, 1979, Dr. Desmond Ford was invited by the Adventist Forum to speak at Pacific Union College. It was this particular talk which became his undoing. The reader may wonder why a man who had spoken on hundreds upon hundreds of occasions, and had written tens of thousands of words concerning his beliefs, should reach crisis point in this particular presentation. For those who had been concerned about Dr. Ford's theological teachings, there was not a single novel relation in that which he stated at this meeting. However, for many who had not clearly perceived the trends in the thinking of Dr. Ford, this was not the case. Many who had stoutly defended him as a godly man preaching the truth in a unique manner, were suddenly confronted with the thought that Ford was far from fundamental in his beliefs. To them, this was a startling realization. Again we would pose the question: Why did Ford choose this particular time to present frankly his inner convictions?

In answer to the first question: It must now be obvious to the reader of this book, that for many years Dr. Ford chose to represent himself as a teacher of orthodox Seventh-day Adventist doctrine. When questions were raised concerning the beliefs of his students, he would simply disown the students, stating that he could not be held responsible for every foolish concept held by those who passed through his college classes. To many, this answer was a fair and reasonable reply. Those who perceived that the vast majority of his students held such beliefs were the only ones to cast doubt upon the validity of such a reply. Further, when Dr. Ford made statements undermining Seventh-day Adventist beliefs, he would couch them in such terms that, when questioned later, there was always an escape route. Thus, when a leader of the Church would question a statement which did not appear in line with Seventh-day Adventist teachings, Ford would, in general terms, be able to point out that he had made another statement which had to be balanced against the one which had concerned the questioner. This statement would be one which was perfectly orthodox. The person who had raised the objection would feel comforted by the fact that he had, by some curious oversight, not given full attention or weight to that which Dr. Ford had presented.

In the light of Dr. Ford's open statement at the October 1979 Forum meeting, in which he revealed that he had not believed the truth on the Sanctuary for over thirty years, many concluded that Dr. Ford must be one of the most deceptive persons that this Church had ever produced. On the surface it is very difficult to escape such a conclusion, but even in what seemed like such an open and shut case, we must be careful lest we set ourselves up as judges of our fellow men.

The authors believe there is little doubt that, in Dr. Ford's mind, he was doing the will of God in being "discreet" concerning that which he stated. He was well aware of the Lord's advice to be as wise as serpents and as harmless as doves. It is our conviction that Dr. Ford felt that he was following this advice, in order to bring "truth" to the Seventh-day Adventist Church in a manner which would be acceptable to the body of believers. He well knew that if he made a frontal attack on the doctrines of the Church in a frank and open way, he would meet the same opposition as had Albion Ballenger, W. W. Fletcher and Robert Greive. He also was aware that the vast majority of ministers and laity within Australia and New Zealand would have had nothing whatsoever to do with his concepts, had he presented them in this manner.

In the 1950s probably no Division in the world field was more fundamental in its Adventist faith than the Australasian Division. It is difficult for anyone visiting Australia and New Zealand today to believe this fact, for it is well known that while many of the lay people are still fundamental in their faith, the majority of active pastors have a very weak evaluation of the function of the Spirit of Prophecy. Further, most do not believe that obedience to the law of God is a requirement, or even a possibility, this side of the Second Coming,[1] and a great number are extremely doubtful about the Sanctuary message. In 1950, it would have been difficult to find one minister who had doubts in any one of these areas. In order to change this situation to conform to his private beliefs, Ford had to show tact of an extraordinary degree. There can be no doubt that he achieved this latter aim.

There is also evidence that Dr. Ford advised senior theology students to be careful in their enunciation of some of those divergent doctrines which he had taught them in the classroom. This caution came after Ford himself was queried on the beliefs and teachings of his students. Pastor Austin Cooke, one of Australia's leading evangelists, has revealed that two interns assigned to him both confirmed that they received such advice from Ford. Further, they stated Ford had told them that eventually the time would come when there would be a sufficient number of believers adhering to the new doctrinal stance that they would be able to be more open in their teaching of this new material. In this revelation we do see a little of Ford's thinking. He was waiting until he was aware of sufficient support before coming out more openly concerning his beliefs. Then, he would judge, the situation would be much more propitious for the open preaching of the *new theology*.

There can be little doubt that Ford chose the Forum meeting to speak with an openness hitherto unknown, because he had judged that the critical moment had arrived. He then considered that the vast majority of leading Adventist theological thinkers, and even some in administrative roles, had come to the place where they valued his new theological positions. A very large number of those teaching theology in our colleges in the United States were in sympathy with Ford's views. This sympathy became apparent after Glacier View, when at Forum meeting after Forum meeting, cautious but nevertheless obvious support for Dr. Ford was found among this class of persons. Ford stated he had found in private discussions that the vast majority of theologians were sympathetic to his point of view. Where he made his tactical mistake was that he did not evaluate their position as thoroughly as he might have done. In all likelihood, he felt that his position would be protected by an overwhelming outcry of support from those who were fellow-thinkers. But he had forgotten his own former situation, where he had feared to jeopardize his position by making frank revelations himself. In that period he had chosen to sow the seeds of error in the classroom, while on the official level proclaiming the truth of God. Perhaps some of his colleagues in the United States were still, at this early stage, awaiting the development of a majority of believers who espoused their views, before they, too, openly admitted to them.

Thus, to Ford's amazement, he found that following the pronouncement of October 27, 1979, he was left high and dry by many of the people upon whose support he had counted. This was the reason it was stated that "privately, a number of S.D.A. Bible scholars who had expressed reservations about Ford's outspokenness, nevertheless, generally agreed with him on key doctrinal positions, and a large number of laymen and young clergy backed him fully." (*Christianity Today*, February 8, 1980, 64)  Since the information used by the editors of *Christianity Today* was provided, in a large measure, by Ford's friends in the Brinsmead organization, the nature of their inner belief in this matter can be discerned.

Some have also conjectured that Ford, following the meeting of October 3–4, 1979, which strongly rejected his positions upon righteousness by faith, may have feared that without some resolute action the doctrinal ground which he had taken would be reclaimed. What is true is that following the Righteousness by Faith Consultation of October 3–4, 1979, Ford's posture was altered. His strident presentation of his views upon October 27 was not the first. On October 20, he had preached in the Woodside Church in Sacramento, California, in terms quite similar to those he was to use one week later. It is possible that, at the Consultation of October 3–4, 1979, Ford felt the initiative slipping away from him, and he decided to bring his assumed supporters out into the open.

However, since Ford had for the first time painted himself into a corner by admitting that for over thirty years he had disbelieved the Adventist position on such key passages of Scripture as Hebrews 9, and he had not, on this occasion, provided himself with a covering counter-statement, he was forced to brave out the situation with minimal assistance from those who had privately assured him of their support. It is indeed possible that Ford later regretted the timing of his announcement of dissent from fundamental Adventist doctrine. Perhaps he recognized that from the point of timing, he was even then ahead of his day. The authors believe that the

Lord had a most definite hand in this, for God had determined that the time had come to put a stop to the evergrowing insinuation of apostasy by one whom many had failed to recognize as a purveyor of error.

In summary, Ford's announcements in the Forum meeting may be presented as follows:

1. That Sister White's role was pastoral, not canonical.[2]
2. That we should accept the Bible and the Bible only. (By this, Ford meant that we should not use Sister White's writings when discussing matters of doctrine.)
3. That Albion Ballenger, who was dismissed from the ministry in 1905 for preaching error on the Sanctuary doctrine, was, in fact, correct in his exposition of this doctrine.
4. That the book, *The Great Controversy*, should be seen only as an "historical account of prophetic interpretation by the Seventh-day Adventists at the time of the birth of that movement."[3]
5. That Sister White taught that Christ entered the Most Holy Place at His ascension.

Ford's assertions were so obviously in error that Pastor Arthur White, grandson of Sister White and Secretary of the White Estate from 1938 to 1978, quickly answered the charges in a most effective way. In a tape prepared at his home in Deer Park, California, November 15, 1979, Pastor White showed the fallacy of Dr. Ford's position in every case. Speaking on Dr. Ford's first point, Pastor White stated: "If he [Dr. Ford] means that Ellen White could not be considered reliable in her comments on doctrine—that she could not show Heaven's approval or disapproval of certain positions specifying what was truth and what was error on broadening our concepts of the significance of certain doctrinal points, he has taken a position out of harmony with her own declarations and the denominational position." (*Ibid.*) Arthur White, in defense of this point, quoted:

> The power of God would come upon me, and I was enabled clearly to define what is truth and what is error. As the points of our faith were thus established, our feet were placed upon a solid foundation. We accepted the truth point by point under the demonstration of the Holy Spirit. I would be taken off in vision, and explanations would be given to me. (*GW* 302)

Dr. Ford had quoted a number of statements from Sister White which emphasized the all-sufficiency of Scripture, but Pastor White pointed out that these were not meant to imply that her writings were to be thus ignored in their doctrinal insights. Pastor White quoted instance after instance where Sister White was used to bring Bible understanding more clearly before those who were seeking truth. Speaking of the light which she received on the matters of the false Sanctuary doctrine of Ballenger and the pantheistic views of Kellogg, Sister White stated:

> Men may get up scheme after scheme and the enemy will seek to seduce souls from the truth, but all who believe that the Lord has spoken through Sister White and has given her a message will be safe from the many delusions that will come in the last days. (Letter 50, 1906)

It did not take Pastor White much effort to counter Ford's view that Ballenger taught the truth on the Sanctuary, for he was able to quote:

> If the theories that Brother Ballenger presents were received, they would lead many to depart from the faith. They would counteract the truths upon which the people of God have stood for the past fifty years. (Manuscript 62, 1905)

Ford's attempt to relegate *The Great Controversy* to a mere account of the thinking of Adventists at an early period of their movement, rather than the truth relevant to our day, was again quickly shown to be false. Speaking of *The Great Controversy*, Sister White had said:

> The Lord has set before me matters which are of urgent importance for the present time, and which reach into the future. The words have been spoken in a charge to me, "Write in the book the things which thou hast seen and heard, and let it go to all the people; for the time is at hand when past history will be repeated." (*CM* 128)

Pastor White also addressed the charge that Sister White believed Christ went directly to the Most Holy Place at His ascension. Ignoring the numerous unequivocal statements that Christ entered the Most Holy Place in 1844, Ford had taken four equivocal statements to "prove" his point. This technique he had used all too often—the technique of explaining clear statements by those which were not specifically addressing the point in question.

Thus the Forum message was the beginning of the end of Ford's ministry within the Seventh-day Adventist Church. It led to a six-month period of study by Ford, followed by an examination of his findings at Glacier View and, eventually, first the removal of his ministerial credentials and later, the annulment of his ordination. It was indeed, as experience has shown, an important moment in the history of the remnant church.

Chapter 60 Endnotes

1. That this unbelief continued to be propagated in the Australasian Division well after Ford's dismissal, was seen in a reply to a question answered in the Australasian edition of the *Signs of the Times*, February 1984, 16. In answer it was stated, "A man is not a Christian unless he keeps God's commandments—but no one keeps them perfectly. See and study 1 John 2:3,4; chapter 5:2,3 and Romans 3:20–24 and verse 31, where a Christian is described as obeying God's commandments while falling short of perfection. Christian perfection is found only in Christ." (*Ibid.*) It would be instructive for each reader to review the texts quoted as support for this theory. They teach precisely the opposite of what is contended. This is yet another instance of the use of false proof texting, a technique fully exposed in *Adventism Vindicated* in the chapter, "Is Obedience Possible?"
2. This meant that her writings were not part of Scripture. The truth of this claim has never been in doubt, but what most theologians mean when they state Sister White's writings are not canonical, is that you cannot rely upon them for accuracy in doctrinal exposition. This is a very different statement, indeed, for God has most certainly inspired Sister White's insight into Bible doctrine.
3. Dr. Ford, *Forum Address*, October 27, 1979

# 61 Glacier View

IT is possible that history will not deal kindly with the Glacier View meetings. We say this, not because nothing was achieved, but because the key doctrinal issues were not resolved. Evidences of widespread dissatisfaction with the results of that meeting are not hard to find. Naturally, those espousing the *new theology* have spoken out sharply against the dismissal of Dr. Ford, which was a direct consequence of these meetings. These people tended, as we later heard, to welcome the so-called "consensus statement" concerning doctrine, perceiving that it made significant concessions to their views of the Sanctuary.[1] Those supporting the Seventh-day Adventist position were in accord with the decision to remove Desmond Ford from denominational employment, but expressed grave reservations about, and objections to, the decided trend to accept some of the erroneous positions of Dr. Ford, as if they were the truth of God.

The unsatisfactory nature of the conclusions reached at this historic meeting was determined by the diversity of belief of the delegates invited. Some of those present were well respected for their fidelity to the fundamentals of our faith. They were men who had fearlessly stood for truth despite some railing accusations. Others were just as firmly committed to the *new theology* as Dr. Ford was himself, while a third group just didn't know where to stand. This assessment is not mere speculation, but is clearly evidenced by the results of a doctrinal survey taken of the delegates before and after the session. For instance, over one-quarter of those present (26%) supported the view that the Old Testament does not set forth the termination of the 2300-day prophecy. Another 11% of those present were unsure about the validity of the year-day principle (15% rejected it outright). Only 64% of these church leaders in attendance acknowledged that they believed that Christ's second apartment ministry commenced in 1844 (31% asserted that it commenced in A.D. 31, and 5% admitted that they did not know). Only 69% of those present believed that the Sanctuary had to be cleansed of confessed sins, while only 67% could agree that the first apartment services referred to Christ's ministry from His ascension to 1844.

Thus many of those present at Glacier View were ill-qualified to make authoritative pronouncements on fundamental doctrine, for too many of them were in opposition to God's truth, or harbored uncertainty concerning it. *Something as sacred as the preservation of the faith should undoubtedly be entrusted only to those known for their deep study of, and unwavering commitment to, the fundamentals of the faith.* Only thus can truth triumph.

Some Adventists hold the view that fairness dictates persons holding truth, along with those holding error, have an equal right to be represented among those who are called upon to examine doctrinal disputes. Such a position is faulty, for it ensures that truth cannot be upheld in its purity. Usually, such meetings lead to the issuance of consensus statements cleverly worded, so that those believing both truth and error can read their positions into the statement and thus accept it. This technique is said to produce unity, but in fact, it simply leads to a most dangerous union of truth and error. Truth is never assisted by such statements; error invariably is, for a statement only supports truth when it contains pure truth, while statements support error when they contain any amount of error, however small that may be. Such a dilution of truth has a disastrous effect upon God's message. All our conclusions should uphold truth and condemn error, leaving neither in doubt. Some have expressed the view that the main aim should have been the preservation of unity among God's people. They maintain that those who have rejected truth but choose to remain as powerful voices in the Church should be heard and, as far as is feasible, their views accommodated. But surely Paul's rhetorical question is pertinent here:

> What fellowship hath righteousness with unrighteousness? and what communion hath light with darkness? (2 Cor. 6:14)

To put forward this view of accommodation is to ignore the fact that God's Church must face a shaking time if it is ever to perform its God-ordained mission. No one, when seeking a union (for it can never be unity) between those who believe the clear words of God, and those who seek to cast doubts upon them, can be performing God's will.

However, there is a very real need for gatherings of another nature bringing together those true to our message and those with growing doubts. God's people must exert every effort in Christian love to present truth before the waverers. Let us not cast them all aside at the first sign of apostasy, but let there ever be a sincere endeavor to set truth before these brethren and sisters in its most powerful light. Thus some who have been led into error by faithless teachers, or the workings of those ignorant of our special truths, may be reclaimed. This goal should ever be uppermost in the minds of God's people. Such meetings as these, however, should not be used to debate these truths.

We would not labor the matter of error accepted in the Glacier View Consensus Document entitled *Christ in the Heavenly Sanctuary*, except to illustrate our meaning with a single specific example. Since the apostasy of Albion Ballenger, and even before that time, those opposed to God's Sanctuary truth have insisted that Hebrews 6:19,20 teaches that at the time of the writing of the Epistle to the Hebrews, Christ was laboring in the Most Holy Place. This text of Scripture states:

> Which hope we have as an anchor to the soul, both sure and steadfast, and which entereth into that within the veil: whither the forerunner is for us entered, even Jesus, made an high priest for ever after the order of Melchisedec. (Hebrews 6:19,20)

The key term in this passage is, *"within the veil."* Citing Old Testament references to this term, all who have sought to overthrow the Sanctuary truth have asserted that it has the exclusive meaning of "within the Most Holy Place." Seventh-day Adventists have always disputed this interpretation, recognizing that to accept it would be tantamount to an agreement with the thesis that in apostolic times Jesus was already ministering in the second apartment of the heavenly Sanctuary. Further, such a concession would cast a decided doubt upon the clearest testimony of God's servant. Sister White, referring to this text, has written:

> The ministration of the priest throughout the year in the first apartment of the sanctuary, "within the veil" which formed the door and separated the holy place from the outer court, represents the work of ministration upon which Christ entered at His ascension. (*GC* 420)

It is perfectly plain why men like Ballenger, Fletcher, Greive, Brinsmead and Ford, in rejecting the Sanctuary message, found it necessary not only to reinterpret the book of Hebrews, but to make every effort to nullify the witness of the Spirit of Prophecy.

Thus it was most disconcerting when, ignoring the specific insights of inspiration, the *Consensus Document* conceded Ford's interpretation of Hebrews 6:19,20, while at the same time attempting to discredit the impact of such an interpretation. It was claimed that this interpretation did not necessitate the conclusion that Christ was ministering in the second apartment before the close of the first century of the Christian era. The actual words of the *Consensus Document* were, "There is no intermediate step in our approach to God. Hebrews stresses the fact that our great High Priest is at the very right hand of God (Chap. 1:3), in 'heaven itself . . . in the presence of God.'[2] (Chapt. 9:24). The symbolic language of the Most Holy Place "within the veil" is used to assure us of our full, direct and free access to God (Chaps. 6:19,20; 9:24–28; 10:1–4)."

The Response Committee set up at Glacier View, while strongly denying Dr. Ford's conclusions regarding this passage, did concede too much to Dr. Ford's interpretation. This committee issued a *Ten-Point Statement* which, in referring to the term, *within the veil*, stated: "We acknowledge the insights of Dr. Ford's study of the letter to the Hebrews; however, we do not agree with the theological implications he draws from the term 'within the veil.'" The authors then went on to affirm their belief in a two-apartment ministry, stating that Hebrews 6:19,20 should not be used to destroy this Bible doctrine, but rather the term '*within the veil*' means that "since Christ's ascension we have full, free and direct access to the very presence of God." Undoubtedly, the conclusion of this Response Committee was absolutely correct and the only reasonable interpretation of the text. However, its reference to Dr. Ford's view, that the term *"within the veil"* has a strict literal meaning of "within the 'most holy place,'" was unfortunate. Since that time, truth has been hampered by some who have used these statements as grounds for rejecting the truth of inspiration, which unquestionably informs us that the term specifically refers to the first apartment.

The Glacier View Meeting was convened on August 10–15, 1980. Its specific purpose was to examine Dr. Ford's 900-page thesis prepared during a six-month period of paid leave. In this manuscript, Dr. Ford set out the reasons for his objections to the Sanctuary doctrine. As had been pointed out by the Concerned Brethren in Australia some years previously, those examining Dr. Ford's manuscript concluded that "in various instances [statements] have been taken out of context or used indiscriminately and thus not in harmony with the quoted writers' original intent. This is true of both secular and Spirit of Prophecy statements." (*Ministry*, Oct. 1980)

It is not the purpose of this manuscript to detail every procedure followed at Glacier View, since any reader who cares to can find a full account in the *Ministry* magazine of October, 1980. Much good arose from the meetings because a number of strong expositions of Bible truth related to the vital doctrine of the Sanctuary were presented. Whatever its shortcomings, Glacier View was an honest attempt by the leadership to come to terms with a very dangerous and most unsettling series of doctrinal deviations.

Its weaknesses were manifold, but two stand out. Dr. Ford's view of the Sanctuary was not formulated without influence upon other doctrines. In particular, it logically necessitated his erroneous view of righteousness by faith. In ignoring this connection, some delegates were blinded to the enormity of the problem they confronted. Some had not sufficiently studied the subject to an extent where they could see that the Sanctuary message is so much an expression of righteousness by faith, that it is a rank impossibility for someone to hold the truth on one of these doctrines and be in error on the other. Yet some at Glacier View harbored the conviction that Dr. Ford's preaching on righteousness by faith had blessed the Church. However, a careful examination of Dr. Ford's teaching on this topic, comparing it with Scripture and the Spirit of Prophecy, reveals that his presentations, based as they are on the premise that obedience to God's law by a Spirit-filled Christian is not possible, are incorrect in virtually every detail. Many overlooked Christ's stern warning to those who do not obey His commandments:

> Whosoever therefore shall break one of these least commandments, and shall teach men so, he shall be called the least in the kingdom of heaven: but whosoever shall do and teach them, the same shall be called great in the kingdom of heaven. (Matthew 5:19)

Some of the delegates even asserted that they had benefited by Dr. Ford's presentations on righteousness by faith, though recognizing that they were not fully truth. (See *Ministry*, October 1980, 4.)

The second major failing was the diversity of belief among the delegates. Within the Seventh-day Adventist Church, theologians represent a relatively minute percentage of the flock. Conversely, lay people represent over ninety-five percent of God's Church. Yet the theologians were represented by large numbers, while the lay people were virtually unrepresented. Some would not see this imbalance as an untoward situation, believing as they do that theologians are the experts on doctrine, while the lay people are relatively ignorant of the subject. After all, it could be argued, a conference on medical practice would naturally call on a proportionately higher representation from physicians than from lay persons, despite the fact that the lay people outnumber physicians several hundred to one, even in Western nations. (Perhaps even in this area, physicians would do well to heed the good insights many of their patients provide, and a first-class physician does indeed do this.)

But in the area of doctrine and Bible study, the situation is very different indeed, primarily because the whole history of theologians in the Christian Church is a sorry one indeed. While occasionally godly theologians, such as Paul and Martin Luther, have been mightily used of God to uplift the truth, the major errors of Christendom have originated in the minds of the theologians. The history of Christianity abounds with theologians who have upheld Sunday sacredness, the immortality of the soul, the secret rapture, futurist and preterist interpretations of prophecy, and even the "death of God" theory.

On the other hand, when God wished to reveal His last great message to mankind, he chose humble lay people—farmers, artisans, seamen, and housewives. This policy did not differ in substance from Christ's in the selection of apostles. The reason is that as a general principle such people, being humble and dedicated to their Lord, are more able than the learned to interpret the Scripture accurately.

> The Bible with its precious gems of truth was not written for the scholar alone. On the contrary, it was designed for the common people; and the interpretation given by the common people, when aided by the Holy Spirit, accords best with the truth as it is in Jesus. (5*T* 331)

Thus it would seem to be only prudent at such future discussions on doctrine to reduce the proportion of theologians and increase the number of lay people in attendance. In our opinion, such would be a surer path to doctrinal purity and would give the discussion the distinct advantage of the insights of those whose views accord best with truth. If this lesson had been learned from the Glacier View meetings, then a substantial matter would have been resolved and the entire expense justified.

## Chapter 61 Endnotes

1. Referring to Dr. Ford, Pastor Spangler, Secretary of the General Conference Ministerial Stewardship Association, stated: "He professed to being able to feel very comfortable preaching under the umbrella of the consensus paper just voted at Glacier View. In his opinion, that paper showed a definite shift away from Ellen White's interpretations of the Sanctuary. He said that the Church had moved considerably from its past position toward his direction, and in a few years the Church will eventually come to see things as he does." (*Ministry*, Oct. 1970) The same author emphasized that "Dr. Ford would not shift his position even on minor points. . . . after meeting with Des for approximately fifty hours, during which time numerous suggestions, both spoken and written were shared with him, the Committee was unable to find any evidence that he had accepted a single suggestion." (*Ibid.*) These two statements should cause grave concern. It was conceded that Dr. Ford made absolutely no concession with regard to any of his erroneous views, yet he found the consensus statement sufficiently close to his errors to be able to preach under it with comfort. Such a reaction should direct us to reexamine the Glacier View Consensus Statement and rid it of doctrinal error.

2. The Consensus Statement here links the term "within the veil" with the Most Holy Place, while Sister White (see quotation from GC 420) specifically states that it refers to the first apartment (the holy place). The rejection of such a precise position of the Spirit of Prophecy should have no place in our Church pronouncements.

# 62

## Editor Denounces the Sanctuary Doctrine

FROM 1967 to 1980, our former headmaster was editor of the church publications in Australia. He had commenced his denominational service as a church school teacher. Indeed, when the authors first attended the Newcastle Adventist School in 1943, he was appointed that year as the headmaster of the school, although he was then quite a young man. He remained at the school for a total of seven years, the exact seven years that we attended the Newcastle Seventh-day Adventist School.

Since the school was only small and boasted at the maximum four teachers for all the grades from grade one to matriculation, we had the opportunity of growing to know the headmaster extremely well. He was a man we admired very greatly. In fact, perhaps one of the reasons that we both followed, initially, a teaching career, was due to his example and our admiration for him. He was a fine teacher and a most enthusiastic school leader. It is always a painful experience when men who have been greatly admired and to whom people owe so much, depart from the faith.

After some years as headmaster of our school and later of the Sydney Adventist High School, he left denominational service to become editor of the Shakespeare Head Press. But in 1967 he reentered denominational service at the request of the Australasian Division, to head the editorial work of the Signs Publishing Company in Warburton in Victoria.

After some time, to our dismay, we noted that the tenor of the articles in the denominational papers was changing, coming very much into line with the teachings and concepts of Dr. Ford. It soon became evident to many that the distinctive truths of God were not being upheld. This change was evident not only to Seventh-day Adventists. On one occasion, shortly before the editor was released from his duties as editor, our father attended a meeting in a country town of Victoria and fell into conversation there with a leader of the Presbyterian Church. This man mentioned that he had received the Australasian edition of the *Signs of the Times* and had done so for many years. Our father warmed to this fact and expressed satisfaction in it. However, he was completely nonplussed when the man turned to him and said: "Well, I want to tell you, you people have changed a tremendous lot of your doctrines in recent years." The embarrassing fact was that our father could not, in all truth, rightly deny the accusation.

How and why the editor changed from his belief in the fundamentals of our Church we do not know, but we can testify that when he taught us Bible doctrines in grade 11, we were not taught the doctrines that he later promoted in the church publications. When he taught us in grade 10 Daniel and Revelation, we were not taught the material that Dr. Ford was permitted to place in the *Signs of the Times* for non-believers to read, as if it represented the Seventh-day Adventist position.

One matter is certain, however, and that is, for reasons best known to himself, this church editor ceased to have any faith in the Sanctuary message. This fact was brought to the fore in a letter which he wrote to Pastor Duncan Eva, who, at the time, was a vice-president of the General Conference. The letter was dated March 11, 1980. It will be recalled that this was almost six months after Dr. Ford had declared his opposition to the truth of God in the now-famous Forum lectures of October 27, 1979. Dr. Ford was at this point preparing his nine-hundred-page defense of his position, and the Church had taken no stand upon it. The timing, we believe, is worth recording so that the letter can be placed in its proper context.

After defending Dr. Ford very stoutly, the editor stated: "'I can be as good a Seventh-day Adventist without the Sanctuary as I ever was with it' is something that I am hearing increasingly. Come to think of it, so can I, and so, apparently, can you, for your article did not mention the Sanctuary, which must have been a surprise to other readers beside myself.[1] (Whether they applauded your stance as much as I did, I cannot say.) Your article, incidentally, has not yet been published. I have taken pains to point out to Alf Jorgensen[2] and to Pastor Parmenter[3] that the publication of your article will bring a storm about their heads; nevertheless, I say to you that I applaud what you have written.[4]

"I, too, have examined myself concerning the Sanctuary doctrine and my relationship to the Church, and come up, as have so many others, with the thought that my standing as a loyal member of the church is in no way compromised if I do not believe that Christ was ministering for 1800 years in a small room in Heaven before He went in to the Father. Indeed, I have not so believed for many a year, but have rather embraced the two-phase ministry of Christ in Heaven as so many have done, but have never promulgated this interpretation in any way. Years ago, I said to my wife, 'You'll never hear me preach about the Sanctuary.' This was mainly because I felt that it was not my place to stir unnecessarily, so I elected to remain silent on a non-essential (as I saw it) issue. That is about all I ever said and even today, when my revelations are being made, I am not jumping into the fray to contribute my two-cents' worth. Better minds than mine are concerned with these issues, but these better minds are bringing information to me which I dare not ignore—and that goes for a lot of people who have spoken to me and written to me.

"Again I say it, my relationship to God's Church is not altered one whit because this cherished doctrine is revealed to be passé. And if 1844 is a non-event, as Cottrell[5] proved to everyone but himself, so what? Why can't we be big enough to come out and say it? That is our trouble—the 'don't rock the boat' philosophy is so ingrained into our thinking, that anyone who dares to trespass on to new territory (to change the metaphor) to seek to mine nuggets of truth is regarded as a villain and as someone who has the upset of the Church as his goal. Believe me, Pastor Eva, I have no brief for Robert Brinsmead, but I admire him for the capacity he had for saying: 'I made a mistake. I am embarrassed by some of the things I put my name to in the past.' Would that we were as honest! And as courageous!" [6]

Here is a clear declaration of disbelief in the Sanctuary doctrine. The writer stated that he had not believed the doctrine for "many a year." How alarming it was that a man who was prepared to continue in such a responsible position as editor of our church papers, frankly admitted that he disbelieved a pillar of the Seventh-day Adventist faith. Manifestly, no man can be a Seventh-day Adventist who does not believe the Sanctuary message, one of the key doctrines of our faith, any more than an individual can be a Seventh-day Adventist who expresses disbelief in the Sabbath doctrine. Most Adventists would never have anticipated the day would come when a man who for many years disbelieved one of the pillars of the faith, could retain his position as a credentialed minister and editor. But upon his own admission, the editor had done so. We could not help but notice his condemnation of those who will not come out and state what they believe, lest they "rock the boat." Yet in the preceding paragraph he admitted that he himself had fallen under such condemnation, for he set forward as a virtue, in his own case, that he had "never promulgated this interpretation in any way." (*Ibid.*) It's strange how that which is a virtue in oneself is a defect in others. Of course, we all suffer from this weakness.

In his letter, the editor was extremely exercised by Cottrell's tape, a tape which to many of God's people represented a very sad reflection on the thinking of a man who should have known much better. In discussing the matters contained in Cottrell's tape, the editor was quite strong in his denunciation of the leadership of the Church. "We have been misled by a hierarchy (an unpleasant word, but that is the term which is increasingly used) which knew these things, but which has elected to cover up the truth. If they have done this, they can hardly be trusted in matters which are equally important." (*Ibid.*) Further on, the editor stated: "I sense, Pastor Eva, a distrust for the leadership which I have never sensed before, and this is not pleasing to me. I regard myself as a completely loyal Seventh-day Adventist, loyal to my own leadership and loyal to the brethren of the General Conference. But this current revelation is doing nothing to bolster one's confidence in the leadership. What can restore it, is not in my province to suggest, but I can only think that complete honesty and forthrightness with the people would be a beginning." (*Ibid.*) The editor continued to voice his support for Dr. Ford. "If Ford is ecclesiastically decapitated, or if he is silenced because of what he said, then justice will be trampled in the dust if Cottrell is allowed to continue his way unchallenged. It is my personal wish that neither of these men should be silenced. God knows that we need scholars who will speak the truth and bring fresh insights to the people." (*Ibid.*) In another statement he described Ford as "the scapegoat."

The editor concluded with a heated finale, "Most of my working life has been in what we call the organized work. But yesterday I was angry because truth had been swept under the carpet, because honesty had been given a deadly wound, because one man has been called to account when another's even more damning evidence has been ignored, because 'peace at any price' has become the slogan, and that price is truth and honesty, because bigotry in high places has been uncovered, because *sola Scriptura,* which the Church has piously intoned for more years than I can remember, has been a mere sham and a fraudulent claim, because the 'little people' of the Church have been misled by men who would not trust them with the truth as they knew it to be, because the grand old lady has been elevated to a place where she would not have allowed herself to be, to the detriment of truth and right. These things, Pastor Eva, stir me to write to you this morning. I regret that I feel this way, but I also believe that I represent the feelings of many of the honest, sincere people with whom I have contact." (*Ibid.*)

This letter stated that copies were sent to only two persons—Pastor Duncan Eva and Pastor Keith Parmenter, yet several months later, copies of the letter surfaced in the United States, initially, among those who had accepted the *new theology*. Some have suggested that, as soon as possible, the editor sent this letter to someone who was favorably mentioned in it and that he saw an advantage to its distribution. However, this view has no firm evidence.

The editor's reply to the exposure of his convictions was to complain very bitterly that his private letter had been distributed. This complaint perhaps was more a cry of despair that his inner disbeliefs were now apparent. What is more perplexing is that before the year 1980 was completed, this man had been elected president of the Greater Sydney Conference. It is true that at the time the constituency was quite unaware of this letter, but it is puzzling to many that the Division did not warn the nominating committee, since it was represented at the constituency meeting.[7] By the 1982 election, however, this matter was well known throughout the Greater Sydney Conference. Indeed, at the constituency meeting, at least four persons forcibly brought the matter to the attention of the gathered delegates. Despite this, the editor was reelected. Perhaps nothing better reflected the state of the Church in Australia than to record that God's people were prepared to elect a self-proclaimed disbeliever to the highest position of trust in their Conference; a position which entails the preservation of the doctrines of the Church, and that this man was prepared to accept the election.[8]

## Chapter 62 Endnotes

1. The editor was referring to an article which he had received from Pastor Duncan Eva for inclusion in one of the church papers. Pastor Eva later reacted to the inferences in the letter by stating that he fully believed the Sanctuary message.
2. Field Secretary of the Australasian Division.
3. President of the Australasian Division.
4. Pastor Eva's paper was never published.
5. Dr. Raymond Cottrell, retired church editor, who had attacked the Sanctuary doctrine at a meeting in California
6. Letter written from the editor of the Australasian *Signs of the Times,* to Pastor Duncan Eva, dated March 11, 1980
7. In fact, it was reported by one of the nominating committee, that when the editor's name was under discussion for the presidency, one of the committee asked the Division president, who was present, how the editor stood in regard to the doctrines of the Church. The Division president's alleged response was that the editor was quite O.K., and yet about nine months before this, the Division president had received the editor's damning letter to D. Eva.
8. See Appendix I.

# 63 Dispelling Darkness

CHURCH leaders are naturally interested in the preservation of unity. It is a very simple matter for people who have not had the burden of administration placed upon them to be critical of this apparent overwhelming urge to preserve unity at all costs. The authors hold positions of administration, and we know all too well how happy we are when there is a contented spirit of unanimity among the workers in our institutions. Indeed, both have worked very hard to establish and maintain such unity. Only those who have been thrust into such positions know how disturbing it is to have bitter controversy within the ranks of those working within one's organization. This fact must be kept in mind when evaluating the reasons behind calls for unity.

While consistently some church leaders in Australia have chosen to declare that the concerned brethren were the source of the disunity in the Church, the plain facts were that those who declared persistent disobedience to the Decalogue was not necessarily associated with the loss of eternal life were the real sources. Yet the hands of those who declare that men will continue to sin until the Second Coming of Christ are those whom the leaders uphold. In Australia and New Zealand, at least three-quarters of the ministers in active service believe that victory over sin cannot be the lot of God's people prior to glorification. It is these men who have caused the greatest divisiveness ever to present itself within the Australasian Division. Yet leaders of that Division have traveled the world declaring that the ministers and leaders in Australia follow a middle-of-the-road course. By the 1980s, many leaders in other Divisions were openly skeptical of these obviously false claims. When the president of the Australasian Division repeated this claim in a worship service at the Far Eastern Division Headquarters in Singapore in June, 1984, he was challenged by his counterpart, who had spoken to a sufficient number of Australian pastors to recognize that the claim lacked veracity.

In fact there is no middle road. God never speaks of three roads. All there is, is truth and error without any dispute; the majority of ministers in Australia were strongly promoting error and thus causing deep divisions among God's people. Sister White declared about unity:

> In the professedly Christian world, many turn away from the plain teachings of the Bible and build up a creed from human speculations and pleasing fables;

and they point to their tower as a way to climb up to heaven. Men hang with admiration upon the lips of eloquence while it teaches that the transgressor shall not die, that salvation may be secured without obedience to the law of God. If the professed followers of Christ would accept God's standard, it would bring them into unity; but so long as human wisdom is exalted above His holy word, there will be divisions and dissension. (*PP* 124)

That the Church of God should and will become a unified force cannot be doubted, for Christ has promised this unity in Scripture. However, let us never overlook that the most divisive force in this world is truth, for it divides those who would follow it from those who would spurn it. Calls for unity must always be based firmly upon a platform of truth. And truth must never be muzzled. It is not surprising, therefore, that some church leaders, in their eagerness to preserve unity, have requested that truth not be spoken lest it cause division. Indeed, there were instances where whole Conferences of ministers were forbidden to say anything about the Sanctuary message until the Glacier View meetings were concluded. Such requests made it appear as if we were ignorant of what the truth was on these matters, and had to wait for a body of theologians to tell us what it was.

In the Australasian Division at one time, the doctrine of Righteousness by Faith was said to be a matter which could not be discussed, for it was *sub judice*, since it was to be discussed at the Palmdale Conference in 1976. It is entirely unacceptable, and indeed appalling, that men would dare to suggest that God's people are so unaware of the truth, that it should not be proclaimed with all the force and veracity to which Scripture attests. The time to present our doctrines with the greatest clarity and with the loudest voices is at the time they are under attack. When Israel adopted the practice of idolatry, would Elijah have fulfilled his God-given calling if he had decided that this was the time to cease speaking concerning the first and second commandments, lest it cause division in Israel? We might well ask ourselves the question, "Did Christ, when he saw hypocrisy and legalistic formalism practiced within the Jewish church, decide that He should not deal with topics related to these areas, lest He be the source of division in God's Church in Israel?" He was unafraid to call sin by its right name, just as Elijah was on Mount Carmel.

When the physicians at Battle Creek chose to keep their counsel concerning the apostasy of Dr. Kellogg, Sister White did not compliment them on their great desire for unity; rather she condemned them roundly for not measuring up to their duty in denouncing error. Writing to our physicians at Battle Creek Sanitarium in the summer of 1904, Sister White put the following question:

> Will the men in our institutions keep silent, allowing insidious fallacies to be promulgated to the ruin of souls? (*1SM* 195)

This question should be pondered by every Seventh-day Adventist. Sister White's condemnation did not cease with this question. She further stated:

> For years our physicians have been trained to think that they must not give expression to sentiments that differ from those of their chief [Dr. J. H. Kellogg]. O that they had broken the yoke! O that they had called sin by its right name! Then they would not be regarded in the heavenly courts as men who, though bearing weighty responsibilities, have failed of speaking the truth in reproof of that which has been in disobedience to God's Word. (*Ibid.* 196)

Let the pillars of our faith be preached with greater confidence and assurance in this time of peril. Let no one hinder the voice of those who would do so, or remove the pen of those who would write in defense of such truths. It is absolutely impossible to find a single text of Scripture or a single passage in the Spirit of Prophecy which admonishes silence in the face of attacks upon God's Church and its doctrines. Indeed, Sister White reminded us that—

> If God abhors one sin above another, of which His people are guilty, it is doing nothing in case of an emergency. Indifference and neutrality in a religious crisis is regarded of God as a grievous crime, and equal to the very worst type of hostility against God. (*3T* 281)

Today our people are thirsting for the precious truths of our faith, and yet many of our pastors spend each Sabbath day in the pulpit preaching those things which could be preached by ministers of virtually any other denomination. It should be a rare event in a Seventh-day Adventist Church that the sermon presented could be given with equal facility by a minister of another denomination. We have a unique message, and it is this unique message alone, which will stir men and women to serve God with the whole heart. May it ever be preached from uncensored lips with the impelling power of the Most High.

# 64    Moral Degeneracy

DOCTRINES are vital. For this reason Scripture admonishes purity of doctrines. The pluralism[1] advocated by many of our theologians is quite contrary to the Bible, for pluralism means that both truth and error may be accepted side by side. This acceptance can never exist in the Christian faith. Error always leads to a lowering of standards and a loss of Christian commitment, leading to eternal loss. One evidence of this degeneration has been the growing acceptance of the practice of homosexuality among Seventh-day Adventists. This sin was overwhelmingly condemned by God on a number of occasions, and regarding it the Scripture states:

> But the men of Sodom were wicked and sinners before the LORD exceedingly. (Genesis 13:13)

It appears to have become a prevailing sin in our Church. One can not but have sympathy for persons who have this weakness, but like other predispositions to sin, the person, under the power of God, can and must have victory in thought and deed. Unless this is so, then God's Word amounts to nothing.

Nothing brought this problem to the fore with greater suddenness than the so-called "Kinship Kamp Meeting," held for homosexual "Adventists" in August 1980 in Arizona. Had this meeting been an effort to find victory over their sin, there might have been some value in it, although meeting together in this way could hardly be viewed as a wise procedure. The General Conference leadership, in the authors' opinion, erred in approving six representatives to this "Kamp Meeting." It is probable that the administrators "may have thought Kinship (the name of the homosexual Adventist group) was appealing for denominational help to escape from homosexuality." (Alvin Benton, "Adventists Face Homosexuality," *Spectrum*, Vol. 12, No. 3, p. 33) But Benton soon put an end to that misconception by stating: "Kinship leaders assert, rather, that they sought only mutual understanding between the church organization and gay Adventists and deny that any attempt was made to let it appear that they were seeking 'deliverance' from their orientation." (*Ibid.*) This assertion is perfectly evident from the workshop topics chosen, which included "It's OK to be Gay," "Ethics for Gay Christians," "Relationships," and "Being Gay and S.D.A." In view of such topics, it should have been obvious that it was improper for representatives of the Church to attend, for this tended to lend church support to these persons in their sin. To take this course to its logical conclusion, let us substitute any other sin and see how these topics might look. Perhaps we could have a workshop entitled, "Being a Robber and S.D.A." or, "It's OK to be an Adulterer" or "Ethics for Murderous Christians." Perhaps it would be proper for us to invite all the so-called Seventh-day Adventist thieves to a camp meeting so that they could discuss how they could be accepted while continuing in their thieving? We would advise, however, that if any church representative should attend such a gathering, he should keep a close eye on his pocketbook lest he, too, become a victim of the continuing sin of the campers.

Sadly, the ministers selected to counsel with these people were, by and large, from the liberal group of the Church, and did little but encourage these people in their sin by asserting that the Scripture could not be properly understood in its condemnation of homosexuality. The three theologians selected were the chairman of the New Testament Department at Andrews University, who was subsequently appointed president of Avondale College; an Old Testament scholar and professor of archaeology at Andrews University; and a professor of theology at the same university. With them were the pastor of the Sligo Church, the pastor of the Rockville Church, and a counselor to homosexuals in Pennsylvania.

It was the New Testament and Old Testament professors who gave indirect encouragement to the homosexuals, but others also made their contribution. The pastor of the Sligo church concentrated on what he termed "Pastoral Bungling" (*ibid*. 34) and what he saw as the ill-advice of ministers to homosexuals which caused "them to believe they are eternally lost." (*Ibid*.)

The pastor of the Rockville Church said that her experience in counseling homosexuals had caused her to ask the question: "Would God require a whole group of people either to change orientation or be celibate when they didn't choose their orientation, and statistics say perhaps only four percent could change even with extensive counseling?" (*Ibid*.) She then went on to say: "It's easy for me, a happily married heterosexual [she and her husband were divorced in 1983], to say, 'You homosexual people must be celibate to be right with God.'" (*Ibid*.)

Only the counselor to homosexuals asserted that he "believed all homosexual relationships are unhealthy and sinful." (*Ibid*.)

The professor of Theology offered to the gathered homosexuals the advice that they should aim to reach "as a goal the highest level of moral behavior of which they are capable." (*Ibid*. 35) Quite clearly, such a standard, if adopted in every area of Christian life, would be tantamount to the perpetual practice of sin. We should never aim for the moral behavior of which we alone are capable. Our aim must be for that level of moral behavior which God in the life makes possible. By placing a trivial human standard before these people, their counselors made it impossible for them to find victory over sin.

The Old Testament professor was given the opportunity to show the clear Old Testament passages which roundly condemn homosexuality. Yet he adopted what was called a bottom-line conclusion, "that the Old Testament *by itself* (without the counsel of the New Testament and a contemporary theology of sexuality, based on the whole testimony of Scripture) is not sufficient to settle the question of the morality of homosexual relationships in today's world." (*Ibid.*)²

This same professor excused his conclusions on the basis that "references to homosexual acts in the Levitical 'holiness code' have been read by religious people to make moral judgments against those acts. However, noted [name omitted], other parts of the same code, such as rules against sexual intercourse during menstruation and against mixing dissimilar fabrics in the same garment are substantially ignored." (*Ibid.*)

This tactic left it to the New Testament professor in his presentation on the New Testament, to show what is clearly stated there. But in fact, he asserted, "There is no discussion in Scripture of homosexual orientation. While there is mention of certain homosexual *acts* unacceptable to the Christian community, none is defined with sufficient specificity for us to know exactly what is being described. One must understand the context of any Scriptural passage, said [name omitted], before the real meaning of the text can be understood. [Name omitted] pointed to clear New Testament disapproval of some kinds of sexual acts, both homosexual and heterosexual, even if determining exactly what those acts were, is difficult. What is clear, [name omitted] maintained, is that sexual acts growing out of lust—misusing people—were patently unacceptable." (*Ibid.*35,36) Despite his reputation as a New Testament scholar, this professor seemed to have had absolutely no understanding of some of the clearest passages of Scripture. Because of this evident lack he offered very poor advice indeed to these needed souls. The New Testament leaves no doubt about God's abhorrence concerning the practice of homosexuality. Two texts will suffice:

> For this reason God gave them up to dishonorable passions. Then women exchanged natural relations for unnatural, and the men likewise gave up natural relations with women and were consumed with passion for one another, men committing shameless acts with men and receiving in their own persons the due penalty of their error. (Romans 1:26,27, RSV)

> Do you not know that the unrighteous will not inherit the kingdom of God? Do not be deceived, neither the immoral, nor idolaters, nor adulterers, nor sexual perverts. (1 Corinthians 6:9, RSV)

The news item of this meeting, which must rank as one of the most deplorable in the annals of the Seventh-day Adventist Church, was sent to our colleges. At least one, the Canadian Union College, published the article and concluded with the paragraph, "more information on Kinship can be obtained" (the name of the president of the group and his address were quoted). ³ One can only pray that no reader was induced to write for this further information.

After the publication of this report, it was only natural that many true believers in Australia were greatly concerned, since the New Testament professor had been appointed as president of the Avondale College. Much pressure was brought to bear on the Australasian Division to investigate his sympathy for the homosexual group. He was then pressed to write a statement which appeared in the *Australasian Record*. One only has to read a paragraph or two to realize that he was saying virtually everything except that the practice of homosexuality is in all instances a sin. This truth the Avondale College president never brought himself to state. He later produced a paper of over twenty pages in which he again, despite much verbosity, failed in a single instance to make such a declaration. His use of careful wording is very obvious, for he combines homosexuality with heterosexuality,[4] knowing full well that within heterosexuality, although he dared not state this opinion openly, "I want to assure you that, as long as I am principal of Avondale College, no person, male or female, homosexual, bisexual, or heterosexual, involved in the practice of sexual behavior that is immoral, as defined either explicitly or implicitly, by the Christian Scripture (both Old and New Testaments) and by the writings of Ellen G. White, will be admitted, knowingly, to Avondale College, as a member of either the administration, staff, or student body, or if discovered to be so involved after admission, continued at the college." [5]

His intent becomes even more evident when we realize that he had already expressed the opinion, "Neither Jesus nor Ellen White said anything explicitly about the issue of the morality of homosexuality." (*Spectrum*, Vol. 12, No. 3, p. 36) Thus his inclusion of the writings of Ellen White is really a smokescreen to make it seem as if he is utilizing all sources of Inspiration. It will be noticed that he stated that anybody who practiced sexual behavior that is immoral, as defined either explicitly or implicitly by the Christian Scriptures, or Ellen G. White, would be removed from the college. Since the College president had claimed that homosexuality is not declared to be a sin by either the Bible or the Spirit of Prophecy, his statement was worthless. Further, at no stage did he attempt to say what were such immoral acts. In his statement to the homosexual group in Arizona, he made it perfectly clear that, as far as homosexuality is concerned, in his opinion, the Bible and the Spirit of Prophecy are totally useless in defining this term.

We live in an age when men and women are seeking to insinuate evil into our Church by the use and misuse of words. It is true they will confuse the superficial reader sufficiently to mislead him. But there is a God in heaven who perceives with exactitude every intention of the heart.

Many believe that they are demonstrating love and Christian concern by failing to point out the sin of individuals and accepting them as they are. Such overlook the fact that sin always brings unhappiness to the sinner. It is no favor to him to leave him in his sin. Further, it overlooks the deep sorrow which it causes our Savior and the heavenly hosts. Furthermore, to suggest that sin cannot cease, is an affront to a merciful God, who promises power to overcome all hereditary and cultivated tendencies to evil.

The question which needs to be faced by each minister of the gospel is whether he has shown kindness to a person who is practicing the sin of homosexuality by encouraging him with the false belief that this sin is not incompatible with his salvation. Such a position defies the plainest words of the Almighty. Further, as such a man lies dying of AIDS and its complication, Kaposi's sarcoma, when victory over the sin of homosexuality would have saved him from this feared disease, will the victim thank the pastor who brought him no word of reproach? Worse still, in the day of the final destruction of sinners, will such a person offer gratitude to his "loving" pastor?

Surely the only proper path is for God's people to point out the sin and to offer Jesus Christ as the provider of complete victory. This victory will bring rewards in this life and eternal life to each repentant, overcoming soul. This fact is true of the homosexual just as truly as it is of the adulterer, thief, blasphemer, evil-tempered or murderer.[6]

## Chapter 64 Endnotes

1. This term refers to the acceptance of the view that several doctrinal positions may be equally valid simultaneously.
2. Lev. 20:13 NEB: "If a man has intercourse with a man as with a woman, they both commit an abomination. They shall be put to death." This text would leave the reader in no doubt as to God's stand on homosexuality between consenting parties, for obviously both were stoned because they consented to the act.
3. *Aurora*, students' paper of Canadian Union College, November 15, 1980
4. He combined these two forms of sexuality with bisexual conduct on well over twenty occasions in his larger paper.
5. Statement by the Avondale College president, *Australasian Record*, March 26, 1983
6. It is worth reporting that the Avondale College president subsequently invited, at suitable intervals, the Old Testament professor, the theology professor and the pastor of the Sligo church to present special lecture series in the college. Perhaps the other two were not invited because the Rockville pastor left the ministry and the counselor of homosexuals supported the correct moral standard on this matter. It is little wonder that the Concerned Brethren saw Avondale College to be in jeopardy.

# 65 American Leader in Australia

IN 1981, Pastor William May, secretary of the Southwestern Union in the United States, was invited by the Adventist Laymen's Fellowship to deliver a series of addresses at their Vision Valley retreat. On his return to the United States, Pastor May made the following report, which he circulated in a newsletter to the retired workers in the Southwestern Union. He gleaned this material from his first-hand observation of the situation in Australia. Because of its perceptiveness, the report will be quoted in its entirety:

"Tragically, the Ford/Brinsmead '*new theology*' heresy is making major inroads into our Church in Australia. For some unexplained reason, believers in the '*new theology*' were permitted to teach at the (Avondale) College for the last twenty years. The results are absolutely astounding:

"1. Avondale teachers are mostly pro-Ford. The graduates are overwhelming Fordites.

2. A large proportion of the pastors are Forditfeaturing, since that is the theology they were taught at college. They teach heresy from the pulpit.

3. Most teachers in our church schools teach heresy to the students.

4. '*New theology*' tapes, books, articles and teachings abound in many workers' meetings, official papers, the Adventist Book Centres, etc., and every effort is made by certain leaders and pastors to prevent the true S.D.A. position from being heard.

5. So many have embraced the *new theology* that in many churches and on many Conference boards and committees, they have the balance of power in voting.

6. The loyal Seventh-day Adventists (about 450) who attended my meetings, are church elders and other local church leaders from all over the country, plus retired ministers (who, incidentally, are extremely distressed over the situation).

7. Their questions to me included the following:

(a) 'My boy is ready for Avondale College, but I can't send him there because of heresy. We have only one college in Australia. What shall I do?'

(b) 'My pastor openly teaches error from the pulpit. Shall I rebuff him?'

(c) 'I have three people ready for baptism, but I'm afraid to take them to church because of heresy. What shall I do?'

(d) 'I can't send my children to church school because of heresy being taught by the teachers. I'm writing all over about this. What do you advise?'

"In all my ministry I have never been so torn in my soul over a situation as with that I saw in Australia. The loyal Seventh-day Adventists feel framed and backed up against the wall. Their hearts are screaming for help, and they feel no one is listening.

"Thankfully, the loyal brethren in administration (and there are some) are preparing a strong counter-attack (it is under-cover, as yet), but it will take many, many months (perhaps years), much trauma, tremendous heartache and crunches and much intervention of the Lord to turn it around. And sadly—pathetically—unforgivably, many will be lost in the process, who would have still been loyal Seventh-day Adventists if the heresy had never been permitted a foothold. Who will answer for these precious people?

"The lesson must not be lost on us here in America. The '*new theology*' is gaining a foot-hold all over the North American Division. It teaches the following regarding the Seventh-day Adventist doctrine:

(i) that we are not the remnant church
(ii) that the three angels' messages are invalid
(iii) that the Seventh-day Sabbath is unimportant. (While I was in Australia, Brinsmead issued the manuscript for a book against the Sabbath. I have a copy.)
(iv) that the 'clean and unclean' foods message is false. All foods are clean.
(v) that Ellen White is not to be believed in anything except perhaps certain suggestions regarding living a good life
(vi) that the Bible itself is unreliable, except in strictly Spiritual matters. It cannot be trusted in history, science, chronology, astronomy, etc.
(vii) it also teaches that all that matters is to accept Jesus. From that moment, one is justified, which they say means Christ's record covers for not only the past but also the future. One never stops sinning, but it doesn't matter! Sin will be removed at the second coming, so don't worry about it. What day you keep holy, what you eat, how you dress, where you worship, what denomination you affiliate with, and what you believe about most other doctrines, are irrelevant and have nothing to do with Salvation. They teach that Seventh-day Adventism is a heresy and that it and its 'gospel' are mutually exclusive. You cannot remain a Seventh-day Adventist and accept the '*new theology.*' It destroys virtually every principle and teaching upon which our church stand. And at the same time, undermines and rejects the authority of the Bible and the Spirit of Prophecy. The '*new theology*' is a definite fulfillment of Ellen White's prediction regarding heresy and apostasy in the last days. It fits her prediction in every detail. No wonder they wish to discredit her testimonies.

"Some here in the States are saying that the '*new theology*' is only a difference of opinion on minor matters and that we should not fight it. 'Let's be loving and not disturb unity,' they say.

"Now for the big question: 'Will we learn from the tragedy of Australia, or will we be criminally sleepy, unconcerned and unfaithful and forced to repeat it?' God forbid!" (Written report presented by Pastor William May on his return to the United States)

As can be imagined, this most accurate report caused a furor in Australia. It was not without significance that one of the groups which was most incensed by it was the *Forum*. Writing in their newsletter, one young pastor suggested: "If this report (that of Pastor William May) does not express your sentiments, it's time you contacted your friendly conference, union or division administrators and express your support for their protection of the ministry." (Written by a young Sydney minister in the *Forum Newsletter*) Protests went from higher sources than this young minister, but the truth of the matter was that Pastor May's findings accorded precisely with the facts.

# 66 Little Change in Avondale College

MANY believed that once Dr. Ford left Avondale College, the problem of doctrine would be solved. Time has shown, however, that this result was not to be. Unfortunately, the predominant thinking, not only in the theology department, but also in most other departments of the college, had been one of disbelief in the Sanctuary doctrine, and in the veracity of Sister White's writings with respect to doctrinal issues. As a result, reports indicate that the vast majority of students have left that institution with less faith in the Seventh-day Adventist message than when they entered it.[1] It is little wonder that there is a continuous procession of young ministers leaving the ministry when they discover that they are out of sympathy with the teachings of the Church, and that their work in the field is largely fruitless.

When Russell arrived in Australia in 1981 for furlough, already a group of very sincere pastors and lay people living in the vicinity of Avondale College had prepared an article entitled *Is Avondale College in Jeopardy?* Russell was introduced to this statement and, concurring with it, added his signature to it. This article was no longer a plea to the leadership of the Church, but a warning to God's faithful people throughout the Division. The reader may wonder why this course was taken. When it is understood that these men had made discreet approaches to leadership expressing their concerns, and these meetings had apparently no positive result, it was felt that their duty to God and His message demanded a more open warning to the flock. No longer could sin and error be covered. Those parents who had been led to believe their children would be confirmed in the faith needed to be acquainted with the true situation.

It was deemed necessary to explain to the laity the reasons that Dr. Ford's teachings had been so strongly supported in the face of the subsequent events which have proved him to be in error. Thus the article stated: "Having sprung to the defense of Dr. Ford with seeming justification on a number of occasions, the Division brethren then tended to regard all later questioning of Dr. Ford's teachings as malicious, and on these grounds persistently dismissed all further warnings by concerned ministers and laymen. When the storm finally broke, it was plainly evident that the same divergent beliefs for which it was found necessary to dismiss Dr. Ford, had already gained wide acceptance among the young ministers and other students going through Avondale College in recent years. From the strong letters of protest by several members of Avondale College faculty to the Division in defense of Dr. Ford's views and objecting to his dismissal, it is also very evident that there is still a strong representation among the staff of Avondale, who have known of and supported Dr. Ford's views for years and are continuing to influence our young people towards these errors." [2]

The document also pointed out that "It is a great tragedy that some of our currently serving Conference presidents have been among the most active in championing the Fordian cause and opposing those who have spoken against what is now officially identified as error. A reluctance on the part of church members to 'criticize the brethren' has allowed these workers to retain their office, but the church cannot prosper while led by men who have convenient convictions that are more responsive to political considerations than the guidance of the Holy Spirit." (*Ibid.* 3,4) It can be seen that, while this statement confined itself to facts and was presented in a Christian tone, it was predictable that it would find a negative reaction in the hearts of those leaders who had chosen to follow Desmond Ford and his *new theology*. Unfortunately, in Australia, this number amounted to quite a large group.

In contrast to the situation in the United States, the average church member in Australia is much less likely to express his concerns about the errors of the leadership. This trait has its obvious good points, but it has also led, in many cases, to men retaining high office in a Church whose beliefs, it is easy to demonstrate, they do not hold. Many Australian believers feel often feel very loath frankly to express any concerns about those in leadership, for they fear the almost inevitable ridicule and ostracism which will follow such representations.

This response can be well illustrated in the case of Desmond Ford. While it is now perfectly obvious that the concern of the senior pastors in Australia was not only kindly but also proper, nevertheless many in the church leadership continued to condemn these men as troublemakers and to ban them, in a number of instances, from the pulpit after Ford was exposed.

This mistreatment was brought to the attention of God's people quite forcibly when the Australasian Division president made an effort to explain the reason for Ford's dismissal. It was obviously very embarrassing to need to explain why a person who had been represented to God's people as being a reliable source of doctrinal exposition, was now being removed from the ministry of the Church for teaching apostate doctrines.

In a meeting held in the Wahroonga Seventh-day Adventist Church shortly after Glacier View, the Division president was asked the question: "Does this not now vindicate the warnings of the Concerned Brethren?" In angry reply to this question, the president quite inconceivably answered, "Two wrongs don't make a right!" This statement was recorded on tape. Thus it will be seen that even when justifiable concerns were expressed, and there were demonstrated to be such, there was still an antagonism toward those who had voiced these concerns. To suggest that there were two wrongs involved, one of which was on the part of those who had stood faithfully in the light that had come to them from Jesus through the apostles and the pioneers of our Church, almost bordered on the absurd.

The article *Is Avondale College in Jeopardy?* then went on to describe some specific problems noted at Avondale College: "Under the guise of scholarship, further light and changing times, a sinister climate of liberalism has pervaded Avondale. Are you aware that under the Fordian regime, homosexuality was knowingly tolerated amongst some of our students—even theological students? This is fact, not hearsay. No wonder many of the students regard the place simply as another College of Advanced Education. No wonder, at the most recent College baptism, candidates were not asked to respond to the statements on the official baptismal certificate, but to an alternative list drawn up by the College church pastor." [3]

Naturally, the distribution of this paper produced a prompt and strong reply from the Division secretariat. It had been signed by sixteen people, seven of whom were ordained ministers. In a reply to the signatories the Division secretary stated: "But, your document is not about doctrine or the Adventist Church. It is about politics! It reaches to the bottom of the bag of political dirty tricks, to use innuendo, half-truths, guilt by association and explicit falsehood in an attempt at character assassination." [4] As examples of innuendo it was stated that there were "strong inferences that the Division president and a number of Conference presidents espouse what you call "the Fordian cause!" (*Ibid.*). In reality, this was not an innuendo in the paper. It was stated as a plain fact, a fact well known to any observer of the situation, both in and outside the country, and one which the reader has noted has been easy to document.

As the reader has seen, the president of the Greater Sydney Conference had endorsed, in writing, the most serious of Dr. Ford's doctrinal errors, and had supported him as well on a personal level. The reader has also seen that the president of the South New Zealand Conference wrote, stating that the beliefs of the theology department of Avondale College were to be followed. In addition to these, there have been many spoken statements of a similar nature.

The Division secretary gave as an example of a half-truth a reference made in the paper to the *Signs of the Times* editor's letter and noted that the editor had subsequently written a letter stating: "I also regret having written the letter. . . . I have had opportunity to do some study on these points of doctrine and I would like to state that I applaud the statement of belief which came from the General Conference in Session at Dallas, Texas. I have also studied the Glacier View Statement, 'Christ in the Heavenly Sanctuary,' and I find that I am able to stand with my brethren on that also." One does not have to have great insight to see the half-hearted nature of this statement. No one denied that the editor (later president of the Greater Sydney Conference), once the matter had been revealed, did regret having written the letter, for it very clearly expressed his position for all to see. It will be noticed how carefully he had chosen his words in stating "he applauded" the statement of belief which came from Dallas. There is a world of difference between applauding and believing. Quite clearly, this letter did not proclaim an unqualified belief in the

Adventist faith. This president did not believe, by his own testimony, the Sanctuary message and he has never, with conviction, withdrawn that statement.[5]

Thus the reference in *Is Avondale College in Jeopardy?* was perfectly correct and not issuing a half-truth. The interesting fact was that the brethren, in reply, were able to quote the Division secretary's own testimony that he was not fully satisfied himself with the Greater Sydney Conference president's statement.

As an example of falsehood, it was stated that the accusation concerning homosexuality was false. Unfortunately, at the time the Division secretary made this remark, the *Spectrum* magazine published a report of the remarks of the Avondale College president, which he made when he attended the homosexual camp meeting for Seventh-day Adventists in Arizona.

The Avondale College president at the time, as has been mentioned previously, has since made efforts to state his position on morality. Never once, despite the writing of numerous pages, has he come out and said that he believes what Scripture teaches—that the practice of homosexuality, under all circumstances, is a sin. Indeed, *Spectrum* revealed that he told the homosexuals that the Bible was unclear on which acts of homosexuality were wrong, thus leaving the strong implication that there were some acts which a Christian could safely commit.

It should be pointed out that in the counterfeit baptismal vows used at the college,[6] many of the distinctives of our faith were greatly watered down on the pretext that this change made them more understandable to the candidates. However, as these alterations were analyzed, it was found that in every instance the changes had been influenced by the teachings of Desmond Ford. That there was grave error being taught at the College cannot be disputed.

At the time this pamphlet was published, Russell spoke to one of the lecturers in the theology department, who had made a statement in writing that he affirmed the Dallas summary of beliefs, but added a rider to the effect that he accepted them, having regard to the Preamble. The Preamble indicated that there would be further study. It was suspected by Russell that the reason this rider was added, was that the person did not, in fact, believe all the fundamentals from Dallas, and that he was hoping that at some future General Conference session there would be a change toward his erroneous views.

In order to test this theory, Russell visited the theology professor and stated to him that he believed "Jesus went into the Most Holy Place of the Sanctuary in 1844 to commence the investigative judgement." He then asked this theology lecturer to reiterate his belief in this fact. This request led to absolute silence on the part of the professor. Russell then, pointing to him as secretary of the Ellen White Research Centre at Avondale College, stated that he believed "Sister White's writings were authoritative, both in the area of spiritual counsel and in doctrine." Once again, the professor could not affirm this view, despite the fact that the essence of both these propositions is found in the Dallas summary. Russell challenged the professor that he, along with other like-minded members of the theology department, should write for the *Australasian Record* a statement indicating that they now had "new light" on these matters, and that when parents sent their children to Avondale College, they would be happy to teach them this "new light," *viz*. That Jesus did not wait until 1844 to enter the Most Holy Place; but He did so at His ascension, and that while Sister White's writings were beneficial for spiritual guidance, they were unreliable, at times, in the area of doctrine. When this challenge was put to the professor, he was aghast and stated: "We could never do this, for it would prevent the advance of Bible truth." He did not elaborate, but Russell assumed he meant that they would be promptly dismissed from their positions and would therefore, be unable to continue to promulgate surreptitiously these errors to the minds of their students. That Avondale, by 1981, was in fearful jeopardy, and continues to be so, is without doubt.

### Chapter 66 Endnotes

1. In a letter from one of the Australasian Division Officers to Russell in 1983, it was indicated that the Division leaders were aware of this fact and concerned by it. The officer, of course, could only indirectly refer to the matter by stating he believed that he had noticed a greater number of students accepting fundamental beliefs than had been the case two or three years earlier.
2. *Is Avondale College in Jeopardy?* pg. 2
3. See Appendix F.
4. Letter written by the Secretary of the Australasian Division to the authors of *Is Avondale College in Jeopardy?* dated August 5, 1981
5. That the belief of the president of the Greater Sydney Conference in the Sanctuary was less than enthusiastic, was borne out by an incident which occurred several months after his apologetic letter. The Board of the Windsor Church, concerned about the publicity given to their Conference president's beliefs, asked to meet with him. At the meeting, questions were put to him about the ministry of Christ, both before and after 1844. Those present reported that the president hedged, shifted ground, and generally attempted to talk his way out of the presentation of direct answers for three and a half hours. Finally, in apparent desperation, he asserted that he supported the fundamental belief on the Sanctuary. This, of course, directly contradicted his letter to Pastor Eva. Those present were left without reassurance. (Meeting in Brother Carl Branster's home, attended by elders of the Windsor Church)
4. See Appendix F.

# 67     Ways with Words

MANY, not closely associated with the spread of the *new theology* and other liberal trends in our Church, may wonder how such a large number of Seventh-day Adventists could fail to perceive the error. The answer lay in the use of clever phraseology which to the mind of the hearer meant one thing, but to the speaker, another. For example, those espousing the *new theology* delighted in affirming that they truly believed in a pre-advent judgment. To the listener this statement may have erased any doubts which he had upon this matter. Here was a clear affirmation of a fundamental belief. The problem was that the listener, quite understandably, perceived the term *pre-Advent judgment* to have the specific meaning applied to it by Seventh-day Adventists, i.e. an investigative judgment commencing in 1844. But the speakers were not in any way supporting the 1844 timing of Christ's entry into the most holy place of the heavenly Sanctuary. They were referring to a judgment (admittedly pre-advent by a long period of time) which commenced in A.D. 31, when Jesus returned to heaven. It was by such "clever" techniques that many true believers were lulled into a sense of false security.

In 1978, Russell spent three hours with an Australian Conference president, known to have reservations concerning Dr. Ford's teachings. On at least five occasions, Russell pointed out some of the errors which were being taught. On every occasion the conference president replied: "Yes, I've heard him say that and I, too, was concerned." But then, in Dr. Ford's defense, the Conference president added: "But I saw him about that statement after the meeting and when I found out what he really meant, I was satisfied that it agreed with our faith." After the fifth such episode, Russell said to the president, "Aren't you concerned just how many times you've found it necessary to ask what he *really* believed?" The president dropped his head and stared in silence. He was indeed most concerned. He agreed that many of these equivocal statements were made at camp meetings and at workers' meetings, and that many others in all probability had been left in great doubt; yet never once at any subsequent meeting was an effort made to right the impression given.

Since 1980, it has become a hallmark of those teaching the *new theology* in our schools and colleges to proclaim loudly that they affirm the twenty-seven fundamentals of faith as adopted by the Dallas General Conference. Strangely, few of those who truly believe our stand on the investigative judgment and the Spirit of

Prophecy find it necessary to make such a statement, for their fidelity to God's truths on these matters is without question. For the new theologians, however, it became popular to make such statements in an effort to allay justified fears concerning their beliefs and teachings. In order to refrain from uttering outright untruths, it became popular among such people in Australia to say words to the effect that "I affirm all twenty-seven fundamentals as accepted in Dallas," but then add a qualifying statement—"having regard to the Preamble."

What did this mean? It will be recalled the Preamble stated that there will be continuing study of our faith. Of course, this statement referred to our search for deeper and fuller understanding, and knowledge of the immovable pillars of our faith. But the new theologians, interpreting it to mean it was possible that at some future General Conference Session these pillars would be removed and their own cherished errors substantiated, used this qualification as an escape for their disbelief in some of the fundamentals. In reality, of course, while it was necessary to have fundamentals listed, we must be careful lest we turn these into a creed. Adventists, rather than assenting to a necessarily abbreviated list of doctrinal beliefs, should covenant to believe—

> every word that proceedeth out of the mouth of the LORD. (Deuteronomy 8:3)

Further, there seemed to be an almost hypnotic aura associated with the preaching of the *new theology*. Devout Seventh-day Adventist have, on occasions, heard it, being fully aware of its dangers, and yet have not recognized it. In January, 1974, one such Sabbath service was presented at the Victorian Conference camp meeting in Australia. Many heard that service, which contained many non-biblical themes, without noticing anything untoward. The speaker, Dr. Ford, for example stated that we were children of God and children of Satan simultaneously. He totally ignored the biblical information that—

> No man can serve two masters. (Matthew 5:24)

It was only when transcripts of the meeting were presented to these listeners, that they perceived the terrible errors in the sermon that had entirely passed them by unnoticed. These people were most perplexed that they had failed to recognize the nature of its message.

On one occasion, a godly friend who loved this message and was vocally in opposition to the inroads that the *new theology* was making in the United States, listened to one of Dr. Ford's tapes for the very first time. His conclusion was that the speaker was being very careful on this occasion, for he spoke no error. Puzzled, we agreed to re-listen to the tape with our friend. Within the first thirty seconds the speaker declared that the converted man cannot keep the commandments for 1/24th of a second. We stopped the tape at that point and enquired of our friend whether he shared this conviction. Of course, he believed in Spirit-empowered obedience and immediately saw the insinuation of Satan's old error, that man cannot under any circumstances obey God's law. We turned the tape off after about five or ten minutes, for we had, by that time, detected a number of clear errors of teaching. Our friend was amazed that the skill of oratory had been such that he had overlooked significant aspects of the content. Jesus' messengers must obey His injunction to—

> Let your communication be Yea, yea; Nay, nay; for whatsoever is more than these cometh of evil. (Matthew 5:37)

Let us fearlessly declare our Bible-based positions in words so clear, so precise, and so simple, that even a child could not misunderstand. There are some in our midst who would so phrase the statements of our belief that those of opposing views could equally affirm each statement. Such a statement is utterly worthless, for it tells us nothing of God's verities and only ushers in confusion. As the late evangelist and church administrator, Pastor J. W. Kent used to love to state, "Truth is like the handle on a cup. It's all on one side." Let us declare such truths, and those truths alone.

Chapter 67 Endnote

1. A published example of this technique appeared in the *Australian Record*. The writer was the Avondale College president.

# 68 The Printed Page

AS has been seen, early in the history of the controversy in Australia, publications warning God's people were produced. It should be noted, however, that these publications appeared only after much behind-the-scenes effort to alert the leadership of God's Church in Australia and New Zealand to the perils which the Church was facing. Those warnings not only went unheeded, but gave rise to stern rebukes for, and even vilification of, those who steadfastly refused to accept error as truth. When it became obvious that some in leadership would not play their God-ordained role in refuting error, it was left to the senior pastors of the Church and a few lay people to remedy this lack. Men like Pastor George Burnside produced a stream of materials upholding the old landmarks of the Church. These writings will go down in the history of God's Church as some of the most timely defenses of truth.

A group of senior pastors published a booklet entitled *Dr. Ford's Dangerous Doctrines*. These men were not minor characters in the Church of God. The eight authors had all held senior positions in the work of God: Pastor J. W. Kent, the president of three conferences; Pastor Herbert White, associate director of the publishing department of the General Conference; Pastor A. W. Knight, senior chaplain at Sydney Adventist Hospital; Pastor R. N. Heggie, mission president; Pastor J. E. Cormack, mission president; Pastor George Burnside, ministerial director of the Australasian Division; Pastor J. B. Keith, president of two Union conferences; and Pastor W. G. Ferris, mission president.

While these men were at that time retired, nevertheless their work of God was never more significant than when they stood and called error by its right name. Sad to report, the first four mentioned at the time of the writing of this manuscript, have already been called to their rest; but they died having fulfilled their ministerial vows to uplift the truth of God in its purity. Their booklet presented clear evidence of Dr. Ford's errors on the Sanctuary doctrine, the identification of the papacy as the man of sin, the infallibility of Scripture, the age of the earth, the authorship of the book of Hebrews, and the finished work of Christ, among other matters. At the time of its publication in the 1970s, the book was regarded by the church leadership as grossly inflammatory, yet all this booklet did was to present in a factual way what Dr. Ford was teaching, and to compare this with inspiration. Truly these men could state, "This is the voice of concerned men. As is well known, we have given our lives in the preaching of the Everlasting Gospel—The Three Angels' Messages of Rev. 14:6–12" (*Dr. D. Ford's Dangerous Doctrines*)

The voice of these concerned men went unheeded by many, but not by all. Other men such as Pastor Frank Breaden, Brother Victor Christensen, Pastor Frank Basham, Pastor Arthur Jacobson, Dr. Winston Kent, Pastor W. M. R. Scragg, Pastor Llewellyn Jones, Dr. David Pennington, and many others, joined the band of those who put pen to paper in defense of the precious truths of God within Australia.

Meanwhile, as the error spread in the United States, men of fidelity there also saw the need to write in defense of the faith. Among the earliest were men such as Pastor Robert Wieland, and shortly after, a group of lay people in the Paradise Church in Northern California humbly set out to deliver the truth of God to those who were hearing little but error. Prominent among these were Brother Lowell Scarbrough and Dr. Wendell Gibbs. Brother Scarbrough subsequently wrote one of the finest defenses of the Adventist position on Righteousness by Faith, entitled *The Three Angels' Messages and Righteousness by Faith and Its Present Rejection*. These men and others with them, set up "Historic Truth Publications," which has published a number of books defending God's truth. It has been the privilege of the authors to have three of their books published by this fine organization.[1]

The late Paul Miller in Oregon, with his wife and some others, also early perceived the appalling dangers of the *new theology*, and commenced what was called "The Final Century Research Foundation." From its location in Central Point, Oregon, this research foundation sent out warnings, both by tape and by the written word.

Perhaps no one has contributed more to the preservation of material concerning the inroads of the *new theology*, than Brother Vance Ferrell with his "Pilgrim's Rest Organization," originally established in Harrisburg, Illinois, and later transferred to Tennessee. Brother Ferrell was able to collect an enormous quantity of original documents, which he made available to those who were serious about defending God's truth. He also conducted an effective tape ministry.

Naturally, the significance of Brother Ferrell's work led to many violent attacks upon him and his character. It was pointed out, quite correctly, that he had been, for a brief period, sympathetic to Brinsmead's early views. Indeed, many good people appreciated the Brinsmead message during this period for, mixed with his error, there was perceptive truth on the nature of Christ, and the validity of the Sanctuary message. Brother Ferrell has continued to believe these valid documents and, unlike so many others, has not supported Brinsmead at every turn of his doctrinal march. One of the difficulties of attacking Ferrell has been that his primary work has involved the production of document after document which set forth the irrefutable evidence of the course taken by the *new theology*. Thus, if men and women have been upset by what Ferrell has produced, they have no one to blame but those whose appalling statements he has accurately quoted.

Many others in the United States have gone into print in order to uphold truth. Pastor Ralph Larson, now a professor at the Theological Seminary of the Far East in the Philippines, ably defended truth in many small publications. A group in Tennessee published *Collegedale Tidings* under the editorship of Theodore R. Barta. This publication set forth the terrible consequences of the *new theology* as it afflicted Southern Missionary College, as well as the basic facts of the Davenport affair.

One of the most influential works has been Lewis Walton's book *Omega*. This most skillfully written book carefully outlined the alpha of apostasy in such a way that no one could have doubted that the seeds of the omega of apostasy were present in the *new theology*. Naturally, this book brought forth another tirade of abuse. Even the archivist of the General Conference wrote a letter of disapproval, dated October 22, 1981. In replying to this, Lewis Walton stated, "Secondly, while I appreciate your expressions disclaiming any intent to confront me, I am forced to conclude that both your letter and your presentation at the Colloquium were indeed confrontational. When I arrived here in Washington, I was met by a welter of reports that you and Mr. Haloviak had rather widely announced that you would discredit the book during the course of the weekend. That by no means discouraged me; I encounter challenges like that five days every week (Lewis Walton is an attorney), but I think that we should at least openly and honestly define what is happening. Having admitted, with all Christian grace and goodwill, that there is indeed a confrontation involved, let's deal for a moment or two with specifics." [2]

Walton made a penetrating appeal to the General Conference archivist, "All of which brings me to my key question: 'Why do you seem to be trying so hard to discredit a book that merely reasserts God's evident supernatural guidance of this Church, and urges people to retain their faith, both in its historical mission and its world leadership?' Coming from someone philosophically or professionally outside the Church, your arguments would at least be understandable to me. Coming from someone in the infrastructure of our world organization, your approach is puzzling." (*Ibid.*)

So strong were many of the attacks on *Omega* that the president of the General Conference, Pastor Neal Wilson, felt constrained publicly to express his support of the book in writing. Perhaps the level of the attack represented the effectiveness of the book in hitting its target.[3]

Dr. LeRoy Moore's book *The Theology Crisis* also caught the attention of many. This book was an able examination of Sister White's teaching on Righteousness by Faith. It left no room to doubt her support of character perfection.

Another who felt called to defend the truth by his voice on tape was Pastor Arthur White, grandson of Sister White, in a tape recording made on November 15, 1979. The specific aim of this recording was to comment upon Dr. Ford's *Adventist Forum* statement of October 27, of the same year. Although this tape was made not very long before Pastor White had to undergo open heart surgery, it nevertheless presented a powerful defence of the Spirit of Prophecy and pinpointed Dr. Ford's misuse of that source.

These writings represent just a small number of the men and women who have, in their devotion to this last message, risen up in its defence. This is a faith worth defending. It is a faith that thousands of Seventh-day Adventists still gladly acknowledge as the precious truths of God.

### Chapter 68 Endnotes

1. "Historic Truth Publications" is now operated by Hartland Institute, P.O. Box 1, Rapidan, Virginia 22733, U.S.A.
2. Letter written by Lewis Walton to the General Conference archivist, dated November 6, 1981
3. As Pastor Kenneth Wood once noted, using an old proverb: "When you throw a stone into a pack of wolves, you discover which one you have hit by noticing the one which howls."

# 69 Adventist Observer

BETWEEN the months of November 1981 and March 1982 three copies of a publication entitled *Adventist Observer* were published. The address given on the first two editions was Hornsby, a suburb of Sydney, while on the third edition, both this address and one in Yeronga in Queensland were cited. The publication grew in size with each edition. It was obvious in the first edition that the concern of the authors, whose names were never made public, was the teaching of Avondale College, and the inroads of the *new theology* into the ministerial labor force. The author stated, "This erroneous position applies especially to Avondale College where liberalism and the so-called *'new theology'* have been taught for so long that ministerial and other workers who have been infected by these views are now moving into influential positions. Because of their numerical strength and political implications, many of our leaders who know the truth are turning a blind eye to the heresy in the hope that peace will prevail." [1]

The publishers set forth their aim as follows: "The object of this paper is to provide a vehicle of communication with lay members. Through it we wish to disseminate Adventist truth, expose error and encourage loyal ministers and laymen to resist apostasy. In general, it will fill a need denied by our leadership." (*Ibid*., 2) These publishers set forth the reason for remaining anonymous. "The *Observer* does not intend to be placed in a position of vulnerability to the abuse and character assassination already dispensed by some of our leaders and others to the Concerned Brethren. We therefore make no apology for preserving anonymity. We shall rely on truth and love for our Church, to preserve credibility. Let the church members be the judge." (*Ibid*.) It certainly seemed to be a very sad reflection upon the situation in Australia that men wishing only to expose the terrible soul-destroying errors in the Church, felt it essential to remain anonymous so that their characters would not become a prime issue in the material that they were presenting.

The first issue, apart from the introductory remarks of the publisher, dealt with but three items. The first of these was a statement on the nature of true love in the light of the current apostasy. The second was a report of the Vision Valley meeting at which Attorney Lewis Walton spoke, and the third article reported the response of readers and leaders to the publication of *Is Avondale College in Jeopardy?* The authors put forward the view that "According to Scripture and the Spirit of Prophecy, the attitude of tolerance and protection that is being displayed by many of our administrators towards those who are in apostasy, is an evidence of a lack of true love." (*Ibid.*, 3) In order to set forth what these authors considered to be true love in such circumstances, they quoted the following statement:

> Jesus Himself never purchased peace by compromise. His heart overflowed with love for the whole human race, but He was never indulgent to their sins. He was too much their friend to remain silent while they were pursuing a course that would ruin their souls. . . . The servants of Christ are called to the same work, and they should beware lest, in seeking to prevent discord, they surrender the truth. They are "to follow after the things that make for peace"; but real peace can never be secured by compromising principle. And no man can be true to principle without exciting opposition. A Christianity that is spiritual will be opposed by the children of disobedience. (*DA* 355,356)

Again, using the same source of inspiration, these authors quoted:

> Those ministers who are men pleasers, who cry, Peace, peace, when God has not spoken peace, might well humble their hearts before God, asking pardon for their insincerity and their lack of moral courage. It is not from love for their neighbor that they smooth down the message entrusted to them, but because they are self-indulgent and ease-loving. True love seeks first the honor of God and the salvation of souls. Those who have this love will not evade the truth to save themselves from the unpleasant results of plain speaking. When souls are in peril, God's ministers will not consider self, but will speak the word given them to speak, refusing to excuse or palliate evil. (*PK* 141)

As one examines these statements, it is possible to see the root of many of the problems which have occurred in Australia. There is absolutely no doubt that some ministers must accept responsibility for the serious schism in the church. Those who cry peace and unity in the Church without first placing truth in its proper position are, in fact, crying for compromise, a compromise which has led to the fateful results in the Church in Australia and in other parts of the world. The basis of true love is the redemption of souls, not the condoning of those doctrines and sins which will bring men to eternal destruction.

The second edition of *Adventist Observer*, dated January 1982, again spent some time in exposing problems at Avondale. A whole article was given over to the teachings of one member of the theology faculty. It stated, "In September 1980 [name deleted] privately admitted that the views he had taught at Avondale College over the last six years were in direct conflict with our Adventist position on the Sanctuary question. This was done with the full knowledge of the Division leadership, he said." [2]

Other accusations which, to this day, remain unchallenged were "At a Ministerial League meeting during the first semester, 1981, [name deleted—the Avondale College theology professor] publicly expressed his disbelief in the 2300 days and the 1844 position as held by the church. He said that if Ellen White and the pioneers were in error in regard to the imminence of the second advent, they could also be in error in regard to 1844. In one of his classes on September 23, 1981, [name deleted] asked the question as to whether we are humanizing God by saying there has to be an investigative judgment." (*Ibid.*) This professor was also quoted as referring to the efforts of the Concerned Brethren to expose his errors of teaching. In doing this he "referred to the Protestant Reformers and stated that Luther and others did not have to speak out and expose the papacy. God would have done that in His own time. Luther was in error in doing it as he did, and so are the Concerned Brethren." (*Ibid.*) Just how God would have done this in His own good time, if nobody spoke out, the professor did not state.

One interesting article was entitled *What Are the Facts About Avondale College?* This article set out to analyze the position of the teachers in the theology department. Two were specifically mentioned. It was stated regarding one of these, "another liberal, he also has a negative attitude to some of our standard doctrines. He rejects the Adventist view of the Remnant Church. However, he is careful to conceal his non-Adventist views. In a 1981 class lecture it was stated that it does not matter whether one takes the Book of Jonah as factual or symbolic." (*Ibid.*, 12)

It is not without significance that, by the beginning of 1983, this teacher had left the college employment, left the Church, and had accepted the position of chaplain at Knox College, a Presbyterian high school in Sydney.

Of the other it was stated that he "has a similar attitude to [name deleted—Avondale College theology professor] regarding the Spirit of Prophecy. At a recent series of meetings in Brisbane, he gave from six to nine reasons why we cannot accept the Spirit of Prophecy. In class he presents the official view of the church, but in a way that leaves doubts in the minds of the students." (*Ibid.*, 11) This teacher had, by the end of 1983, been transferred. His replacement also strongly supported the *new theology*. Yet when these matters were brought out only one year earlier, the authors of the *Adventist Observer* were vilified for their conclusions.

The other departments of the College were also stated to be in serious trouble. "English Department—All three teachers are extremely pro-Fordian. These are [names deleted]. The last two are destructive of students' faith in Adventism. [Names deleted] constantly criticize Adventist theology and make aspersions against theology students. At times [name deleted] deliberately creates difficulties in his classes for mature-age students. This is because many are not pro-Fordian. One book he uses is entitled "An Introduction to Language." He cites one page to study [page number given]. This deals with—(1) Four-letter words, (2) euphemisms for 'urinate,' (3) metaphors for sexual intercourse. He emphasizes this page, he admitted, for the sake of young girls at the college!! In 1981 [name deleted] was confronted by a Conference president on his use of [this] page [number deleted]. He has now changed his approach. He refers his class to the same page, but because of the letters of protest, he informs the class that he did not write it! In this manner he still subtly draws attention to the sordid material." (*Ibid*. 12) The article also asserted that the majority of the members of the Education Department were in favor of the Fordian doctrines and this was the reason that the church schools were infected by such doctrines.

It was only natural that *Adventist Observer* would create a furor among those supporting the *new theology*. The commonest effort to discredit the facts contained therein was to assert that the magazine was full of inaccuracies. For example, it has been stated in edition number 2 that Pastor Barry Crabtree had been appointed to the Bendigo Church in Victoria. Since he did not take up that appointment, this statement was cited as an example of error. Yet there is no doubt that, at the time of writing, the *Adventist Observer* had been perfectly correct, for later it was stated, "Pastor B. L. Crabtree was appointed to Bendigo next year from U.S.A. This call has been rescinded." (Victorian Conference News Bulletin *Intravic* No. 6)

Also, edition number two had reported that the Church was taking government funds for operation of our schools. This again was cited as being in error, since no money was being taken for paying the teaching staff. However, the *Adventist Observer* had not made any claim about payment of teaching staff. It had simply stated that operating expenses were being funded by government money, and it was able to state accurately that operating expenses such as removal of teachers from one location to another were, in fact, coming from government funds. It was able to quote the minutes of the Australasian Division of November, 1981, which said, "All general educational operating expenses at Conference and school level, excluding regular teachers' wages . . . may be funded from recurrent [government] grants."

It is interesting to note that by 1983 the Australasian Division had publicly proclaimed in the *Australasian Record* that it was now prepared to accept government funds for the payment of teachers' salaries, provided that the Conference maintained two years' salary in reserves. In that particular article it was pointed out that already they had been paying the salaries of relief teachers from government grants for a period of time.

Thus it appeared to many that these and other complaints about the veracity of the revelations of *Adventist Observer* were used in an attempt to sidetrack earnest members from their concern about the degenerating state of the Church in Australia. *Adventist Observer* was all too accurate.

By 1983, for example, one Conference worker in Victoria had stated with evident accuracy, that no more than four of the ministers in the Conference believed the basic doctrines of the Seventh-day Adventist Church. Since this conference was one of our largest, the situation was grave indeed. Yet in early 1982, the *Adventist Observer* had warned that this situation prevailed. It was pointed out that the "Orbost Church pastor [name deleted][3] has long been trying to destroy the confidence of his flock in the message of the Remnant Church. He says that the Ten Commandments are not applicable to our times, for they are transitory and impossible to be kept. When his long-suffering parishioners were shocked into action and reported this apostasy to their president, what did he do? Well, get ready for another shock—he exonerated the wolf and told the sheep to demonstrate that they loved their false prophet." [4] *Adventist Observer* pointed out that the Conference president had written very mildly in discussing the work of Walter Rea, at the time he came to Victoria in order to take away our believers' faith in the Spirit of Prophecy. He had written, "We also have had a visit from Brother Walter Rea, who is rather a controversial figure in our ranks today. Undoubtedly, Walter Rea has brought to our attention thought-provoking material that is being studied by our brethren, and many problems in its train. We can only wish that the differences he seems to have with the Church will one day be resolved." [5] This was hardly the type of warning necessary for God's people, and it showed a somewhat sympathetic leaning toward Walter Rea's attacks upon God's Church.

It is little wonder that the present situation in Victoria is so serious. Nor is it any wonder that in 1982 the Victorian Conference had fewer members on the thirty-first of December than it had on the first of January. These matters are not just of transitory interest. They are life-and-death matters, matters of eternal consequence.

Until men and women stand up and recognize these facts and stand for the upholding of the precious truth, there can be no progress in God's work in Australia, and no finishing of the task assigned to us.

The third edition of *Adventist Observer* was its last. This outcome was foreshadowed in the paper in an article entitled *Discontinuance of Observer*. There were a number of reasons for the decease, but in reality, the chief reason was the tremendous effort by some in leadership to use other persons in an attempt to discover who were the editors of this paper so that legal threats could be made against them. So far did these efforts go that some who had absolutely nothing to do with the publication, e.g. Brother Neil Foxcroft, were accused of being involved. Dr. Pennington, the editor of *Landmarks*, was also falsely accused of involvement, simply on the basis that his wife was seen by some "spy" attending the post office at which the *Adventist Observer* had its box number. Such was the anxiety of some to see this publication eliminated that truth was not considered as a high priority in the process.

One church member undertook to investigate the matter as a type of private detective, and in the process, passed himself off as a policeman, an offense with which he was charged by the police under the New South Wales law. Under extreme duress the postmaster of the post office, at which the *Adventist Observer* held its box, was coerced into revealing the name of the person by whom the box was held. Quite understandably, this person had nothing to do with the editorial work of the *Adventist Observer*. Nevertheless, accusations were made concerning him and his relatives. All these efforts were bent upon discrediting, and bringing ecclesiastical pressure to bear on those persons who had brought a warning of truth before God's people.

Although the editors had nothing to fear from an examination of the facts which they had revealed, being sound Adventists, they felt it was not desirable for the matter to be taken to the courts. Indeed, when this matter was finally taken up before the courts with a charge of defamation, the magistrate spoke to the person who had brought it, and quoted to him from the following passage of Scripture:

> Dare any of you, having a matter against another, go to the law before the unjust, and not before the saints? Do ye not know that the saints shall judge the world? and if the world shall be judged by you, are ye unworthy to judge the smallest matters? Know ye not that we shall judge angels? how much more things that pertain to this life? If then ye have judgments of things pertaining to this life, set them to judge who are least esteemed in the church. I speak to your shame. Is it so, that there is not a wise man among you? no, not one that shall be able to judge between his brethren? But brother goes to law with brother, and that before the unbelievers. (1 Corinthians 6:1–7)

This passage was certainly a stunning rebuke to one claiming to be a Seventh-day Adventist and bringing his brother to court. Fortunately, the case was later dismissed, court costs being awarded to the complainant.

It is pertinent to record that Mr. Michael Newcity, a former New York lawyer and currently lecturer in law at MacQuarie University, reported that his research had revealed that "Defamation law in N.S.W. [New South Wales] has been designed largely to protect public figures, the wealthy and the prominent from scrutiny and criticism." (*The Sydney Morning Herald*, Aug. 7, 1984) It seems that the case against the *Adventist Observer* simply verified the findings of this University law lecturer. Such a purpose is of dubious validity indeed.

Chapter 69 Endnote

1. *Adventist Observer,* Nov. 1981, pg. 1
2. *Adventist Observer*, Jan. 1982, pg. 3
3. This pastor subsequently spoke at Dr. Ford's Good News Unlimited meetings in Victoria, as the guest speaker. He has left the Church.
4. *Adventist Observer*, No. 2, Jan. 1982, 15
5. Victorian president's Pastoral Letter, Oct. 1981

# 70 God's Work Falters

FOR decades the Australasian Division was looked upon as a fine example of rapid growth. This period occurred when the work was slow in many other areas of the world field, some of which now have extremely high growth rates. Because of the blessing of Sister White's presence in Australia and New Zealand for nine years, God's work got off to a very strong commencement. It did not take long before the number of Adventists in Australia and New Zealand was double that in the United States on a per capita basis. But times have changed with the spread of the *new theology* from our pulpits. It is quite understandable that failure to preach the message which God has designed for us can bring little blessing upon our efforts. This truth is emphasized by one of our present leading evangelists who, after studying at Avondale College, found that his ministry, so far as soul-winning was concerned, was absolutely impotent. Being a godly young man and one who felt that the Lord had called him to the ministry, he was unprepared to follow his calling in such a fruitless manner. Thus in order to bear fruit he decided he would sit at the feet of one of the senior evangelists of the past—Pastor George Burnside—to learn the true Adventist message and the successful presentation of it. Immediately he became fruitful in his work, and God has greatly blessed his ministry. He is now known throughout the Division for his success in soul winning.

An examination of the Australasian Division statistics indicates that the growth of the Church is occurring mainly in the Pacific, with close to zero growth in Australia and New Zealand. Indeed, indications are that the Church is fast losing ground by comparison with population growth, and this matter should be of great concern. Let us analyze the figures for two years, 1981 and 1982, as examples. Within Australia and New Zealand there are eleven conferences. In the year 1981 three of those conferences had fewer members in the conclusion of the year than they did at its commencement. The North New Zealand Conference lost 78 members, the South New Zealand Conference lost 26 members, and the South New South Wales Conference lost 2 members. A further four conferences had a gain of fewer than 20 members. These were North Queensland Conference, 3; South Australian Conference, 9; Victorian Conference, 14; Tasmanian Conference, 16. Only two conferences exceeded an increase of 100 members: North New South Wales Conference, 194, and the South Queensland Conference, 149. These two conferences are by far the largest retirement areas for Seventh-day Adventists, and if the excess of transfers-in over transfers-out were deducted, neither reached the one hundred mark increase.

The church membership at the beginning of 1981 in Australia and New Zealand was 50,203. The increase for the year in membership was only 448, partly due to the fact that there was a net gain of 66 within Australia and New Zealand by transfer. Thus the real gain for the year was a mere 382, an increase of approximately 0.7%.

The situation was even more serious in 1982. In that year four conferences had a net loss of membership at the conclusion of the year. These were the North New Zealand Conference, 126; the South Australian Conference, 71; the Victorian Conference, 32; the Tasmanian Conference, 17. Three conferences had net gains over one hundred: South Queensland, 174; Greater Sydney, 168; North New South Wales, 164. The largest of these, South Queensland, in fact would have had a loss had it not been for its net increase by transfer of 176 members. Only the Greater Sydney Conference, which actually had a net loss by transfer, truly exceeded the one hundred mark. In this conference the largest and most expensive evangelistic program ever mounted by the Church in Australia and New Zealand was carried out in 1982.

It will be seen that in the two years 1981 and 1982, six of the eleven conferences in one year or the other, had net losses of membership. Four of these had less membership at the end of 1982 than they had two years earlier, at the commencement of 1981. Thus, the total conference evangelistic effort resulted in a negative growth in four conferences: North New Zealand Conference, a two-year net loss of 204; South Australian Conference, a two-year net loss of 62; Victorian Conference, a two-year net loss of 18; and the Tasmanian Conference, a two-year net loss of 1. Indeed, in 1982, the entire Trans-Australian Union Conference that year had a gain of 448, but this statistic must be measured against a net increase due to transfers of 211. Thus the real increase for that Union was only 237 souls.

Even in some areas of the mission field, there were some disturbing trends, while in others, good progress continued to be made. In the Cook Islands, for example, the membership which stood at 865 in the beginning of 1981, dropped to 488 at the end of 1981—an enormous loss. This loss of 270 members was due to a net loss from transfers. But nevertheless, this decrease was still large. In 1981 the French Polynesian Mission lost two members for the year, and the Southwest Papuan Mission lost 111 members during the year.

Those who have observed the trend at Avondale College in preparing men and women with doctrines that do not reflect the truth of God, and which lead the graduates to question the veracity of the Spirit of Prophecy and the Sanctuary Message, cannot doubt that this fact is a major reason for the unprecedented lack of progress in the Australasian Division.[1] While the nation, as a whole, continues to progress and increase its population, the Church of God is falling behind that growth. This fact, if nothing else, should bring us to the realization that only the presentation of God's truth will suffice to win souls to the Adventist message and to keep our children within the precincts of God's Church. Surely men such as those who have been banned from the pulpit are God-ordained, as they call for a reevaluation of the teachings of the theology department at Avondale College, so that men and women can be prepared to preach the Adventist message in its purity.

## Chapter 70 Endnote

1. It is not denied that other sources of secularism have contributed, such as materialism, conformity to the moral codes of the world, and the usual declension in faith within the church which possesses a majority of members born into the faith. Indeed, all such factors have no doubt interacted.

# 71 Prophetic Fulfillment

IN 1964, a most remarkable "prophecy" was made. This "prophecy" stated:

> Those who teach that Christ took a superior human nature draw the logical conclusion that it is impossible for the rest of mankind to perfectly obey the law of Jehovah in this life. Those who accept this "new view" of the incarnation, logically take the side of Satan in the great controversy over the law, claiming that God has not made provision for us to obey it perfectly. If God's people accept this delusion, then there will be no third angel's message, no sealing of the saints, no finishing of the mystery of God, no cleansing of the Sanctuary, no community of the saints prepared to live without a Mediator, no first fruits of the harvest, and no people ready for translation—at least as far as they are concerned. Ellen G. White saw that God had three steps to the platform of truth (*EW* 258). Satan has three steps down from the platform. The first step is the teaching that Christ took the human nature of man as it was before the fall. This leads to the second step—to the teaching that man cannot find grace to obey perfectly the law of God in this life. This will inevitably lead to the third step—giving up the Sabbath. This last step must logically follow the original premise, for if it is conceded that we cannot obey all the law all the time, then there is no point in the Sabbath being a test question." (*The Incarnation of Christ, Adam's Human Nature versus Fallen Nature*, 7,8)

This reasoning was an excellent exercise in doctrinal logic. Once a person believes that Christ has a nature superior to his own and thus had a marked advantage over mankind in the battle with Satan, then logic demands the acceptance of the belief that obedience to the Decalogue is impossible in this life. Once that doctrinal aberration becomes part of one's belief, then by yet another step of logical deduction it becomes superfluous to keep the Sabbath day holy, for this concept would necessitate the logical conclusion that it cannot be achieved. Second, obedience to the fourth commandment is a sign of holy living, an attainment which this view teaches cannot be attained, even by a Spirit-filled Christian.

The pattern of doctrinal belief adopted by Robert Brinsmead most certainly has fulfilled this "prophecy" to the letter. Having once been a strong exponent of the fact that Jesus took our nature, he later, in the early 1970s, entirely reversed this belief. In this doctrinal turnabout, he was followed in a rather sheep-like fashion by a large number of his followers. Brinsmead now declared that Christ indeed had a nature superior to our own, namely, that of Adam in his pre-fall condition. From this point, Brinsmead commenced boldly to preach that obedience to the Decalogue was impossible, and then in 1980, he took the third logical step which had been foretold in the "prophecy" by abandoning the Sabbath. This defection was made public in his book, *Sabbatarianism Re-Examined*.

The amazing fact is that the "prophecy " quoted above came from the pen of Robert Brinsmead himself. Thus with unerring accuracy he had predicted the very road which he was to tread some years later. This prediction surely must be one of the most amazing in recent church history. One can never accuse Robert Brinsmead of being illogical in his beliefs. What had occurred was that he had accepted a non-biblical premise—that Christ did not take our fallen nature—ignoring the powerful facts of Scripture—and from thence drew logical conclusions from this false premise. Desmond Ford up to now has continued, somewhat illogically, to defend the Sabbath. In many areas, Desmond Ford has not been as logical as he might have been. His continued support of the Sabbath is one of those areas. The Sabbath, in reality, is absolutely superfluous to his beliefs, since he has accepted the other two steps noted by Brinsmead. Indeed, it is difficult to see how Ford could truly believe in the Sabbath, for he believes in a Sabbath which cannot be kept holy. Such, as has been pointed out, is not Sabbath keeping but Saturday keeping. Thus his defence of the Sabbath is greatly weakened.

Strangely, many of Brinsmead's followers have accepted every twist and turn of his doctrinal changes. In 1973, Russell first suspected that Brinsmead was weakening in his faith in the Spirit of Prophecy. Noting this, he wrote to Ray Martin, Brinsmead's unofficial leader in the State of Victoria. Ray was a former youth leader in the Adventist Church in Australia, but was dismissed from the ministry when he accepted Brinsmead's early views. Believing Ray to be a sincere Christian, Russell wrote to him, pointing out the dangers of the trend in Brinsmead's thinking. In return, he received a rather strongly worded reply, in which Ray Martin insisted that no one more courageously supported the Spirit of Prophecy than did Brinsmead, and that Russell was entirely imperceptive in his judgment. Of course, subsequent events have shown that Russell's fears were more than justified.

When Russell again met Ray in 1979, he reminded him of the correspondence of 1973, and asked Ray whether now he would return to the Church, since Brinsmead had completely shown his true colors at that time. This request Ray refused on the ground that they now had much more evidence about the Spirit of Prophecy, especially that coming from the researches of Walter Rea, which were beginning to be made known.

Russell then turned to Ray and asked him, "Ray, what are you going to do when Brinsmead gives up the Sabbath?" Ray Martin replied that Russell had posed a foolish hypothetical question and that he would refuse to answer it, particularly as Bob Brinsmead was, in his view, a very devout Sabbath-keeper. Russell pointed out that history was against Brinsmead, for everyone who had adopted the views which he held had eventually lost faith in the Sabbath. At that stage, Russell was unaware of Brinsmead's self-defeating "prophecy."

Russell pressed the issue and asked Ray to state quite categorically that he would never give up the Sabbath, irrespective of Brinsmead's future stance upon it. In order to encourage Ray to make such a statement, Russell remarked that he himself was prepared to state that, under God's power and blessing, he would not give up the Sabbath irrespective of any other person's doing so. However, Ray refused to provide such an assurance, asserting that the question did not merit a response since it was illogical and foolish. Of course, within one year Robert Brinsmead had followed the path that had been predicted by himself, and, sad to state, Ray Martin completely followed Brinsmead's new direction once more. This path has been typical of many persons who have followed both Ford and Brinsmead. They have provided evidence of having followed men rather than the God of heaven.

# 72 China Enlightens the World

IN apostolic times, the truth of the death and resurrection of Jesus Christ was taken to China. Thousands upon thousands of Chinese capitulated to the claims of Jesus Christ upon their lives. So strong did Christianity emerge in China that when Marco Polo visited there, he found many cities containing numerous Christian churches. Furthermore, these Christian churches were not steeped in the paganism of Roman Catholic Christianity, but were true to the apostolic faith—keeping the Sabbath and adhering to the basic doctrines of Scripture. The history of the Christian church in China during the Dark Ages of Europe is a thrilling one. At a time when European Christianity was steeped in superstitious paganism, the light of truth shone just as clearly in far-off China as it did in the valleys of Piedmont inhabited by the Waldenses.

It should not surprise us then, that one of the most perceptive analyses of the retreat to the *new theology* over the last three decades, was made by a man isolated in China. Indeed, in one respect, this isolation was a great advantage. For many who have lived through the changes in the Church over the last thirty years, these have been so subtle that they have passed by unperceived. But for David Lin this was not so. Having been isolated in the People's Republic of China during this period, and having spent fourteen years in prison for his fidelity to truth of God, he was not subject to the gradual encroachments of the *new theology* upon the faith of God. Therefore, when he became aware of what was being taught by Ford and Brinsmead and many others in our theology departments throughout the world, it came as a sudden shock to a man who knew only the faith of God as believed by God's people prior to the Barnhouse-Martin affair. He could see the gigantic degeneration in doctrinal belief which had occurred over that period.

From his home near Shanghai, David Lin, a graduate of Pacific Union College[1] and former secretary of the China Division, began to use his pen to defend the truth of God. This material, little by little seeped out of China and spread throughout the world. Those who read it stood amazed at the freshness and the perceptiveness of the material presented. Lin, a skillful writer in the English language, had lost none of his brilliance during his period of incarceration. Nor had he lost the least knowledge of the great truths which have been the hallmark of the Seventh-day Adventist faith. His love for these truths constrained him to write very directly in opposition to that which he now perceived to be destroying God's Church throughout the world.

Indeed, the light which issued from Shanghai proved to be a great help and blessing to many souls concerned by the trends of doctrine within the Church.

In a series of papers such as *Victory or Fiasco?*, *Is Adventism "Patchwork Theology"?*, and a series of analyses of Desmond Ford's *new theology*, Pastor Lin set forth his defense of the Adventist faith. One of his strongest attacks was against what he termed "patchwork theology." He was quoting from an article in the April 1981 issue of *Sligoscope* entitled, *Can We Trust Our Theologians?* This article was written by the senior pastor of the Sligo Church. David Lin objected to three aspects of this article by the Sligo Church senior pastor:

> (1) It explicitly denies but implicitly affirms the existence of "an elite corps of theologians" in the Church who comprise an "expertise" in matters of faith and doctrine. (2) It asserts that "Ford's right to raise questions and offer solutions without fear of reprisal is an important one for most scholars." (3) It deplores the present state of Adventist theology as "only adequate for a certain level of discussion, the level at which Jehovah's Witnesses and fundamentalists do their work," asserting that "if we do not, so to speak, get our act together, theologically, many scholars believe that Adventists will not be a viable option in the twenty-first century for anyone but the most simple-minded. Like the Amish we will be a curiosity with interesting practices that few take seriously." (David Lin, *Is Adventism "Patchwork Theology"?*).

Pastor Lin, reminding us of his oriental background stated, "The Chinese have a saying that a full canister makes no sound, but one half-full will rattle. And the loudest rattle is this concluding remark: 'Give trust and freedom to our scholars and the uniqueness of Adventist thought may yet shine in all its brightness.'" (*Ibid.*)

This statement of the Sligo Church pastor manifestly stirred David Lin, for he commented that the pastor labors under two misapprehensions: "(1) that 'our scholars have no freedom and are not trusted, and (2) that 'uniqueness of Adventist thought' has heretofore never shined in all its brightness, but the new elite corps of modern Adventist theologians, if given trust and freedom, will make it shine at last.'" (*Ibid.*) Lin's answer to this assertion was—

> He [the Sligo Church pastor] is talking of an imaginary situation, for Adventist scholars have always been free to choose between truth and error. If one thinks that Adventism is not the truth, he is free to repudiate it and openly denounce it, but he should not then call himself an Adventist, or receive Adventist pay to teach non-Adventist doctrines in Adventist schools. Secondly, the "uniqueness of Adventist thought" (this is [the pastor's] nomenclature for what we call the third angel's message) has been a shining light ever since the inception of our movement, but if any man is blinded to its light by a worldly outlook and imagines himself sinking to the depth of Jehovah's Witnesses and the Amish, then we advise him to abandon ship before his fears come true. Face-lifting Adventist theology won't save him. (*Ibid.*, 1,2)

The title of Lin's paper came from a statement in the *Sligoscope* article in which he described the Adventist faith as "a 'patchwork theology' that is inappropriate for the main work of the Church." The pastor's article was typical of the response of many theologians in the Church, for as Lin points out:

> Not a word is said about combating Ford's errors, because [name deleted] apparently sees no errors in Ford's proposals. On the contrary, they will probably form the embryo of the new Adventist theology and eventually lead up to "Adventism's greatest days of proclamation." By that time the antiquated "rug" we now have will be relegated to the rubbish heap—if [name deleted]'s dream comes true.

David Lin's strident tone is well exemplified in his analysis of the nature of theology. The Sligo Church pastor—

> informs us what theology is and what it is not. It is not "merely proving a collection of doctrines from texts in Scripture." (All who do this are simpletons, not theologians.) "Theology is the task of interpreting the will of God for the whole of human existence as we experience it." (This interpreting is the task of experts; and because our pioneers did not have the benefit of such expertise, they failed to interpret the will of God for the whole of human existence as we experience it. The best they could do was to sew a patchwork rug.) . . . "Detailing the ritual and furniture of the sanctuary is not theology; it is biblical history. Only when we show how the symbolism of the sanctuary service helps us understand God's will for us now, helps us grasp the reality of his purposes for the whole cosmos, does the work of theology begin."

> Impressive verbiage and scholarly, to be sure, but not a word about the three angels' messages and the investigative judgment. (These are just unsightly patches in that old rug.) Here [the author] gives us a sampling of what we will be confronted with when and if he and his peers begin "doing theology" for us. We will have to grapple with such vague abstractions as "the whole of human existence" and "the reality of God's purposes for the whole cosmos." A liberal spate of such sophisticated verbosity will perhaps impress other theologians that we are their equals, but the third angel's message will be swamped and finally liquidated by this flood of "words of wisdom."[2]

That David Lin's mental agility was in no wise dulled by his years of imprisonment is seen in his response to the suggestion that Desmond Ford should have a hearing involving his peers, because he has raised important questions. Looking for these important questions, David Lin hit upon the apotelesmatic principle. This principle of prophetic interpretation suggests that single prophecies can have several fulfillments. It was pointed out in the *Ministry*, October, 1980, p. 32, that Desmond Ford had quoted about a dozen possible fulfillments of the prophecy of Daniel 8:14. It seemed as if the only fulfillment which he would not accept was that of the commencement of the investigative judgment in 1844.

Commenting on this "important question," David Lin said:

> Scanning through the October 1980 issue of *Ministry*, we come across a word which strikes us with awe—"apotelesmatic," the "apotelesmatic principle." Indeed, this looks like a term reserved for experts—out of our depth. . . . How much true scholarship is manifested in Ford's application of this principle is self-evident. It does not take a "scholar's peer" to recognize the complete lack of sound, honest reasoning in Ford's wild guesswork. We are sadly disappointed. Here we see no wisdom, only folly; no depth, but shallow, irresponsible thinking. Any college sophomore who has read enough history can apply the apotelesmatic principle, simply by giving full reign to his imagination and thus become an easy peer of Desmond Ford, or even excel him.
>
> Perhaps we were looking in the wrong place. Let us continue our search for the "important questions" Ford has raised. It is known that he denies the heavenly Sanctuary has two apartments. This is indeed an important question. But strangely enough, in the next breath he asserts that the "anchor of the soul" of Hebrews 6:19 enters into the *second* veil. But how can there be a second veil if there is only one apartment? Perhaps he would explain that this is a figurative veil. Yet we read, "Whither the forerunner is entered, even Jesus." Jesus is a real person having entered a real veil. Did He enter the first or second veil? Let Ford extricate himself. We can't help him. (*Ibid.* 3)

David Lin was also critical of those who, after Des Ford had shown himself to have been deceptive in covering up the fact that he did not believe the Sanctuary truth for the past thirty years, still wanted him to remain as part of God's ministry. Lin focused in on two such requests as presented in the *Ministry* magazine. "Please come with us, Des. For the sake of the Church and its people and for your own sake. Your ministry is of great value to the Church." (*Ministry*, October, 1980, 9). "Des, I know you are a man of integrity. . . . Our great desire is to see you preserved for the ministry." (*Ibid.*, 10)

Commenting on the statements made by delegates to the Glacier View meetings, David Lin stated:

> These words would have been appropriate before he made his open challenge. But after he had denied the doctrinal positions he held when he acted the orthodox Adventist and has demonstrated to all that he has been working under an Adventist camouflage and duped us all these years, how can we still believe in his moral integrity and want to retain him in the ministry?
> (*Victory or Fiasco?*, 3)

David Lin also brought forth important questions of his own.

> We need to ascertain the extent of the influence of the Fordian heresies within our ranks. Why have we given Desmond Ford grounds to say that our statement of "Fundamental Beliefs" voted by the Church at Dallas, showed a definite shift away from Ellen White's interpretation in the area of the Sanctuary? And

he declared that the statement on the Sanctuary voted at Dallas says nothing about two apartments in the heavenly Sanctuary. Was this a deliberate concession on our part to accommodate the Fordian heresy and preserve an appearance of unity? Does this apostate still have sympathizers and secret agents among our leading men? (*Victory or Fiasco?*, 5)

Naturally, this article caused much upset among those who strongly supported the *new theology*, yet David Lin was simply using the type of straight testimony which was formerly used by our leaders and the biblical prophets when confronting damnable heresy. David Lin himself stated: "I just got a letter . . . stating that *Victory or Fiasco?* is not well received by many people at P.U.C., because Ford has many sympathizers there." [3] David Lin noted it had been assessed that "my 'stocks' are affected by that outspoken article [*Victory or Fiasco?*]. But I feel I was not acting from personal animosity against Ford, because I've never met the man. And I made no scruples about calling him for what he really is. It is strange that so many people still think well of a man who has done God's cause so much damage. . . . Anyway I'm not worried at all about my 'stocks,' I just feel we should hit this dangerous heresy with all we have." (*Ibid.*)

Quite obviously, a man with the faith of David Lin, who was prepared to spend fourteen years in jail rather than compromise his commitment to his Savior, will be little influenced by the scorn of a few men and women of much lesser dedication. Indeed, it is for the lack of this dedication that the *new theology* has found a place in the hearts of so many. The acceptance of the *new theology* does not prepare men to suffer intense persecution for their faith as David Lin did. His testimony against this error is a living witness to the power of the truth of God in the life of an individual.

Indeed, with David Lin, we have been given the unique opportunity of enjoying the perspectives of a dedicated Adventist, who, for virtually thirty years, was preserved apart and thus able to furnish a knowledge of the thinking of God's true people of an earlier era. Truly he, too, was preserved for such a time as this.

## Chapter 72 Endnotes

1. Lin's papers clearly show what students at Pacific Union College had been taught in the 1940s.
2. It is disconcerting to find that the pastor, whose views Pastor Lin so properly condemned, has been frequently asked to present a series of talks to our young people. For example, he was invited to speak to the homosexuals at their meeting in Arizona. He presented the 1984 Week of Prayer at Avondale College, and he was the chief speaker at the All-Europe Youth Congress in England in 1984. Surely our youth deserve much greater care in the selection of those who minister to their needs.
3. Letter written by Pastor David Lin to Dr. Russell Standish, dated September 21, 1981

# 73 The Atlanta Affirmation

ON June 12 and 13, 1981, a group of seventeen teachers from seven different Seventh-day Adventist colleges and universities met in Atlanta, Georgia. These teachers stated they were seeking "ways in increasing mutual confidence among its various groups." (Letter signed by the seventeen in attendance)

The declaration noted that two others from Southern Missionary College had attended the Friday session, but were not present to add their signatures to the letter. After expressing a number of altruistic concepts concerning their ministry and their love for the Church, the signatories expressed concern about the following matters:

1. That dismissal or withdrawal under pressure of certain teachers and pastors from denominational employ has given rise to grave concern among many members of our Church.
2. That loyalty to the Church is now often measured with reference to certain personalities or publications rather than to Scripture.
3. That well-meaning attempts to respond creatively to theological questions now confronting Adventism have been interpreted in some circles as jeopardizing the integrity of the Church and its message.
4. That the credibility, and therefore, effectiveness, of seminary and certain other religion faculties—made up of the very persons prepared to serve the Church theologically—are now being eroded.
5. That the treatment of the recent theological controversy in the *Adventist Review* and *Ministry* has not always reflected the variety of viewpoints that exist in the Church, and that this one-sidedness has fostered an attitude of suspicion and a sense of impotence among a substantial number of members.
6. That both critics and defenders of currently dominant expressions of Adventist doctrine stated their views in a manner tending to divide rather than to heal.
7. That energies which should go into the building up of the Church are now being wasted in dealing with the consequences of the present climate of distrust and alienation.
8. That frustrations associated with developments, we are noting, have engendered hurt, dismay, and cynicism among our students, our col-

leagues in other academic disciplines and the general membership of the Church. (Atlanta Declaration dated June 13, 1981)

The purpose of these meetings was clearly perceived. One comment upon it stated: "Thank you for sending me a copy of the minutes and plans of the June 13 meeting in Atlanta. The minutes provide clear evidence that an organized effort is being made to undermine the historic doctrines of the Church. Fortunately these minutes are now in the hands of church authorities so they will be alert to what is happening." [1] (Letter written by a General Conference Committee member working in the *Adventist Review* office, dated August 24, 1981, and quoted in the *Collegedale Tidings*, 7)

A similar letter stated, "I think we already had the minutes from the Atlanta Affirmation meeting, also some interpretation of this from Bible teachers who were sickened at what went on there. There is no doubt but that a lasting warfare is on within Adventism regarding the theological truth of our message. Certainly we are living in the last days, and Satan is going to make every attempt to overthrow God's truth, if not one way, then by another route. The kind of evangelicalism which is being promulgated will eventually destroy the Sabbath, the state of the dead, the imminent coming of Jesus, as well as the investigative judgment, and responsible Christian living based on a concept of sanctification." (Letter dated August 19, 1981, written by a member of the General Conference Committee from the staff of the *Ministry* magazine quoted in the *Collegedale Tidings*, 7)

The expressed concerns of those who put their signatures to the *Atlanta Affirmation* are worthy of analysis, since men representing seven of the ten Seventh-day Adventist Colleges in the United States added their names to the document. These Colleges were Andrews University, Columbia Union, Loma Linda University, Pacific Union, Southern Missionary, Southwestern Adventist and Walla Walla. Only Atlantic Union, Oakwood and Union Colleges were unrepresented.

One matter stood out. At no time did these men express a concern for the preservation of the pure faith of the Seventh-day Adventist Church. Their concerns may be summarized as twofold, *viz.*, the preservation of their denominational employment and the freedom to teach that which pleases them. They described their "well-meaning attempts to respond creatively to theological questions now confronting Adventism." What was not admitted was that it was these very theologians who themselves had, because of their own personal doubts, posed these theological questions. Now they asked the right to be the ones to settle the doubts they had expressed and endangered. Such is not their right. A halt must be called to theologians using this means to alter the doctrines of the Church. Such is the prerogative of the General Conference in full session, alone. If those men have doubts about our faith, honesty dictates that they cease to teach our young people and that they seek alternative employment. There they can contemplate their doubts further if they so wish.

These theologians complain about the lack of credibility of our religion faculties. It is entirely in their own hands to bring back that credibility. It is their irresponsible disregard of the Adventist message which has precipitated this woe upon themselves.

Their call for a reflection of "the variety of viewpoints that exist in the Church" in our denominational publications is, in reality, a call that error as well as truth be foisted upon God's flock. Our literature must never become the vehicle for the expression of men's doubts, nor the avenue by which error is offered to the people of God.

The cynicism among their students is a matter that these men would have done well to keep to themselves. Their mention of it only reminds the Church that this cynicism is increasingly the result of the mode of theological teaching they have adopted.

Yet these men continued long after this period to present doubt to many of our young people in the various colleges that they represented. One from Loma Linda University was invited by the Australasian Division in 1983 to present special messages to the National Convention of Seventh-day Adventist University Students' Societies. In his presentation there, he was quoted in the *Australasian Record* as stating that Jesus did not present the signs of His coming as noted in Matthew 24 to indicate *when* He would come but merely *that* He would come. This statement was just one means of proclaiming that my Lord delayeth His coming. How glaring is this falsehood! The very question of the disciples was, "*When* shall these things be?" And over and over again the time factor is mentioned. University students hear sufficient error in their lectures day by day without Adventists being brought half way around the world to reinforce such error.

In the S.M.C.[2] *Southern Columns*, one of the theology lecturers at Southern Missionary College prepared an article entitled "Some Observations on the Present Theology Crisis." In this article he stated "that the so-called new '*theology*' essentially agrees with the official General Conference position and the Defense Literature Committee." (*Southern Columns*, 1st quarter 1982, 12) Surely this theologian knew this assertion to be an utter falsehood, for the *new theology* had done absolutely nothing but attack the doctrines of the Seventh-day Adventist Church. His thesis in this article was that those defending the truth of God were simply reiterating the errors of Robert Brinsmead's early position. That a man claiming to be a scholar could demonstrate such a mistaken view was staggering. Attacking an article in the publication, *The Layworker*, he said: "A reading of *The Layworker* soon brings the conviction that what they earnestly desire is a revival of this era [the era of the old Brinsmead movement] or something like it. Even the tapes listed for sale on the back page of *The Layworker* evoke memories of the old Brinsmead movement. Such names as William Grotheer, Wieland (of Wieland and Short fame) and new names appear, too. A series of tapes called *The Bangkok Series* refers to the tapes of the Standish brothers. Their scathing attacks on the scholars and institutions of the Church are highly prized and eagerly digested by the continuers of the old Brinsmead tradition, whether in the form of tapes, unofficial mimeographed sheets, or the new unofficial book, *Adventism Vindicated*. Another name appearing is LeRoy Moore, whose tapes and unofficial book, Theology in Crisis,[3] are considered grist for the theological mills of the perfectionists. Yet another person coming into print in recent months, who appears to be reviving the old S.A.F. [this stands for *Sanctuary Awakening Fellowship*, the name of Brinsmead's first movement] message is Vance Ferrell."

In referring to Attorney Lewis Walton's book, *Omega*, this theology professor stated, "We are surprised to note that even some very recent books from denominational presses contain implied criticism of present denominational schools by drawing false contrasts between them and Battle Creek College. The historical inaccuracies of some of these books amount to a serious misrepresentation of the situation." (*Ibid.*, 14,15)

Thus it can be seen that these men are not merely passive purveyors of error, but they are prepared to jump into the attack whenever the opportunity presents itself. The presentation of the *Atlanta Affirmation* marks a point at which dissident Adventist theologians decided to assert their right to pursue the proclamation of their errors, and to use guile and stealth of word in order to convince church leaders and others of the nobility of their purposes. The reader himself must be the judge of this claim.

### Chapter 73 Endnotes

1. Despite this assurance, one of the signatories was later invited to lead the Theological Seminary of the Far East in the Philippines. This was a most careless selection to a vital and most responsible post. Providentially, the theologian refused the appointment.
2. Southern Missionary College (now Southern College of Adventists)
3. Actually the title is *The Theology Crisis*.

# 74 The Spirit of Prophecy

EVEN during Sister White's lifetime, there were a number of people who questioned her inspiration and who denied that her revelations were from God. This fact should cause no surprise since disbelief has been the lot of every prophet since the days of Enoch. The basic reason for disbelief in prophets is, of course, that their messages rebuke, and many are unprepared to face the realities of the lost lives they are living.

Ronald Numbers, in his book *Prophetess of Health* set out to show that Sister White's insights into the health message were little more than flagrant copies of the teaching of many of her contemporaries. Of course, it cannot be denied that many of the truths which Sister White enunciated were propounded by various men living in her time. In fact, some of these principles were well known for centuries. What Numbers failed to do was to explain why Sister White incorporated in her writing the valid principles of health found in these works, but omitted the numerous foolish concepts which had crept into their writings.[1]

It is safe to say that, apart from the health principles enunciated in the Bible, there has been no body of preventive medicine principles put together which compares with those of the Spirit of Prophecy. In those writings, superb principles for the maintenance of physical health, mental health and spiritual well-being are placed side by side in a manner unsurpassed. For this, Numbers in his attempt to discredit Sister White's works gave no credit whatsoever. One of the authors is a physician and the other a psychologist. We stand truly amazed at the magnificent collection of health material provided by Sister White. There is only one possible explanation, in our opinion, and that is that it was divinely derived.

The pastor of the Long Beach Church in Southern California, Walter Rea, left the ministry after losing faith in the Spirit of Prophecy. His research indicated that Sister White had used a large number of reference books in the writing of *Desire of Ages* and a number of her other works. Apparently Walter Rea[2] imagined that proper scholarship and inspiration were mutually exclusive. There is no reason to believe that God cannot inspire a person in his research, or in any other way that He chooses to reveal truth. Furthermore, Walter Rea put forth the fallacious notion that Seventh-day Adventists had adopted a view of inspiration which depended upon God providing every word used. One day, in the 1950s, our father came home from his work with the Sanitarium Health Food Company. He had been serving in the retail shop in the city of Newcastle. During the day, someone had brought in a book written by d'Aubigne: *The History of the Reformation*. The person stated that his deceased relatives had been Seventh-day Adventists and they had bought this book from Mrs. White prior to her departure from Australia in 1900. This statement was confirmed by the fact that her name was found in the inside front cover printed on a small personal library card. Our father gladly bought this book. In showing it to the authors as young men he stated: "It is very likely that this was the book that Sister White used for some of the information on history which she included in the *Great Controversy*." As young people we felt no shock concerning this matter. It seemed a perfectly proper use of a valuable source of material. Our father expressed his supposition in terms which indicated that he had known for years that Sister White relied for some of her information upon truth that was already available.

In some ways Walter Rea acted almost as if we should believe that uninspired persons cannot be relied upon for truth. But let us never forget that even the most evil men have enunciated numerous precious truths. A simple reflection by the reader will call to mind many scientific truths which did not demand special inspiration for their discovery. Similarly, many historians, both evil and godly, have written truthfully concerning the topics upon which they were concentrating. Who are we to dictate to the God of heaven that He may not direct His servant to use such sources as they relate truth?

Walter Rea titled his book *The White Lie*. This title was no doubt clever and catchy, but one that brought no honor to the author when the title is related to the topic considered. It seems very tragic that a man coming toward the close of his ministerial service should end it in an attack upon the very truths that have made his life worthwhile. It is hard to believe that Walter Rea now possesses the joy of service in the Master's cause. We can only trust and pray that he, along with the hundred of others who have apostatized, will one day find their way back into the fold of God and embrace the precious truths which at present they seem to despise. Such a return a loving God would not refuse.

It was probably inevitable that the General Conference would seek to blunt Rea's attack on Sister White as a plagiarist. This was attempted by asking a legal opinion from Vincent L. Ramik, senior partner of Dillar, Ramik, and Wight, Ltd. Ramik is an expert in patent, trademark, and copyright laws. It could be argued that, naturally, a man who is retained by an organization in these circumstances, would be predisposed to please those who were paying his fee. In fairness to those who would take this view, it should be stated that legal opinions are traditionally quite variant, and seem to be greatly influenced by the interest of those who hire the lawyer. Thus perhaps it was no surprise that Ramik concluded "that the charges concerning Sister White's alleged plagiarism simply were not true." (*Adventist Review*, Sept. 17, 1981) However, it must be said that Ramik seemed to show a greater passion than necessary for his subject. Indeed, he asserted he had become absolutely engrossed, even changed, by what he had read. We should not be surprised that Sister White did not commit any act of plagiarism, for God would certainly not have utilized His servant in such a manner. However, Walter Rea and those who followed his line of reasoning could justifiably state that even if Sister White did not breach the laws of plagiarism, this fact would not necessarily negate their other claim, that she was a false prophet. However, the whole facts of the case totally dispel such a conclusion. Sister White must be judged by her life's work, and her prophetic gift must be tested by Scripture. By such criteria her standing as a prophetess of God stands unchallengeable.

## Chapter 74 Endnotes

1. Dr. Bernard Richardson, Medical Director of the Northern European-West Africa Division, 1975–80, and a colleague of Russell's at Enton Medical Centre, has recounted his own experience. As a young physician, newly graduated from Edinburgh, he had little faith in the Spirit of Prophecy. However, this changed when he found a copy of a medical book, written in the 1890s by Queen Victoria's personal physician. As Dr. Richardson read this book, he found it to be full of ludicrous suggestions for medical care, suggestions found by the 1940s to be quite unscientific. He shortly after took the opportunity to read Sister White's book, *Ministry of Healing*. This book, written at a similar date, Dr. Richardson discovered to be full of medical information which has remained current. This formed the basis for his lasting faith in the testimonies of God's servant.
2. This chapter does not intend to completely rebut Rea's material, since that has already been done in *The White Truth* and materials circulated by the White Estate. The reader is referred to these publications. This chapter simply passes over this matter in its historical setting, since it bears relevance to the claims of the *new theology*. Most supporting this view uncritically accepted Rea's accusations.

# 75 The Davenport Affair

WHILE this sorry episode in the history of the Seventh-day Adventist Church is not directly related to the doctrinal controversy, it found itself being pushed into a central area of that controversy. Briefly, the situation was that Dr. Donald J. Davenport, a California physician, was involved in large investment projects principally associated with the building of post offices. Much of his funds came from Seventh-day Adventist sources. By offering attractive interest rates, he was able to induce many Adventists to place their funds into his projects, even though they were poorly secured. That this occurred on an individual level was serious enough, for when the inevitable happened, and Dr. Davenport was declared bankrupt, naturally those private investors who had placed their money into these funds had less means to support the work of God.

The situation was much graver than that, however, for Davenport managed to encourage a number of church leaders to flout denominational policy and standards by investing church money in his very risky ventures. In at least one instance, tithe money was placed into his hands, but in general, the money was from trust funds.

Despite the fact that the General Conference treasury issued warnings, a number of leaders persisted in this dangerous utilization of church funds. Part of the reason may be attributable to the fact that Davenport offered some of these people interest rates reported to be as high as eighty percent per annum on their personal investments in his ventures. These accusations have been made in writing[1] and have not been denied. If they are correct, then the conference presidents involved have succumbed to something which was a not-too-subtle form of bribery, in order to increase their own personal wealth. Since the total money lost by the Church was something on the order of twenty million dollars, the gravity of the situation can be understood.

Unfortunately, the news of the financial strife within the Church traveled very quickly through the news media and was reported in many countries of the world. Incredibly the common reaction was to associate this situation with the theological problems. Thus it was stated: "Already divided by theological differences, the [Seventh-day Adventist] church has been plunged into a financial tangle that may cost it and its members millions of dollars and, conceivably, ensnarl it in legal battles." (*Washington Post*, Aug. 24, 1981)

According to this same article, Davenport's preliminary bankruptcy petition listed twenty-seven Adventist institutions and more than two hundred individuals, the majority of whom were Seventh-day Adventists. A number of newspapers (e.g. *The Spokesman-Review*, July 29, 1981, and *The Sunday Oregonian* of August 2, 1981), placed the estimated loss to the Church from its bankruptcy as high as over forty million dollars.

Naturally, there was a widespread reaction from the church members. Many expressed a lack of confidence in sending their funds for church projects, and there was a noticeable drop in Sabbath School and some other offerings. This outcome was really a quite understandable reaction, even though the final result was to damage the work of God, which many of these people wished to uphold. It also led other persons to ask, "Why do we build up huge reserves for stock market investments as well as investments in real estate and at the same time continue to plead with the members to give and give to finish the work? Faith! In God, or mammon?" (Statement made by Final Century Foundation, Oregon)

Others, especially in Tennessee, moved to publish far and wide the names of those ministers who had received extremely high interest rates for their personal loans to Davenport, and had then invested much larger church funds at a fraction of the interest they themselves were receiving. That these publishers were not challenged in court for misrepresentation, does give veracity to their assertion. Furthermore, they reproduced photocopies of the letters alleged to have been written by the culprits. What is true is that the leadership of the Church was compelled to take the matter very seriously indeed, and to take disciplinary action against those who had so failed their Church.

Initially, Neal Wilson, president of the General Conference, stated, in writing, in the *Adventist Review*, that the names of the individuals punished would be listed,[2] but this decision was later rescinded. It was widely rumored that enormous pressure had been brought to bear upon Pastor Wilson to effect this reversal of intention. What is certain is that, by and large, the treatment of these persons may be considered light in relationship to the enormity of their failure to do that which was expected of them as stewards of God's means. Some of them were removed from their positions. Some also went into early retirement, and others into positions not involving financial matters. It is only to be hoped that for their own sakes, every effort will be made by these men, who failed to measure up to the trust of their fellow believers, to make full and appropriate restitution.

In reality, the Davenport affair was only tangential to the theological conflict, despite the repeated association of the two in the public press and among many of those supporting the *new theology*. The financial crisis, however, may indicate a lowered level of integrity engendered by the drift from commandment keeping, seen to be a common consequence of the influence of the *new theology*. God's work will most surely survive this unfortunate event, and we can only hop that it will lead to the learning of important lessons.

Perhaps the Davenport affair highlighted more than anything else that it appears there are many workers in the Church of God, who are not motivated by the high calling that God has bestowed upon them, but rather by very low mercenary ideals.

### Chapter 75 Endnotes

1. *S.D.A. Press Release*, Vol. 1, Nos. 8 & 9: "I would appreciate your arranging the 50% rate on the enclosed $25,000 and would have liked very much to have gotten on the 80%, but as you told [name deleted, president of the Georgia Cumberland Conference], there's another year coming." (Letter from Sabbath School and Stewardship secretary of the Georgia-Cumberland Conference to Dr. Donald J. Davenport, dated August 7, 1980. Photocopied from *S.D.A. Press Release*, Vol. 1, No. 9) The conference president's letter investing $50,000 at the same interest rate was also photocopied in the same report.
2. This measure had been recommended by a task force consisting of laymen appointed to examine the Davenport scandal. Prexad, the officer committee of the General Conference, had accepted the recommendation.

# 76 Column Inches

OVER the last quarter of a century there has been a steady increase in the desire of the Seventh-day Adventist Church to obtain favorable publicity in the secular press throughout the world. Press secretaries at various levels were commended for the number of column inches which each could gain in their respective areas. Little could the Church have envisaged the dramatic increase in the number of these column inches which was to bring the name Seventh-day Adventist and of the Seventh-day Adventist Church to the fore. It could hardly be anticipated, however, that much of the adverse publicity to which the Church was subjected, was included in the report of our press secretaries as they reckoned their achievements in column inches.

In 1978 when Geoffrey Paxton was in the United States, the authors took the opportunity to speak with him. At that time, he stated that he and others were determined to have the doctrinal controversy within the Seventh-day Adventist Church brought before the world. With this in mind, he had already spoken to editorial staff of *Time* magazine and *Christianity Today*. He assured us that these magazines would be taking up the matter in their publications. There is absolutely no doubt that there was an orchestrated attempt on the part of some to shame the Seventh-day Adventist Church before the world at large. Just what Paxton's real aims were is difficult to evaluate. Why should it matter to an Anglican minister whether or not the Seventh-day Adventist Church was well thought of by the Christian community as a whole, remains a puzzle. No doubt, a number of dissident Seventh-day Adventists were able to exploit this method of "punishing" God's Church for what they perceived to be its unacceptable attitude toward them.

As the months went by and there was no fulfillment of Paxton's prediction, it was wondered whether he had not taken himself more seriously than necessary.

By February 1980, however, the first prediction was fulfilled. An article entitled "The Shaking Up of Adventism" appeared in the February 8 issue of *Christianity Today*. Colin, along with other proponents of the historic Adventist faith, was contacted by the author of this article prior to its publication. It is assumed that those contacted, including many promoting the *new theology*, had their names supplied to the author by those anxious to see the controversy within God's Church aired before the world and to see the Church under fire. Colin, sensing that the expression of his views could not, in these circumstances, help the cause of truth, refrained from contributing.

This article predictably expounded the viewpoint of those who were opposing the truth of God. The article pointed out what to us was fully evident, that "privately, a number of S.D.A. Biblical scholars who express reservations about Ford's outspokenness, nevertheless generally agree with him on key doctrinal positions, and a large number of laymen and young clergy back him fully." (*Christianity Today*, Feb. 8, 1980, 64)

In Australia, since it has been regarded as a sign of gross disloyalty to God's Church to equate Desmond Ford's teachings with those of Robert Brinsmead, it was interesting to observe that this article stated: "For some reason, Ford has been under heavy pressure from unnamed officials to condemn Brinsmead and his teachings publicly. Ford, however, agrees with Brinsmead on many positions and has declined to rebuke him." (*Ibid.*, 67) It does seem strange that the leadership of the Church in Australia refused to believe this perfectly obvious fact.

When John Clifford and Russell wrote *Conflicting Concepts* in 1976, they put forward their observation that the teachings of Ford and Brinsmead were essentially the same. This similarity, of course, can no longer be denied. But at the time the Australasian Division spokesman wrote a highly condemnatory statement, indicating that to unite the two names was an attempt to use smear tactics against Dr. Ford. No room was left for the view that perhaps the authors were simply perceptive of an established fact.

The *Christianity Today* article also referred to Walter Rea's attack on the Spirit of Prophecy, and Sister White's writings were disparaged. Furthermore, it was falsely claimed that "early in S.D.A. history, though, many of the Church's members placed Mrs. White's teaching on a level with Scripture, and they tended to require the Bible to square with her views, a practice that persists amongst some Adventists today." (*Ibid.*, 65)

It wasn't long before *Time* magazine and *Newsweek* both went into print, outlining the doctrinal problems within the Church. It was patently obvious that the information was supplied from inside sources, and undoubtedly, these sources were those of the Brinsmead-Paxton-Ford axis, whose point of view was accepted almost without question. Very shortly, the Davenport affair and the work of Walter Rea were integrated into the doctrinal controversy, in an effort to make it appear as if the Church was about to fold. This attempt reminded us of Sister White's statement that this condition would indeed be reached, but she provided the assurance that such a destruction of God's remnant Church would not occur.

*Newsweek*, in covering several aspects of the problems in the Church, noted:

> In this massive study, Ford argues that Scripture simply does not support White's interpretation of Daniel. "No scholar seriously believes that Jesus Christ is sitting in heaven turning pages to investigate Christians' lives," he argues.

Specifically, Ford contends that Mrs. White's notion of a "judgment" phase in Christ's redemption violates the orthodox Christian doctrine that Jesus' atonement for sin was completed with His atonement on the cross. (*Newsweek*, Jan. 19, 1981)

The authors of this article did leave the Church with one matter to ponder:

> The dilemma facing the Adventist Church in 1981 is how to reconcile its commitment to the Bible with its doctrinal dependence upon the charismatic Mrs. White. For if it loses its founding mother, the church may find it has also lost its distinctive visionary soul. (*Ibid.*)

Later, *Time* devoted a full article to Walter Rea's attack on the Church, but it did not overlook the other problems troubling the Church. It stated:

> The 3.8 million-member Seventh-day Adventist Church is normally the most doctrinally placid and prosperous of faiths. Lately however, it has fallen into unaccustomed uproar. For starters, church members are suing Adventist officials in an Oregon court for fraud and breach of fiduciary trust, stemming from the 1981 bankruptcy of fellow Adventist, Donald Davenport, a Los Angeles developer.... On top of this, the Church has been hit by a second scandal: the charge that the theological writings of its most important figure, which ranks second only to the Bible, may have been plagiarized from other authors. (*Time*, Aug. 2, 1982)

Even prior to the announcements in these international magazines of the news of the problems in the Church, they had spread worldwide. *The Los Angeles Times* of Jan. 12, 1980, proclaimed the headline, "Theologian Called to Defend His Views." This became a type of catch-cry through numerous newspapers in many countries of the world.

In Australia, which was having its own private problems with the trial of the wife of one of its ministers, accused of the murder of her child, and the concomitant accusation that the pastor had aided and abetted with this event. The *Sydney Sun* of July 19, 1982, headlined "The Chamberlain Teacher [Dr. Ford] who Split the Church," referring to Pastor Michael Chamberlain, who was accused of complicity in the murder. The newspaper pointed out that he had been taught by Dr. Ford in the theology department of Avondale College. It then set out the problems in the Church.

The *Sydney Morning Herald* of Aug. 14, 1982, devoted a full page and a half of its large page-style newspaper to an article which linked the alleged murder with the Sanitarium Health Food Company and with many problems within the Church, including Dr. Ford's challenge, the Davenport affair, and Walter Rea. It also linked all this with the *It Is Written* program which it unfairly described as "the worst religious programme on Australian television."

In Australia, the unfortunate death of the child of Pastor and Mrs. Chamberlain which had captured the imagination of the Australian public and made Mrs. Chamberlain's trial for murder the most publicized and notorious in the history of Australian crime, did much to provide an unflattering picture of our Church. That

Mrs. Chamberlain was convicted unanimously by the jury of the crime with which she was charged, and that Pastor Chamberlain was convicted of aiding her, did not help matters. Yet, to any unbiased person, it should have been plain that Mrs. Chamberlain was not found guilty beyond reasonable doubt. Indeed, it is almost certain that in no other city of Australia would it have been possible to have found twelve persons who could have so misread the evidence presented.[1] Nevertheless, it is probably correct to say that the majority of Australians were convinced of Mrs. Chamberlain's guilt, while the vast majority of Adventists believed in her innocence.

The Australian Broadcasting Commission also gave prominence to the problems within the Church in its radio broadcast of the program, *Broadband*, on July 2, 1980. In this talk, Geoffrey Paxton took up the matter of Ford and Rea and also mentioned Robert Brinsmead. Unfortunately, Paxton was able to point to Seventh-day Adventists, such as Raymond Cottrell, Ronald Numbers, William Peterson and Walter Rea, whose words had caused more difficulty for God's people than a score of non-Adventists could have done.

Thus the Church was certainly able to score a record number of column inches. But these were a series of publicity statements which it could well have done without. Nevertheless, we must never overlook that God can bring the worst intentions of the enemies of His truth to the point where they prove to be a blessing. There can be little doubt that, out of all this ill-publicity, God's plan will not be deviated and His work will not be thwarted.

One fact is certain, there can be little doubt now that, in Australia, virtually all its inhabitants have at least heard the name, Seventh-day Adventist.

Chapter 76 Endnote:

1. The nine-week-old child, Azaria Chamberlain, disappeared from a camping site in the desert in Central Australia. Mrs. Chamberlain testified that she saw a dingo (a wild dog) take the child. The case was a most mysterious one, for only the baby's jumper-suit was ever found. All evidence indicated that the child had been buried and subsequently disinterred and the jumper suit taken off. It had been mutilated subsequently by a sharp object in order to make it appear as if a dog's teethmarks had caused the tearing. Naturally, the attempted deception was easily detected at the forensic tests. The jumper-suit was so stained with blood, that medical evidence presented at the trial indicated that the baby must be dead. Forensic witnesses also testified that they found traces of blood in the Chamberlain car and camera bag, which was fetal in type. This type of blood is present in babies under six months of age. The Chamberlains did not deny human involvement in the death of their baby. Some supporters suggested that the dog was owned by a resident in the vicinity and that he buried the child in self-defense. Then, sensing that the Chamberlains were under suspicion, the owner repented of the deception and attempted to assist the Chamberlains, without revealing his own identity, by recovering the jumper-suit and attempting to bolster Mrs. Chamberlain's contention. Some forensic scientists also witness to the fact that the tests for fetal blood were inconclusive. One interesting sidelight was that the forensic dentist who witnessed against the Chamberlains, was a Seventh-day Adventist. What is certain is, that Mrs. Chamberlain was sentenced to life imprisonment without the production of the body or the murder weapon and without the establishment of a single, plausible motive, a situation unique in the annals of murder trials in Australia. Darwin, the city in which the trial was heard, is a sort of frontier city two thousand miles from the population centers of Australia. The authors, as well as the majority of Adventists, and a large number of Australians are convinced of the Chamberlains' innocence.

# 77

## Cartoons Return

ONCE again, in 1981, there was resort to the use of cartoons in order to object to Dr. Ford's dismissal. Some of these cartoons were directed specifically to Pastor Neal Wilson. One showed him in a motor vehicle in an advanced state of dilapidation—a 1920 vintage vehicle in such a state of disrepair that one of the back wheels was off and the terrified passengers in the back seat were making moves to abandon the car. This car was entitled: "S.D.A. Remnant Church and the Kingdom—or Bust." The vehicle was situated in a very stony road on the edge of a precipice and had just come to a dead end which stated: "Route 1844."

Perhaps the most detailed cartoon was one which set out to represent the Glacier View examination of Dr. Ford as a travesty of justice. This cartoon was entitled: "Drama of the Sages," or "Will They Do It?" To the left of the cartoon was a group of church leaders who attended Glacier View, sitting in a jury box. Over the jury box was an advertisement entitled: Coming Attractions—Walter Rea," and in the minds of the "jury" was projected the thought: "We think we'll do it." The center of the cartoon was taken up with the judge, who was Neal Wilson holding what was called the Glacier Gavel. He was quoted as saying: "Dr. Ford is not on trial here—Ideas are!!" In his mind he was saying: "*We've Got To Do It*," and then again he stated, "And therefore, Prexad[1] is recommending to the Australasian Division . . ."

On the witness stand was the title "Traditional Witness Stand" and Wood was seen holding up Ford's book on Daniel as an exhibit. Behind the "judge" was a dove, titled Sola Scriptura, flying out the window.

On the defendant's stand stood Dr. Ford who was saying, "Here I stand," an obvious effort to present his errors in a similar light to the truths enunciated by Luther. In his mind Ford was thinking, "They really *might* do it!!!" His defense stand was entitled: "Idea Box," and also contained the commencement of the words: "Sola Scriptura." Below Dr. Ford was Dr. Cassell, then president of the Pacific Union College, who was thinking: "They *did* it!!" To the extreme right of the cartoon we could see Dr. Ford behind a wall which was being built by a man with the name "Review" on his jacket. The name on the wall was "Outer limit SDA theology (traditional variety)." Behind this wall Dr. Ford said: "They really *did it*!!" And then he also said, "Come, let us reason together." Below him is a picture of Pastor

Wilson; Pastor Keith Parmenter, president of the Australasian Division; and the authors of this book who were reputed to be thinking "We did it."

Another cartoon consisted of a satire on Kenneth Wood, then editor of the *Adventist Review*. It was entitled, "Ken, the Sandwich Man." It showed a caricature of Pastor Wood carrying sandwich boards entitled "Adventist Review." Beneath this heading were the following statements: "SDAs Are It!"; "E.G.W. Proves 2,300 days"; "Bible writers plagiarized too"; "SDAs give more tithe than anybody"; "SDAs are the remnant"; "Infallibility of E.G.W." Pastor Wood was claimed to be saying: "This is MY Board—I'll write on it what I please!"

A third cartoon in a similar vein depicted three sailors in a rowboat entitled "The Remnant Church." The boat was among a large number of mines, contact with any one of which it may be assumed would destroy the boat. The sailors were termed "The Curia SDA." Three of the mines were named as follows: "Justification by Faith Alone," "Walter Rea Research," and "Hebrews 9." Above the sailors hovered a helicopter which could have saved them and was entitled "Brinsmead, Paxton." One of the occupants of the helicopter was entitled "Brinsmead, Paxton." Another of the occupants of the helicopter was calling out, "May we help?" The response of these sailors was "Go away!"

Such efforts, in this instance, while humorous, contributed, of course, nothing to the serious debate within the Church.

Chapter 77 Endnote:

1. Prexad is the committee consisting of the General Conference president, vice presidents, secretaries and treasurers.

# 78 Pacific Union College

WHEN Desmond Ford was transferred to Pacific Union College as a professor of theology in 1977, very few involved in this transfer had the least perception of the damage that would be perpetrated upon that college by his brief stay of two years. Perhaps only those who had stood for the truth of God in Australia recognized that, in such a short period, enormous damage could and would be achieved. One of the reasons for the success of Desmond Ford was that there were a number of professors, chiefly in theology but not excluding other disciplines, who had already accepted erroneous Protestant views similar to those held by Ford. They were in a situation similar to that in which Ford had been placed at Avondale College. They were quietly going about the task of insinuating their ideas into the minds of the students, but outwardly, they were apparently supporting the Adventist beliefs. In Ford, they found a rallying point for their secret convictions.

The truth is that many leaders in our Church were very reluctant to believe that Desmond Ford was causing anything but progress to the Church of God. Despite much warning from many lay people, the president of the Oregon Conference persisted in his plan to have Desmond Ford speak at meetings there. That the truth of God has had a rather rough passage in Oregon in recent years can be attributed, in part at least, to the failure of the conference president to take heed of the proper warnings of some of his flock.

The Nebraska Conference invited Ford to take every evening meeting at its camp meeting. These are just two instances of many that could be quoted. At these meetings Ford was permitted to speak to large Adventist congregations. Of course, the radio station at Pacific Union College was also used as a medium to take his message, not only to Adventists, but to those non-Adventists who listened to it.

Little by little men of perception and fidelity realized that something must be done. Questions were passed around. Among them was a series of ten questions which included the following:

"Is it right for ordained S.D.A. ministers, who are paid from tithe money, to undermine the Church openly, or by underhanded methods?

"Is it right for parents to pay thousands of dollars to send their children to S.D.A. schools to unlearn the S.D.A. message?

"Is it right for S.D.A. employees to serve on editorial boards and staffs of
*Spectrum* . . . a magazine published by dissident 'Adventists' with anti-Adventist articles and propaganda in the name of 'scholarship'?"

It was not surprising that, shortly after this, several petitions were circulating with the purpose of bringing more vividly to the attention of the administration of the college, the problems which were existing. It was absolutely amazing to many, that a college president and academic leaders would continue to support the role of a dissident teacher in their midst in the face of overwhelming evidence of infidelity to spiritual truths. The minds of God's people could only have been laid to rest if it had been frankly admitted by these leaders that they had erred in their original assessment of the situation. But, tragically, such admissions are rarely forthcoming.

One petition signed by many stated:

"1) As loyal and contributing Seventh-day Adventists, we have a right and a responsibility to insist that Pacific Union College train our youth to be loyal, believing Seventh-day Adventists. We want teachers and administrators, who, by word and practice, show a complete confidence in the inspired authority of the Bible and the writings of Ellen G. White. We do not want our college to have those who lend support to conflicting doctrines, or who foment distrust in proper leadership. We want educational leaders who will not compromise any details of a conservative Adventist life style in the face of secular pressure.

"2) The present program as being followed by some of the personnel of Pacific Union College openly violates the historical Seventh-day Adventist position in the areas of theology, attitude toward leadership, Seventh-day Adventist life style and support of the Spirit of Prophecy.

"3) As a steward of God's blessing, it appears to me to be incompatible to continue my support of Pacific Union College, if the present program continues as it is. I urge Pacific Union College Board of Trustees to exercise their solemn responsibility to see that the true Seventh-day Adventist principles are followed at Pacific Union College."

In response to the outcry against the problems at Pacific Union College, which predictably continued after Ford had been released from there, a Fact-finding Committee was appointed in November 1981. This committee consisted of nine persons: John Cassell, college president; Gordon Madgwick, vice-president for academic affairs and academic dean; David Igler, vice-president for student affairs; Robert Strickland, vice-president for financial affairs; Herbert Ford, vice-president for public relations and college relations; Caleb Davidian; Charles Cook; Janice von Pohle; and Marion Williams. Since five of these nine members of the committee were the top administrators of the college, it is hard to believe that this selection could be seriously taken as an unbiased committee.

Very shortly the composition of this committee was questioned in a constituency petition presented to the Fact-finding Committee on March 24, 1982, by a group of concerned Pacific Union College constituents from Sacramento, Bakersfield and

Redding. Among other concerns they stated: "Many people who have examined the composition of the investigation committee are not comfortable with its makeup and do not have confidence in it. The committee, in the opinion of many constituents, is not properly constituted. It has a built-in conflict of interest. The majority of its members are members of the administration which, in our view, is the major part of the current deteriorating condition of Pacific Union College. The committee has shown its bias in statements made by its representatives in the *Campus Chronicle* and to numerous people. These members should disqualify themselves. The committee should be reconstituted, if it is to conduct an honest and honorable investigation. Watergate would never have ended the way it did if Nixon had set up an in-house investigation committee to investigate Watergate! It is especially important that a church-related institution be honest with its constituents. Watergate and the Davenport incidents should teach us that to take constituents for granted is a dangerous thing."

This same constituency petition made the accusation that some of the key members of the Investigation Committee had used their position and influence to muzzle and intimidate students and faculty. These persons pointed out that "just a few years ago, Pacific Union College was admired and sought-after by parents. Now its very name is synonymous with controversy and irresponsible faculty conduct."

Perhaps nothing brought more disrepute upon Pacific Union College than the shameful treatment meted out to one of the members of their theology faculty, Dr. Erwin Gane. Dr. Gane, an Australian by birth, was a highly respected member of the department. Being true to the Lord, however, he could not accept the teachings of Dr. Ford and others. He spoke of his concerns in a Christian but responsible manner. Naturally, because those who were destroying the doctrines of the Church did not appreciate being exposed, they commenced a smear campaign against Dr. Gane. Untruthfully, it was stated that he was causing trouble in the college. The accusation had about as much validity as did Ahab's accusation that it was Elijah who was troubling Israel. In psychology, this type of behavior is known as *transference*. This term means that an individual who has a particular problem, compensates for that problem by transferring the defect to the character of another. Thus several members of the theology department, who were indeed bringing dishonor to the college, and causing problems, transferred their own defects of character to the shoulders of Dr. Gane. Incredibly, the administration and Pacific Union College leadership listened to these false and malicious accusations and Dr. Gane, after first of all being seconded to the White Estate, was eventually dismissed from the college. Thus a voice of truth was effectively silenced and the reputation of Pacific Union College appeared to suffer as a result.

An effort, which some have termed scandalous, was made to discredit Dr. Gane prior to his dismissal, by holding psychotherapy group discussions. The use of this foolish, worldly concept, in which individuals throw accusations at one another in a no-holds-barred context, was a discredit to the college. It has absolutely no part in

Christian conduct. "A clinical psychologist[1] was hired to be present at these weekly sessions, in order to give them the appearance of a commonplace, orderly procedure. The stated reason for the session was that problems in the Religion Department were not due to doctrinal differences but rather to personality clashes. The sessions were initiated and carried on at the request of the administration of the college. And the two most influential leaders in the administration were present at the first session. The faculty members of the department of Religion were *required* to attend these once-a-week meetings. They knew they had to attend, or thus give grounds to the administration to terminate their employment. And these sessions did not last a week or two—they went *on for months*! The psychologist, in effect, explained that the way to resolve the problems within the religion department was for the teachers to freely spend each weekly session in direct discussions of what they thought of one another. The plan of action was, that if they did this for enough sessions, all the entanglements would be solved, all would think very highly of one another, and the problems of the religion department would be entirely eliminated." (Constituency Petition presented to the Fact-finding Committee, March 24, 1982)

The naiveté of those who were attempting to follow this approach with the hope of settling the problem is but too plain.[2] If, indeed, men did believe that the problem was a clash of personalities rather than deep conviction of the truth of God, then they were sadly deluded.

Chapter 78 Endnotes:

1. A Seventh-day Adventist psychologist.
2. A careful analysis of the use of this type of confrontational group sessions can be found in the book, *Adventism Jeopardized* by the authors of this book, published by Hartland Publications, P. O. Box 1, Rapidan, Virginia 22733, U.S.A.

# 79 Songs of Blasphemy

NOTHING more vividly underlined the tragedy of the apostasy to which Pacific Union College had descended than the blasphemous "hymns" which, on Friday evening following the Vespers service, a number of college faculty composed. After writing these poems these members of the faculty sang them together with great gusto. The level[1] of blasphemy involved can be seen by the two poems composed to the tune of "The Church Has One Foundation." The first one commenced with the words:

> The Church has one foundation, 'Tis Ellen White of old.

The second was equally blasphemous:

> The Church's new foundation is Ellen and her brood;
> She is a prophet chosen to lead out by her mood.
> From somewhere came a "well done" to bless her every act;
> For everything she taught, by vision was a fact.
>
> Elect from every portion of this old sinful race
> Would by her gospel given, be a new view of grace.
> The Sanctuary above would not replace the cross,
> And eighteen forty-four would supplant the hapless loss.
>
> The church; a corporation will not be found at fault.
> "Spirit of Prophecy"; the earmark of her own cult.
> Ellen G. White inspired, new life to everyone.
> So, following her briefing, the battle soon is won.

There were other verses likening Sister White to the great Diana, Greek goddess of Ephesians. The ridiculous turn of the whole set of songs can be guessed by such silly lines as "What a dud we have in Wilson," sung to the tune of "What a Friend We Have in Jesus." An attempt to discredit the inspiration of the Spirit of Prophecy by implying that Miss Marian Davis[2] wrote her books for her from other sources, was made into a puerile song sung to the tune of "Tom Dooley":

> Take down your book, Miss Davis
> Take down your book and write.
> Take down your book, Miss Davis;
> That's what we call new light.

Desmond Ford was eulogized in a song sung to the tune of "I Saw One Weary." This song also referred to Lewis Walton, the attorney who wrote the book *Omega*:

> I saw one weary, sad, and torn,
> His frock no longer could be worn;
> He smiled a friendly smile at me
> But Lewis Walton said to flee.
> I gasped and gaped, and with a shout
> I asked him What's this all about?
> He said, My friend, what can I do,
> I went on trial at Glacier View.

There were many more similar songs which blackened the night and which indicated a most childish attitude. It is hard to believe that these men were seriously passing themselves off as intellectuals and Christians when they had reduced themselves to the level of activity associated with little school boys behind a school toilet. If it were not for the fact that these men were showing contempt, not only for our message but also for God, the matter could be dismissed as the foolish escapades of immature adults. But here is clear evidence that these men had no respect for God and the messages He gave through His prophetess. Furthermore, they blasphemed by placing Sister White's name in the place of that of our Redeemer, Jesus Christ. No sincere Seventh-day Adventist could but be appalled at the situation where Sister White's name was so substituted. It is well recognized that she was mortal, a sinner, just as much in need of divine grace as any reader of this book. To put her name in place of that of Jesus Christ is a most shocking disgrace. To imply that God's people put her in such a position is libelous and contrary to the facts.

Perhaps nothing emphasized the deep-seated inroads that the *new theology* had made into the administration of Pacific Union College more than that two of the theology faculty who took part in this blasphemous episode, were within six months of the event promoted from the rank of assistant professor to associate professor. At the same time, Erwin Gane, the member of the theology department who had spoken most strongly against the *new theology*, had his post at Pacific Union College terminated. It is little wonder that parents were looking elsewhere that they might send their children where the influence of Christ existed.

### Chapter 79 Endnotes:

1. The words of the most blasphemous songs have not been included in order to prevent a further publication of songs which degrade Christian principles.
2. Marian Davis was Sister White's secretary for a number of years, including the years she spent in Australia. During that period *Desire of Ages* was written.

# 80 Efforts to Shake Student Confidence

THE constituency petition presented to the administration of Pacific Union College set out to detail some of the disastrous effects of efforts which were made to shake the confidence of the students in the truth of God. A member of the teaching staff of the department of Biological Sciences was reported to have written in the *Campus Chronicle* of January 28, 1982, an article entitled, "The Second Coming— Does Imminence Influence Our Behavior?" In this article he disparaged "the doctrine of an imminent Second Advent, asserting that such a notion threatens Adventist credibility, and tends to undermine the philosophy of responsible Christian living, and is not clearly taught by the weight of Scripture." In this article, the biology professor stated, "The idea that the return must be imminent seems somewhat peripheral. It might be well to examine whether it enriches or detracts from the main article of faith. I suggest that our continuing emphasis upon an imminent return of Jesus may be unwise, for it has the potential to ultimately threaten confidence in the promise of the Second Coming itself."

The writer went on to state: "Many believers who take imminence seriously, however, are reluctant to become engaged in service opportunities. There's never enough time." He even mentioned his own father, in order to emphasize his point, asserting that his father had said to him of at least six cars purchased in his childhood and youth, "probably the last car I'll ever own, Son." He stated that by forgetting the imminence of the Second Coming, we "avoid commitment to the task of escaping into the haven of end-time thinking. Paralyzed by the perception of inadequate time, we have become spiritual heirs of the unprofitable servant (Matthew 25:24–30)— useless on earth and unsafe for heaven." (*Ibid*.)

The subtle techniques of this professor of biology can be clearly analyzed. He cites gross exceptions to the rule—persons who have sat back and done nothing because Jesus is coming soon. He then extrapolates to the point that he asserts this to be the procedure of all people who believe in the imminence of Christ's return. Surely he must be well aware that the majority of people with such belief are vastly more energetic in their witness for God than those who believe that the Lord could come any time in the next fifty million years. The work of our pioneers is testimony to that fact. Any man who will make a thesis upon a gross caricature and exception, does not deserve serious consideration of his work.

Another article which appeared in the *Campus Chronicle* of Feb. 29, 1982, was written by a professor of the Religion department. In this article he was quite strong in his condemnation of those students who were unprepared to listen to his day-by-day demeaning of the Spirit of Prophecy. He asked the question, "Am I completely off target when I suggest that some of these students may not want to know about recent Ellen White research because they are unwilling to reexamine (or examine for the first time) their understanding of Ellen White's authority?' ("The Imperialism of Ignorance," *Campus Chronicle*, Feb. 25, 1982) Speaking of the Spirit of Prophecy and the manner in which he saw that fundamental Adventists did not investigate Sister White's writings, this writer stated, "In a sense we championed ignorance, encouraged ignorance, enlisted ignorance, and outfitted it for battle, and then rewarded it." (*Ibid.*)

Perhaps one of the most disturbing episodes also reported in the *Campus Chronicle* was the visit of the lecturer and his class in Comparative Religion to Napa Roman Catholic Church. In a disgraceful oversight of the real blasphemy of the mass, some of these students participated by carrying the wafer to the participants. One matter is certain, devout Seventh-day Adventists do not send their children to Pacific Union College in order for them to participate in such blasphemous services. Incredibly, it was reported in the *Campus Chronicle* that, at the conclusion of the program, the class partook of a meal at a Chinese restaurant and during this meal, discussed their experience, each apparently asserting he or she felt perfectly comfortable in the church service which they had witnessed. How the angels of God must weep when they see theology lecturers leading young people in an appreciation of that which God has declared to be hateful to Him.

These statements, of course, are ones which are easily verifiable, since they are in print. However, by far the greatest number of statements which have undermined the faith of many of the students at Pacific Union College, are those for which exact verification is impossible. Nevertheless, they have done their dastardly work in unsettling young minds. We can argue back and forth that there is no direct evidence for these. But, in fact, there is in black and white ample evidence of the sort of material which is being thrust upon the student body, even if this is just the tip of the iceberg. There was little doubt that the administration of the college was in sympathy with much of what had occurred. The fact was that they were prepared to host Adventist Forum meetings on campus, where one speaker denied that the Scriptures teach the doctrine of the investigative judgment, and took the opportunity to criticize the findings at Glacier View, and presented a view of creation and the age of the earth unsanctioned by either Scripture or the Spirit of Prophecy.

It was observed that despite cries for the preservation of academic freedom, any speaker who wished to present the truth of God at Pacific union College, had the greatest difficulty in being heard. Thus both Lewis Walton[1] and Margaret Davis were barred when attempts were made for them to present the truth of God. It is quite obvious that to those believing the *new theology*, the term *academic freedom*, in practical terms, meant license for them to present any error that came into their minds, and a refusal to listen to those who believed the old Adventist faith. This is indeed a most curious definition of academic freedom.

Chapter 80 Endnote:

1. Later, after much effort, Lewis Walton did conduct the Sabbath service at the College Church.

# 81 Moral Laxity at Pacific Union College

INEVITABLY, when doctrinal impurity is espoused at a college, there is a moral decline in the conduct of students. Thus there was a serious decline in student morality at Pacific Union College. This development was partly due to lax rules at the College. Both the Dean of Men and the Dean of Women were, however, fine leaders and were not responsible for this unfortunate state of affairs. Since students were permitted to stay out late on Saturday evenings until 1 a.m. without explanation (in the case of female freshmen, this privilege was restricted to six Saturday nights per quarter, but in the case of the others it was permissible every Saturday night), it was understandable that opportunities arose for conduct unbecoming Christians.

Dr. Erwin Gane, in a report proffered to the investigation committee, stated that "young women who have had abortions are retained as students, and so are the young men who cohabited with them." This charge is very serious indeed. However, it was reported that up to seventy such abortions were occurring annually among young ladies attending Pacific Union College. Reports circulated that it was the practice of the administration of the college to assist young women who had become pregnant, by arranging for them to have an abortion in a clinic in Napa without any notification to their parents. Since the laws of the United States now permit such procedures, even for under-aged persons, there would be no restraining factor from legal authorities.

Such a situation should not surprise us, for the lowering of moral standards within our colleges seems to have become widespread. A confidential survey of the students at Walla Walla College about 1980, indicated that at least ninety percent admitted to participating in premarital sex and that over fifty percent of the young ladies admitted that, when they were invited to a date, they commenced appropriate contraceptive procedures in anticipation of participating in sexual activity. How far the ideals of our Christian education have fallen! And this decline can be directly attributed to the dilution of doctrinal purity.

Some may argue that this influence is due to the prevailing mores of our society. Clearly that connection cannot be denied, but it does seem distressing that the pathetically low standards of our society have now become the standards of many of our young people in colleges. However, where the unsurpassed ideals of Jesus are said to be uplifted, it is difficult to understand why such conduct should be so prevalent among those seeking to prepare themselves for service in the work of God. What this means in reality is that many of those who become our pastors and our teachers and our administrators have, during their college period, participated in conduct offensive to a pure God.

A survey published in 1984 indicated that the majority of our college students in North America show little discrimination in the viewing of movies. Only 2% never watched movies on television, and 33% did not attend theaters. This survey was undertaken by *College People*,[1] a North American Youth Ministries publication, produced by Union College. The survey covered eight of our colleges in North America. The results of this survey indicated a particularly low standard of principle on the matter of entertainment. For instance, only 6% indicated that prior to deciding to attend a movie, they always considered the effect it would have upon their relationship to Christ. Further, only 22% always avoided films opposed to Christian principles, while 15% always avoided movies featuring a lot of graphic violence, and 18% always avoided film featuring nudity and/or explicit love scenes. Yet 53% of those interviewed stated that they regarded themselves as strongly committed Christians. Only 10% of those interviewed believed that movie attendance inevitably weakened their Christian experience. Indeed, 37% felt it sometimes strengthened them spiritually, and 2% believed that it always did. In addition, 51% asserted that movie attendance had little effect upon their Christian experience. Since most of our college students appear to be ignorant of God's standards in entertainment and the principle of guarding the avenues of the soul, it is little wonder that moral degeneracy of all forms abounds.

In October, 1983, at the A.S.I. (Adventist Laymen's Services and Industries) Convention in Guntersville, Alabama, in answer to a question Pastor Neal Wilson, president of the General Conference admitted that a recent survey in Seventh-day Adventist academies and colleges indicated that over fifty percent of the students had participated in the taking of alcohol and/or other drugs. It is thus that Gane could state, "No wonder our young people have moral and drinking problems No wonder they are to be found in night clubs, discos, and other places of worldly entertainment." (Submission of Dr. Erwin Gane to Investigation Committee) One parent who sent her daughter to Pacific Union College was appalled to find that, on a number of occasions, her daughter's roommate returned home drunk. On one of these occasions, the girl vomited all over the room. When in desperation the daughter complained the next morning to her dean, she was informed that nothing could be done, since the episode of drunkenness had not been observed by the dean.

When one looks at the philosophy of the vice-president for student affairs and dean of students during the period 1970–82, it is little wonder that this deterioration in student conduct occurred. This person, who held both posts, was quoted as stating that he saw the dean's role as "assisting individual students to take charge of their own lives—to shift the responsibility of making choices from the institution to the individual." (*Campus Chronicle*, Jan. 4, 1982) He stated he had been able to make this change despite the "tension resulting from the marked increase in doctrinal and lifestyle differences among laity and clergy in the Seventh-day Adventist Church; and, second, that tension resulting from the sharp conflict between the narrow *in loco parentis*[2] view of some church constituents and the view held by most students—that persons who were legally adult, not only have the right to take charge of their own lives, but should be expected to be self-directing and responsible for their own lives." (*Ibid.*)

It was not surprising, then, that many people were asking the question, "Is it safe to send our children to Pacific Union College?" This question has been asked of more than one college. It was no surprise when one church leader was forced to voice his concern about the standards of our colleges. Kenneth H. Wood stated:

> We confess that we are alarmed by the fact that some of our colleges seem to be drifting away from the standards and objectives established for them by their founders. We are alarmed by the secular climate that prevails on some campuses. We are alarmed by the strange winds of doctrine that blow on some campuses. We are alarmed by lax moral standards that prevail on some campuses. We are alarmed by the feeble efforts put forth by some administrators and faculty members to create a spiritual climate that will prepare students for the greatest event in earth's history, the second coming of Jesus." (Kenneth H. Wood, "Colleges in Trouble," *Adventist Review*, Feb. 21, 1980)

Wood quoted Sister White's statement concerning Battle Creek College at the time of the apostasy there:

> I must again say to our people, Keep your children away from Battle Creek. Some of our medical missionary workers are becoming leavened with infidelity. Specious heresy has been taking hold of minds, and its threads have been woven into the pattern of the figure. (Letter T-208, 1906).[3]

That Sister White meant what she said cannot be doubted. Indeed, the first Seventh-day Adventist graduates from the University of Sydney in Australia were two physicians, Dr. Margherita Mary Freeman and Dr. Thomas A. Sherwin, who completed their courses in 1911. "What were the circumstances surrounding their decisions to enter Sydney University? Several Australian Adventists, who had desired to pursue the medical course about this time, had gone to the United States to study in our own institutions. Indeed, such were the plans of Drs. Freeman and Sherwin. However, because of the problems encountered at the time in Battle Creek with respect to Dr. Kellogg, Sister White strongly advised against the venture. Thus it was that entry into Sydney University was envisaged."[4]

Noting Sister White's advice of 1906, Wood counseled:

> Clearly, parents have an obligation to know what is being taught even at Adventist schools, and to send their children only to those schools that teach

historic Adventism and will strengthen the faith of the young people who are sent there." (*Adventist Review*, Feb. 21, 1980)

Wood's editorial caused a tremendous furor. Over seventy-five percent of the large correspondence which he received concerning this editorial was condemnatory in nature. One member of the General Conference Educational Department even referred to him as the Adventist Khomeini.[5] To a man, all the presidents of the Adventist colleges in North America took exception to the editorial. Rather than humbly accepting the justifiable rebuke and instituting measures to restore the colleges to the high ideals planned for them by God, most chose to ignore the valid remarks, and to attack the one who had sounded such a reasonable warning. That there was ample evidence for Wood's concerns in undoubted. Indeed, the reactions of the presidents only verified this matter in its fullest light. Until our college and school leaders offer authentic Christian education to our young people, they are in no position to protest valid rebukes and counsels.

Other leaders also openly expressed their concerns. One officer of the General Conference wrote, "Dr. Standish, I deplore what is happening to our churches in this nation [The United States]. I firmly believe that we have been failing in taking some clear stands in the face of some theological trends. The Church has not been harmed by enemies from the outside. The world is not against a church that seems willing to compromise its theological views or lose its sense of mission.

"It is true that we officially are not making theological concessions, but influential individuals, engaged in the task of training new ministers, under the influence of liberal views, are consistently undermining our foundations. As a result, we are producing a generation of preachers without conviction, and the consequence we are seeing is a regrettable statistical slow-down in this division." [6]

God's people take courage when leaders fearlessly identify error in our midst. However, equally, there are leaders who have facilitated the terrible doctrinal downfall of our colleges. Of another officer of the General Conference, one of his colleagues wrote: "I really fell out with him over his support of our more liberal teachers. . . . He continued to defend Ford after I had decided I could no longer support his trends (when he came to P.U.C.)" [7]

Understandably, there is a close correlation between the diminution of student count in many of the colleges and the low standard of conduct within those colleges. This outcome is indeed proper. One could only hope that, where possible, our people would unanimously send their children to only those colleges where truth and fidelity are upheld. To do less is to show a crass disregard for the eternal destiny of our children.[8]

Chapter 81 Endnotes:

1. Published in *College People*, April 1984
2. *In loco parentis* is the Latin term for 'in place of the parent.' What the vice-president for student affairs was stating was that the college did not see as its duty the need to take the place of a parent, but rather to permit the students to run their own lives.
3. It should be stated that by 1906, the Battle Creek College was not a church-sponsored institution, the original Battle Creek College having been relocated at Berrien Springs and renamed Emmanuel Missionary College. Nevertheless the college leadership still claimed to uphold Seventh-day Adventist principles. Sister White clearly did not countenance the sending of our children to Adventist colleges which undermined God's truth.
4. Bulletin of the Sydney University Adventist Student Society, Vol. II. No. 5, July, 1961
5. This reference was to the Ayatollah Khomeini, the head of the Islamic republic of Iran and a Muslim religious fanatic.
6. Letter written to Dr. C. Standish, June, 1984
7. Letter dated Dec. 7, 1983
8. Russell, as father of three college-aged sons had to address this dilemma, and full well appreciates the problems Adventist parents face today. Being committed to the principles of Christian education, Russell naturally desired an Adventist education for all his sons. He also desired that they be spared the need to study in non-Adventist institutions. During one academic year, one of his sons attended an Adventist college without studying a single Bible course. This was an alarming situation. Yet, in all truth, Russell, knowing what was taught by some of the theology professors, was not a little relieved at this lack of instruction in religion. Surely our parents deserve better than this. They should be able to send their children to our colleges and rest content that only Bible truth is taught. That some theology professors deliberately deprive our children of hearing the Seventh-day Adventist faith in the classroom reflects poorly upon the characters of these teachers.

# 82    Students Respond at Pacific Union College

ONE fourth-year theology student made complaints based on his personal observation at the college. These correspond accurately with those of Dr. Gane and the group of constituents who had made other representations. He stated that "during the course of the discussion [at a theology colloquium], a student courteously asked if [theology professor's name deleted] believed there was a change in Christ's heavenly ministry in 1844, in harmony with the Dallas Statement. Rather than responding in the affirmative, [professor's name deleted] launched into a tirade, claiming that the student had threatened him." (Statement by Kevin D. Paulson, senior theology student at Pacific Union College, submitted to the Fact-finding Committee on Jan. 28, 1982) Paulson confirmed much of what has been said concerning this theology professor's aberrant doctrines and his attacks upon the truth of God. He also confirmed that this man had stated: "The Church has not proven that Dr. Desmond Ford's theology on the Sanctuary was wrong" (*ibid.*), and also that "The church should restore Dr. Ford's ministerial credentials to help heal the breach in the Church." (*Ibid.*)

Paulson further cited a number of other lecturers who were damaging the faith of the students. One, from whom Paulson took a class in Pastoral Leadership, was quoted as stating, "The Church once stood for individual freedom; it is now destroying it." (*Ibid.*) "Truth is undefinable; it is only as you perceive it." (*Ibid.*) Paulson quoted this second professor as stating to a student that "He should reply to Conference presidents who asked about the date 1844 by simply just telling 'them' that 1844 was the date our Church began." (*Ibid.*)

Another matter upon which Paulson threw some light, was that of the persistent attempts to ban Lewis Walton from the Pacific Union College campus, lest the students hear a little of the truth of God. Paulson stated, "From my knowledge of the affair, the effort was initiated by a letter from the college president, insisting upon cancellation and/or reduction of the Walton invitation. This was followed by the notorious business meeting, in which this group coalesced so as to pass a resolution that Walton be denied the Sabbath pulpit." (*Ibid.*) Walton had been invited to speak at Pacific Union College on Jan. 29 and 30, 1982. The church business meeting of Nov. 9, 1981, voted by a majority to rescind the invitation, after a most unpleasant meeting in which accusations were exchanged between those of opposing views.

However, the pastoral staff eventually had its way and Walton was privileged to speak on Jan. 30, 1982.

One letter to the *Campus Chronicle* precisely summed up the situation: "I am writing to you in deep concern. I understand that Lewis R. Walton, author of the book *Omega* was going to be asked to speak this January. I understand that if he has an invitation from the church, he will come. I also understand that there is a movement by some of the faculty of our school, including members of the history department and the religion department, to keep Mr. Walton away. I have one question: Why? Other churches have asked him to come and, from what I can tell, his fruits produce unity. Why may we not benefit from this also? He has a message that confirms the belief of our beloved Church. Are we to assume that the members of our faculty, who are opposing his coming, do not want our beliefs confirmed? At prayer meeting, all I hear is unity, love, and reformation, and yet here is a man willing to bring all three to us and some members of our faculty do not want him to come. Why are we afraid to hear Lewis Walton? Can somebody answer me?" (*Campus Chronicle*, Nov. 19, 1981, p. 20) Of course, the probable answer to the question posed, was that those elements at Pacific Union College supporting the *new theology* were afraid that truth would be presented to the student body in such a way that it would have exposed their erroneous positions and placed them in a face-losing battle before the students. While it is true that these same people were crying for academic freedom and, indeed, an article had been printed in the Oct. 15, 1981, edition of the *Campus Chronicle* entitled, "Freedom of Choice Is a Responsibility," it was manifest that such freedom was envisaged only for those who wished to spread the dissident views. In the article, "Freedom of Choice Is a Responsibility," the thesis was propounded that the college students had a God-given right to hear all sides of the doctrinal controversy within the Church. However, it was obvious that in the minds of many, there was one side which they had no right to hear, and that was the truth of God.

This observation was not lost on Paulson, for in his presentation he noted: "It was indeed ironic that those loudly trumpeting the cause of so-called academic freedom were prepared to deny this freedom to one not sharing their perspective. Moreover, the charge of divisiveness leveled at Mr. Walton by this group seems strange, considering the fact that a number of this very group had taken part in perhaps one of the most divisive events ever to occur in campus history—the notorious 'hymn-singing' incident." (Kevin Paulson's Submission to the Investigative Committee)

Paulson also took exception to the treatment of Dr. Erwin Gane. He asserted that: "The real roots of the affair extended to a number of comments made by Dr. Gane in his classes, that no theology student disbelieving the doctrinal authority of Ellen White or the two-phased ministry of Christ in heaven, could be recommended by him to the Seventh-day Adventist ministry." (*Ibid.*) This led, of course, to complaints by those students who were not in a position to be recommended by a teacher using these criteria, and shortly after this, a straw vote was taken among the members of the theology department. Incredibly, of those present, only two other members of the religion department supported Dr. Gane. These two were Drs. Paul Bork and David Taylor. It is sad to relate that Dr. David Taylor, the chairman of the religion department, was promptly removed from his post. The reason given was so transparent as to be almost humorous. "A majority of the religion faculty felt Taylor was working too hard, said Madgwick." (*Campus Chronicle*, May 27, 1982, p. 3)

The unfortunate happenings at Pacific Union College led some students to distribute a document which asked several cogent questions. This document has been referred to previously, but the reader is reminded of some of its salient questions, e.g. "Is it right for ordained 'S.D.A.' ministers who are paid from tithe money, to undermine the church openly or by underhanded methods" (*Is It Right?* P.U.C. Students, 1981) "Is it right for 'S.D.A.' ministers to be licensed when they continue to avoid preaching certain S.D.A. doctrines, because they no longer believe in them?" (*Ibid.*) "Is it right for parents to pay thousands of dollars to send their children to S.D.A. schools to unlearn the S.D.A. message?" (*Ibid.*) These rhetorical questions were very pertinent to every Seventh-day Adventist.

One matter which was certain was that the level of integrity among many of those entrusted with the training of our young people at Pacific Union College was at an all-time low.

# 83 Southern Missionary College

IT must not be imagined that the problems of false theology were confined to Avondale College in Australia and Pacific Union College in the United States. Indeed, the vast majority of our colleges in western nations have, to a greater or lesser extent, been influenced by men whose doctrinal positions have been unsound. Southern Missionary College enjoyed a reputation for being, perhaps, the most fundamental of our colleges in the United States. It was only natural that the arch-enemy would seek to undermine such a bulwark for truth. Dedicated parents from all parts of the United States often send their children to Southern Missionary College, believing that there they would be taught the truths of God in their purity.

However, by the late 1970s and early 1980s, the situation degenerated to such an extent that, with the arguable exception of Pacific Union College, Southern Missionary College became the college most openly challenging the Adventist faith. Once again, the problem centered in but was not limited to the theology department. The obvious implications need not be stated. So desperate did the situation become at Southern Missionary College that a group of lay people published a newspaper entitled *Collegedale Tidings*, which set out their genuine concerns. Under the editorship of Theodore Barta, this publication made many disturbing accusations. In a front page article the following questions were asked of leading college faculty:

"WHY—did [name deleted] advertise Ford tapes in his classes?

"WHY—did [name deleted] teach from the apostate magazine, *Evangelica*?

"WHY—did [name deleted] say in a chapel address that there was no temple in heaven?

"WHY—did two of our theology professors attend the 'Atlanta Forum' featuring the apostate professor Smuts Van Rooyan?

"WHY—was the 'Atlanta Affirmation' meeting held in such secrecy?

"WHY—did [name deleted] say that Dr. Ford was teaching a valid message?

"WHY—did Walter Rea state in his recent meeting at Covenant College that [names of two theology professors deleted] helped him produce his book, *The White Lie*?

"WHY—did Walter Rea state in his recent meeting: 'I don't see any theology professors at my meeting, but I'll have to go "underground" with them'?

"WHY—was the apostate magazine *Evangelica* passed out to theology students last year?

"WHY—are concerned people who have much evidence of apostasy taught at S.M.C. not allowed to state their cases before the College Board?
"WHY—has [name deleted] given an order for no visitors to be allowed in theology classes?" (*Collegedale Tidings*, 1)

These questions by their very nature underscore the sympathy of a number of the members of the theology department with the *new theology*. Four theology students at Southern Missionary College had the courage to present their firsthand reports of what was occurring behind the scenes in the theology classes. One of these publications was sworn before a Notary Public on September 18, 1981, in Asheville, North Carolina.

Some extracts from these open letters will indicate the alleged methods used by these disloyal professors in their destruction of the faith of our young people: "I took Life and Teachings of Jesus from [name deleted] during the first semester. In this class he attempted to teach me that Christ was not my example, that forgiveness of sins was all that was really important in salvation, that you could keep on being a sinner after probation closes and that Adam and Eve sinned because they wanted perfect characters like God. . . . At every chance he would attack men like Herbert Douglass, C. Mervyn Maxwell and Kenneth Wood for upholding Christian character perfection! In a two-hour interview with me, he even told me I couldn't believe in everything that Sister White presented as being truth." (Open letter written by Thomas L. Tucker, published in *Collegedale Tidings*, 2)

"Next semester I took Righteousness by Faith with [name deleted]. . . . I got graded down by him for writing too effective a critique of Heppenstall's paper on Christian Perfection. He would mark me off for not believing that character change comes instantly at translation, not before translation. What really shocked me was when one day I came and he started teaching the class that the Holy Spirit does not indwell the believer, and if you believe any part of the Godhead will actually come into the believer—you are a pantheist! (John 14:17,18) I asked him for a biblical statement as a basis for such a belief, to which he replied with a nasty attack on me. He said that I hadn't heard all the argument before in the classes I had missed. He was in such a nasty temper that I decided to shut up. . . . The next day I received a three-page letter from him attacking my ability to learn, my morality and character. He threatened to flunk me if I didn't change, and accused me of attacking him and the faculty. Other students have come to me with their classmates, very confused by the doubts and attacks made by the teachers on the Spirit of Prophecy, 1844, and Daniel 8:14. I had to spend a lot of time helping these young people see through the clever twistings of these men and open the Scriptures to them to show how sound are the S.D.A. positions. For this I was accused of making personal attacks on the teachers in this letter. . . . One of the favorite tactics of these men is to accuse you of not being a Christian if you disagree with anything they believe in. They claim you're attacking them. You have a grudge against them, and you're not following the counsel of Christ to come first to them. The purpose of this is to induce guilt and to discredit whoever happens to be merely presenting truth." (*Ibid.*) "I did well on tests, and made the fourth highest grade on the final, but still got a 'D'." (*Ibid.*)

Eventually, this young man was called in before the college president. "He [the college president] called me insolent, stupid, and incapable of comprehending deep philosophical matters. In a very gloating way he said, 'You can't point out anything we have said that is pro-Ford.' . . . I, at this point, reminded him of what he had said at one of his chapel talks about the Spirit of Prophecy statements on masturbation, the Testimonies (which E. G. White herself said we should read), and about even some of Paul's writing not being 'everlastingly authoritative.' Needless to say, he became very angry, and mean to me. He told me how there were deep problems with Mrs. White's writings and how come I was so sure about them? I said, 'Try me,' but he refused. That's the problem with these great intellects like him and Walter Rea (and the teachers). They claim to have great evidence which would devastate our simple faith in God's messenger, keeping it hidden in their boxes as too deadly for us uneducated mortals. In the meantime, they dropped doubts here and there, while claiming to have the 'goods on Sister White.'" (*Ibid.*)

"Last July 4th, my wife and I were walking by the C-K when [name deleted] of the religion department called us over to his table. He proceeded to talk very rudely to us, calling us names, even using vile language. He mocked my wife and called me arrogant, for daring to disagree with their theology." (*Ibid.*)

"My first semester in 1980 took in [name deleted] class of Principles and Origin of Education. The class denounced the use of the Spirit of Prophecy in education, health message, and went so far as to say that Mrs. White's visions and dreams finished in 1896." (Letter written by Robert McMullin, published in *Collegedale Tidings*, 2)

"The year-day principle was also attacked [in a class of 'Revelation'] in praising Des Ford that he thought our position weak in having only two weak texts. . . . In referring to Dan. 7, it was inferred to be Antiochus Epiphanes and when I questioned this by referring to verse 25, the answer I got was 'Des Ford and Heppenstall apply it and I agree with them." (*Ibid.*)

"I have been taught by [name deleted] that Jesus Christ is *not* our example." (Open letter written by Ted Barta quoted in *Collegedale Tidings*, 3)

Another theology professor "taught that the indwelling of the Holy Spirit is symbolic and believing in it is pantheism." (*Ibid.*) "I have been informed by four professors in the theology department that they are paid to interpret Ellen White and the Bible, and that I do not have the interpretative right to highlight copies of her writings or the Bible and post them [on the notice boards]. They have told me that we have deep theological problems with Ellen White because, for example, over two full pages of her vision in Testimonies, Vol. 5, beginning on page 62—*are copied*. This, they say, is not for laity to attempt to handle. They have told me they have enough material to blow away simple faith like mine." (*Ibid.*) "Yet another theology professor has told me that there is no Sanctuary in heaven and as one of his proofs, he cites that most theologians don't believe it." (*Ibid.*)

One student in her open letter asserted that a theology professor had made the following statements in the classes she attended: "The Traditional Adventist view is 1844—Dan. 8. The judgment has nothing go do with the saints. The emphasis is not on the people of God, but on the judgment of the little horn." Speaking of the two-apartment Sanctuary in heaven, he was reported as saying, "That view may be OK for those in kindergarten." Regarding the investigative judgment, "My view is that it is a weird doctrine that has come in to fill a need of the disappointment." On another topic, the Spirit of Prophecy (this professor was quoted as saying): "Not one Adventist minister who deeply studied E. White has kept his faith—to me, this seems to be saying something." Other statements attributed to this professor in his classes, include "I do not think our Church has a strong biblical position on the year-day principle." "I do not believe in the investigative judgment, but in a pre-Adventist judgment. I don't think anyone would quarrel with me about that." The statements were written by Florence Woolcock and published in *Collegedale Tidings*, 3.

That young people in their unsophisticated ways, were able to highlight the surreptitious teaching of men who were not true to our faith, emphasizes the reason why there was such a paucity of truth in Southern Missionary College.

During the height of the theological crisis at Southern Missionary College, Colin was invited to present a weekend series at Ringgold, Georgia, located a few miles from the college. A number of incidents at that time amply illustrated the atmosphere on campus. Colin was invited by a theology professor to be interviewed by him for a program on the college radio station. Unfortunately, this interview was not broadcast directly, but was taped for airing at 9 o'clock Friday evening. One of Colin's friends who listened to the interview predicted that it would not be broadcast. He expressed the view that Colin's Bible-based answers were too damaging to the *new theology*. On the other hand, Colin had stated nothing which could have been construed as offensive to, or critical of, the college or its administration. The friend's prediction proved to be correct. Whether his reasoning was right or not, cannot be stated. A request for a copy of the interview was subsequently denied. This episode did appear to breach the oft-demanded freedom of expression requested by a large number of theologians.

Though Colin, as an act of courtesy, did not address any remarks to the tragic teaching of error in Southern Missionary College, nevertheless the overflow crowds which forced a transfer of the meeting to the large Southern Baptist Church in the town contained those who were anxious to express their concerns. The words of three students highlighted the plight of many:

1. One young female religion graduate of the college stated (through her tears): "I've just graduated from Southern Missionary College with a major in religion. Why haven't I been taught the things you preached this weekend?"

2. A young man from Arkansas stated that, in his home church, he had been "taught what you preached tonight, but after attending religion classes at Southern Missionary College, I thought I must be wrong." He twice expressed his appreciation for Colin's messages.

3. A young married man from Florida, who was a freshman, stated: "I knew there was something wrong with the Bible classes I've been attending. I've only been an Adventist eight months. Thank you for coming."

The name of the college was subsequently changed to Southern College of Seventh-day Adventists—probably more accurately reflecting the fact that many of the professors had lost their missionary zeal. That men would make a defense of those who taught such matters, and try to blacken the characters of the young people who brought these problems to the light of day is very tragic indeed. That many of those named continued to be favored as workers in the Church, despite their clear departure from doctrinal truth, is a tragedy of the highest order. It is little wonder that many dedicated parents now fear to send their children to such a college, and have sought to satisfy their education requirements elsewhere.

According to latest reports, it appears that at last something has been done to bring reform to Southern College. A new president, John Wagner, has been installed and already he has given evidence of proper leadership. Reports indicate that several of the suspect lecturers in the theology department have been replaced. For this we thank God. One report tells us that three of the lecturers mentioned in the students' letters cited previously are no longer employed by the college. May this work of reform continue in the Southern College, and also commence and continue in the other Adventist colleges throughout the world where liberalism and the *new theology* have penetrated.

# 84 Consensus

ONE of the severe limitations of the thrust for truth has been a desire by many to obtain consensus, so that persons, even of diametrically opposed views, can ascribe to a carefully-worded accord. The truth of God, quite understandably, does not leave space for such manipulation of words. For example, it would be possible to make a statement on Sabbath-keeping which could, if sufficiently vague, be accepted by both Saturday- and Sunday-keepers. Similarly, a statement on the state of the dead could be so cleverly constructed, that those who believe in the immortality of the soul and those who believe what Scripture teaches, *viz.* that man sleeps until the resurrection, could concur. We see this often in the hymns which we sing. For example, the hymn, "Rock of Ages," was written by Augustus Toplady. He was a man who had no faith at all in free choice and believed in predestination and the "once saved always saved" concept. It is, in fact, this doctrine which he is eulogizing in his hymn, yet his words may be so construed that Seventh-day Adventists can sing them with a clear conscience, because we can place our own special interpretation upon that which Toplady has penned.

As has been pointed out, this technique has been used as a deceptive measure by a number of those following the *new theology*. These men have made the bold assertion that they believe in a pre-advent judgment, knowing full well that their timing of that judgment differed very widely from the special meaning that Adventists ascribed to that term. Adventists have always meant by the pre-advent judgment, that judgment which commenced in 1844. But deceivers have used the term to cover up their faith in the view that Jesus entered the Most Holy Place upon his ascension. That surely is truly pre-advent, in fact, 2,000 years pre-advent. But these men knew full well that the term *pre-advent* was not meant to indicate just any time prior to the Second Coming of Jesus.[1] Its meaning was much more specific than that. Thus it would be possible for two groups of people, one believing the truth of the 1844 message and the other rejecting that message and accepting the error that Jesus entered into the Most Holy Place ministry at His ascension, both to assent to a consensus statement which reads: "We affirm our belief in the pre-advent judgment." This type of word manipulation is common in politics, but should have no part in the Church of God. We should be as specific as words will allow. We should leave no doubt as to the nature of our belief, nor should we leave room for those accepting error to hide under the cover of orthodoxy. Even politicians, from time to time, become averse to this type of deception.

In 1983, the heads of the British Commonwealth countries met in New Delhi. They had to prepare a statement of their views to be issued at the conclusion of the meetings. At least one prime minister in attendance, Mr. Lee Kuan Yew, the Prime Minister of Singapore, expressed his disgust at the use of these techniques of compromise. He stated: "One painful price that has to be paid for an agreed communiqué is the endless arguing and compromising, then debating, maneuvering, and again compromising, to water down positions and to fudge meanings in order to agree on a form of words which synthesize as much as possible the divergent views." (*Bangkok Post*, Dec. 5, 1983)

The time has come for some of our men to rise up and make similar outspoken attacks on this form of foolishness. Surely we must acknowledge that absolutely nothing is to be gained by using words to cover up the fact that two groups are espousing diametrically opposed doctrines. There is no place for error hidden under any cloak in the Church of God, and the time has come for us clearly and specifically to say so in the presentation of our faith. It is the devil whose policy thrives on an admixture of truth and error. God's Word depends upon pure truth.

There was even some hesitance to be as specific as we should have been in 1980 in Dallas, when the new statement of our fundamental beliefs was adopted. Any person reading the statement, for example, on the heavenly Sanctuary, will notice that on no occasion is the two-apartment nature of the heavenly Sanctuary set forth. Since there was much discussion beforehand, this did not appear to be a matter of oversight, nor was it likely to be due to a lack of space, requiring summarization of this belief. Some even believed that it was a deliberate omission conceived by a group of theologians, in order to accommodate a lack of faith on the part of many of our leading theologians in the clear, scriptural testimony that such a two-apartment Sanctuary exists in heaven. Whether this view is correct or not, the wording was remarkably beneficial to the rather large group of theologians who reject the presence of a two-apartment Sanctuary in heaven.

Unfortunately, this accommodation has led to a further step. In a Forum meeting in Cooranbong in 1981, the field secretary of the Australasian Division stated that it was not essential to believe in a two-apartment Sanctuary, since this was not spelled out in the statement of beliefs accepted in Dallas in 1980. The danger of such a statement becomes very obvious. First of all, by his statement, this church leader has, in effect, converted the statement or summary of our beliefs into a creed, indicating that we have to believe no more and no less than that which is written in the statement. But Seventh-day Adventists have no creed but the Bible, and thus our beliefs are not limited to a mere summary of them.

Naturally, it is impossible to put every last detail of our faith into a few brief words, but that does not negate the obligation of every Seventh-day Adventist to adhere in every detail to the truth of the Holy Scriptures. Since the Scriptures teach a two-apartment Sanctuary, irrespective of whether this truth is included in the Summary or not, it is mandatory for Seventh-day Adventists to acknowledge belief in this fact. The statement of fundamental beliefs does not mention specifically that Seventh-day Adventists must not kill. Would anyone dare to stand up before a congregation and say that because of the failure to spell out this fact specifically, it was permissible for Adventists to murder? This line of argument is so fallacious that it is difficult to understand why men still use it.

The authors plead with leaders in God's Church to eschew this practice of attempting to cover up the errors of its members by the construction of statements of consensus in such a way that those far from the truth of God can ascribe to them. Let truth, instead, be stated in clear, precise and unequivocal terms.

Chapter 84 Endnotes:

1. Editor's observation: in the previous chapter a theology professor was quoted as saying he believed in the "pre-Advent-*ist* judgment."

# 85 Publications

NATURALLY, with the eroding of faith within the Seventh-day Adventist Church, the standard of its publications became a very important consideration. Our leading publishing houses certainly should have had the added responsibility to ensure that only the truth of God was published by them. As has been mentioned, under the editorial leadership of Kenneth Wood, the *Adventist Review* set an admirable example in this respect. However, the disturbing trend to place on book review committees men of various doctrinal persuasions has not helped in the presentation of truth. The concept that we must have a balance between those who are "conservative" and those who are "liberal" meant that, in general, only books which are not addressing vital doctrinal matters in the Church, have much opportunity to be published. It is far easier, it will be noted, to obtain in our Adventist Book Centers, books of a devotional nature, or books telling stories, than it is to obtain books which stoutly defend the most distinctive doctrines of our Church.

This bias is easily explained on the basis that persons with a leaning to the *new theology* are not likely to write complimentary reports upon books or publications which are upholding the precious distinctive truths of the Church. One must admit that, at any time, it is a difficult matter to obtain uniformity of opinion, particularly when it comes to the selection of manuscripts for publication or their rejection. There appears to be a distinct bias on the part of book reviewers to recommend material which is written by someone who is renowned within the organization, or who holds a position of authority within it.

Some interesting studies have recently been undertaken in secular areas which attest to this fact. Perhaps nothing underscored the personal bias of the average book reviewer more than a statement written by T. H. Huxley, concerning a paper he had presented to the Royal Society in England in 1900:

> I know that the paper I have just sent in is very original and of some importance and I am equally sure that if it is referred to the judgment of my "particular friend" X that it will not be published. He won't be able to say a word against it, but he will pooh-pooh it to a dead certainty. You will ask with some wonderment, Why? Because for the last twenty years X had been regarded as the great authority on these matters, and has had no one to tread on his heels, until at last, I think he has come to look upon the Natural World as his special preserve, and "no poachers allowed." So I must manoeuvre a little to get my

poor memoir kept out of his hands. (Quoted in Zuckerman, H. Merton, R.K., Patterson of Evaluation in Science, *Minerva*, 1971, Vol. 9, 66–100 [sic])

An interesting study was conducted by Peters and Ceci. These men randomly selected twelve articles from important psychological journals, which had been written by respected authors from some of the most prestigious institutions of the world. By simply altering the title of the articles and giving fictitious authors from fictitious, and thus unknown, institutions, these articles were resubmitted to the twelve journals which had published them eighteen to thirty-two months previously. The editors and referees were not told about the project. Only three of the twelve manuscripts were recognized as having been previously published. Of the remaining nine articles, eight were rejected. It is pertinent to note the reasons given for these rejections. Naturally, reference was not made to the fact that the authors and their institutions were unknown. Rather, they were rejected for reasons of poor methodology, inadequate statistical analysis, or poor writing technique. Yet they had been accepted quite freely for publication from their renowned authors in eminent institutions.[1] It is interesting to note that this article of Peters and Ceci was itself rejected by prominent journals, *Science* and *American Psychologist*, before being accepted by *Behavioural Brain Sciences*.

A former editor of the prestigious English medical journal, *The Lancet*, Sir Thomas Fox stated: "When I divide the week's contributions into two piles—one that we are going to publish and the other that we are going to return—I wonder whether it would make any real difference to the journal or its readers if I exchanged one pile for the other?" (Sir Theodore Fox, *Crisis in Communication*, 1965)

In the Seventh-day Adventist Church, the answer to such a question is indeed vital. If there is no difference between the two piles, this is indeed tragic, for we are dealing with eternal verities, truths far more important than those affecting the present life of men and women. There is surely a case for reviewers being denied the knowledge of the identity of the author, of the organization, or institution he represents. This policy, of course, may bring some distress to persons in prominent positions, but it may also provide publication opportunities for works of merit by lay people and others in our midst who are less known. But even more important than this, it is vital that those selected to review articles and books for denominational publications, should hold fundamental positions on the truth of God.

The authors have had personal experience with the difficulty of publishing manuscripts which, in a simple and orthodox manner, set forth the truth of God. One book which they privately published, *Adventism Unveiled*, was originally submitted to the *Review and Herald*. To cite the thoughts of one of the reviewers who, incidentally, presented a very favorable overall report of the manuscript, will underline some of the difficulties many authors face in the presentation of truth. This reviewer was prepared to recommend the publication, so long as one or two adjustments were made. However, the authors could not, under any circumstances, agree to these adjustments, since there was strong evidence in Inspiration to support what had been written. In his report the reviewer stated: "The Standishes apply the phrase, 'within the veil' (Heb. 6:19) to the outermost veil of the sanctuary, not to the most holy place." Thus it was requested that we change our view and state that 'within the veil' referred to Christ's entry at His ascension directly to the most holy place. In fact, this reviewer also stated: "I think we have to admit that Hebrews does not teach that Christ went into the most holy place at His ascension. We as a Church did so at Glacier View,[2] but now the Standishes want us to back away from that." However, regardless of what was decided at Glacier View, Inspiration states:

> The ministration of the priest throughout the year in the first apartment of the sanctuary, "within the veil" *which formed the door and separated the holy place from the outer court*, represents the work of ministration upon which Christ entered at His ascension. (*GC* 420, emphasis supplied.)

Here Sister White unequivocally refers to the term, 'within the veil' and states without hesitation that this represents the holy place and that it was here that Christ entered upon His ascension. Thus the authors would have denied Inspiration, had they made the adjustment to their manuscript.

Another change which was requested was that we delete the section which stated that the atonement was not final until the cleansing of the Sanctuary. The reviewer stated, "The authors state that Christ's sacrifice was complete at the cross, but the atonement is not final until the cleansing of the heavenly Sanctuary. To me, this seems like double talk; if something is complete, then it is final. I think the Church now teaches that Christ's atonement is both complete and final at the cross, and the investigative judgment is viewed as an application of the benefits of the completed atonement. I would hate to see anything going into print from the *Review and Herald*, suggesting that Christ's atonement was *not* completed at the cross. We settled that question years ago when *Questions on Doctrine* was being written." [3] Once again, Inspiration has spoken on this point. Speaking of 1844, Sister White stated:

> So when Christ entered the holy of holies to perform the closing work of the atonement, He ceased His ministration in the first apartment. (*GC* 428)

It can be seen perfectly well from this statement that Sister White does not close the atonement at the cross. She is referring, of course, to Christ's entry into the holy of holies in 1844, to complete the work of the investigative judgment and to make atonement for the sins of His people. As we have seen, the book, *Questions on Doctrine*, is a most unsafe guide to Adventist doctrine, for it is written in order to please a group of Evangelicals who had no faith in the full doctrine of the atonement. Rather than change items of revealed truth, the authors published their manuscript through Historic Truth Publications.

Truth, quite naturally, is not dependent upon the false thinking of manuscript reviewers for its propagation. Nevertheless, the time has surely come for us as a people to reexamine the matter of selection of articles and books for denominational publication. That Ford's book, *Daniel*, could be accepted by one of our publishing houses (*The Southern Publishing Association*), surely testifies to the fact that some reorganization of our methods is essential. That men in secular areas of study are looking more objectively at their peer-review techniques should encourage us to do no less in the cause of God.

## Chapter 85 Endnotes:

1. Report published by D. P. Peters and S. J. Ceci, "Peer Review Practices of Psychological Journals," *Behavioural Brain Sciences*, 1982, Vol. 5, 187–195
2. It will be recalled that, in fact, at Glacier View, while it is true that it was erroneously stated that the term, *within the veil*, referred to the most holy place, nevertheless it was still maintained that Christ entered the holy place at His ascension. This reviewer's claim that Glacier View accepted that Christ entered the most holy place, is quite in error. However, it does demonstrate the peril of accepting the erroneous meaning of *within the veil*.
3. See the chapter entitled "Fundamental Doctrinal Changes," where the failure of *Questions on Doctrine* on this point was discussed.

# 86 Another Sabbath School Quarterly Controversy

IN the first quarter of 1983, a *Sabbath School Quarterly*, written by a theologian on the faculty of Southern College of Seventh-day Adventists again roused enormous controversy, reminiscent of the Douglass *Quarterly* of the second quarter of 1977. However, in this case, the roles in the controversy were reversed, meaning that those who accepted the fundamental Adventist faith were outraged, while those supporting the *new theology* were jubilant. The reason was that again the matter of Christ's nature was addressed, and the author, an original signatory to the Atlanta Affirmation (he did later rescind his signature), obviously believed the erroneous view that Jesus took the nature of Adam prior to his fall.[1]

How the errors of this *Quarterly* were passed by the screening committee is hard to understand. What is true though, is that by the time Dr. Leo Van Dolson became editor of the *Sabbath School Quarterly*, this *Quarterly* was in an advanced stage of preparation. Since Van Dolson had written the teacher's helps for the Douglass *Quarterly* of 1977, it was perfectly obvious that he would quickly perceive the problem in this *Quarterly*. Van Dolson, in attempting to explain his approach to the problem in a widely circulated letter, stated that he tried to make modifications which would at least present both sides of the picture. This action was clearly well-intentioned on his part to bring truth before the worldwide student body of the Sabbath School.

However, despite his undoubted good intentions, Van Dolson's efforts backfired, for they led to much confusion among God's people, many of whom reacted by believing the truth was not discernible, while others assumed that the position one takes is of no importance in Christian understanding.

The approach adopted by Van Dolson was underlined in the third lesson, entitled, "The Incarnation," in the study guide for Monday, Jan. 10, 1983. Two questions were asked. The first was, "Can the Bible be used to support the 'after-the-fall' position of Christ's nature?" (Sabbath School Quarterly for Jan. 10, 1983) The second was, "Can the Bible be used to support the 'pre-fall' position of Christ's nature?" (*Ibid*.) The lesson then set out to answer both questions in the positive, and to set out, in answer to each question, a few Bible texts which apparently the author felt supported the particular view questioned. The danger of this approach is obvious, for it appeared to make the Bible indecisive in the matter. Yet the fact is that never once does Scripture state that Christ took the nature of Adam before he fell, whereas time and time again it does state that He took the nature of fallen man. As usual, inconclusive statements were used to support the pre-fall position (for there are none of a conclusive nature); while the texts from the Scripture and the statements from the Spirit of Prophecy that were used, with the exception of Hebrews 2:14–17, did not include the most clear-cut evidence available. Since Russell was in the mission field (Thailand) at the time, he was well aware of the confusion that this approach caused among God's people. The people had been taught by us, as missionaries, that the Bible does not contradict itself; yet here in the *Sabbath School Quarterly* was an apparent instance of biblical contradiction. It was most unfortunate and embarrassing indeed.

One Division president reported that, for the first time the farmers of Africa were questioning the General Conference as a result of this *Sabbath School* Quarterly. At least this reaction does indicate a sound knowledge of truth by these believers. The Teachers' Helps were no better. In this, the editor of the Teachers' Helps stated: "The question about Jesus' spiritual nature is not specifically addressed in the New Testament." (*Sabbath School Quarterly*, Teachers' Edition, 1st Quarter, 1983, p. 40) He also admonished, on the controversy arising between the divergent views, that "teachers should not try to resolve this issue, as they teach today's lesson or any other lesson this quarter." (*Ibid.*) Yet the Bible does resolve the matter as does the Spirit of Prophecy:

> Concerning his Son Jesus Christ our Lord, which was made of the seed of David according to the flesh. (Romans 1:3)

> Forasmuch then as the children are partakers of flesh and blood, he also himself likewise took part of the same, that through death he might destroy him that had the power of death, that is, the devil; and deliver them who through fear of death were all their lifetime subject to bondage. For verily he took on him not the nature of angels; but he took on him the seed of Abraham. Wherefore in all things it behoved him to be made like unto his brethren, that he might be a merciful and faithful high priest in things pertaining to God, to make reconciliation for the sins of the people: for in that he himself hath suffered being tempted, he is able to succour them that are tempted. (Heb. 2:14–18)

> It would have been an almost infinite humiliation for the Son of God to take man's nature, even when Adam stood in his innocence in Eden. But Jesus accepted humanity when the race had been weakened by four thousand years of sin. Like every child of Adam He accepted the results of the working of the great law of heredity. What these results were is shown in the history of his earthly ancestors. He came with such a heredity to share our sorrows and temptations, and to give us the example of a sinless life. (*DA* 49)

> Satan had pointed to Adam's sin as proof that God's law was unjust, and could not be obeyed. In our humanity, Christ was to redeem Adam's failure. But

when Adam was assailed by the tempter, none of the effects of sin were upon him. He stood in the strength of perfect manhood, possessing the full vigor of mind and body. He was surrounded with the glories of Eden, and was in daily communion with heavenly beings. It was not thus with Jesus when He entered the wilderness to cope with Satan. For four thousand years the race had been decreasing in physical strength, in mental power, and in moral worth; and Christ took upon Him the infirmities of degenerate humanity. Only thus could He rescue man from the lowest depths of his degradation. (*DA* 117)

In fairness to Dr. Van Dolson it must be stated that he is a fine Christian with an unshakable faith in Adventist truths. He has never wavered in his fidelity to them. He was forced into a situation not of his own devising. That his attempted solution to the awkward situation did not assist in no way alters these facts. He is a fine choice as a *Sabbath School Quarterly* editor, and God's people can expect a series of excellent studies in the years to come.

Chapter 86 Endnotes:

1. See the chapter entitled "Robert Brinsmead" for the true position on this doctrine.

# 87     Smokescreens

IT is vital that sincere Seventh-day Adventists understand the various ways in which concerted efforts were made to prevent them from understanding the serious nature of the prevailing doctrinal aberrations. It is only as these are perceived in their true light that godly people can be forewarned and will be able to stand shoulder to shoulder with their brethren in defense of the glorious truths of the gospel. Let us illustrate the way in which smokescreens were placed in front of the eyes of God's believers, with a few specific examples of what has occurred in the past several years.

In November, 1983, a two-part paper entitled *Australasian Takeover* was circulated worldwide, including Australia, and this was printed in the United States by Brother Vance Ferrell of Tennessee. However, it was quite plain to anyone reading the material that there had been considerable Australian input into it. As the authors read the historical account that was presented, they could testify that it was only a very modest picture of the problems that existed in Australia. Indeed, over and over again, there were understatements of the problem, rather than exaggerations of it. One criticism of the paper that may be made was that the author made little attempt to present documentary evidence of that which he revealed, despite the fact that accurate documentation of the vast majority of the history was available. Indeed, the documented evidence is far stronger than that which was presented in his paper. Those who have read this present book will be aware that there are documents confirming, point by point, that which the author of *Australasian Takeover* presented. When he gave an analysis of the situation in several conferences, these, we believe, were very mild compared with the actual situation in these conferences. Nevertheless, this honest and factual presentation which, we would add, mentioned no names, apart from those of Desmond Ford and Walter Rea, and the three Australian Division presidents during the period: Pastors L. C. Naden, R. R. Frame and K. Parmenter, was roundly condemned by those who apparently wished to see a continuation of the *new theology*.

By way of example, the condemnation of one church pastor in his church bulletin is cited: "In recent weeks, many have indicated concern over the receiving of unsolicited material from the United States, from a group professing much zeal and orthodoxy, but clearly deficient in knowledge and lacking in the spirit of 1 Corinthians

13. It is possible to show each case to be either untrue or grossly exaggerated. However, I would suggest we look at the wider issues and judge the material on the basis of Christian ethics of whether it is right or wrong to engage in misrepresentation, exaggerations, fabrications, character assassinations and the bitter, critical spirit evident. We would do well to bear in mind that an earlier publication of Australian origin, was, following a successful defamation case against the publishers, proscribed by Australia Post and banned from distribution through the postal service.

"The use of the U.S. dispatch route can be seen as an attempt to circumvent this ban.

"You would also possibly be aware that use is being made of tapes, printed material and gatherings to spread the idea that 'the Seventh-day Adventist Church is not the remnant Church of prophecy and that those preparing to meet the Lord need to come out of her.' This line of attack is not new and Mrs. White addressed this attack in no uncertain manner in four *Review and Herald* articles between August 22 – September 12, 1893. This material is available in *Testimonies to Ministers*, pp. 32–62, and completely destroys any suggestion of its validity. Other E. G. White statements can be found in *Selected Messages*, book 2, 66, and quotations in the *Australian Years* by A. L. White, 80–85.

"Space does not permit the copying of this material here, but I would urge all to read the material mentioned, so that we can be clear in our minds in this matter, and so remain unmoved in the faith.

"In closing, just a sample of the comments made by Mrs. White ( *2SM* 66) 'the message to pronounce the Seventh-day Adventist Church Babylon and call the people of God to come out of her, does not come from any heavenly messenger or any human agent inspired by the Spirit of God.'" [1]

Let us analyze this statement. It will be found that there was never the slightest mention of the view that the Adventist Church is not the remnant Church, nor that it is Babylon, nor was there a call in the *Australasian Takeover* to come out of her as a people. As this church pastor must have been fully aware, it is the teaching of the *new theology* that the Seventh-day Adventist Church is not the remnant. Those standing for the old principles of our faith believe that the Seventh-day Adventist Church is God's remnant with the fullness of their hearts. The authors are well aware that Brother Vance Ferrell believes the Church is the remnant of God,[2] and we have no doubt that those from Australia, who gave input for that publication, believe exactly the same. This then appeared to be an effort to direct the readers away from the plain facts presented in the material.

The authors believe that there is no group of Seventh-day Adventists more firmly committed to the remnant status of the Seventh-day Adventist Church and the fact that it will never become Babylon, than those who truly believe the Spirit of Prophecy. It was surely the men and women who have little faith in that source of inspiration who needed the counsel which this pastor offered.

There are further causes for concern. In his article, the church pastor stated that these people profess "much zeal and orthodoxy but clearly [are] deficient in knowledge and lacking the spirit of 1 Corinthians 13." This demonstrates a very shallow understanding of Christian love. Christian love does not condone the spread of heresy. Those pastors who encourage their congregations to continue in the errors of the *new theology*, who put their arms of love about them, and assure them of salvation in their sins, are so far from fulfilling the spirit of 1 Corinthians 13, that this passage of Scripture has to be meaningless to them. There are others, on the other hand, who in righteous concern, spread a warning to God's fold out of love for their souls. This warning may be urgent, it may be forceful, it may even be given with righteous indignation, but it is nevertheless completely in accord with the spirit of 1 Corinthians 13.

Surely these men have confirmed the truth that love—

> rejoiceth not in iniquity, but rejoiceth in the truth (1 Corinthians 13:6)

The author of *Australasian Takeover* has surely fulfilled this criterion of love.

In the Bible we see illustrated very vividly this principle. No doubt if those who falsely accuse God's people of lacking the spirit of 1 Corinthians 13 had been present at the time of the apostasy in Israel at Sinai, they may have felt that Moses was most defective in this matter of love. On the other hand, they would also have been able to observe "the loving attitude" of Aaron and would have felt that he was a man inspired by the sentiments of 1 Corinthians 13. But let us quote from God's servant, who reveals God's assessment.

> When Moses, on returning to the camp, confronted the rebels, his severe rebukes and the indignation he displayed in breaking the sacred tables of the law, were contrasted by the people with his brother's pleasant speech and dignified demeanor, and their sympathies were with Aaron. To justify himself, Aaron endeavored to make the people responsible for his weakness in yielding to their demand; but notwithstanding this, they were filled with admiration of his gentleness and patience. But God seeth not as man sees. Aaron's yielding spirit and his desire to please, had blinded his eyes to the enormity of the crime he was sanctioning. His course in giving his influence to sin in Israel cost the life of thousands. In what contrast with this was the course of Moses, who, while faithfully executing God's judgments, showed that the welfare of Israel was dearer to him than prosperity or honor or life.
>
> Of all the sins that God will punish, none are more grievous in His sight than those that encourage others to do evil. God would have His servants prove their loyalty by faithfully rebuking transgression, however painful the act may be. Those who are honored with a divine commission, are not to be weak, pliant time-servers. They are not to aim at self-exaltation, or to shun disagreeable duties, but to perform God's work with unswerving fidelity. (PP 323,324)

The reader is left to consider which man, Aaron or Moses, demonstrated the spirit of 1 Corinthians 13 and which one contravened it. As far as the people were concerned, there was no doubt, but in God's judgment, the picture was very different indeed. Unfortunately, this magnificent lesson has been largely lost upon God's people, for today we uphold Aarons and condemn those who, like Moses, warn of sin. We cannot escape the observation that the church pastor who wrote this scathing condemnation of the author of *Australasian Takeover*, made not the slightest effort to condemn those who were taking God's people along the road of perdition. This is a serious failure of duty. The arguments used by this church pastor are, of course, self-condemnatory. He stated that, in his view, the author has been lacking the spirit of 1 Corinthians 13. But what he has written concerning that author may appear to be lacking in the very same spirit.

A further smokescreen was placed before the reader: "It is possible to show each case to be either untrue or grossly exaggerated." As has been mentioned, the author of *Australasian Takeover*, in our view, obviously understated the situation rather than exaggerating it, and to the best of the knowledge of the authors, there was only one small error of little consequence in the whole paper.[3] However, the most significant fact was that the writer of this appraisal omitted to give even one instance to add veracity to the charge which he had made. The truth is that it is possible he was not very conversant with the matters which were discussed, and was thus not in a position to know whether they were true or false. Certainly he could not have been in possession of any documentary evidence which would have proved the material to be either substantially untrue or grossly exaggerated.

These revelations should have been enough to arouse any pastor to the defense of the faith. When we recognize that the material in *Australasian Takeover* does not fully expose the gross problems in Australia, then surely no ordained minister should have a restful night while failing to stand up against an apostasy which is taking his flock away from its eternal reward.

The pastor then proceeded to defame the material by describing it as "misrepresentations, exaggerations, fabrications, character assassinations and [a] bitter critical spirit." This was another smokescreen, for once again he gave no documented evidence to support these extreme assertions. If someone supporting the truth of God were to refer to a pastor representing the *new theology* in Australia as being guilty of misrepresentation, exaggeration, fabrication, character assassinations and in possession of a bitter critical spirit, there is little doubt that full ecclesiastical ire would be brought to bear on the head of such an accuser. This would be produced as evidence of a "bitter, critical spirit." But this pastor, even though unacquainted with the editor and unable to cite any proof of his assertions, felt no compunction about emphasizing these qualities as being characteristics of the one who possessed sufficient love for his Church and its truth so firmly implanted in his life that he was prepared to warn when such were under attack.

From that point, the pastor moved to a matter concerning which he clearly had only scant knowledge. He said that an "earlier publication of Australasian origin, was, following a successful defamation case against the publishers, proscribed by Australia Post and banned for distribution through the postal service." The facts of the case are that one church member did take out a defamation case against the publishers of *Adventist Observer*. This was a rather curious action in a number of ways. In the first place, the brother who took out the action had never been mentioned, nor referred to, in *Adventist Observer*. Thus he had no personal reason to lay the charge of defamation. Second, the charged men were not in the least involved in the production of the magazine.[4] Thus it would have been very surprising if such a curious action could have succeeded. The fact of this situation, which appeared to be unknown to the pastor in his attack on the *Australasian Takeover*, was that the magistrate was shocked to find a Seventh-day Adventist church member bringing a defamation action against his brethren. He did not even stop to find out that the accuser had charged the wrong men. The magistrate simply picked up the Word of God and challenged the complainant by reading:

> Durst any of you, having a matter against another, go to law before the unjust, and not before the saints? Do ye not know that the saints shall judge the world? and if the world shall be judged by you, are ye unworthy to judge the smallest matters? Know ye not that we shall judge angels? How much more things that pertain to this life? If then ye have judgments of things pertaining to this life, set them to judge who are least esteemed in the church. I speak to your shame. Is it so, that there is not a wise man among you? no, not one that shall be able to judge between his brethren? But brother goeth to law with brother, and that before the unbelievers. Now therefore there is utterly a fault among you, because ye go to law one with another. Why do ye not rather take wrong? Why do ye not rather suffer yourselves to be defrauded? Nay, ye do wrong, and defraud, and that your brethren. (1 Corinthians 6:1–8)

With this rebuke, the magistrate dismissed the case and the complainant had no option but to drop it. Not only did he drop the case but he was left to meet the cost which he had incurred in bringing it. Thus the church pastor's statement is totally without foundation. To state that Australia Post banned the publication from distribution is again without any foundation. Thus, we can summarize the smokescreen which was utilized in this particular case:

1. There was a condemnation of those standing for truth, suggesting that they were not loving.
2. It was stated, without proof, that their material was untrue or exaggerated.
3. The author's character was defamed by suggesting that he had the most sinful and devious motives.
4. Erroneous statements were made, which made it appear as if some persons had lost a lawsuit over this matter.[5]

5. A straw man was set up indicating that the author of *Australasian Takeover* had leveled the most terrible charges against our Church, and then statements from the Spirit of Prophecy were utilized to show correctly that such charges would be highly contrary to the plain Word of God. The fact was, however, that the author had never brought such charges against God's Church. He is a fundamental Spirit of Prophecy believing Seventh-day Adventist, who has spent years defending the view that the Seventh-day Adventist Church is, indeed, God's remnant. It would appear to be less than Christian rectitude for a pastor to bring such patently false charges against another brother. Truth does not require such tactics.

Undoubtedly, the church pastor sincerely believed he was doing his best to uphold the leadership of the Church and perhaps the Church itself. These in themselves are noble ideals. But God's truth must be upheld above all. God's Church and its leaders do not need smokescreens to uphold them.

The authors, themselves, experienced another effort to minimize the effectiveness of the work of those who would present God's truth. Their book, *Adventism Vindicated*, although not advertised to any large degree, has now reached the fifth printing. This book set forth the true Adventist position on Righteousness by Faith in a manner which was understandable to all Seventh-day Adventists. Only a small portion of this book was given over to citing the error which had come into the Church. It should be noted that this book was written in the early part of 1979, although not published until 1980. At the time of writing, Dr. Ford was still a professor on the staff of Pacific Union College and the authors could not have known that so soon he would be discredited within the Church.

The book made an immediate impact. A number of conference presidents in North America recommended the book to their ministers and/or members. In other conferences, departmental leaders took the initiative in distributing the book to the workers within their conferences. In Canada, each school teacher was provided with a copy by one Adventist Book Center manager, who was very enthusiastic about the contents of the book. In the Far Eastern Division the ministerial secretary[6] and the stewardship director[7] distributed copies to each Union leader in their respective departments. The ministerial secretary of the Central Philippines Union,[8] in turn, bought copies for the 150 pastors within his Union.

This support for the book reached the ears of one of the Australasian Division officers. Although almost three years had passed since Dr. Ford had shown his true doctrinal colors, the officer contacted the president of the Far Eastern Division[9] and expressed his great displeasure that men in the Far Eastern Division were showing appreciation for the book. He objected to the statement:

> The bitter attacks on the *Sabbath School Quarterly* of 1977, *Jesus, the Model Man*, authored by Dr. Herbert Douglass, were engendered by those who chose to believe the theories of man in contrast to the simple truths of God's Word. That the leadership of a whole Division sought to change the impact of that lesson series, emphasizes the serious nature of the errors in our midst.

We can praise God that our General Conference leadership did not yield to this pressure and permitted truth to be presented. (*Adventism Vindicated*, 3rd printing, 82)

In his communiqués, the Australasian Division officer insisted that there had been only a very minor problem over that *Quarterly* in the Australasian Division and that the Division officers had been misrepresented. Since he had been an officer at the time of the discussion, there was no possibility that he could not have known the enormous implications of the controversy over this *Quarterly*.

The Australasian Division officer had written, "At no time did I, my fellow officers, the Union presidents or local Conference presidents try to do what we are accused of doing. In fact, I encouraged our people to study the pamphlet referred to and to my knowledge, there were only one or two sections in the pamphlet that anybody took exception to." [10]

The Division officer was obviously unaware that the authors had extensive documentary evidence of the reaction of himself and numbers of others to the *Sabbath School Quarterly*. His challenge demanded an answer which was given with full documentation. There was no further correspondence on the matter following the provision of this material to the Division officer.[11]

Here again was an apparent effort to provide a smokescreen by denying the presence of any major problem. This course was taken over and over again. We do not overlook the possibility that, in his busy term of office, this Division officer may have forgotten many details. However, in this instance, full documentation was available to reveal the real nature of the upheaval over the *Quarterly* in Australasia. The same officer had stated: "Neither I, nor my fellow leaders, agree with the deviations to our message that have been introduced by Ballenger, Fletcher, Greive, Brinsmead or Ford and their followers." [12] The facts, however, appear to be otherwise. This officer was one of those leaders who, on the Biblical Research Institute in 1976, assented to Ford's aberrant doctrines by agreeing to the statement "that Dr. Desmond Ford ably demonstrated that such stances as he takes which appear to diverge from what some senior men hold as 'Present Truth' can be justified by reference to majority positions taken by current Seventh-day Adventist authors and scholars." [13]

To those outside the Australasian Division who were not in a position to know the details and the depth of the problems, it was an easy matter to place a smokescreen over the gigantic spiritual problems within the Division, but for those close to the situation, the dense smoke could not obscure the reality of the problem.

Thus, in many ways, efforts were made to denounce truth, while very few efforts were made to warn God's people of the perils of the *new theology*.

A further popular smokescreen used was to accuse those who were attempting to warn of the perils within the Church of failing to follow the admonition of Jesus in Matthew 18. It will be recalled that in this passage Jesus said:

> Moreover, if thy brother shall trespass against thee, go and tell him his fault between thee and him alone; if he shall hear thee, thou hast gained thy brother. But if he will not hear thee, then take with thee one or two more, that in the mouth of two or three witnesses every word may be established. And if he shall neglect to hear them, tell it unto the church: but if he neglect to hear the church, let him be unto thee as an heathen man and a publican. (Matthew 18:15–17)

Of course, many of those who were making this complaint, were quite ignorant of the fact that on numerous occasions, godly men had approached the persons concerned in a private way.[14] They have later approached these persons as the Scripture indicates in twos and threes before finally bringing the matter into the open before the Church. The readers of this manuscript will now be acquainted with many of the pleading letters and interviews which did occur prior to the Church, at large, being informed of the deceit which was being practiced in the name of Jesus. However, we must be careful that we do not misapply Matthew 18. Sister White, it will be recalled, was also accused of breaching this command of Jesus. She had presented a testimony in the church at Tuscola, Illinois, in which she stated that one sister lacked discretion and caution and did not fully control her words and actions:

> Her husband seemed to feel unreconciled to my bringing out her faults before the church, and stated that if Sister White had followed the directions of our Lord in Matthew 18:15–17, he should not have felt hurt. (*2T* 15)

Pastor James White then brought out the true biblical position involved:

> My husband then stated that he should understand that these words of our Lord had reference to cases of personal trespass and could not be applied in the case of this sister. She had not trespassed against Sister White, but that which had been reproved publicly, was public wrongs which threatened the prosperity of the church and the cause. (*Ibid.*)

James White then went on to quote a Scripture which seems to be overlooked by many of those defending the new *theology*:[15]

> Them that sin, rebuke before all, that others also may fear.
> (1 Timothy 5:20)

Thus there is a plain directive from God that sins against God's church should be rebuked openly. Those who would accuse God's spokesmen of a failure to follow God's commands are, in fact, totally in error in asserting this charge.

## Chapter 87 Endnotes:

1. *Church Bulletin*, Tamworth Church, North New South Wales Conference, December, 1983.
2. Indeed, Bro. Ferrell had stated that one reason his organization was used to print *Australasian Takeover* was "that it was concerned with reforming the church, not forsaking it." (*Pilgrims' Waymarks* No. 70)
3. The author stated that Dr. Bernie Brinsmead was a brother of Robert Brinsmead. In fact, he is a nephew. It will be agreed that this error was not of any consequence whatsoever.
4. One of these was Brother Neil Foxcroft whom he quite erroneously guessed was one of the editors. In fact, Brother Foxcroft had not made the slightest contribution in any way to *Adventist Observer*. Another falsely accused was Brother Dallas Wilson. During his futile investigation, the church member revealed his true character by impersonating a police officer. This is an offense of a criminal nature and he was subsequently charged with this offense by the New South Wales Constabulary.
5. It is almost certain that the pastor had no idea whether the authors of the two manuscripts were the same. It is doubtful whether he knows the Australian author of either manuscript. Certainly the complainant's efforts showed how far off most people were in establishing the authorship of *Australian Observer*. We ourselves suspect a different authorship.
6. Pastor James Zachary
7. Pastor Doyle Barnett
8. Pastor Bacola
9. Pastor Winston Clark
10. Letter from Australasian Division officer to Pastor W. Clark, president of the Far Eastern Division, dated May 24, 1982
11. For those who wish to see some of this documentation, it is found in the chapter entitled: *Australasian Division Responds*. No fair-minded person could deny the accuracy of the statement in *Adventism Vindicated* after reading the documentation available. It will be noted that the name of the Division was not even alluded to in the passage which offended. The fact that this Australasian Division officer felt impelled to defend the Australasian Division leadership in such circumstance, will not have been overlooked by the astute reader. It is worthy of reporting that the leaders of none of the other world Divisions reacted in this way.
12. Letter from Australasian Division officer to Pastor James Zachary, ministerial director of the Far Eastern Division, dated July 14, 1982
13. Report of Australasian Division, B.R.I. on meeting with Dr. Ford and sixteen Concerned Brethren, Feb. 3, 4, 1976—see chapter entitled "The Findings of the B.R.I."

14. In this book the reader will have noted the reproduction of much private correspondence between concerned believers and those misleading God's children.

15. Although, incongruously, little care has been taken to preserve the reputations of many seeking to uphold truth. On many occasions these people have been openly condemned without any sense that Matthew 18 has been breached.

# 88

## Lack of Fundamental Faith: A Phenomenon of the Eighties

IT must not be thought that the Seventh-day Adventist Church was unique in having its fundamental doctrines attacked during the 1970s and 1980s. The trends within our Church simply reflected that which was occurring in virtually every faith in Christendom. The one difference was that we believe the Seventh-day Adventist Church has been called out, in a most specific way by God, to present the last message to mankind. Thus the problems within the older churches were minor compared with those within the Seventh-day Adventist Church. Even if those faiths should collapse, it would be of only minor significance[1] in the plan of taking the great gospel commission to the whole world, since they have not shouldered the task of preaching God's last message.

It is well known that the Baptist, Lutheran, Methodist and Presbyterian Churches, among others, have long been haunted by liberalism and by those destructive influences which have reduced the majority of their colleges to the place where they are producing men with barely a semblance of faith in the Word of God, let alone in the fundamental doctrines of their faith.

Even in the Roman Catholic Church, where there has been considerable dissent about the centuries-old traditions of their faith, problems have surfaced. Archbishop Hunthausen, Roman Catholic archbishop of Seattle, has adopted a most liberal attitude in this archdiocese. *Time* magazine reported that at one funeral conducted in Seattle, there was dancing, and a clown entered into the ritual; people were calling out in ecstasy at the commencement of the service. Such liberal trends are an affront to human dignity, let alone to Christian fidelity. It is only natural that some more fundamental Roman Catholics are revolted by such practices.

Interestingly, Roman Catholics have resorted to the type of response which seems to be universal in such circumstances. Letters continually are passing to Rome exposing the lack of orthodoxy on the part of these Roman Catholic clergy. It is interesting that some of the most vocal have been Roman Catholic laymen who have, to their credit, desired to maintain the standards of their faith, even though that faith be vastly removed from the pure truth of God. Alfonse Matt, Jr., edits a newspaper called the *Wanderer*, which consistently includes "Curia names and addresses to which disgruntled can write." (*Newsweek*, Nov. 28, 1983) Naturally, Matt is vilified for his effort to keep American Roman Catholic bishops on the straight and narrow path. "Much of the misunderstandings between Curia and the American bishops may be traced to the *Wanderer*, whose mischievous reports, says a Vatican official, are accepted 'as gospel' by a small group of like-minded curia prelates. That group includes Cardinal Angelo Rossi of the Congregation for the Propagation of the Faith, Archbishop Augustine Mayer of the Congregation for the Religious, and, in particular, Cardinal Oddi. Indeed, in a recent *Wanderer* interview, Oddi agreed that any Roman Catholic who doesn't accept the literal truth of the Creation narrative, or who practices contraception, is automatically 'out of the church' —a proposition that could reduce the number of American Roman Catholics to not much more than the 36,000 who subscribe to the *Wanderer* itself." (*Ibid.*) According to the article, only two American bishops accept the *Wanderer* ideas, and both of them are near to the retiring age of seventy-five years.

Even smaller churches, such as Jehovah's Witnesses, had a defection by one of their Headquarters' men over the matter of doctrine. There have also been large-scale defections of rank-and-file members. The Mormons, whose scholars in Salt Lake City are questioning much of their fundamental beliefs, have also suffered the indignity of having their doctrinal crises well covered by *Time* and *Newsweek* magazines.

On July 6, 1984, Professor David Perkins was consecrated Anglican Bishop of Durham, despite much protest from the laity against his appointment. Bishop Perkins "was quoted as saying that he was 'pretty clear' that the virgin birth was a symbolic story. 'I would not put it past God to arrange a virgin birth if He wanted to, but I very much doubt if He would,' he said." (London *Times*, May 24, 1984) That Bishop Perkins was not alone among Anglican bishops in his doubting of the authenticity of the New Testament miracles, was shown by the fact that thirty-one of the forty-two Anglican bishops interviewed, admitted that they did not believe in the actual occurrences of the recorded miracles of Scripture (London *Daily Telegraph*, June 27, 1984) Further, John Sarum, Bishop of Salisbury, who, despite his knowledge of Perkins' stand, claimed that he looked "forward eagerly and thankfully to the contribution he [Bishop Perkins] will make as a bishop to the life and thinking of the Church, and I know that when, at his consecration, he affirms his loyalty to Bible and creeds as his inheritance of faith, he will be speaking the truth." (London *Times*, June 27, 1984)

The Anglican Church, despite still having some most sincere members, has had difficulty with many of its bishops. In the early 1960s it was the Bishop of Woolwich, John Robinson, who shocked the religious world with his book, *Honest to God*, a book which commenced the "God is dead" movement. All that can now be said about Bishop Robinson's contribution is that *he* is now dead, having died in 1983.

Another to cause a stir in the Anglican Church has been Bishop Hugh Montifiore. He was first consecrated a bishop in 1970 (Bishop of Kingston-upon-Thames). At that time, many parishioners protested his appointment, some even threatening in letters to the London *Times* that they would never attend an Anglican Church in the diocese while he was its head. The reason for the uproar was that it was asserted, nine months earlier, Dr. Montifiore, a converted Jew, had put forward the view that Christ was a homosexual. When interviewed on national television, Dr. Montifiore would neither deny nor affirm the charge. Later, he was promoted Bishop of Birmingham. In 1984, when interviewed by the press on television, one pressman offered the opinion that the bishop seldom referred to God. The pressman challenged Bishop Montifiore to convince the agnostics in his audience of the existence of God. The bishop, in asserting there were many evidences, commenced, by way of example, with evolution! Undoubtedly, the Anglican Church has major problems with its hierarchy.

However, Seventh-day Adventists can take scant comfort from this universal trend. It does seem that there are many within our Church who are accepting society's norms as being the standards for the Church, and this is true also regarding matters of doctrine.

The trend to follow social norms is occurring as well in the area of moral conduct. Thousands of Seventh-day Adventists today see no wrong in abortion on demand. Yet twenty years ago, in most civilized countries of the world, any person practicing such operations was sentenced to penal servitude.

When Russell graduated as a physician in 1964, he would have been promptly jailed had he performed an abortion upon the demand of the mother, and furthermore, his name would have been struck off the medical register of the State of New South Wales for an indefinite period.

Such were the standards even of such organizations of low morality as many governments appeared to be.[2] When divorce was obnoxious to society as a whole, Seventh-day Adventists followed such a conviction. Now that divorce has become a matter of social acceptance, many Seventh-day Adventists wish to accept the guilty party in a divorce into church fellowship. The same may be said of homosexuality. Only recently have most Western governments failed to see this practice as a crime against society. Now the degraded standards of our society have seriously eroded the thinking of many of our people on this matter.

Surely God's remnant people should have a standard which far surpasses that of the miserable standards of the world. When thirty or forty years ago, the standards of the world were very much higher than they are today, Adventists were still far removed from the practices of the world. Now that these standards have reached an all-time low, there are many among us who want us to match these appalling moral levels within our communities.

Let us not forget the high and holy trust God has bestowed upon His remnant people. It is little wonder that some are seeking to reduce the remnant status of God's people, for they themselves no longer wish to conform to the exalted standards required of such a calling. But as Seventh-day Adventists we cannot, indeed, we dare not shrink from these enormous responsibilities. Thus we must always, under God's power, irrespective of the social standards about us, reach the highest attainments of doctrinal purity and moral conduct.

Chapter 88 Endnotes:

1. Editors note: With this edition, sixteen years later, it is possible to see great apocalyptic significance in the collapse of Protestantism in some major churches and their consequent movement to coalesce with the Great Apostasy.
2. Perhaps no Seventh-day Adventist has studied the problem in greater depth than Dr. Robert Dunn. His paper, *The Nature of Man in the Early Stages of Life and Our Responsibility*, is highly recommended. Dr. Dunn, a dedicated former missionary physician to China, Burma, India, Pakistan and England, has made detailed biblical analysis of the evil of abortion. With Dr. Dunn, the authors unhesitatingly accept the view that abortion is a breach of the sixth commandment. Dr. Dunn's address is, 7180 Old Pipe Stone Road, Box 223, Eau Claire, Michigan 49111, U.S.A.

# 89

## God's Word

THERE is no doubt that the Bible is the source book for every aspect of the Seventh-day Adventist hope. Without it there would be no Seventh-day Adventists; indeed, no Christians at all. Within its pages are the words of life, the very truths conveyed to us through human agents of the God of the universe. It is quite natural that these messages, crucial as they are to man's salvation, are the target of satanic attacks. Nothing would serve the arch-deceiver better than to pervert and alter the word of Scripture. This goal he achieved very early in the Christian era.[1] There is little wonder that God saw fit to invoke the most fearful condemnation upon those who would alter God's Word.

> And if any man shall take away from the words of the book of this prophecy,
> God shall take away his part out of the book of life, and out of the holy city,
> and from the things which are written in this book. (Revelation 22:19)

Ignoring this divine anathema, men, first in the city of Alexandria and later in Rome, felt content to pervert the Word of God. Most of these were men influenced by the gnostic heresy, and they attempted to delete references in the New Testament to Christ's divinity. Men such as Justin Martyr and Origen were foremost in this counterfeit. As a result, early in the Christian era, altered manuscripts became available from the centers of Christianity in Alexandria and Rome. In many ways, these counterfeit manuscripts closely resembled the truth, but here and there produced little changes and omissions which altered the sense of God's Word to suit their doctrinal bias.

Fortunately, the Lord did not permit the accurate truth to be lost, for the church in Syria and in other parts of the Eastern world did not accept these heresies and faithfully preserved, in a manner akin to that used by the Jewish scribes, the precise words of Scripture. Thus the Greek and Syrian texts have come down to us in an unbroken chain of accuracy preserved by the hand of God. It was upon these texts that the translators of the King James version of the Bible relied, for they represented the most accurate rendition of Scripture. These were collected together by Erasmus, who produced what has been known as the Textus Receptus.

The counterfeit manuscripts have been concentrated in Rome, the most famous of which is the Codex Vaticanus. Another corrupt text which has received considerable notoriety is the Codex Sinaiticus. This codex was discovered in the Sinai peninsula in 1844. These two manuscripts date to the fourth century, Christian Era, while the earliest Greek manuscripts used by those translating the King James version date to the fifth century C.E. The fact that these two manuscripts are dated about one hundred years earlier than any of the Greek manuscripts used by the King James translators, has been the basis of a most complicated theory put forward by two leading British Bible scholars of the nineteenth century—Bishop Westcott and Dr. Hort. In simple terms, their theory was that the older the manuscript, the more accurately it represented that which was written by the apostles. However, the fallacy of this argument is, as we have seen, that very early in the Christian era, counterfeit manuscripts appeared. It also overlooked that the translators of the King James version were able to examine many Greek translations of the Scripture, going back to the second century C.E. Most of these were in the Syrian or related languages and came from a Christian tradition where the Word of God was preserved with virtually unerring accuracy. Also, the translators of the King James version were able to refer to the writings of numerous church fathers of the period prior to the fourth century C.E. These men obviously quoted large passages of Scripture in their writings and it was possible to compare these with the Textus Receptus, thus further confirming the accuracy of preservation in the manuscripts.

Unfortunately, today, the vast majority of translations accept the Westcott and Hort theory and thus base their translations upon a corrupted Greek text. This is true of the Revised Standard Version, the New English Version, the New International Version and numerous others of the most popular translations. It is not a difficult matter to examine quickly to determine whether a translation is from a corrupted manuscript or not. There are two texts of Scripture which are inevitably perverted by those who are using counterfeit Greek texts for their translations. The first of these is,

> For there are three that bear the record in heaven, the Father, the Word, and the Holy Ghost; and these three are one. (1 John 5:7)

It will be noted that this text very precisely sets out the place of Jesus as part of the Godhead. Naturally, this was offensive to the Gnostics, since they did not believe that Jesus held such a position. They therefore deleted this text from their manuscripts. The translators of the King James version were too alert to the errors harbored by the papacy to be fooled by such an omission and have marvelously preserved this great truth for us.

But this is not true of the translators of most modern versions. What they do is to take the eighth verse and divide it into two verses, thus preserving the correct number of verses. Therefore, any person wishing to know whether his version is translated from corrupted sources, need only to look at verse seven of first John, chapter five and note whether this is included or omitted.

The second text which is the hallmark of those who would change the truth of God is,

> And without controversy, great is the mystery of godliness. God was manifest in the flesh, justified in the Spirit, seen of angels, preached unto the Gentiles, believed on in the world, received up into glory. (1 Timothy 3:16)

Once again it will be noted that this passage specifically testifies to the divinity of Jesus Christ, for He was God manifest in the flesh. However, if we look at most modern translations, based upon the counterfeited Greek text, it will be seen that the word *He* is substituted for *God*. This, of course, takes away the message of the passage that Jesus, indeed, was God. The reader is invited to check these two texts in any versions of Scripture which he possesses.

Today there are numerous ministers within the Seventh-day Adventist Church who are pressing their congregations into accepting the use of translations other than King James versions. The Revised Standard Version is very popular with many preachers now. But this change must be resisted by all who want to study the pure truth of God. The authors are not suggesting that alternative versions are unworthy of consultation from time to time, but one must always have in mind that while much of what is written in these versions contains the truth of God, there are vital areas of change which submerge precious truth. We are not suggesting that the King James version is an inerrant translation. It most certainly is not. There are instances where modern translations more clearly and, in a few cases, more accurately translate the Greek found in the received text (Textus Receptus). But one matter is certain, and that is, that few modern versions, as a whole, are nearly as accurate as the King James version. The complaints that it is archaic in its expressions are fallacious. Even young children of four and five can understand the *thee*'s and the *thou*'s which occur within the King James version. The use of words with meanings different from that of today, e.g., the use of "meat" when meaning food, do not require more than an elementary school education in order to understand them.[2]

Unfortunately, many Adventist academics prefer other translations, for they are most inaccurate in their representation of the matters dealing with the Sanctuary. For example, the New International Version has a very poor translation of Hebrews 9, a passage which is so misunderstood by those who would destroy the Sanctuary truth. There are some who believe that the present emphasis by many on these new translations is based upon the need felt by some theologians to take away from the people a version of the Scripture which much more powerfully presents the distinctive messages of the Adventist faith. One just has to read Daniel 8:14 in the various translations to become aware of this trend. The concept of cleansing of the Sanctuary is omitted from most, yet the translators of the King James version very perceptively saw this primary meaning, as they compared the words used by the Jews themselves in translating the Old Testament into Greek.

Thus we must be aware that when we are using these modern translations, in most instances we are using texts which have been deliberately altered in order to change some of the truths of God. Further, the insights of a number of the translators into the passages which are vital to the proper understanding of the Sanctuary truth have often been poor indeed. There is great safety in utilizing the King James version, based as it is on the non-corrupted texts of the Eastern Christian Church, rather than the corrupted texts of the Western and Roman Churches.

Chapter 89 Endnotes:

1. "I saw that God has especially guarded the Bible, yet learned men, when the copies were few, had changed the words in some instances, thinking that they were making it more plain, when they were mystifying that which was plain, in causing it to lean to their established views, governed by tradition." (1SG 117)
2. The New King James Version uses modern terms, while providing a translation based upon sound manuscripts.

# 90   Conclusion

THE question on the lips of every dedicated Seventh-day Adventist is, how can the present apostasy be stayed? As doctrinal declension has been translated into loss of moral fiber and standards, and weakening of our evangelistic, publishing, educational and medical witness, some have despaired, believing that the Seventh-day Adventist Church has crossed that invisible division between God's Church and Babylon. Such a sentiment is not new. After the rejection of the great message of 1888, there were good men and women who made a similar judgment. But Sister White has laid to rest such conclusions. Writing to a brother in 1893, only five years after the Minneapolis Conference, Sister White warned against calling the Seventh-day Adventist Church Babylon:

> The Lord has not given you a message to call Seventh-day Adventists Babylon, and to call the people of God to come out of her. All the reasons you may present cannot have weight with me upon this subject, because the Lord has given me decided light that is opposed to such a message. (*2SM* 63)

Fortunately, only a very few of those who express confidence in God's message have chosen to separate from the Church at this time of crisis. This is a time, as never before, when God's people should support His Church with all their vigor and with greater dedication than ever. It is not a time to withdraw our means from those spreading the gospel of truth. If ever such funds were needed by the Church, it is now. This is not a time to withdraw our presence from the congregation of the saints. It is not a time to utilize our talents elsewhere. This is the time of all times to give all to Jesus and His Church.

This book has presented clear documentary evidence of the problems confronting our Church. Some will read this account and complain that it is unscholarly. Others will seek to ignore the heavy weight of documentary evidence, and still claim its facts to be false. In doing this they will seek to turn God's people away from a much needed reformation. Such overlook that if even ten percent of the contents of this book were correct, it would portend a crisis of the greatest magnitude within God's Church. But the facts, as presented, cannot be disputed, for they are fully documented. Yet others, noting that the evidence is too strong to refute, will cast aspersions upon the motives of the authors, or the spirit in which this book has been written. Such judgments are not objective and simply seek to draw the reader away from the tragic fact of apostasy by introducing judgmental arguments. The authors can only state with all conviction that they have written from troubled hearts, hearts filled with love for their Savior and the certainty of the precious truths of Scripture. We are jealous for the faith. We are deeply distressed when we see friends whose convictions have been destroyed by this terrible apostasy. Our hearts ache when we see former colleagues and men and women once nobly standing for the truth sink into the mire of doubt and confusion and finally become alienated from those truths which they once held so precious.

It would not reflect our faith to pen knowingly a dishonest word. Nor would we uplift Jesus by writing from motives of personal animosity. We love the brethren. God does not put within our hearts hate or vengeance. But those leading out in this apostasy are not assisted by a mute response to their work of destruction. At our ordinations each of us assented to the ordination charge. This, in part, stated:

> Son of man, I have made thee a watchman unto the house of Israel: therefore hear the word at my mouth, and give them warning from me. When I say unto the wicked, Thou shalt surely die; and thou givest him not warning, nor speakest to warn the wicked from his wicked way, to save his life; the same wicked man shall die in his iniquity; but his blood will I require at thine hand. Yet if thou warn the wicked, and he turn not from his wickedness, nor from his wicked way, he shall die in his iniquity; but thou has delivered thy soul. (Ezekiel 3:17–19)

Isaiah was further commanded to a ministry of strong reproof:

> Cry aloud, spare not, lift up thy voice like a trumpet, and show my people their transgressions, and the house of Jacob their sins. (Isaiah 58:1)

It is not love that motivates men to silence when apostasy abounds. Usually such silence is motivated by regard for one's self-esteem, for the ministry of reproof is one hardly designed to promote appreciation from those who have digressed.

To those who would seek to bypass the plain evidence of this far-reaching apostasy within our Church by concentrating upon trivial matters, we would urge that this book be reread, and that the documentary evidence be given close attention, and that guidance be sought from above so that one's duty to God may be fulfilled.

The Health department of the Far Eastern Division in 1983 faced up to the problem of employing missionaries who were unfaithful to the message of God. Led by men such as Dr. Everett Witzel, Division health director, Mr. Laurie Dunfield, president of Adventist Health Services, Asia, and Dr. Harold Butler, director of Dental Services for the Far Eastern Division, steps were taken to remedy this problem. This consisted of a simple written inquiry concerning the potential missionary's doctrinal convictions in certain controversial areas.[1] The Division had always made a thorough investigation of the academic qualifications of its missionaries, but until recently it was assumed that each was in possession of the truth. As this assumption became increasingly untenable, this new procedure was devised.

Of course, such a questionnaire is open to falsification. And no doubt in the course of time, such will occur. But in most cases it will assist those making appointments to find men and women prepared to preach the three angels' messages. An occasional person will feel affronted by the questions. Rarely will this be a person filled with a burning love of truth and proud to proclaim his convictions.

It is suggested that this lead of the Far Eastern Division be followed worldwide. It could save us from perhaps ninety percent of the problems that we now face. When Colin was president of Columbia Union College, he, along with Dr. Jack Blanco, academic dean, and Pastor Gordon Bullock, business manager, interviewed potential staff members, specifically seeking their doctrinal views. While they did not find this method faultless, it did nevertheless protect the college at that time from much of the drift toward the *new theology* so markedly evident in some other colleges. This result can be seen in that extremely few attended Paxton's meeting for Columbia Union College students in 1978, as compared with the full houses he enjoyed in some other colleges.[2]

Some have expressed the view that virtually nothing can be done to retrace the steps of apostasy already taken. In their view, since the institutional Boards control these institutions, and the Boards consist largely of men and women who favor the current trends within the institution, the matter is beyond repair. We do not share this pessimistic view. The Church is not as impotent as this concept suggests. The views of the leadership, even in this age of dissent, are still valued by the majority of our believers.

Let us hasten to state that the authors believe in the decentralization of church policy making. It is proper that the local Boards be in charge of the operation of the institution. To deny this plan would be to fly in the face of the counsels of the Spirit of Prophecy. But when these Board members and the institutional administration can no longer perform their duties as faithful Seventh-day Adventists, then it is time for outside action.

Furthermore, we do have the machinery available to make such changes. The Seventh-day Adventist Church follows an affiliation procedure for colleges and medical institutions. Within the Far Eastern Division, the Adventist Health Services Asia has taken God's commission for hospitals so seriously that the Board has voted a plan whereby hospitals which do not meet the ideals of Seventh-day Adventist medical work, are deprived of accreditation by that failure alone. It is thus perfectly possible for a hospital in the Far Eastern Division to uphold the highest of medical standards and yet fail to meet our church accreditation criteria.

This situation should prevail in our other institutions. If, after counsel and guidance, institutions fail to measure up to minimal denominational standards, wisdom dictates that they lose denominational accreditation and be no longer listed in official publications, as being representative of our faith. This procedure will alert God's people that they can no longer, with safety, support these institutions. God's people, by and large, are loyal. They would appreciate such information. Certainly we could anticipate a hue and cry from those supportive of lowered standards. But they would soon learn that the only course open to them, in order to return these institutions to their former denominational status, would be to reform them, so that they again become worthy of the name Seventh-day Adventist. It is unthinkable that we have institutions proclaiming denominational approval, while their leaders flout the very standards and aims of the Church.

Pastor Kenneth Wood demonstrated that straight writing concerning deplorable conditions in some of our colleges, while arousing the ire of the college presidents concerned, did alert many good people to the peril in which they had placed their children. Had Pastor Wood's voice been reinforced by those of many others who held similar convictions, it is likely that of necessity a transformation would have occurred.

We would reemphasize that our concern for those following the *new theology*, which is in such contradiction to the Word of God, is destructive. Firm denunciation and exposure of error do not denote a lack of Christian affection for those holding and promoting such doctrines. Our own relationship to those on our staffs and others of our acquaintance will bear testimony to this affection. Following Glacier View, Colin and his wife, Cheryl, happily entertained Des and Gillian Ford at their home in Weimar. They also accepted the Ford's return invitation to dinner. Russell and his wife, Enid, enjoyed Robert Brinsmead's company at their dinner table in Australia in 1978.

On one occasion in April 1978 Russell was invited to preach the Wednesday evening service at the Campus Hill Church in Loma Linda. He was booked to stay in Loma Linda Motel. To Russell's surprise, the first person he met there was Geoffrey Paxton, who was staying at the same place. A friendly chat of fifteen minutes ensued. Shortly after, Des Ford was found to be rooming next door. This led to a ninety-minute conversation in Ford's room. We were still Australians meeting abroad, still old college friends. Pastor Jim Wolter, pastor of the Ontario Church, was accompanying Russell. He met Ford, whose views he quite properly opposed, for the first time on that occasion. Pastor Wolter expressed surprise at the amiable tone of that meeting between Desmond and Russell. But surely Christian standards demand nothing less. We long to see Des and Bob and all others influenced by this new thinking return to correct doctrinal convictions. We hope to share eternity with them.

We will not, however, condone their erroneous postulates while awaiting this return. To do so would not help them, nor would it be honorable conduct in view of each Christian's duty to obey his Lord in holding truth aloft. We would urge care in acting against those misled by these errors. Precipitous actions may harm a person who, with loving care, would again walk in the light. In urging this course, we would not extend this view to those teaching our young people. So crucial are the souls of our youth that their salvation cannot be jeopardized by the acquisition of error represented as truth. Thus such teachers must be promptly required to step aside, and efforts to reclaim them must, of necessity, take place while these men and women follow alternative professions. Only thus can our youth be spared.

It now cannot be disputed that the influence of Desmond Ford and Robert Brinsmead is but a faint echo of their influence in former years. This inevitably occurs when men openly spurn the Church of God. The lives of Canright, Ballenger, Kellogg, Jones, Fletcher and Greive may be studied by anyone interested in documenting this phenomenon. We can see in the lives of these men persons whose influence within God's church has been profound, and whose reputations had been high, yet by their course they have lost with great rapidity the esteem of God's people. Not one of these men has lived to see his reputation enhanced by dissociation from God's people.

But now the dangers to God's Church are even more insidious. We have within the Church a widespread network of men and women dedicated to promoting the errors of apostate Protestantism. That which Ford and Brinsmead proclaimed, these persons promote. Yet many of our people appear to be blinded. The course of those who follow this error is now apparent. None need fall into apostasy for lack of knowledge. Only those who deliberately choose the path of error will forsake the narrow road which leads to life eternal.

Many place the blame for the apostasy in the Church upon the leaders. This accusation is unjust and untrue. Inevitably the blame lies with God's people in the pews. Church leaders are simply the servants, first of God, and second of the flock. If God's people permit faithless leaders to continue in office, then clearly the fault is with themselves. Paul laid the blame for the situation we now see in the Church squarely upon the shoulders of the laity. It is through the laxity of a laity, too busy with material matters, which has permitted such a loss of scriptural knowledge, that error comes in undetected by those lost in Laodicean slumber.

> For the time will come when they will not endure sound doctrine; but after their own lusts shall they heap to themselves teachers, having itching ears; and they shall turn away their ears from the truth, and shall be turned unto fables.
> (2Timothy 4:3,4)

Today is this prophecy fulfilled in our ears!

Time is short. *Jesus is coming soon.* This book has been written with the aim of alerting every true soul to the dangers within our midst. It has been written by men fully cognizant of the nearness of the hour and the perils of the time. Speaking of God's truths, Inspiration has declared:

> These words are trustworthy and true. The Lord God who inspires the prophets has sent his angel to show his servants what must shortly happen. And remember, I am coming soon! (Revelation 22:6, NEB)

Chapter 90 Endnotes:

1. This procedure was unanimously approved by the twenty-two hospital presidents in the Far Eastern Division (representing citizens of ten nations—Japan, United States, Great Britain, Korea, Hong Kong, Philippines, Australia, Malaysia, Indonesia and Canada). The selection of questions was carefully made in consultation with the Division officers and others.
2. In fact, the total attendance was less than twenty, and this number included Russell and Dr. Norman John, head of the Religion department of Columbia Union College, who attended as observers.

# Appendixes

# A Worldwide Concern

IN order to show that even by 1976 and 1977 the problem of the *new theology* was seen by a number of people throughout the world, a selection of extracts from some of the letters received by Drs. Clifford and Standish in response to the reading of *Conflicting Concepts* follows:

May 31, 1976—from the wife of an Avondale College teacher:
"I had the privilege for a couple of days, of looking through the book you and Doctor Clifford compiled on the current doctrinal controversies in Australia. For what my humble opinion is worth, I thought it an excellent effort in every way. It shows the differences of opinion very plainly. We pray earnestly that God will bless and guide the distribution of this work. . . . The point that really distresses me is that the Palmdale statement is being claimed up here as a great victory for our college. . . . Dr. Ford claims in one of his chapel talks on tape, that this is a historic new pronouncement."

December 20, 1976—from a college professor in Canada:
"In the last year [1976] there has been a growing interest in righteousness by faith—perhaps I should say that there has been a growing debate on the subject."

March 17, 1977—from a pastor in British Columbia, Canada:
"It would seem that the Australasian Division is facing its greatest crisis ever, and surely now is the hour for God's watchmen to give a certain sound to the trumpet of God's eternal truth."

June 29, 1977—from a lay woman in Canada:
"I wish to say that, as a third-generation Adventist, with grandchildren, I thank the Lord for raising up younger people who will stand for the right though the heavens fall. . . . Recently I have done a good deal of research myself on the errors being taught, not only by Brinsmead but by those who have imbibed the waters of Babylon and are bringing them to our people. . . . We shall continue to praise God for giving you men the burden to meet the Omega of apostasy, and shall pray for your continued guidance in the future. We know it is not easy to stand up and be counted, but how much that courage is needed now!"

November 28, 1976—from a layman in England:

"I have now returned to England after my long tour through the Far East and Australia. It was good to meet with the group at Melbourne, and to discuss some things of mutual interest. I have found your book—Conflicting Concepts of Righteousness by Faith—very stimulating. I write now on behalf of two friends who are anxious to have a copy."

January 17, 1977—from a layman in Great Britain:
"Even in Britain there are quite a number 'bowing the knee to Baal.' The Fordian views are, I suspect, being spread by young Australian evangelists and students at Newbold. Even our local minister, an otherwise excellent young pastor [name deleted] is suspect on righteousness by faith."

January 28, 1977—from a lay woman in Great Britain:
"The more I hear of the Australian situation the more I think of the statement, 'many there be but few will be chosen,' or words to that effect. Last Friday night I really sat down with your book on righteousness by faith and started to read it, and the more convinced I became that it is Truth."

August, 1977—from a layman in Great Britain:
"When we first learned of the conflicting views which have gained such credence in Australia, and especially so in the Theological Department of Avondale, we were astounded, not only with the views propounded but also with the seeming lack of definite action as to safeguarding the training of young members of the ministry at Avondale. . . . We feel very grieved about the situation which has arisen and the effects which will result from it, but are thankful to our heavenly Father that he has raised you and Dr. Clifford up to combat this error. . . . Having nursed and lived in the home of a Plymouth Brethren of the exclusive order, I know how adamant they are in their beliefs and how appealing divorcement from the need of endeavouring by the help of God's Spirit to live a sanctified life can be."

Undated letter—from three lay women in the Greater Sydney Conference and one layman in Queensland:
"We have just read your book on the discussions of 'Justification by Faith' disproving some of Dr. Ford's views. We are very interested."

April 1, 1976—from a pastor in the Greater Sydney Conference:
"I fully appreciate your position in meeting the many criticisms and charges. The one thing I fail to understand is that so many who, in the past, have shared our conceptions and convictions on righteousness by faith are, today either silent or quite vocal—the one in defense of the Church's historic and fundamental position, and the latter, in their support of a view that cannot be denominationally sustained."

May 4, 1976—from a pastor in the Greater Sydney Conference:
"It seems as now the Australasian Division will have to do something with Des. I cannot see how they can continue to hold him in his present position. I would not be surprised that before long he is a leader in the Brinsmead movement."

July 14, 1976—from a pastor in the Greater Sydney Conference:
"I do not see any reason why you should desist with the production and circulation of the said thesis [*Conflicting Concepts*]."

August 15, 1976—from a layman in the Greater Sydney Conference:
"I want you to know, Russell, that I completely support the principles you have been upholding. I am appreciating more clearly the basic concepts Avondale is supporting and yet these come across broadly in such a plausible manner that they are misleading. The tragedy is, however, that the debate on this issue is being focused on personal factors."

November 29, 1976—from a lay woman in the Greater Sydney Conference:
"The devil is working with great power and he knows where to attack at the head of the work—the training of the ministry. . . . We that are older and have had years in the message know the fundamental teaching of this movement, but our young people know practically nothing of it. This is the greatest deception that has ever come into the Seventh-day Adventist Church. One thing I cannot understand is that our leaders have allowed it to go so far. I have been impressed with the Christian way you have handled this serious situation."

March 16, 1977—from a lay woman in the Greater Sydney Conference:
"We have a fresh minister here. You may know him. Just a young man in his early thirties, [name deleted]. He preaches what Des Ford teaches on the Nature of Christ and other subjects. He nearly drives us silly with Greek, Latin and Hebrew, and changes the meaning of words in the Bible such as repentance as that doesn't mean sorry for something we have done, or for sin."

July 7, 1977—from a brother in Holland:
"From time to time I read in literature about you and Dr. Standish. From this information it seems as if you both have written something about the doctrine of justification as taught by Brinsmead and Ford. After the Palmdale discussions and the stand taken by the Brinsmead-Ford wing in our church it was good to read about your remarks of the experience of justification in the *Review* of June 2."

June, 1976—from a lay woman in Avondale:
"I am astounded to know that Dr. Ford is teaching students that Robert Brinsmead has the true light on the subject [Righteousness by Faith]. . . . Thank you for the great service you are doing for God's truth and may it same many from accepting false doctrines."

June 16, 1976—from a pastor in the North New South Wales Conference:
"It troubles me greatly that the B.R.I. Committee appointed to sniff out error and properly deal with the erroneous, has itself become unanimously agreed to advocating error. As long as these minutes which were written up some weeks ago remain to be later passed on to the Australasian Division Committee as that researched and supposedly carefully studied and recommended for official adoption in this Division, the whole of the 'Message' is so threatened with possible

modifications as to become ineffective in rescuing men and women from the fast-flowing current of sin and false religions on this old planet."

July 8, 1976—from a layman in the North New South Wales Conference:
"Recently I received a copy of your Ms. on righteousness by faith. I want to tell you that I was very pleased to see someone at last making a protest in a positive manner."

July 27, 1976—from a lay woman in the North New South Wales Conference:
"Please send me two copies of your paper *Conflicting Concepts of Righteousness by Faith*—I have been so worried by all this and must give one to my daughter just out of Avondale."

October 18, 1976—from a layman in North New South Wales Conference:
"I am glad to know that others are protesting against the teachings of Dr. Ford and R. Brinsmead. I am greatly concerned that Dr. Ford is still allowed to teach at Avondale. Does this mean that the Division has accepted his teaching? The mistake was to allow our men to go to evangelical universities. They are certainly leading our church back to Babylon. . . . I think we have reached a crisis in the S.D.A. Church. It could take us into the Shaking Time. . . . Have you read '*How to Be a Victorious Christian*' by T. A. Davis? I was sorry that H. E. Douglass left the *Review*. These men were upholding Truth."

October 21, 1976—from a layman in the North New South Wales Conference:
"May I ask why Mrs. Ford is allowed to use the College facilities to put out her book which is so opposed to the clear teachings of this Church? And why is Dr. Ford allowed free, unhindered play to advertise the book?

October 23, 1976—from a layman in the North New South Wales Conference:
"It is very encouraging to know that there are others who are willing to stand for God in these perilous times. . . . Are there many pastors teaching the truth now, or are they mainly only the retired men who are understanding the truth? . . . I feel I could place quite a few [copies of *Conflicting Concepts*] with S.D.A.s who are confused over this issue of Ford-Brinsmead theology."

October 25, 1976—from a lay woman in the North New South Wales Conference:
"Truly our Church is asleep, for the sin is creeping in to many of our churches, and even our Pastor here has been indoctrinated by the Ford heresy. . . . What I can't understand is why had Ford not been shifted long ago? Either our leaders do not know the Word of God, or they are in agreement with is being taught. I am praying daily that the Lord will take a hand and shift not only Des Ford but [a pastor who is still active in the leadership of the church in Australia was mentioned] who promotes Ford every chance he gets. . . . I was called to Norfolk Island . . . and lo and behold! it had reached the church there and my relatives, through the young minister that was there. On returning home I wrote to Dr. Ford through the Principal and Committee at Avondale telling Ford he was teaching fallacy at the College and that he would be held responsible for the lives of these young people. . . . I . . . told them that I was over seventy and had known

the message most of my life and what they were teaching was wrong. As for Brinsmead, he and Ford have been working together for some time."

November 21, 1976—from a lay woman in the North New South Wales Conference:
"Believing the teachings of Brinsmead would ultimately develop into the false latter rain and loud cry. I am extremely interested in its progress, knowing that the Truth will follow very closely."

December 5, 1976—from a lay woman in the North New South Wales Conference:
"My husband and I would like to tell you how happy we are that you and Dr. Clifford have stepped out and presented the truth. We only hope that the eyes of those being deluded will be opened. For five years we have waited for something to happen. . . . We had a visit from Pastor [named deleted], an author of several articles on righteousness by faith printed in the *Australasian Record* in 1976]—he asked us our beliefs on the Nature of Christ [note the same as the Sabbath School pamphlet of next quarter] and righteousness by faith [note identical with the *Review and Herald* Extra on Righteousness by Faith] and when we told him he said 'The Church would never accept that.' I could hardly believe what I heard coming from a pastor."

December 5, 1976—from a layman in the North New South Wales Conference:
"Ford's theory was preached a couple of Sabbaths ago by an ex-missionary who is a church school teacher in this area. . . . There are quite a few of us in this North Coast area who are not in harmony with the theology of Ford-Brinsmead-Paxton; but prefer Scripture and the Spirit of Prophecy. We rejoice with you in the truth and have studied Waggoner and Jones' message."

January 25, 1977—from a layman in the North New South Wales Conference:
"Having listened to cassette tapes of Bob Brinsmead's Melbourne Meeting and Llewellyn Jones' interview with yourself and Doctor Clifford and read the report of the February meeting with the Division Committee, I feel a greater concern regarding the present controversy in the S.D.A. Church. I have a granddaughter going to Avondale this year and I am concerned that she will inevitably have to listen to this erroneous teaching now being fostered by the Theology Department. Is it possible that some move of protest could have these men suspended?"

March 1, 1977—from a layman in the North New South Wales Conference:
"We encountered controversy over Righteousness by Faith at Tamworth and Glen Innes. It will be very interesting next quarter when we study Dr. Douglass' lessons."

March 23, 1977—from a lay woman in the North New South Wales Conference:
"Firstly we wanted to tell you that we were able to hear a tape of Bob Brinsmead's answer to your manuscript. . . . We were shocked at the way Bob went on—we were saddened at the way he made a mockery of everything. Something that

really shocked us was that Bob said that Sabbath keeping had nothing to do with our Salvation—what a statement to make."

October 3, 1977—from a Division worker, Singapore:
"I am deeply interested in what you have to say. I have been distressed to hear many popular preachers and theologians present righteousness by faith as though it has only to do with justification. They minimize the law. Their messages do not ring true although they are very appealing to many who think they, at last, had been freed from guilt complexes, etc. To my mind this is a serious heresy."

February 7, 1977—from a pastor in South Africa:
"The thesis is clear enough. There are men in our midst bringing in strange doctrines.... You have pointed out the utter confusion of the Ford-Brinsmead position. Where do we go from here? ... Having rejected the beginning of the Latter Rain and the Loud Cry in 1888 we are in grave danger of accepting false doctrine. It would appear that such a situation now faces the church in a marked way."

April 22, 1977—from a pastor in South Africa:
"How can S.D.A.s become so completely confused as the evidence shows they have? It would seem to me that Paxton is trying to say 'You people are pretty good—you just need to fix up a few things, bow down to my theology, and I will be with you as well as all the Evangelicals. In fact I think the whole Christian world will be yours.' Dare I say, all too much like Matt. 4:8,9. May the Lord help us to know how to reply, 'It is written.'"

July 20, 1977—from a brother in South Africa:
"I recently came across a copy of your booklet, '*Conflicting Concepts of Righteousness by Faith in the S.D.A. Church, Australasian Division*,' and would very much appreciate receiving a copy. If you are interested, I could send you in return a paper on 'Sacred Chronology I, II, III, which establishes the 6,000-year age of the earth. Just let me know if you could use the material and I will send it on. From a declaration made by you and a number of our senior workers in Australia I notice that this is also an issue in Australia, just as it is in America."

November 2, 1976—from a pastor in the South Australian Conference:
"I have a copy of your Biblical Research paper ... and I must say that I am in complete harmony with its subject matter and refutation of the erroneous ideas that are being taught on the subject at Avondale College. We are reaping the results of such teachings in the preaching of the younger pastors who have been educated at Avondale since Dr. Ford has been there by putting forth his questionable views."

June 5, 1977—from a pastor in the South Australian Conference:
"As a student of God's Word, and being particularly interested in Righteousness by Faith—I am conducting a series of church services on the subject—I would like to obtain your book *Conflicting Concepts of Righteousness by Faith*. Also if you have other literature of interest along similar lines. There is, without

doubt, a dangerous type of theology coming into our midst. It is not unsuspected, for Ellen White has warned us of the dangers from within and the heresies that will come in order to wake up the church. It is vitally necessary to take a stand in these things as deception on the Sanctuary and Righteousness by Faith will increase as the end approaches."

Undated letter from a pastor in the North New South Wales Conference:
"We recently had Dr. Ford at our Bible Camp in this conference at which time he went into detail on the subject of Righteousness by Faith. The young people really appreciated his approach.... I am sure you will agree that this is a subject that none of us can afford to be astray on."

September 20, 1976—from a layman in the South New South Wales Conference:
"I feel much in common with people like you who lament that in some circles nearly anything that could be described as distinctive Adventism seems to be considered to have scant importance."

June 24, 1976—from a pastor in the South Queensland Conference:
"As pastor of [large church named] I am meeting a little of the conflict of differing views on this subject [righteousness by faith] and will be most appreciative of any possibility of obtaining a copy of your book."

August, 1976—from a layman in Queensland:
I have mentioned this manuscript to many of our local church, and many have expressed interest in reading it."

November, 1976—from a layman in South Queensland Conference:
"On the weekend some brethren recommended to me a manuscript which you have co-authored. ... I am concerned about the unity of our Church and the irresponsible teaching propounded by some members of our Church."

November 9, 1976—from a layman in the South Queensland Conference:
"On Sabbath 4th inst. my wife and I attended [name of church deleted]. Pastor [name deleted] attended to the spiritual needs of the people. He touched on things new to the wife and me of happenings in and around Avondale which astounded us. Further conversation with the church folk later revealed they had known for a long time of these things. I got into conversation with Pastor [name deleted] after the service. ... Finally he suggested that if I was to contact you, you would be able to supply me with some materials which would inform us of the trend in things today."

June 14, 1977—from a pastor in the South Queensland Conference:
"There isn't the slightest doubt that Ford imbibed quite a stomach full of the Brethren teachings on Futurism. This of course is evidenced by the fact that he quoted so much from the Futuristic Commentators. He claims that there is good in every form of prophetical interpretation including the Jesuitical interpretations. Why doesn't the General Conference call a special conference and decide once and for all the teaching of the Church on these matters? The so-called academics then would have to conform or get out."

Undated letter from a layman in Alabama:
> What do you think of the accuracy of Ray's [Martin's] *'Objective Digest Report'*?

Undated letter from a layman in California:
> "We have a group of about twenty-five out of a thousand in our church that know and understand what is going on in our church, because our pastor has accepted the new teaching on Righteousness by Faith."

Undated letter from a literature evangelist in the Northern New England Conference, USA:
> "There are many of our S.D.A. members here in the Northern New England Conference who are earnestly seeking God's plan for our lives."

August 27, 1976—from a retired Division president. Speaking of the Ford-Brinsmead view the writer stated:
> "They are promulgating a false and most dangerous philosophy; one that is anti-Christian, anti-biblical, anti-denominational and a serious subversion of our Lord Jesus Christ. A philosophy such as this should be strongly challenged and opposed by every believer in, and lover of, the truth which is the power of God unto the salvation of sinners. It pains me that our leadership here in Australia permits this kind of anti-biblical theory to be taught in our college, in our churches, and at our camp meetings. What is wrong with our leadership? I can foresee the development of a serious division in our ranks and a terrible apostasy on the part of many of our church members, unless the issue is handled immediately, wisely, strongly and effectively."

September 5, 1976—from a college president, U.S.A.
> "Of course I am delighted with the final thesis. I am delighted that you recognize the truth of sanctification by faith and give to imparted righteousness its true importance. Glad also that you recognize the value of the 1888 message as presented by the messengers that Ellen G. White endorsed. This is crucial. You show a good Christian spirit."

November 4, 1976—from a conference departmental leader, North Dakota, U.S.A.
> "Recently I was talking to Elder [name deleted] on the telephone and he told me briefly that you . . . were involved in the discussions on Righteousness by Faith that are so common among Adventists in these days. . . . I have been led to believe that a paper written by the two of you would be of assistance to me in developing a true concept of Righteousness by Faith."

December 2, 1976—from a pastor in California:
> "Recently editorials in the *Review and Herald* very strongly support the position that you brethren have taken. Oh, may the Lord help us to keep in tune with heaven, and not run ahead nor lag behind the angels."

January 4, 1976—from a lay woman in California (representing four families):
> "Our church here of 1,000 members is in a spiritual turmoil because our new pastor is preaching and teaching Dr. Ford's views. Consequently some of us

who are studying are very much concerned as you are, for we too feel that this will hinder the finishing of God's work in the earth and delay the coming of Jesus."

January 19, 1977—from a conference departmental leader in the Northern New England Conference, U.S.A.:
"At our workers' meeting in the North New England Conference Elder [name deleted] presented the topic of Righteousness by Faith. In talking with him he mentioned your book. . . . I would love to receive a copy."

February, 1977—from a layman in California:
"I thank God over and over for guiding you brethren in its preparation. I have never read so much clear, beautiful truth in one manuscript. The Ford-Brinsmead teaching is getting a strong following in some of our churches. It is tragic. We *need* your manuscript desperately in order to counteract this."

February 2, 1977—from a pastor in California:
"You gentlemen are not in this battle alone. We are with you. Keep your strength in the Lord and continue to defend Righteousness by Faith as found in the Bible and the Spirit of Prophecy. . . . Our prayers are with you."

February 8, 1977—from a pastor in New Mexico:
"I want to reaffirm my great appreciation of Russell and John's burden and their treatment of the subject. I think they were wise in preparing the summary as they did which permits a sharp focus on the contrast between the various statements of Ford, Brinsmead versus the Word of God. I also appreciated the attitude revealed in the conclusion."

March 11, 1977—from an academy student in California:
"I am deeply concerned with the theological controversy occurring in our church over righteousness by faith, and I tend to side with the position you and Dr. Clifford, as well as most of our leading men, have taken on this issue."

March 25, 1977—from a physician in California:
"Please send us one [copy of *Conflicting Concepts*] . . . we understand that Dr. Desmond Ford will be coming here to P.U.C. in the next few months, and we are very much interested in studying into the various concepts of righteousness by faith in Jesus."

April 20, 1977—from a surgeon in Idaho:
"We have learned from secondhand reports that you have stood stiffly for the truth in recent months during the doctrinal upheavals taking place in Australia."

April 22, 1977—from a layman in California:
"Recently I have received a letter from one of my childhood friends in Germany who is a Conference president [name of conference omitted]. He writes 'Too bad that Dr. Ford has teamed up with Brinsmead and with his false doctrine has poisoned many people in all of our churches in Holland, Germany and Austria.'"

## Appendix A: Worldwide Concern 399

April 22, 1977—from a conference worker in Maine:
"May God bless you as you continue to present this most important subject. It's nice to hear the true message coming from Australia for a change. I just finished reading a manuscript by Dr. Desmond Ford, and I almost cried as I see how well the devil can use the Bible and the Spirit of Prophecy to confuse and mislead people. I'm not saying Mr. Ford is the devil, but he was used by him at Palmdale, although I don't think Mr. Ford knows it. I believe Mr. Ford is very sincere, but he is sincerely WRONG. . . . I have three or four doctors that would like one [a copy of *Conflicting Concepts*] also. If you can, send five copies."

April 24, 1977—from a pastor in U.S.A.:
"Nevertheless, we have a phenomenon on our hands. Certain leaders of our Church in Australia kneeling at the feet of a brilliant Anglican and a gifted, but divisive, ex-church member to discover what truth is! Where is our ringing concern for the development of truth as E. G. White has given the world?"

June, 1977—from a pastor in Arizona:
"I understand that you and Dr. Clifford are in the middle of a war between thruth and error in Australia with Desmond Ford and Brinsmead, etc. . . . It is very encouraging to know that God has men to teach the truth of Righteousness by Faith while error is multiplying. . . . I understand you have done exceptional work in contending with the Brinsmead forces in your land. . . . I know the Ford, Brinsmead theology is a denial of the truth. . . . This heresy is also in America and threatening God's people here. . . . Carry on, brother, for until the battle is over, the victory, this truth will bring us to the true Jesus."

July, 1977—from a lay woman in the West Australian Conference:
"No doubt this letter will surprise you but small groups of loyal Adventists in Perth suburbs have become aware of the controversy regarding the incarnation and righteousness by faith. There are pastors who have openly disagreed with the last *Lesson Quarterly*, and have preached against it. I myself have heard a fearful distortion of the doctrine of justification by faith, also the denial of Christian perfection. I have taken the liberty of writing you as literature from the Brinsmead people is coming in regularly and absolutely nothing from the opposite camp."

July 24, 1977—from a pastor in Ohio, U.S.A.
"I saw your book *Conflicting Concepts of Righteousness by Faith in the Seventh-day Adventist Church* recently on a trip. I am greatly interested in what is happening in the Adventist Church and am looking forward to reading your manuscript."

September 12, 1977—from a lay woman in West Virginia, U.S.A.:
"I appreciate the facts clearly presented in your research paper—*Conflicting Concepts of Righteousness by Faith.*"

October 10, 1976—from a pastor in the Victorian Conference:

"I have been much disturbed at the turn of events in Melbourne, and in respect of the Brinsmead-Ford situation in particular. You are dealing with two very clever and able men who, it seems to me, are careless in the means to the end."

January 24, 1977—from a layman in the West Australian Conference:

"Many of our people over here have been aware of something developing, but were not clear on it. We have a strong Brinsmead movement here in Perth also."

April 5, 1977—from a layman in the West Australian Conference:

"The present controversy in the church is beginning to rage over here. This last week or so it's been laid open for me to see. The Western Australian Seventh-day Adventist Students' Society has accepted Ford-Brinsmead theology it seems."

May 14, 1977—from a pastor in the Western Australia Conference:

"This pastor stated that a Division officer 'told me that a good number of our workers [more of the senior ones] are aware of the issues [on the doctrinal controversy] but are not buying into it yet but will come out into the open later on. It is a pity that they don't come out now, as we surely need them.' . . . We do have some workers who are against the brethren at G.C. and R&H. Some have been writing rather bold letters to the brethren over there."

July 10, 1977—from a pastor, Washington, D.C., U.S.A.

"In the afternoon Elder [a General Conference officer] asked me about the Australian situation. He was recently in Europe and said many times he was asked about the terrible split in the Australian Church. He seems very solid and said he was thinking of writing to Des Ford about it."

August 4, 1977—from a lay woman in Western Australia Conference:

"The book *Questions on Doctrine* was a real sorrow to me, causing me many nights of bitter tears. *Movement of Destiny* whilst containing much valuable truth and information contains also 'The sting of the serpent.' As I ponder these things in my heart I cannot blame Dr. Ford entirely. The seed in infidelity was sown in our conversations with Martin and Barnhouse."

August, 1977—from a layman in the Western Australia Conference:

"Sadly the position is quite poor here in the west. Many ministers hold error as truth and are successfully sowing seeds to this effect. Still, there is a small number holding fast to the truth and undoubtedly there are many others scattered throughout the west."

# B  Conflicting Concepts

BELOW are the significant objections which the authors received to the manuscript, *Conflicting Concepts*:

September 20, 1976—from a layman, New South Wales:
"I believe that you err in denying that real sin remains (though does not reign) in the hearts of the regenerate."

July 10, 1976—from a pastor, Greater Sydney Conference:
"I think you are entitled to know that I think I stand on the opposite side of the fence to you on the question but I am anxious to be fully informed on both sides of the question."

September 14, 1976—from a lay woman, South Queensland Conference:
"Would you please check with Dr. Des Ford of Avondale College on what he is teaching? I think if you had personal contact with him you would find that the book *Conflicting Concepts of Righteousness by Faith* is not worthy of you as it contains many misquotes and twistings of his actual teachings."

August 12, 1976—from an Avondale College theology student:
"Although I do not support the theology of this paper, I must say that this book is doing a lot of good here at Avondale in that it is making students study and digest what they themselves believe. It is very true that there are a good many people who would accept anything that Dr. Ford or Robert Brinsmead teach, and this is something I despise in a person."

August 20, 1976—from an Avondale College theology student:
"I came across many inconsistencies . . . my concern is not alone for Avondale's good name and that of its faculty. It is also for those young church members, still partaking of the milk of the word, who may be caused to stumble because of *Conflicting Concepts*."

August 5, 1976—from a pastor, Victorian Conference:
"It would seem that in your desire to give credibility to your views, subtle and deceptive methods have been employed. . . . Brethren, it is my firm belief that your questionable methodology, inaccurate quoting, your erroneous exposition of Scripture, are all explained by—and consistent with—your misunderstanding of the Gospel."

## Appendix B: Conflicting Concepts 402

Undated—from a pastor, Victorian Conference:
"I am amazed, Russ, at the horrible caricature of the Ford-Brinsmead position which the paper manages to create. It is a masterpiece of misinterpretation, in short, a lie (a lie is any perversion of truth . . .). To say the least, I am distressed that a man of your intellectual and spiritual nature would put your name to something so evidently lacking in truth, lacking understanding of the real issues, lacking in scholarship, sensitivity, something betraying a heinous pretense of acquaintance with dogmatic theology and history, and so inept with Scripture and E.G.W."

October 12, 1976—from a layman, Victorian Conference:
"I am sorry to have to say so but I believe I have demonstrated good reason for my concern."

May 4, 1977—from a layman, Greater Sydney Conference:
"Your book itself is more concerned with the *Conflicting* of the concepts, rather than the concepts themselves. And when you continue (and probably your next publication will support my statement even further) to refer to the Ford-Brinsmead theory, which you should know is an emotive expression aimed at short-cutting your cause into lay people's sympathies."

March 29, 1976—from a Division officer.
"I would appeal to you and to all who share your concern to refrain from discussion that would tend to lead to hasty action which might be regretted at a later date."

September 21, 1976—from a pastor, Victorian Conference:
"However, when you do engage in a crusade, at least you must expect it to be bloody and two-sided. . . . Your magnum opus *C.C.* is nothing but a violent attack on the theology department of Avondale College and Des Ford in particular. . . . I can only say that if I were the devil I would be doing exactly what you are doing."

August 20, 1976—from a pastor, Victorian Conference:
"In the area of Medicine I look to you and John as professionals. In the light of the material you have produced I am led to the conclusion that in the area of Theology you are laymen and amateurs."

November 29, 1976—from an Avondale College theology department lecturer:
"You have heard correctly that I have been most grossly misrepresented in your book."

# C  Correspondence with Church Editor

IN order to obtain a background for this letter from the editor of the *Australasian Record*, it is important to quote in full the letter which generated the comments. This letter was addressed to Dr. Desmond Ford, but a copy was also sent to the editor of the *Australasian Record*.

"Greetings from this side of the world! I trust that all is well with you and your family.

"I have tried to read carefully your article in the *Australasian Record*, December 13, entitled 'Scripture Can Be Dreadful,' and as you might anticipate, I find it difficult to accept at least some of it.

"Your last paragraph in the first column certainly is of concern to me. It seems the references you use in reference to 'the erroneous nature of all theories of sanctification which teach erradication [sic] of carnal propensities', are not directly relevant to this theme. In fact, the reference in the second volume of *Spiritual Gifts*, page 14, certainly seems to infer as the paragraph continues, that *there is* to be this change. Ellen White says on page 15, 'I must experience the soul-purifying effects of the truth, that when it was preached, it would find a response in my own heart.' Her whole burden in many of these articles is how she will find that fuller relationship and experience with Christ. Certainly the references that you have used here do not in any wise allude to the eradication of the carnal propensities. I believe your comment to be contrary to both Scripture and Spirit of Prophecy. As, for example Romans 8:6–9 expressed a viewpoint in the opposite direction.

"Even more plain is *3T* 475's assertion that the carnal mind must die. Because of the critical importance of the present controversy I am deeply concerned that no misrepresentation of the Bible or Spirit of Prophecy reference be made. The issues are vital.

"With you I want to see truth triumphant that Jesus might soon come. With personal best wishes and New Year greetings." (Letter written by Dr. Colin Standish to Dr. Desmond Ford, December 21, 1976)

Below is the complete reply of the editor of the *Australasian Record*.

"You will kindly stay in after school and write out twenty times the word eradication; then, when you have learned it, you may go home to your supper.[1] And, perhaps, you had better get your secretary to write it out twenty times too, the naughty girl![2]

"I see you are still combing the *Australasian Record* for peccadillos and grosser sins; ah well, I will try to smile under the chastening rod of correction. Russell, bless his evil old heart, espouses the cause of instant sanctification![3] Do you go along with that also? I hope you murmur to yourself ten times every night before dropping off to sleep 'they chucked Brinsmead out of the church twelve years ago because he preached perfection; watch your step, dear Colin, that might even happen to you!' Such a salutory recital each night might have a beneficial effect, who knows?

"Of course, I can see your problem. The sad tome which John Clifford and Russell jointly fathered,[4] was quoted [though not mentioned by name] as defining sin as 'the *wilfull* transgression of a known law' and therein, of course, our brotherly nature (sanctified albeit) came to the fore. Col, what would we do without you? as a corrector of heretics and as one who keeps his evil eye on the Australian brethren from the dizzy heights of Columbia Union College, noting every minor *abberation* and minute heresy. I commend you, and I shall have a citation made for you to be presented at the next G.C. conference. Such diligence, such earnest dedication, should not go unrewarded. A better idea strikes me! I shall award you the Gold-plated Cuspidor Award so that you may spit in disgust whenever you see a theological discrepancy in the AUSTRALASIAN RECORD. That ought to relieve your pent-up feelings somewhat, and allow you to get rid of your repressions.

"It so happens, that, *inspite* of your carefully documented letter, I would still present Des's article exactly as it is, and point out to you that the great mistake in the paragraph to which you allude is not the string of quotations that he makes, but that pathetic and heretical definition cooked up by those amateur theologians who insist on burning their fingers in the white heat of theological discussion. Any half-pied theologian can shoot holes through that weak old definition. I am sure you must have blushed to the roots of your theological hair to see such a thing as that. To say that sin is 'the willful transgression of a known law' must be the faux pas of all time. What about the sins of ignorance that God winks at?[5] What about sins of omission?[6] I could go on, but I have no wish to embarrass.

"Col, I gave Russell a little advice some time ago, and I am sure you must have read it somewhere, but I am going to repeat myself at the risk of ruining a beautiful friendship. For pity's sake, stop being conscience to your brethren; stop appointing yourself as the authority of theology. Above all, stop thinking that you have the sole right to determine what is right for your brethren. Believe me, I offer this suggestion sincerely. You are going to get hurt this way, and I for one would be very sorry to see it happen. I may have sounded a trifle browned off, even to the point of flippancy, in the earlier part of this letter. Browned off I admit to being; I am browned off because I see a good man whose theology is sound and Scriptural, whose dedication to the Spirit of Prophecy is second to none, being shot at whenever he puts pen to paper. I can tell you that I have listened to Des Ford either personally or on tape as much as most people, I would think. I have never been able to bring a charge

## Appendix C: Correspondence with Church Editor

against him of theological dishonesty, loose thinking, or even incipient heresy.[7] Moreover, I find that, unless he is drawn into a discussion, he is happy to let a man have his own feelings about theological matters and his kindness in dealing with his detractors must surely be a lesson to even yourself. I suggest, dear boy, that you mull over that lesson; I suggest, too, that in gray areas you ought not to see only black and white. There are some things, you know, where it is impossible for even you and me to be wrong. Again let me sound a clear warning against the perfectionism which you seem to be mesmerized by. Let me say it, and say it loudly; We threw Brinsmead out for this. Why are you courting the same fate? Do you have a death wish, or something? How can you expect to be perfect until these old bodies of ours are changed at the moment of glorification? On second thoughts, I think it might be better if you didn't bombard me with ten pages from the Spirit of Prophecy by way an answer; I guess I have them all on file anyway.

"In spite of all I have said, please understand this; I have said what I have said to prevent disaster overtaking you. I believe that the Lord has called you to do a job at C.U.C. Why don't you get on with it, and stop reaching your long arm across the Pacific to box the ears of anybody who speaks contrary to what you think ought to be said. Think about it; people have got the reputation for being humbugs for far less than this.

"In spite of all I have said, my best wishes, believe me, accompany this letter." (Letter from Editor of *Australasian Record* to Dr. Colin Standish, dated February 8, 1977)

This letter does reveal the uncritical support which Dr. Desmond Ford received from a large number of the church leaders. Of course, when Desmond Ford was exposed by the General Conference there was a rush of ministers protesting that they did not believe all that Dr. Ford taught. The authors soon found that those making this protestation believed 99.9% of what he did teach and continued to do so.

Appendix C Endnotes:

1. Undoubtedly the editor was utilizing as the basis for this statement the fact that he had been Colin's respected teacher for five years in high school.
2. It will be noticed that the second time the word *eradication* was used in Colin's letter it was spelled correctly. [Note my italics (*abbreviation, wilfull, inspite*) on the same page—ed.]
3. Of course, Russell believes no such thing.
4. *Conflicting Concepts*
5. The writer seemed to be confusing a text of Scripture. Actually the text says,
   > And the times of this ignorance God winked at. (Acts 17:30)

   This text actually teaches that without knowledge there is no sin. It complements Christ's own statements:
   > If I had not come and spoken to them, they had not had sin: but now they have no cloak for their sin. (John 15:22)

   Paul also affirmed,
   > For until the law sin was in the world: but sin is not imputed when there is no law. (Romans 5:13)

   Sister White was directly told exactly the same thing by an angel of God:
   > Said the angel: 'If light come, and that light is set aside or rejected, then comes condemnation and the frown of God; but before the light comes, there is no sin, for there is no light for them to reject.' (*1T* 116)

   The editor was in error in complaining about the definition of sin as being the willful transgression of a known law. This is precisely what God has revealed to us through the Spirit of Prophecy.
   > No man can be forced to transgress. His own consent must first be gained; the soul must purpose the sinful act, before passion can dominate over reason, or iniquity triumph over conscience. Temptation, however strong, is never an excuse for sin. (*5T* 177)
6. If one decides to omit to pay his tithe, that is just as much a willful transgression of God's law as if he performed a sin of commission. To categorize sins of omission as non-willful is incorrect.
7. Subsequent events have demonstrated just how poor this judgment was.

# D  Reply to Australasian Division Spokesman

a. On a number of occasions you[1] discussed the current Australian Theology problem with me in Sydney at the end of 1974 and beginning of 1975. I hesitate to place on paper the full details since you always spoke to me at the conclusion of a medical consultation in the Fox Valley Medical Centre. For purposes of confidentiality I would require your permission to reveal this information in a letter, copies of which may be revealed to others—a simple signed note from you will be sufficient. In the meantime I will protect your confidentiality.

b. As you know, Pastor L. Jones has openly stated to you in writing, in a letter dated 10th May 1976 that while you were still a member of the Theology Department of Avondale College you said that you were teaching one aspect of doctrine in your classroom and Doctor Ford was teaching the opposite. You further stated that when the ground swell of concern grew to sufficient levels you would be found standing with the Concerned Brethren.

c. A senior Division Officer[2] in December 1975 confided to me that prior to the 1975 General Conference session, you had, in expressing your concern for Avondale College Theology, stated that you intended to mute your concern at that time so as not to jeopardize your chances of re-election as Field Secretary of the Australasian Division. He stated that you expressed your admirable desire to serve for a further five years, so—you said—you could more effectively use your influence against what you believed to be the false theological teachings emanating from Avondale College. This conversation occurred at 148 Fox Valley Road, Wahroonga.

d. A senior Officer of the General Conference[3] while in Melbourne in January 1976 in the presence of Pastor O. K. Anderson, Pastor Llewellyn Jones, Pastor J. B. Keith and myself, stated, in your defense, that you had expressed to him your concern about the errors being taught by the Avondale Theology Department. We also enclosed a photostat copy of your article (January 23, 1975) in the *Review and Herald* to remind you of your stance which was formerly so clearly in line with the General Conference position and that also presented in our manuscript."

Appendix D Endnotes:

1. See Chapter entitled Curious Questions.
2. In fact this was a poor use of terms. The person concerned was not a Division officer but an Australasian Division departmental head.
3. Pastor N. Dower, ministerial secretary of the General Conference. Once again a poor term was used due to an inadequate understanding at the time, of the restricted meaning of the term *officer* in denominational parlance.

# E   Misinformation

PASTOR Maurice Peterson was a mature man when he accepted the message of the Seventh-day Adventist Church in New Zealand. His initial interest in the faith was generated by his study of Uriah Smith's book, *Daniel and the Revelation*. After a brief period as a literature evangelist Pastor Peterson attended Avondale College to study for the ministry.

During one of his classes under Dr. Ford the class members were informed that Uriah Smith's book was a most unreliable exposition of prophecy. Naturally, this statement disturbed Pastor Peterson since he felt indebted to Uriah Smith for arousing his interest in our message. Because of this fact he questioned Dr. Ford concerning this opinion. In so doing Pastor Peterson mentioned that he believed that Sister White had stated that Uriah Smith's book would last until the end of time and that she advised God's people to study the book.

In his reply Dr. Ford stated that Sister White had advised Uriah Smith to revise the book. Still not satisfied with this reply Pastor Peterson asked for documentary evidence of this fact. Dr. Ford was evidently not pleased with this questioning of his statement. With most students, Dr. Ford's word was sufficient evidence of itself. "You asked for a reference! I'll give you three!" Dr. Ford quickly provided that which he had promised.

The younger members of the class appeared to be appalled by Pastor Peterson's questioning of Dr. Ford's word. They felt he was decidedly put down when Dr. Ford not only supplied the single reference requested but met that request three times over.

When Pastor Peterson, who had somehow managed to record all three references, examined the pages indicated, he found that they made absolutely no mention whatsoever of Uriah Smith or his book, much less Sister White's alleged request for a revision. Puzzled by this fact, Pastor Peterson sought Dr. Ford privately and mentioned his finding. When confronted by his obvious inability to supply proof of his assertion, Dr. Ford simply stated, "Yes, I know, I just wanted you to learn the lesson that you cannot believe everything you hear." It was indeed a lesson which Pastor Peterson immediately learned. It led to his thoroughly examining all that he heard within the classes of Dr. Ford.

However, since Pastor Peterson did not disclose his findings to the class as a whole, yet another generation of ministers was led to doubt the prophetic truths within Uriah Smith's book.

# F    Counterfeit Baptismal Vows

THE following is a portion of the letter sent to the Secretary of the Australasian Division concerning a dangerous incident in which a modified form of the baptismal affirmation was used by the pastor of the Avondale College Church.

"Another evidence of the continued acceptance of non-Adventist doctrines at Avondale College is the use of counterfeit baptismal vows at a college baptism held June 20, 1981. On what pretext could the College church pastor presume to usurp the authority of the General Conference in plenary session? Pastor Taylor, since you have kindly supplied us with a copy of the counterfeit baptismal vows, the fact of their use cannot be disputed. We wish to express our deepest concern that you would defend such a serious breach of Church procedure. This leaves the door wide open for all ministers to construct baptismal vows in accordance with their own and/or candidates' wishes. Such a course could only lead to doctrinal chaos within the Church.

"The explanation provided by the Avondale College Church pastor in which he claimed his counterfeit format was 'adapted in the style to reflect the personalities of the three young people' is totally unacceptable. Again, upon what line of correct thinking could he believe it prudent to omit the specific requirements to abstain from alcohol, tobacco and drugs on the grounds of there being Pathfinders present in the congregation? We would have thought that you, as a former Director of the Division Temperance Department would have been in strong opposition to this substitution. Further, when the subtle changes from the authorized vows are analyzed, it becomes obvious that this is no coincidence, but a designed attempt to substitute counterfeit vows which are acceptable to those who persist in promulgating the unscriptural views of the Fordian theology in defiance of the church. Below, an analysis of these vows clearly unmasks this effort.

"1. **GENUINE**. Do you accept the death of Jesus Christ on Calvary as the sacrifice for the sins of men, and believe that through faith in His shed blood men are saved from sin and its penalty?
**COUNTERFEIT**. Jesus has died for my sins, and by faith in Him I am saved from sin's guilt and penalty.
**COMMENT**. Note that "saved from sin" is amended to "saved from sin's guilt." This is no accident, for the hallmark of the Fordian theology, espoused by many

## Appendix F: Counterfeit Baptismal Vows

lecturers at Avondale, is that God cannot give power to overcome sin and that God removes the guilt alone.

"2. GENUINE. Do you accept the Ten Commandments as still binding upon Christians and is it your purpose, by the power of the indwelling Christ, to keep this law?
COUNTERFEIT. Because Jesus has won my heart I will honor his [sic] law.
COMMENT. Note that the word "keep" has been replaced by "honor."

"3. GENUINE. . . . Is it your purpose, by the power of the indwelling Christ, to keep this law, which requires the observance of the seventh day of the week as the Sabbath of the Lord?
COUNTERFEIT. I will honor his [sic] law, including His commandment of love to respect his [sic] Sabbath.
COMMENT. Notice once again "keep" is replaced, this time by "respect." Since the president of the Greater Sydney Conference, who is known to be an ardent exponent of the Fordian theology, claims that he has never kept a Sabbath day holy, the significance of this change is apparent. Further, it is most unfortunate that at a time when many espousing the Fordian theology are questioning the need to keep the seventh day as the Sabbath, that this is not specified. It is an ominous omission.

"4. GENUINE. Do you believe that your body is the temple of the Holy Spirit and that you are to honor God by caring for your body, avoiding the use of that which is harmful, abstaining from all unclean foods, from the use, manufacture, or sale of alcoholic beverages, the use, manufacture, or sale of tobacco in any of its forms for human consumption and from the misuse of, or trafficking in, narcotics or other drugs?
COUNTERFEIT. Jesus has all there is of me, including my body and my physical strength. I will not spoil its beauty or dishonor Him by habits that defile.
COMMENT. To disregard the specific matters of temperance opens the door to a grave reduction in standards within the church. Further, the omission of prohibition of unclean foods is significant since unclean foods may be eaten in New Testament times.

"5. GENUINE. Is the soon coming of Jesus the blessed hope in your heart and are you determined to be personally ready to meet the Lord?
COUNTERFEIT. Jesus is coming soon, I long to meet Him.
COMMENT. Note the failure to emphasize personal readiness for Jesus' coming. This is consistent with the belief that God does not empower obedience." (Letter to Division Secretary, signed by ten pastors and lay people, dated 24 August, 1981)

# G  Changed Convictions

"IN his address to the now famous P.U.C. Forum Meeting of October 1979, Dr. Ford stated that he had not believed the doctrines of the Investigative Judgment and the heavenly Sanctuary as taught by Adventists, for over 35 years. Some of the questions (below) show that during that time he clearly did declare himself in print in favor of these very doctrines. Either the truth was being mishandled back then, or he was mishandling it in his statement at the Forum meeting: there can be no other conclusion. How sad that it has come to this! How difficult does Satan make it for us to perceive our own selves objectively." (Robert Kalinowski, Doctrine, Deviation and Delusion: *Landmarks*, June 1983)

A comparison of Ford's two differing views in four vital areas of doctrine is presented. It will be seen that in the mid-1960s Ford expressed himself openly as favoring the truth. However, by the mid-1970s he had become bolder in the presentation of his errors. This comparison was made by Brother Kalinowski.

**RIGHTEOUSNESS BY FAITH**
Pre 1967—"Our message has to do with Sanctification. The Reformation dealt with Justification. Our message is Sanctification. God wants a people such as described in Rev. 14:1–5, without fault before the throne of God, without guile. They are people in which Sanctification has had its perfect work. The Sabbath is a sign and seal of it. The Sabbath tells the power of God and the love of God. In other words, the gospel." (D. Ford, *Sermon at Greater Sydney Camp Meeting*, Blacktown, 1966) Post 1975—"Righteousness by faith is only another way of saying Justification by faith." (D. Ford, *Extract from a letter to an enquirer*, c. 1975) "To accept Christ and stress holiness and experience is essentially legalism." (Mrs. D. Ford, *The Soteriological Implications of the Human Nature of Christ*, p. 10) "That other [false] gospel says . . . Righteousness by faith is both Justification and Sanctification." (*Ibid.*, 9)

**THE SECOND COMING**
Pre-1967—"Paul's second epistle to the Thessalonians expressly warned the Christians of his day that the second advent of Jesus was not imminent." (*Signs of the Times*, Aug. 1, 1964)

Post-1976—"The evidence is overwhelming that Christ was saying He planned to return to that very generation He was addressing." (D. Ford, *Glacier View Thesis*, 297)

## THE YEAR-DAY PRINCIPLE
Pre-1967—"The believer in the year-day principle has just as much evidence of truth of his belief as he could expect. He will admit that objections can be raised to this theory, but realizes that these are few compared with the objections that can be raised to the rejection of the principle. Truth here, as in every other philosophical matter, is determined by the weight of the evidence." (D. Ford, *Ministry*, July 1964, 19)

Post 1975—"It is quite impossible to prove the year-day principle is a Biblical datum." (D. Ford, *Glacier View Thesis*, 278)

## THE INVESTIGATIVE JUDGMENT
Pre 1967—"The cleansing of the sanctuary referred to in Daniel 8:14 has reference to Christ's final work in heaven for His people, a work of investigative judgment which parallels the last work of the typical high priest of Israel." (D. Ford, Australasian *Signs of the Times*, June 1, 1964)

Post-1975—"God does not need books and 140 years to settle the destiny of men. Neither do the angels and unfallen worlds or inhabitants of the earth stand to profit by an investigative judgment." (D. Ford, *Glacier View Thesis*, 278)

# H Pastor W. W. Fletcher

IT is instructive to examine the prompt method of dealing with Pastor W. W. Fletcher when he proposed virtually identical views on the Sanctuary and the Spirit of Prophecy to that taught by those promoting the *new theology*. Pastor A. G. Daniells, who spent time traveling with Pastor Fletcher in New Zealand in 1928 reported the following summary of Pastor Fletcher's beliefs:

"1. He [Pastor Fletcher] does not accept our teachings on Christ's two-fold ministry in the heavenly Sanctuary.

"2. He knows nothing that was to take place in the heavenly Sanctuary at the close of the 2,300 years prophecy.

"3. He does not believe the judgment began in 1844.

"4. He has nothing to show that the three-fold message of Rev. 14:6 was to begin in 1844 or at any other definite time.

"5. He does not accept our views of the Spirit of Prophecy as applied to Sister E. G. White." (Letter written by Pastor W. G. Turner, president of the Australasian Union Conference to Church leaders in Australia dated Dec. 4, 1930)

Pastor Fletcher not only had long discussions with Pastor Daniells, who had been General Conference president 1901–1922, but he also entered into a long correspondence with Pastor Daniells' successor, Pastor W. A. Spicer, in 1929. He also held discussions with Pastor C. H. Watson who was appointed General Conference president in 1930.

The Australasian Union Conference appointed a sub-committee which met March 11–13, 1930 to examine Pastor Fletcher's doctrinal position. It is significant that this small sub-committee included a very able lay Bible student, Brother C. H. Pretyman. Brother Pretyman's utilization should be an example for present day Biblical Research Institutes. Other members of the sub-committee were Pastor A. H. Piper (chairman), Pastor C. M. Snow, Pastor Robert Hare and Pastor E. H. Guilliard. Apart from Pastor Snow, the authors have met all these men. Pastor Piper (father-in-law of Pastor Eric Hare of Burma and General Conference fame, was a member of the first family to accept the Adventist message in New Zealand. Pastor Guilliard was known to us because he performed our parents' wedding ceremony.

Pastor Arthur Knight, another of the Concerned Brethren, typed Pastor Fletcher's presentation to this committee. Pastor Knight perceived enough error in that manuscript to keep him true to the principles of our faith for the remaining fifty years of his life.

It may also be noted that in addition to a lay member on this sub-committee, it was not hampered by the presence of men who shared Pastor Fletcher's doubts. This was a great distinction from present examining committees. The men in 1930 were selected for their fidelity to the truth. There was no resort to theologians, perhaps because they were few within our ranks at that time. Pastor Snow, an American, was editor of the Australasian *Signs of the Times*. We could learn lessons from the composition of that committee.

This sub-committee not only upheld the sanctuary doctrine but it also reaffirmed "that the expression 'the testimony of Jesus' indicates the manifestation of the prophetic gift in the remnant church." (Report of the sub-committee on Pastor W. W. Fletcher's Views, 9)

Later Pastor Fletcher was given the opportunity to present his understanding to a committee of the General Conference. This committee consisted of O. Montgomery (chairman), C. P. Bollman, W. H. Branson, I. H. Evans, L. E. Froom, W. E. Howell, C. A. Irwin, M. E. Kern, J. L. McElhaney, F. D. Nichol, E. R. Palmer, W. A. Spicer, and F. M. Wilcox. Pastor Fletcher's views were, interestingly, closely examined by men who led God's Church for over half a century—A. G. Daniells (1902–1922), W. A. Spicer (1936–1950) and W. H. Branson (1950–1954).

The conclusion of this sub-committee was, "We believe that Brother Fletcher's principal propositions are fundamentally wrong; that therefore the conclusions he has reached and to which he holds tenaciously, believing in these propositions, are also wrong." (Quoted in letter written by Pastor W. G. Turner, Dec. 4, 1930)

Had the Australasian Division acted as promptly with Dr. Ford and had its Biblical Research Institute done its duty as did this committee, the hurt of the *new theology* would have been greatly reduced. Many souls now desperately confused and others perhaps lost eternally might have been saved.

# A Statement of Protest Concerning a Letter to Elder Duncan Eva from the Australasian Signs Editor

PRESENTED to Australasian Division president at Wahroonga on December 19, 1980, by Pastors Needham, Cooke, Burnside and Breaden.

This protest was presented by the four retired pastors as a result of a request by a group of forty experienced and proven ministers and laymen, who were greatly disturbed at the appointment of the ex-editor of the *Signs* as president of the Greater Sydney Conference.

"We appreciate this opportunity to talk with you, as the leader of our Church in the Australasian Division. Our approach is made within the provisions of the Denominational Working Policy, pages 30, 31, point 5, which reads: "Thus our organization makes provision that every agency in the work, from the individual in the remotest mission station, to the responsible committees at every stage of the organization, is assured full privilege, without prejudice, of representing opinion and conviction, and asking consideration and counsel in matters affecting life and service."

"Copies of a letter from *Signs* Editor to Elder Duncan Eva, dated March 11, 1980, have been in our hands for several days. We understand that copies of this letter are currently being circulated in the U.S.A. We have not viewed the original letter, but its authenticity appears to have been established by your visit to Pastor Burnside's home on Wednesday morning, December 16.

"Because we have one-hundred percent commitment to the published doctrines of our Church, as found in such documents as the CHURCH MANUAL, the BAPTISMAL CERTIFICATE and the October 1980 MINISTRY MAGAZINE, and because we have been ordained as guardians and defenders of the original Seventh-day Adventist faith, we are shocked and alarmed by the *Signs* Editor's letter. The grounds for our alarm are as follows:

"GROUND NO. 1
The open skeptical and critical sentiments expressed in the *Signs* Editor's letter.
(a) His apparently unquestioning acceptance of Raymond Cottrell's tape-recorded criticisms of our historic doctrine of the Sanctuary and the Judgment.

(b) His open repudiations (based largely upon Cottrell's criticism) of key elements of our original Sanctuary doctrine.
Examples:
Cottrell completely blows the lid off the 2300-days doctrines.
Cottrell makes it abundantly clear that Scripture does NOT teach the 2300-day prophecy to mean what we have traditionally taught.
Cottrell has proved that it is impossible to substantiate the Sanctuary doctrine from the Scriptures.
The 2300-day doctrine, with the traditional view of the Sanctuary doctrine is untenable from Scripture, etc., etc.
(c) His unmistakable inference that Elder Duncan Eva has abandoned the original Seventh-day Adventist concept of an actually existing Sanctuary in heaven.
(d) His statements that gravely impugn the credibility—and the honesty—of past and present leaders of our General Conference.
Examples:
Cottrell has proved that we have known this—i.e. the insupportability of the 2300-days doctrine—for many years, but have been guilty of a gigantic cover-up.
We have been misled by a hierarchy . . . which knew these things but which has elected to cover up the truth.
I was angry because truth had been swept under the carpet, because honesty had been given a deadly wound . . . because bigotry in high places has been uncovered . . . because the 'little people' of the Church have been misled by men who would not trust them with the truth as they knew it to be, etc.
(e) His repeated claims that many Australian Adventists share his own skepticism concerning the Scriptural validity of our Sanctuary truth and the ethical integrity of our General Conference leaders.
(f) His admission that his skepticism concerning key-elements of our Sanctuary truth has been part of his mentality for years past and that, long ago, he had resolved not to preach on this doctrine.
(g) His plea that sharply conflicting interpretations of the Sanctuary doctrine be allowed to have equal status under the umbrella of Seventh-day Adventist orthodoxy.

"GROUND NO. 2
The fact that the *Signs* Editor's criticisms of our historic Sanctuary positions were made known to Elder Duncan Eva—and apparently to you—in March of this year, which is nine months ago.

"GROUND NO. 3
The fact that since the *Signs* Editor's letter was written, and after prayerful and intensive Bible study, the world leadership of our Church has, on two historic occasions, publicly reaffirmed its unchanged and unqualified allegiance to our original

doctrines of the Sanctuary, the Judgment and the unique doctrinal authority of the Ellen G. White writings.

"The two occasions were (1) at Dallas, in April, and (2) at Glacier View in August. These reaffirmations of the faith of our pioneers have been so deliberate, so specific and so unequivocal that, in the October MINISTRY, for example, our Church leaders have 'burned their bridges behind them' in an unqualified commitment to our original Sanctuary doctrine.

"GROUND NO. 4
The fact that you, as chief shepherd and watchman over God's flock in the Division, have failed to implement the mandates of Dallas and Glacier View, and to discipline the *Signs* Editor, as a self-confessed antagonist of some of the cardinal features of our published Seventh-day Adventist faith.

"However, through the columns of the RECORD and in public statements made at Avondale, Wahroonga, Yarrahappini, etc., you have repeatedly declared your own unqualified allegiance to the fundamental articles of our historic faith—as specifically defined at Dallas and at Glacier View. You have also publicly voiced your conviction that no person can honourably remain in the Seventh-day Adventist preaching or teaching ministry who does not give one-hundred percent allegiance to the published tenets of our historic faith.

"We are senior Seventh-day Adventist ministers, who have given the best years of our lives to expounding and defending the original, unchanged Seventh-day Adventist Message. We are also pledged to support you in the faithful discharge of your duty. Yet, in this present situation, we cannot support your course of action, in what seems to be an inexplicable failure to deal decisively with a privileged and articulate purveyor of error, whose doctrinal sentiments, if given free expression, must irreparably sabotage and destroy our beloved faith.

"Accordingly, we now present to you:

"1. **A SOLEMN REMONSTRANCE**
"In the name of Christ, and His pure Biblical truth, as uniquely committed to the Seventh-day Adventist people, we solemnly protest at the fact that the *Signs* Editor has been permitted to retain until now his privileged position as Editor of the **SIGNS OF THE TIMES** and the **RECORD**, and has recently been allowed to accept a position as president of the Greater Sydney Conference—all without written evidence that he has totally repudiated the damaging doctrinal sentiments expressed in his letter of March 11 to Elder Duncan Eva.

"2. **AN URGENT REQUEST**
"We request that steps be taken, without delay, to call the *Signs* Editor to account in terms of the provisions of our **CHURCH MANUAL** and our **MINISTER'S MANUAL**, governing the activities of professed Seventh-day Adventists who are

found to be teaching contrary to 'the established faith of the body.' (See references at the end of this letter.)

"Also, we request that you give us your personal assurance, in writing, that the *Signs* Editor will be required to submit a specific, written repudiation of his skeptical comments concerning the Sanctuary, the Judgment, the 2300-days prophecy and the doctrinal authority of Ellen G. White's writings—or risk the review of his ministerial standing.

"We request, further, that he be required to make a written disavowal of all the erroneous material that he has allowed to be printed in the Australasian **SIGNS OF THE TIMES** and the **RECORD**, for many years past.

"We have converts to Adventism in all parts of Australia whom we have indoctrinated in strict accordance with our Church's Baptismal Certificate, and who are confused and distressed by the known doctrinal aberrations of influential Adventist spokesmen such as the *Signs* Editor. These converts turn to us for reassurance and guidance. But we cannot reassure them unless we can have in our hands an unequivocal statement from you that you cannot and will not support those Adventist workers who are expressing themselves in harmony with the doctrinal sentiments set out in the *Signs* Editor's letter.

"The precedent upon which our request is based is found in the recently published section of the Australasian Division Committee, relative to the withdrawal of Dr. Desmond Ford's ministerial credentials. This action reads as follows:

> Dr. Ford did indicate that he would be prepared to be silent on these issues (i.e. his criticism of historic Adventist positions on the Sanctuary and the Judgment), but the brethren told him that a minister cannot be silent on two such distinctive matters of doctrine, and still represent the Seventh-day Adventist Church. (Letter written to Australasian Division president by Pastors A.C. Needham, A. P. Cooke, G. Burnside & F. Breaden, Dec. 19, 1980)

In verbally replying to the above letter, which was read to him in the presence of the Division secretary, and the Trans-Tasman Union Conference, the Australasian Division president said that when he received the copy of the *Signs* Editor's letter to D. Eva, he wrote to the editor informing him that his letter "was a mistake." He then said that the *Signs* editor answered his letter admitting his mistake and that he had written the same to Eva.

The Division president then turned on the ministers and said: "Which of you have not erred in your preaching?" as if to equate such minor matters with the *Signs* editor's calculated and deliberate disloyalty. The Division president then implied that the ministers were pharisaical and legalistic (a familiar ring) and that the ministers would not be satisfied until there was blood and slaughter (meaning until every heretic was fired).

The Division president then referred to the incoming editor of the SIGNS and said that he was more troubled about the new editor, for he was too straight, or words to that effect.

Later, the Division president was asked by Pastor Needham as to how the ex-editor could put in the SIGNS answers to questions about the year-day principle which were contrary to the Adventist position, after he (the ex-editor) had allegedly repented? The Division secretary replied by saying that the editor had told him that he had had numbers of questions in his drawer for some considerable time, and seeing he had to set up the SIGNS two months before hand, he had pulled out these questions and included them in that SIGNS.

When the Division president was again pressed to consider why, if the editor had repented of his "mistake" so many months before, he had published further subversive material in the SIGNS of October and November 1980, he (the Division president), in trying to defend himself and the editor, finally said that he had made no move in regard to this editor without first consulting the General Conference president, who was fully aware of the situation. He said that he was in constant touch with the president of the General Conference.

The Division president also stated to the four ministers that if they re-published the editor's letter to Eva and distributed it among our people, it would split the Church. Pastor Arthur Needham replied, "The Church is split already."